Snowy & Co

Insights into pet behaviour

Snowy & Co

Insights into pet behaviour

John Paling

Colour illustrations by
Oxford Scientific Films Ltd

Line drawings by
Joan Sellwood, The Garden Studio

Collins . London

Collins 15.97 May 82 -V

William Collins Sons & Co Ltd
London · Glasgow · Sydney · Auckland
Toronto · Johannesburg

First published 1981
© John Paling 1981
© in the photographs Oxford Scientific Films 1981
ISBN 0 00 216872 3

Filmset by Randall Typographic, Chiswick
Colour reproduction by Adroit Photo-Litho Ltd, Birmingham
Made and Printed in Great Britain
William Collins Sons & Co Ltd, Glasgow

Contents

Dedication

To Wendy, my new super pet, to my parents, with my life-long gratitude for their influence on my puppyhood, and to all our friends, old and new, animal and human.

Foreword

One year in a lifetime can provide encounters which open the door to a whole new world of awareness. Such experiences have been the basis of many previous books. Some people have discovered significant events in their lives while living with a tribe of Aborigines. Others have described what they learnt from a period in a Tibetan monastery or on one-man expeditions to the far-flung corners of the earth.

This story is similar only in that it relates to the personal revelations which accrued from one fascinating year of my life. In every other way it is completely different. It is an attempt to record the discoveries and new perspectives that resulted from me staying at home in the English countryside in the seemingly commonplace company of three domestic pets. It represents a study of wildlife in the home, an attempt to look at domesticated animals through the eyes of both the animal lover and the objective scientist.

For me, this experience represented the fulfilment of a wish I had nurtured for many years, ever since I had filmed and written about my experiences in desocialising a tame squirrel ready for its return to the wild. What, I wondered, could be gained from studying the reverse of this process? What has domestication done to what were previously wild creatures?

Surprisingly, very little work has been done in scientific circles in observing the behaviour of animals such as cats and dogs in a domestic setting. Though pets seem to have an exaggerated (some might say perverted) importance in many people's lives, it is only recently that we have begun to consider them worthy of the same serious study that we have for many years accorded to animals living in the wild. This book is intended to remedy some of that imbalance. I make no pretence that it is a definitive study. Instead, my main intention has been to produce something that will be of interest and relevance to any pet owner, with or without specialist knowledge of the subject. For instance, I have commonly used the pet lover's shorthand of imputing human feelings to my animals when simply describing anecdotal behaviour. I am aware that every critic who flicks through these pages will claim that I can't *possibly* know that my animals behave 'arrogantly', 'cheekily', 'happily' or whatever. Of course I agree. But in the same way as there are compromises in all aspects of life, there are compromises here between my own constant wish to avoid anthropomorphism and the need to write an accessible, readable story which would appeal to a wide range of readers, and not just to the few members of the scientific fraternity who are studying pets. If nothing else, I hope this book serves to stimulate many other people to study the human-pet relationship more sensibly so that future writers will have more hard facts readily available for them to use as the basis for elaborating their own hypotheses.

Acknowledgements

Most of all, I want to express my gratitude and greatest respect for all my friends at the Guide Dogs for the Blind Association. In Snowy, they provided me with a truly magnificent companion and, on a personal level, Derek Freeman, Alison Hornsby, Derek Carver and Barry Stocks fascinated and intrigued me by sharing with me their years of experience with dogs. My colleagues at Oxford Scientific Films contributed much to the project and in particular Joan Tompkins, Philip Sharpe and Georgina Cox all helped in looking after the various members of my pet family during different periods of the year. Their caring, concern and time all were generously given to the benefit of Snowy, Chilly, Motley—and me.

On the scientific plane, I was fortunate to have the ear of Dr Peter Messent in England and Dr Aaron Katcher in America, both widely informed and perceptive experts on our animal companions. Though I have talked long into the night with these and other consultants, I need to make clear that in this popular account of my year's adventures, the observations and interpretations are my own responsibility.

Finally, there is a whole gang of friends and collaborators who gave me valued time, advice and assistance during the year's film project: Isobel Scott, Peter Jones, the liberal and generous TV producer, Nigel Ashcroft the film editor, Rosemary and Janice Warner, Charlie and Tony Creasy (all numbered among Snowy's best friends) and my sons Mark and Sean who are now getting blasé about sharing their lives with animal film stars.

Snowy & Co

This book has been nurtured by Robert MacDonald and Tim Shackleton and most of the pictures were taken by George Bernard, Philip Sharpe and David Thompson. To these and all my pet-orientated helpers, I give my sincere thanks.

1

Snowy For Christmas

The BBC television crew, the newspapermen, the photographers and all the children had left to go home. I returned to the quiet solitude of my sitting room where, amid the disarrayed chairs and the glittery Christmas decorations, two dark eyes looked at me from a white, furry face. We stared at each other in silence for a time, initiating a two-way bond that was to become far deeper over the year ahead.

I couldn't guess what this strange puppy was thinking as he coolly and almost impassively studied me with a look of mild curiosity. He showed no fear, no concern for the strangeness of his new home—only a confident attitude suggesting he was ready to take on anything that we might encounter together in the future.

While his thoughts were unfathomable to me as we looked across the room space at each other, my own reactions were clear and poignant. What had I let myself in for in agreeing to look after this white Alsatian puppy for the British Guide Dogs for the Blind Association? I had undertaken to take him into my home for twelve months to get him used to human company and to begin his training before he finally returned to kennels to learn how to become the eyes of a sightless person.

My first impression was of the strangeness, apprehensiveness perhaps, of having a dog in the house once more. Twenty years ago I had been the owner of a cocker spaniel, but from the moment I first saw Snowy I was struck by the fact that, at nine weeks old, he seemed about as big as my spaniel had ever been even when full grown. His ears seemed excessively large and pointed and his fur was so soft that it resembled lambs-wool.

Bathed in the comforting ticking of the old bracket clock we continued to weigh each other up in silence. Then Snowy rustled his front feet, wagged his tail across the carpet and whined invitingly. I responded by dropping to my knees, hugging him in my arms and greeting him warmly—this time away from the artificial atmosphere of the film cameras. I was conscious that I spoke in tones and with sentiments that no young puppy could be expected to understand in any way except in mood and feeling. However, that didn't stop me chatting to him, explaining how I was going to look after him and make him a film star and how we were going to share our home with other animals in the near future. As I stroked his warm fluffy coat his dark eyes looked searchingly at me and then he started to lick my hand. Soon, despite my affectionate monologue, he was struggling in my arms, wanting to bound across the room and investigate the Christmas present which lay invitingly below the tree.

As he snuffled around, I sat back. Already I was trapped. Like many other pet owners, I was facing two totally different worlds, reflecting two conflicting attitudes. One impulse led me immediately to fondle Snowy, to treat him as any other pet owner would, with love, with an awareness of his personal feelings, with empathy between us. On the other hand, the voice of the scientist was whispering in my ear. I wanted to retain some sense of objectivity, some impartial detachment, so that I could view the behaviour of this young male dog as he grew to maturity through the eyes of a biologist observing his research animals. For I planned that my relationship with Snowy was not simply to be that between a dog and his master.

My aim was to learn as much as I could about my new companion by filming his behaviour in my household and with other animals in the streets and parks around my home. The fruits of our labours took the form of an hour-long documentary called *Snowy, Chilly, Motley and Me*. It was to be made on behalf of the BBC by the film company of which I was then a director, Oxford Scientific Films. OSF has many years' experience in high-technology film work: we did a lot of the filming for the immensely successful *Life on Earth* series, while our technical knowledge and facilities have repeatedly been used in creating special effects for films like *Superman*.

Making a film about pet behaviour would mean that not only would we be able to share our experiences with others but also that we could use the film as a valuable tool for analysing animal behaviour. Film has many advantages for the scientist: you can look at the same action repeatedly and alter the apparent speed of actions that normally take place too quickly for the unaided human eye to see. Snowy was to be both the link to enable us to view other pets and to serve as an example of a 'typical' dog.

Because they are all about us, we tend to think we know a good deal about our pets. Yet the very fact of their abundance probably blinds us to much about their lives, their habits and, even more interestingly, our own responses to them. We, as pet owners, so easily take them for granted and scientists for their part seem to have decided that companion animals are not worthy of serious study and have consequently pretty well ignored them. Indeed, I reckon that if the world's cat or dog population were to be limited to a dozen or so wild creatures living in the remote plains of Syria, scientists would probably know more about them than we really know for sure about the millions of similar animals mankind keeps as pets.

So fulfilling and widespread is our association with animals that nowadays over 50% of all the people in the western world share their homes and their lives with a pet animal. Yet this is no phenomenon of our affluence or a newly acquired ecological consciousness which says we ought to care more for the other creatures which share the globe with us. Though it may be hard for present day man to take in, the human race has in fact kept and bred animals as companions for some 12,000 years. So long established and deep seated is this bond that an even more difficult task for us is to try to perceive reasons why mankind—above all other animals—seems to need such an emotional relationship with another species. Of course, man does not indiscriminately lavish his affections on each and every animal which crosses his path, but rather chooses a particular animal, typically a dog or cat, with whom he may develop a special, exclusive emotional bond.

But despite this, I am quite convinced that the vast majority of pet owners have only the vaguest idea of what is going on in the minds of their pets. Let us try to put this into perspective. Any independent observer—a visitor from outer space, say— would note that the living population of the average Western household is a man, a woman, two children and a cat or a dog, and possibly a bird, a few houseplants and a goldfish or two for good measure. Yet it seems to me remarkable that we know so very little of these creatures with whom we share our daily lives so intimately. It strikes me that this integral relationship with another species probably has a far greater significance than we have so far understood. As a former lecturer in biology at Oxford University now turned film-maker, I had long felt the need to stand back and investigate our major pets as objectively as possible. In particular I was fascinated by the idea of confronting our comfortable folklore interpretations of animal behaviour with the hard scientific evidence derived from objective study, and in so doing I hoped to probe the compulsive willingness with which so many of us keep pets as close members of our families.

Do our stated motives for keeping pets really match up to reality? What do our pets do for us and what do we do to our pets? If I could succeed in balancing my instinctive feelings as a pet owner with the scientific objectivity I wanted to achieve in the making of the film, I was hopeful of being able to offer a greater understanding of why our cats and dogs really behave as they do. The tendency is for us to view our pets through our own eyes: to judge their behaviour as we would judge human actions, to interpret their feelings against the kind of emotional response a human would make. Few people who keep pets have been able to break away from this 'humanizing' attitude and try simple, harmless tests to see if our most widespread views on pets are, after all, valid. By filming this process, we would be able to communicate our findings to a large and, we hoped, very interested section of the pet-owning public through the medium of television. And for my own part, having had many years experience of the analytical filming of wildlife and having also been, at various times in my life, a pet-owner myself, I would now be able to combine these two often quite different approaches for the first time. In so doing, by strengthening the bond between the animals I was filming and myself in a wholly natural way that had not previously been possible (in the film-making business, there are lots of reasons why you don't befriend a Bengal tiger!) my own knowledge of and attitude to the animal kingdom would inevitably be improved.

If the menagerie of pets I wanted to film and study was to include a dog, it seemed from the very start impossible for me to take on any ordinary animal. For a start, we had decided to set aside a year for filming. But once this period was over, I could not guarantee to be around to look after my dog. My job as a wildlife film-maker involves extensive periods of foreign travel and because at the time we were making the film I lived on my own, there would be no one else available to look after him when I was away. I was fully aware of the responsibility one takes on in keeping a pet, and I was determined from the outset that the dog should not suffer. Every conscientious pet owner will be aware of those ill-disciplined, potentially dangerous animals whose unhappy state is a consequence of their owners neglecting them. But what kind of animal could I keep for only twelve months?

The solution came to me out of the blue in, of all places, the library of the *QE2*. Having been invited on board the liner to show passengers extracts from Oxford Scientific Films' wildlife programmes, I was making notes for the proposed television feature that eventually gave us this book as well when I suddenly thought of the guide dogs which act as the 'eyes' for blind people. The Guide Dogs for the Blind Association in Britain regularly lets its specially bred puppies go into ordinary homes for the first year of their lives to accustom them to family life. On completion of this, they are taken back into the Association's kennels and trained intensively for several months before being paired with a blind person. The idea struck me that perhaps I could become one of those people looking after a Guide Dog puppy, or 'puppy-walker' as they are called. The more I thought about it, the more this seemed to suit everyone concerned. For a start, puppy walking a guide dog for a year would be a great help not only to the Association but to the blind person with whom the dog would eventually be paired. Seeing the dog arrive and depart would provide a time structure for the film and would leave me without the social responsibility of looking after the dog after twelve months of filming. And, perhaps most importantly, if I wanted to try to reach some understanding of the behaviour of pets as seen through their eyes instead of our own, there seemed no better starting point than to join forces with a dog who himself was destined to act as the eyes for a sightless person.

I left the *QE2* full of enthusiasm for this idea. Back in Oxford, having had time to consider, I put it to my colleagues. They recognised the logic of the plan, but there were still many questions to be answered before we could begin to fill in the bare bones of my outline. For a start, what breed would we choose? Most of the guide dogs used in Britain are Labradors, and they certainly make affectionate and devoted pets. Collies, recognised as one of the most intelligent of breeds, are also popular, but Lassie's image still hangs over the film world and it seemed inappropriate to base a straight documentary upon yet another collie. 'What about Alsatians?' someone asked. Alsatians, or more correctly German shepherd dogs, as they are now known in the show ring, make up about 10% of the guide dogs employed in Britain (the percentage is far higher in many parts of America) and the more we thought about it the more advantages we could see from the point of view of the film's structure in choosing one.

Firstly, the breed superficially resembles the likely ancestor of all dog breeds, the Asiatic wolf. Second, German shepherds are very intelligent and highly versatile at demonstrating all the basic doggy phenomena I hoped to investigate in the film. Thirdly, they are large and tame enough to permit a small movie camera to be attached to their harness in order to get a detailed 'dog's eye view' picture. Fourthly—and crucially for a film star—there is one colour variety which is very rarely seen in Britain: the white German shepherd. One of these would constantly stand out and engage the attention of our audience. In addition, a white animal would have certain technical benefits for high-speed photography. And hadn't we thought of beginning and ending the film at Christmas, a time when a white animal would be very appropriate? So what else could we choose?

In the end, the animal picked himself. The Guide Dogs for the Blind happened to have just one lone white German shepherd remaining, a male awaiting a home. Because he had had to stay in kennels for some minor veterinary treatment, he was later than the usual six or eight weeks of age in going out to a puppy walker. Although it was simple for me to decide that I wanted him (at this stage, I hadn't actually seen him), it was a much slower process to get the Association's officers to agree to our scheme. Very sensibly, they treated my application like any other and sent down an inspector to sound me out and to see if my home would be suitable. At first, his questions seemed daunting. Wasn't Bladon, a small country village eight miles north-west of Oxford, rather too quiet to give the dog regular experience of traffic noise? Wouldn't the boisterousness of a large family setting be preferable to my being on my own for the greater part of the week? Would I agree to put a secure fence around my acre of lawns and woodland? But in the end, after I'd undertaken to erect a fence, walk the dog regularly in traffic and encourage other people to walk and play with him as well (so he didn't become attached to just one person) these reservations were set aside and I was thrilled to be told that the Association had accepted me as a puppy walker.

*   *   *

'A dog is for a lifetime, not just for Christmas,' read the sticker on the back of Alison's van as she arrived to deliver Snowy on a mid-December morning. After all the conscience-searching I had undertaken since conceiving my idea of filming a year in the life of a dog, I felt confident that this message was not directed at me, but rather at those owners whose momentary enthusiasm for the idea of having a cuddly bundle of fur in their living rooms is changed, after a few short months, into a mutually destructive mood of carelessness and ill-feeling. Nevertheless it was a salutary warning.

Sadly, it didn't snow the day that my puppy arrived, but this little piece of would-be stage management was soon forgotten once I first held Snowy in my arms and carried him indoors.

I held Snowy in my arms and carried him indoors

My two boys and their friends were with me at the time and the new arrival was almost submerged in a sea of patting hands from the moment they set eyes on him. Little wonder, I thought, looking on this extraordinary display of petting and human affection, that we refer to our tame household animals as 'pets'.

Other people responded equally lavishly when they met Snowy for the first time. But also they were struck with his colour. 'How unusual to see a white German shepherd,' they would say. 'Why don't you see so many whites around?' 'Is he an albino?' Especially when they discreetly asked, 'Where can we get one from?' I detected a note of envy in their voices. The answers I gave to such obvious and immediate questions immediately began to shed light on some of the illogicalities that surround the pet world.

For a start, Snowy is not an albino. He does have a dark pigment in his eyes (in an albino they would be pink) as well as

straw-coloured tinges to his ears and back. But his colouring
certainly is unusual and that comes about largely because of
the attitude of the British breeders. They view whites as highly
undesirable and they make a strong effort to avoid producing
animals of this colour. No white German shepherd would ever
stand a chance in the show ring and only a handful of the
breeders who deliberately try to produce dogs of this colour
would ever use a white animal to breed from. This dog apart-
heid has reached such a pitch that, I am told, some breeders of
German shepherds would rather put a white puppy in a bucket
of water at birth than admit that their breeding stock has the
potential for 'throwing a white'.

This sad situation would be understandable if the white
variety was associated with some genetic weakness of body or
temperament. But the experts on genetics will tell you that
there is no reason at all why white German shepherds should
not be as intelligent, as healthy and have as good a disposition
as any coloured dog. The guide dogs and military dog breeders
both have a high level of experience in such matters and they
would certainly not reject a dog on the grounds of colour. In
fact Snowy was born as a result of a very carefully matched
mating which was known in advance would be likely to produce white animals but which promised to make excellent
guide dogs nonetheless.

Outside such specialist working-dog kennels only a very few
breeders are prepared to resist rejection in the dog world by
continuing to breed white German shepherds. Sadly, when the
range of animals available for breeding is artificially limited
there is an increased chance of bad faults showing up in the offspring of such breedings as a result.

Intrigued by this curious prejudice, I decided to seek enlight-
enment from the governing body of the dog-breeding world in
the U.K., the Kennel Club. From them, I received a courteous
letter giving the written standards for German shepherd dogs
which, at first sight, did not seem to put a colour bar on whites.

'The colour of the Alsatian is in itself not important,' the
standard read, 'and has no effect on the character of the dog or
on its fitness for work and should be a secondary consideration
for that reason.'

All well and good, I thought. Perhaps I've formed the wrong impression. But then my eye caught a telling phrase: 'All white or near-white animals unless possessing black points are not desirable.' The paradox left me completely baffled (and it continues to do so to this day). Was this yet another example of bureaucratic double-think? Technically it *is* possible to register the Snowies of this world with the Kennel Club but it remains clear that the white colour is disapproved of because of wording specifying the desirable standard of the breed. If the colour 'is in itself not important,' why then should colour be even 'a secondary consideration'? Why, in other words, doesn't the Kennel Club simply say that the colour of German shepherds doesn't matter at all? The reason, I am sure, is that the breeders have decided that their ideal German shepherd should be some shade of brown and as a result no top breeder is going to encourage white ones. It is the same thing as Pekinese breeders deciding that they don't want long-nosed dogs. Comparable arbitrary standards exist for every breed. A simple human preference for looks means that dogs get chosen and prized for physical features almost without consideration for the fitness or temperament of the animal. In nature different traits in animals are chosen by the simple expedient that those that are fittest to survive can live to breed. With pedigree pets, however, humans now control the breeding and the ones that are encouraged to breed are chosen mainly on their looks.

All of which is to say that Snowy tends to stand out as a very distinctive animal because he flaunts the fashions that the policy-makers in the dog world have decided upon, albeit for no logical reason. Yet many people would agree that the breed standard for top show dogs produces German shepherds that tend to have weak backs and a serious tendency for the hip joint to give way, which causes many animals to be killed before their old age. Also, the temperament of dogs bred purely for show standards is reputed to be less than ideal. Will we ever reach the stage when the Kennel Club will be able to take temperament into account when it decides on standards?

Perhaps my biologist's sense of admiration will always be reserved for an animal well fitted to its environment. Certainly my familiarity with wild animals leaves me offended by our uncritical willingness to breed animals that are highly susceptible to medical problems (such as bulldogs with respiratory diseases). Surely it is illogical to turn a blind eye to this, and yet to reject animals of some breeds on coat colour alone? How about introducing simple tests for temperament and fitness into the 'best breed' classes at Crufts.

*   *   *

Snowy may not have had the stamp of approval of the top breeders but he soon showed himself to have a confident and adaptable temperament as well as a healthy appetite and a great sense of fun. Within a few days he seemed to me to be one of the most obedient and well adjusted dogs anyone could wish to have. And certainly he was most attractive! But where was my scientific objectivity going? Wasn't I falling into the same trap as everyone else who takes in an animal as part of their

We galloped around the frosty garden together

close family and gives him a name? Everything about their pet is described in terms of favourable superlatives. I thought that anyone who voiced any criticism of my dog seemed to be criticising me, and I would automatically leap to Snowy's defence.

The strength of my personal bond with Snowy was undoubtedly there after only a few hours and it was going to be hard constantly to stand back and try to look at his development with the unemotional eyes of a scientist. I couldn't deny that my feelings were already involved and I felt suppressed excitement at the prospects of the year ahead, sharing my family life with pets once again. The eventuality of losing Snowy was twelve long months away and it promised to be an exhilarating year. I could hardly wait for it to begin.

On New Year's Eve, I didn't accept any of the party invitations but instead stayed at home with Snowy. I built a large log fire, watched the build-up to the year's end on television and then, as the chimes for a brand new year began, I hugged my bleary warm puppy into wakefulness. Then I carried him outside in my arms, set him down on the lawn and we galloped around the frosty garden together in our own New Year celebration.

2

A High-Born Lady

I can't say for sure when the idea first came to me—it must
have been in the very early stages of planning—but I'd been
aware for some time of the need to balance my observations of
Snowy with studies of another animal. This would not only
keep me from falling into the trap of speaking about 'pets' in
general when I was really only basing my suppositions on my
experience with dogs, but would also give me some indication
of the social interactions between different species of animals.
For practical reasons, I decided to limit the study to two
species, both carnivorous: I didn't want my home turned into a
zoo overnight!

Once Snowy and I had got to know each other, the next step
was to decide on an animal to co-star with him. I had done
some research into the statistics of pet ownership in Britain,
and had unearthed some very interesting figures. For a start, I
learned that though as many as one in five homes has a pet cat,
dogs are even more popular, being found in a quarter of all
households. Their only serious competitor turns out to be the
budgerigar (which has fallen steadily in popularity until it now
is found in only 7% of homes) so it becomes obvious at a glance
which are our most popular pets, and which would be most
suitable to film.

Many families, of course, have both a cat and a dog, but if
you separate owners into categories of cat-only and dog-only,
several interesting differences are revealed. 13% of dog owners
keep more than one dog in their homes. For cat owners, on the

other hand, the figure is nearly doubled; 23% of this group have two or more cats and of single people who own a cat, the figures show that 95% are women. Why this should be we will hint at later, but the simple statistical fact is that single men in general do not go in for cats. Indeed, in the stereotyped imagery of the entertainment industry, a single man with a pet cat is decidedly suspect in one form or another: think of Blofeld, the villain in the James Bond film *From Russia With Love*.

When I started this project I was living on my own and, being a good, statistically average sort of fellow, I wasn't particularly fond of cats. I had never looked after one for more than a couple of months and, as a boy, I had grown up in a home where cats were unwelcome because they dug up small plants and scattered soil all over the garden pathways. So when I came to take a cat into my home I felt that I'd had so little direct experience of them that I might be able to look at their behaviour more objectively than if I had been or already was a cat owner. In any case, having at various times in my life looked after creatures as diverse as rabbit fleas and salmon, the idea of keeping as accessible and as simple (so I thought!) an animal as a cat had a very strong appeal.

Just as I'd found with Snowy, the question of what breed to choose became a very important consideration. At first I fancied an ordinary street mog, the kind of cat you could find on any corner, nosing around the dustbins or sitting watchfully on your garden wall. After all, I reasoned, such a cat would be entirely typical of the sort of animal the average viewer would keep, and its run-of-the-mill looks would be the perfect foil to Snowy's unusual white colouring. But in the end, Joan Tompkins, a colleague at Oxford Scientific Films, persuaded me to think differently.

'It's a Siamese you want,' argued Joan. An elegant cat, she suggested, was the epitome of feline character. Who was I to argue? As I say, I'd never been a keen cat owner myself, but Joan had three and was obviously far more of a cat person than I was. If anyone ought to know, it was Joan. She told me that Siamese are typically the most loyal and affectionate of cats – almost dog-like in this respect, it seemed. This appealed very strongly to me. But it begged an important question which, as

A high-born lady

I'd already discovered in Snowy's case, was not the easiest one to answer.

If this affectionate, exotic cat was going to form a strong bond with me, what was going to happen when the year of filming ended? Prepared as I was to do all I could for the animal, I couldn't suddenly change my globe-trotting job so I could be around seven days a week to look after it. This wasn't callousness; it was a very real practical consideration. I'd been very fortunate in discovering the guide dog scheme, but as far as I was aware nothing remotely similar existed for cats.

But once again, luck was on my side. One of Joan's cats, coincidentally a Siamese, was getting on in years and she knew that it wasn't going to live for more than another year at the outside. She felt three cats was an ideal number for her and had decided that, when her ailing Siamese died, she'd get another cat in its place. We felt horribly cynical working out how long the poor animal might expect to live, but it was becoming increasingly obvious that the natural solution to both our dilemmas was for me to take on a Siamese for a year and then let Joan take it over when her old cat died. Seeing me hovering on the brink of a major decision, Joan dug out some photographs of Siamese cats. I gazed at their beautiful blue eyes and slim, regal lines. That clinched it: wanted, one seal-point Siamese kitten.

We soon found, though, that in the middle of winter few kittens of any description were to be found. One after another all our local contacts shook their heads. 'The wrong time of year,' they said. 'Really John,' they advised, 'you ought to wait until the first new litters of the year start coming through in early spring.' But time was not something we had in abundance and we redoubled our efforts. Many phone calls later we were recommended to a breeder living some sixty miles away near Bedford who had Siamese kittens for sale.

At the end of the first week in January I drove across country into Bedfordshire with a brand-new cat basket beside me. I found our contact living in a large, beautifully maintained home. Although I hadn't known it at the time, she turned out to be one of the country's top breeders and her cats had, over the years, carried off all the major awards in Britain. By

A lively playgroup of three-month old Siamese kittens

chance, then, our Siamese would not just be the queen of cats that Joan had intimated; she would be a queen of queens, an aristocrat by birth and breeding.

After having coffee, I was left in the sitting room in the company of several aloof Siamese adults and a lively playgroup of lanky, three-month-old kittens. I could have gone for any one of them, but I had automatically limited the available choice by deciding on a female, if only for it to be different from Snowy. Having watched the kittens gambolling together for a few minutes I picked out the one that seemed the most playful on the grounds that she might be expected to provide the most interesting behaviour to record on film. If I knew then . . .

When the breeder returned, I indicated my choice. She murmured agreement. Already, on the phone, I'd had a long and detailed conversation with her about who I was, what I wanted from the cat and what I could offer in return. No security vetting for the Bank of England could have been more thorough, and I felt quite pleased that I'd evidently passed the test. Now she followed this up with detailed feeding instructions, lengthy and impressive notes on the kitten's pedigree, and a request for frequent progress reports.

All this, and especially the last point, made me realise the enormous amount of care and dedication that our top cat breeders give to their animals. As I drove away with my new charge I noticed tears in her eyes and a slightly quivering lip. Driving back to Oxfordshire I began to think, not so much of pets themselves, but rather of their owners and the extraordinary ties they form with their animals. The statistics I had consulted earlier had given me some information to work on, but I was constantly being surprised, now that I was meeting them in the flesh, by how durable and deep-rooted those human-pet relationships were. This breeder of Siamese kittens, I had learned, had a husband whose job took him to the Middle East for long periods of time. She could either go with him, or stay at home with her cats. She chose the latter.

This extreme devotion to pets (or 'petishism' as one American author, Szasz, has dubbed it) at the expense of human relationships was something which I very much wanted to investigate further over the next twelve months. It is something we are all aware of but, I think, slightly embarrassed by. Why else would we make the figure of the little old lady surrounded by her cats into a joke, a situation comedy cliché? It may well be true, I thought at the time, that some people, for one reason or another, sublimate their feelings for real people into their concern for their pets—there are a number of psychological explanations for this—but scientific rationalisations of this kind of crankiness do not explain the cases where, for instance, apparently normal parents will not put down a pet which has severely mauled one of their own children.

Anyway, back to the kitten. I now had to give serious thought to the business of giving her a name. Joan had provided a list of seasonal suggestions, ranging from Frosty to Nippy, and other colleagues at OSF had added their own inspired alternatives, most of which merited high marks for ingenuity but scored low on practicality. Whoever heard of a cat called Mandu, for instance? I wanted a name that would complement my German shepherd's and, as I neared Oxford, decided that

Chilly would do the trick. Though this name might seem quite arbitrary, it's actually very appropriate for a Siamese.

We're all familiar with the characteristic dark tips or points to the nose, ears, feet and tail of a Siamese cat. Most of us, I'm sure, think this is just the way they're born. But, as with many things in nature, there's a good reason for this phenomenon. The extremities of a Siamese cat have a lower temperature than the rest of the animal's body. The natural colour of a Siamese is dark brown all over but the cat's body will only assume this colour when it lives in an environment that is consistently below a particular temperature range. If the habitat gets warmer than this, then the colour changes. Britain, believe it or not, is too warm for a Siamese to take on its natural colour and so the fur assumes a creamy colour. It is still chilly enough, however, for the extremities of the cat's body to be so much cooler than the rest of the animal that they naturally produce the colour pigments which give the familiar dark tips. But if the temperature rises so high that the tail, paws, face and ears of the Siamese lose that little bit of coldness, then the dark points will disappear. There are numerous instances on record where Siamese cats from England have accompanied their owners to the tropics, where they have progressively lost their dark tips and become all-over white cats.

We had an interesting demonstration of this phenomenon when Chilly was six months old and was taken to the vet to be neutered. This minor internal operation involved clipping a triangle of creamy fur off Chilly's flank so an incision could be made. Later, when this fur began to grow back, it took on a significantly darker colouration because the exposed part lacked the warming effect of the normally close fur and so the new growth took on a pigmentation which compensated for the temperature loss.

So it was that Chilly got her name. I'd left Snowy at home while I went to fetch her and when I got back to Bladon I made him sit quietly on the sitting room floor before bringing in our new companion. The breeder had told me that Chilly had never seen a dog before, so I was anxious that they should get on well together from the start. I put Chilly down on the floor and then knelt by Snowy with my hand on his back to reassure him and keep him calm. His tail wagged furiously as the kitten cautiously walked up to him. His ears were pricked up, his eyes alert and he made repeated whines of suppressed excitement. Quite suddenly, Chilly seemed to lose confidence. She moved her body back, though she did her best to keep her front feet firmly planted on the carpet as though glued to the spot. Her tail turned into a bristling brush and, with her eyes still fixed on Snowy, she turned the rear of her body sideways on to the dog and arched her back. This curious, right-angled stance was the classic threatening gesture of the cat, one designed to make the body look as large as possible while still looking straight ahead.

Snowy struggled to get up and this scared Chilly into action. With a yelp, she leapt back a foot or two and then held her ground, still showing her threatening display and staring straight at Snowy. I held on tight to the puppy and shortly I sensed both animals had begun to relax. Chilly assumed her normal shape once again and shuffled off to inspect the Christmas tree. So the initial crisis was past and the introductions were over.

The three of us stayed close together for the rest of the afternoon. Most of the time I sat on the floor with Chilly in my lap, with Snowy under firm control in a 'sit' position nearby. Both animals were making idiosyncratic sounds, Chilly purring softly in response to my stroking while Snowy whined impatiently, as though inviting play. So far scientists don't seem to have bothered to analyse the distinctive sounds our pets make in different situations; indeed, we still don't know for sure precisely how a cat makes its purring sound. We think purring means the cat is contented, but I'm not entirely convinced of this. A cat will purr under various circumstances, including ones where contentment may not be the most logical interpretation. With Snowy too, I had already noticed quite a repertoire of whines and barks which he varied to suit the occasion, and I made a mental note to see if other dogs made recognisably similar sounds under the same conditions.

It was also fascinating to see how the two animals communicated by gesture. Snowy would repeatedly wag his tail, hold his neck and head high and then push his head forward and try to bite Chilly's head gently, without closing his jaws. I'd seen him do this earlier while playing with my children. Sometimes he varied this by substituting an upwards prod with his nose, as though trying to nudge the cat into action. Plainly he wanted Chilly to do something, if only so he could watch what a cat did in response and thus learn a little more about such a strange creature. Maybe, being an affectionate sort of dog, he simply wanted Chilly to play with him. But Chilly, however, would have none of it. Rather than hissing, putting her back up or trying to run away, she showed no outward response at all. In a way, I felt, this nonchalant behaviour was itself a form of communication, designed to achieve a particular effect. Rather like a parent studiously ignoring a pestering child, Chilly seemed to be thinking 'ignore it and it will go away'. In this case, her approach worked—at least for a time.

Snowy trying to trample Chilly with a heavy paw—a friendly rather than an aggressive gesture

But Snowy wasn't to be fobbed off so easily. In his curiosity, he soon evolved another strategy which Chilly had to learn to tolerate, one of trying to trample her with a heavy paw. It was a friendly rather than aggressive gesture, forming part of a behaviour pattern which has close associations with what we presume were happy experiences in the animal's past. You see the same sort of thing in a dog 'shaking a paw'. Though many owners pride themselves on having, as they see it, taught their dog to perform this action, it's basically instinctive. Paw-shaking and Snowy's trampling gesture are deep-seated remnants of a juvenile behaviour. If you watch a four-week-old puppy suckling from its standing mother, you'll see it push the mother's breast with one paw while its mouth takes in her milk. This helps stimulate the milk flow in the mother, but in the puppy's mind the gesture seems to be bound up with the pleasurable experience of feeding. As it gets older, it continues to associate the pushing gesture with a feeling of contentment. Just as a breast-fed baby finds, once it is weaned, that thumb-sucking is a comforting substitute, so the adult dog seems to have the same feelings when it pushes out its paw.

Little by little, then, I grew used to watching the behaviour of Snowy and Chilly as they settled down in the household. They soon made themselves at home. It wasn't long before I was watching television with my dog asleep at my feet and my cat curled on my lap (or draped around my neck, another favourite position). Chilly usually liked to keep herself to herself. She had the image of a refined, delicate lady. What a surprise it was to be for all of us, then, when Motley burst on to the scene.

3

One For The Set

Weeks passed, and Snowy and Chilly seemed to arrive at a mutual acceptance of each other's existence. But it was Snowy who made all the running in trying to strike up some sort of a relationship with the Siamese. The openness of his approaches, however, was not reciprocated: Chilly would either ignore him completely or, worse, pointedly snub him by walking arrogantly away.

After a while, Snowy began to get the message. He would paw or mouth Chilly only half-heartedly, and it was becoming very evident that he was getting bored with a companion who never showed any inclination to play. Whatever affection he had for Chilly soon disappeared when food was put down. If Chilly ventured within range of Snowy's dish, there would be a deep and unmistakeable growl of warning followed, if need be, by a snap in the cat's direction.

There was also some conflict over sleeping arrangements. Snowy bedded down in a specially made wooden box with a blanket, fitting neatly on the floor between two kitchen units. Chilly, meanwhile, had two options; one was a cat basket on the floor near to Snowy and the other was a box on the counter top close to the central heating boiler (cats always find the warmest spot, don't they?). Not content with having a choice, Chilly would sometimes climb into the German shepherd's box and go to sleep. When Snowy returned he would eye the unwelcome intruder with what I can only describe as a pained expression, and then climb in himself. He would lie down

Snowy forced Chilly to get out of his box

either right on top of Chilly or very close to her, with his head disdainfully facing the other way. If this didn't shift the cat immediately he would scrunch himself around until the poor Siamese was jammed between the side of the dog and the box. Faced with such acute discomfort, she had no choice but to get out, but it didn't stop her trying again before long.

I'd never really expected the animals to get on like a house on fire but by this time I was beginning to get more than a little worried about Chilly. It wasn't just that she had very little interest in playing either with me or, still less, with Snowy. She seemed to have decided on a policy of complete non-co-operation whenever the cameras were turned on her. Maybe she resented the intrusion on her privacy or was nervous of all the comings and goings, but she just would not do what we

S. & C.—B

wanted her to do when the time came. The sort of cameras and lighting equipment used at Oxford Scientific Films can't be set up at a moment's notice and even though we had all had many years' experience of waiting patiently for animals to go through their paces Chilly really took the biscuit when it came to foiling our plans. I, as the director, wasn't the only one who was beginning to get more than a little frustrated by Chilly's whims, either. It seemed that the only time we could rely on her to produce the behaviour we wanted to film—playing with a soft toy for example—was when I was trying to cope with Sunday lunch for six people or all the lights and cameras were set up in a different room.

Though I tried not to admit the feeling, a gulf was developing between us because of my frustration. On the one hand, as a pet, she wasn't living up to the reputation for affection I had expected of Siamese cats. On the other, as the subject of a serious scientific film, she was rapidly beginning to rival some famous Hollywood actresses in her unreliability. It began to dawn on me that we were possibly expecting too much of her, that being such a highly bred pedigree cat she might be just too sensitive and temperamental to fulfil the role we'd cast her in—that of demonstrating typical cat behaviour. More and more I wished that instead of this highly-strung fashion model, I'd taken in some perfectly average moggy from the street. What if all these cameras and lights finally proved too much for her and she ran off? That would be a disaster for the film; though we have very little usable footage of Chilly as yet, she still had her part to play.

We decided, though, that it would be a good idea to get in another cat alongside her and so our plans had to be changed. This is how Motley came to join the set and I to enter the ranks of the two-cat families.

Having made this decision the search began for the archetypally ordinary litter of kittens. Based on our experience with Chilly, we thought it a good idea to have not one but two extra animals. They should be tabby for preference and, more importantly, exact lookalikes. One should be the subject of most of the filming; the existence of the other, which we would use when needed, we would keep a secret. The reasoning behind this was that if anything went wrong with our principal tabby, we could rapidly substitute the 'ringer'. This insurance policy, it turned out, was not necessary in the long run.

But where could we find these animals? I once spent weeks tracking down a pregnant male sea horse in the waters of Jamaica but that was child's play compared to trying to locate two lookalike tabby kittens in the Oxford area in the middle of January. Once again, we encountered the problems we'd faced before getting hold of Chilly. After a week of solid searching the only leads I'd had were an offer from someone with two black kittens—an impossible colour to do justice to on a film—and a breeder who could give us the pick of her new litter of—believe it or not—Siamese. Not again, I thought, and carried on searching.

Someone once said that it's not *what* you know but *who* you know that counts. After several fruitless days I began to realise the truth in this. Over the years we'd collaborated a good deal with the BBC's Natural History Unit in Bristol and talking to them one day about quite a different matter I casually mentioned the problems we were having in finding our tabby kittens. They sounded amazed. 'Why didn't you tell us before?' they asked. Within minutes they'd agreed to broadcast an appeal on our behalf at the end of one of their programmes. So we sat back and waited, while I made hurried arrangements with a local doctor and his wife, James and Tricia Falconer-Smith, to take in the ringer alongside their two present cats. I didn't have time to make advance arrangements for my own new cat and what would happen to it in a year's time. In fact, this problem was to be resolved in a way I'd never really anticipated.

Pretty soon the BBC came up trumps. A family near Bristol had heard our appeal, and had phoned in to say they had two eminently suitable kittens for us. In the last week of January then, Tricia and I went down to Bristol to see what was in store for us. It was no small surprise to find our destination was an exquisite fifteenth-century manor house in a superb setting. Somehow I'd expected that our perfectly ordinary domestic cat would come from a perfectly ordinary English semi. The whole thing resembled a Hollywood film mogul's vision of an English gentleman's home and we were led through solid oak doors,

In a humble shoe box were four kittens

past vast hanging tapestries, suits of armour and stained glass windows with ancient crests which filtered the sunlight into gaudy patterns on the floor. Seated in deep comfortable armchairs in the book-lined study we finally met our charges. In a humble shoe box were four kittens. Only two had the same markings, one male and the other female.

I let Tricia make her own mind up about which she wanted. After a little hesitation she chose the female and by default I became the owner of a bouncing, endearing tabby tom. The name Motley sprang to mind almost immediately and thus he was christened on the spot.

Driving home, Tricia and I talked about her own cats. It had been mainly her idea to keep one in the first place, whereas her husband had been initially somewhat uncertain what to expect since he had had little contact with cats before. Though she said that James soon began to take a strong interest himself in the family pets, I felt that this was further confirmation of my idea of the predominances of the bonding process between women and cats. She also said that, when they were discussing the possibility of getting a third cat, James had expressed a preference for a tom, since this seemed potentially a more harmonious combination than three queens, and might reduce the number of undistinguished but noisy toms that came calling. This brought out a nagging doubt in my mind. When we'd seen the whole litter at the manor house, it had been the female tabby who had caught my eye as the most playful and affectionate. To my mind, she'd seemed more like a potential star of the show, while Motley looked like making a good stand-in. By giving Tricia first choice, had I done the right thing for the film? I began to think, somewhat guiltily, if I could somehow suggest a swap. After all, both animals would make excellent pets, but one looked more of an actor than the other—and this was the one Tricia had chosen. Was Tricia perhaps thinking about what her husband had said, and having second thoughts too?

'You don't have to stick to the female,' I ventured tactfully.

There was no response. 'Why not talk it over with James when you get back?' I went on, trying to press the point home.

Still no come-back. 'I'll gladly take either of them when you've both decided,' I added hastily.

Tricia stirred from contemplating possible names for her new kitten.

'Well, yes, of course,' she said, somewhat disinterestedly. 'I'll certainly ask James. After all, I want it to be the right choice for him too.' I felt a slight tremor of hope. 'But I really think we'll hang on to this one.'

That was it. Her eyes turned to the little lady in the basket behind us. I was left with no chance of making an exchange. I sensed that she was hooked. Barely thirty minutes ago we had made a somewhat arbitrary choice between the two animals. Now, though I was wavering a little, Tricia had already formed an invioble bond with one particular kitten and I knew that wild horses, let alone my tactful hints, wouldn't separate them.

Ah well, I thought, and concentrated on the road ahead. I stole a glance at Motley in the rear view mirror. I wondered if

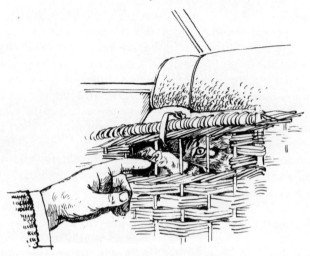

Motley stretched out his paw...

he would be more sociable than Chilly; I thought of him curled contentedly on my lap as I watched television. I imagined him playing with Snowy, and wondered how he and Chilly would get on. I looked over my shoulder at the cat basket. He was stretching out his paws through the opening in my direction. Looking back to the road, I offered my left hand towards the back seat. His claws grabbed my fingers.

I was hooked too.

*   *   *

Why Motley should so readily have become my favourite instead of Chilly I shall probably never know. Their first meeting, though, passed off uneventfully, and I found little on which to base any future predictions. As I placed Motley's travelling basket on the kitchen floor and opened the lid there was a rustle from the other basket and a Siamese head appeared peeping over the top. Motley froze in the act of getting out of his basket and the hairs on his back and tail went up. This bold display of self-aggrandisement evidently disguised considerable nervousness for, with a plaintive miaow, he began alternately to seize and let go of the blue blanket in the travelling basket with his front paws. Neither animal moved for some time, but the atmosphere seemed nowhere near as intense as it had been when Chilly first met Snowy.

Motley soon relaxed his grip on the blanket, enabling me to lift him out of his basket and place him side by side with Chilly. The two cats promptly walked away from each other, Chilly to sniff the stranger's basket and Motley to eat the remains of Snowy's lunch! Such cheeky behaviour, I soon learned, was to be entirely typical of Motley's roguish, outgoing character.

So my household complement was now up to scratch and I was left with the problem of getting Motley's arrival on to film. Because he was intended to represent the average sort of cat, I didn't think it would be appropriate to make mention of his being 'to the manor born'. Instead, I thought it might be a good idea to give the impression of him as just one among millions of cats in back streets around the world, in contrast to Chilly's immaculate pedigree. This was obviously stretching the truth but I felt it was fully justifiable in the context of the film.

I had long decided that I wanted the film to say something about the responsibilities of pet ownership. I therefore toyed with the idea of dummying up an advertisement in the 'lost and found' section of the local paper to use in the film, to give the impression that Motley was an unwanted Christmas present who had been thrown out onto the streets. This not only enabled us to give a brief profile of Motley ('...charming, outgoing') before the viewer even saw him, but allowed us the opportunity of making an editorial point about negligent owners. I wanted to show that it's a bad idea to give any sort of pet to a person who has only a dim awareness of the long term commitments he is taking on. Our programme was originally scheduled to be broadcast on Christmas Day, a time when there would probably be quite a number of new kittens and puppies bouncing around amid the discarded wrapping paper. If I could hammer home a point and make all those new pet owners aware of what they were taking on, I hoped both they and their animals would benefit.

The pet rescue services always find a clear increase in the numbers of abandoned cats and dogs found wandering in the streets between March and June. The surplus is apparently caused by owners growing tired of their Christmas novelties and ditching the poor animals. Strays such as these are a major social concern in all our cities, and are the cause of most of the road accidents involving animals and incidents of biting. They also add to the problem of the fouling of public places. There was a moral issue at stake, too: I wanted to pinpoint the indifference, amounting to sheer callousness, of people who take in pets as prospective members of their families and then throw them out, like a discarded toy, when they have tired of them. Such negligence places an overwhelming burden on our already overstretched animal care organisations and if I could, through the film, make just one such person think a little more deeply about his or her responsibilities at a time when the novelty of their pet had not yet worn off, then I would have done something to help.

So our film played on the viewer's conscience by showing the ad for our 'lost' kitten, followed by a shot of Motley peeking out (suitably forlornly, we hoped) from his basket. Nothing could have been further from the truth, of course, but my cats weren't there just to entertain me and my film wasn't to be pure entertainment either. I had an important educational function to carry out, and if this involved taking a minor piece of artistic licence, I thought the overall results would be well worthwhile.

*   *   *

From the moment each of my pets arrived I made a conscious effort to sit back and scrutinise their activities, just as an animal-behaviour expert might do if he were given the privilege of studying some rare and distant creature for the first time. It was surprising what stood out. Within the first few days of his arrival Motley would perform a distinctive behaviour which has since got me arguing with my pet-scientist friends. Standing or walking slowly in a stiff-legged posture, Motley would repeatedly extend and contract his front claws over any surface he happened to be on. I managed to catch him on film doing it on the hard, shiny kitchen floor.

Many people I have discussed this with agree that their cats do a similar thing and that it is distinctly unlike the intense 'claw sharpening' that their cats seem to be performing on fur-

Could claw extension have nothing to do with 'sharpening' claws?

niture, scratching posts or trees. Immediately Motley started to do it, it seemed out of place on such a smooth surface and so I made a note of the occasions on which it occurred. He would do it when Chilly was in the room and the two animals were apparently not relating to each other. He would do it almost in greeting when I returned to the house having been away. He would do it in any new, unfamiliar place and I got the impression—the non-scientific 'feel' again—that he would do it when somewhat ill at ease.

For generations cat owners have seen their animals 'sharpen their claws' for the obvious purpose of keeping them ready for the essential job of catching their prey. Perhaps we have missed the fact that many cats start this behaviour as youngsters when they are feeling tension—maybe matching the tensions experienced just prior to a pounce? It can be fun to weave such tantalising theories from a few observations in our efforts to understand our pets. However, in this case, I now suspect that we have got it all wrong and that our cats aren't really sharpening their claws at all! Couldn't it be just as likely that Motley's paw extensions had nothing much to do with his claws? One of my main realisations about our interpretations of dog and cat behaviour is that we usually tend to find explanations based on our own senses. Yet we know that our pets live in a different sensory world from ourselves and therefore what we see as a primarily visual piece of behaviour may in fact be carried out by the animal for, say, the noise it produces.

Suppose, just suppose, that the 'sharpening' of a cat's claws as it scratches on a tree or your furniture *not* designed for that purpose at all. Suppose instead that the cat has glands producing distinctive scents with which it marks the surface when it extends its paws as far as possible. That could explain what Motley was doing when he was 'ill at ease'. Perhaps he was stating an emotional condition that would only be comprehensible to animals attuned to such odours. At first I thought such an idea may well *seem* far fetched until I considered other evidence that I became aware of during the year. An Iranian family I know recently returned to London and brought back with them several priceless Persian carpets. Sadly they left their cats behind them but, as 'home didn't seem like home without a cat', they soon obtained two new cats over here. It wasn't long before, to their dismay, their most exquisite and luxurious silk and wool carpet had been ruined by one of the cats scratching a section of it to shreds. They actually caught the culprit red-handed and felt an intense sense of anger towards the animal. The carpet had been worth thousands of pounds and yet, once the initial reaction had passed, so tolerant were these owners of their pet's anti-human behaviour that they didn't get rid of the cat. In fact they were even able to see a positive side to the incident by feeling glad that, as they'd actually seen the cat causing the damage, the animal didn't have a chance to do any more harm before it was banned from the sitting room.

This story on its own simply stresses how tolerant some humans are to the pets that are part of their families. However, it took on a new dimension when learned that the very next day the other cat was allowed in the room and did exactly the same thing to the same carpet! Could this be chance or could the first cat have scent-marked (possibly territorially) the carpet when it was so vigorously extending its claws? In that case it would be little wonder that the second cat had come along and scratched there too. Cats that scratch trees, for example, may be providing a fresh surface (no doubt with the smell of newly scored bark) on which to add their paw scents. My mind was again turned to this topic during a recent holiday in America, where I stayed with a lady who had two cats whose claws had been surgically removed from their front feet. Although I had never heard of this before, it is apparently not uncommonly performed on cats which are to be kept totally indoors all their lives. Putting aside the ethics of carrying out such an operation, it did give me an unusual opportunity to observe how cats without claws behaved. To my astonishment, they both carried out 'claw sharpening' behaviours on favoured posts and on carpets, even though they could only be wiping their pads on the materials concerned! I am aware that even this in itself is not one hundred per cent proof, for there could be other scientific explanations of this phenomenon. But it does lead me to ask that cat owners consider precisely what their pets are *really* doing when they extend their claws.

Finally, before leaving this topic, some cat owners may puzzle over why their cat seems to paw them, sometimes with claws extended, when seemingly happily settled on their knee. This behaviour, I am told, is thought to be a throwback to the contented behaviour pattern that the kittens adopted when they gently pummelled their mothers' breasts to stimulate milk flow. In a way it is a similar remnant behaviour to the behaviour of dogs we mentioned earlier. And if your cat happens to scratch you as it pummels, perhaps it is also marking you as part of its own territory! Maybe it doesn't love you as a person after all!

4

Starting From Scratch

Making a wildlife movie based on pets had some clear advantages from the start. Less obvious, though, were some of the disadvantages. We set out with the immediate bonus of knowing that, because so many people choose to live with pets, the subject would have great popular appeal with a large number of television viewers. However, as owners know their own pets so well and have their own theories about why they do what they do, we were likely to tread on the toes of a lot of people who had spent their lifetimes building up their own working folklore about what made their animals tick.

Even more frustrating was the fact that, even though the subjects were my pets and we knew each other's habits intimately, they could still be just as unreliable as any wild animal in performing certain behaviours that I wanted to demonstrate, whenever the cameras started to run. Thus I spent ages trying to film my cats 'sharpening their claws' on my furniture. In fact, I never managed it, yet I know there will be thousands of readers thinking, 'He should have come and filmed mine. She always ruins the chair covers, no matter what we do...'

Maybe. But if I were to arrive, set up my camera and filming lights and sit with you and wait I could almost guarantee that nothing would happen. It's happened like that so often that I would go so far as to say that cats are *the* most difficult form of 'animal life' I've ever tried to film.

When you 'know' they always do something in a particular

way, you find that the day you go there with a camera they don't even show up. And the same the next day! Alternatively you can sit and stick it out. Wait and wait every day for a week or a month and film just what happens. By now you 'know' a cat will only do something in its own time. Still it won't oblige for the camera. It is bad enough when you are filming alone but if your colleagues are also bound up at the twitch of a whisker, then it is also difficult to face up to their disgruntled glares at the end of a boring and fruitless week.

A further classic situation is that of trying to film a cat reacting to another person or object when all it really wants to do is to come over and endlessly rub itself over the camera and the camerman's body as he lays on his belly for the best filming angle! Or your cat has got itself stuck up a tree and ignores all the sweet encouraging calls of a frustrated owner. One's voice has the same strained affection of an international telephone operator trying to get a three-year-old to put down the phone and fetch her mother!

But I must give credit where it is due. There was one behaviour that Chilly – but never Motley – would perform fairly reliably on cue. This involved her rubbing herself persistently against my hands and arms as I tried to write at the study table. Finally she would sit down or stand right on top of the page I was working on. Needless to say, she wouldn't do this to anyone else and, in any case, I couldn't really film the incident myself at the same time as it was happening! So I gained the assistance of my colleague David Thompson and, on one of the four full evenings we set aside for the filming of this particular behaviour, Chilly engaged in a frantic bout of rubbing. When the action started, she jumped up on to the table and made a pass in front of me, her tail held high, wiping it under my chin. As she passed by, she lowered her head and lightly brushed the hand holding the pen. Then, having crossed over the writing pad, she did an about-turn and marched sedately across in front of me again, this time leaning into my hand and brushing firmly with the side of her head as she continued on her way. Again the stiffly held tail flicked across my face. She now paused, standing partly across my writing pad, before repeating the process over and over again. It almost seemed

Chilly made a pass in front of me, her tail held high

like a self-stimulating addiction. She would forcefully rub, almost scratch her head against my hand, the fountain pen or my body as she paraded to and fro. In time, it became a nuisance. What at first sight might be considered a sign of affection became an annoying disruption of my train of thought. It was almost as if the more I concentrated on what I was trying to write, the more insistent became Chilly's attentions.

This brought to mind an observation made by a well-known American doctor who had carried out extensive research on the definite medical benefits of a regular practice of meditation techniques. He found, as a minor sidelight on his studies, that if a cat was in the room when a subject set about meditating, more often than not the cat would not let the person alone but rubbed him or her continuously.

Some cat lovers may seize upon this as evidence that their pets are sensitive to human brain waves or to some other 'psychic vibrations'. For my part, I certainly feel that there is far more to cats' rubbing than meets the eye, but much of it is capable of less ethereal explanations. For a start, my non-catty background led me immediately to challenge the idea that when a cat rubs itself upon you, it is showing its love for you. Like everyone else, I have often had the experience of walking into a room in a strange house and having the resident cat stalk up, tail furry and high, and proceed to treat my leg to an unhurried and pleasurable caress. The cat may well pause by the legs of the newcomer and then repeat the action, curling its flank, rear quarters and tail over the legs being rubbed.

So common is the belief that this demonstrates the cat's affection for the person concerned that the owner will often venture a remark such as 'Oh, you're lucky. She normally doesn't care for people immediately.' And this happens, so I am told, especially to people who actually dislike cats intensely! To my mind, cat owners get so much pleasure and such a deep feeling of being loved by their cats as they are gently rubbed by the soft and sensuous fur that they automatically assume that it is their pet's way of showing warm feelings for the owner. Yet to my sadness, apart from these intense rubbing bouts, Chilly didn't strike me as being at all closely attached to me emotionally. Motley, on the other hand, did give me an intuitive feeling that he cared for me, but he never rubbed on me or any other person during all the time he was with me. However, he would occasionally rub his head and neck on the furniture and the edge of the doors, just as millions of other cats do although, for obvious reasons, their owners don't interpret this as signifiying the cat's expression of love! So what's going on, I wondered. Why do cats rub inanimate objects like doors as well as visiting legs, and do they all mean the same thing by their actions?

Chilly's antics gave us a chance to look at it all repeatedly. As she strutted to and fro, it was clear that there were definite regions she used for her rubbing. Particularly favoured were the areas at the side of the head, the throat and behind the ears.

In addition she would wipe the sides and top of her tail across my body but, while I was writing, she did not rub the sides of her body or flanks on me as cats commonly do when encountering human legs at floor level.

If you watch two cats that know each other you may well, when they meet, then see them rub each other too. They commonly do it around the face, particularly in the region between the nose and forehead. One body area they never seem to use in relating to each other is the sides of the body, the flanks and tail, the very region most humans get treated to and consider as being reflective of their cat's affection!

The explanation for all this seems to be based more on the cat's sense of smell. It has been found that there are glands under the fur in these areas which secrete odours. By rubbing against us our cats are probably depositing a scent of which we are unaware.

As one cat responds to another known friendly cat by rubbing the nose-forehead region, we can guess that this particular sort of rubbing is the nearest in cat language to actually showing the affection that we humans seem to crave. And yet when I

When friendly cats meet they rub their heads against each other

tried to rub my forehead gently on Chilly's forehead region, she repeatedly pulled her head away. The same was true for Motley. Neither of them would permit such familiarity and so, presumably, never regarded themselves as members of my family at all—a somewhat disillusioning realisation that cat owners might like to risk for themselves.

Having dared to cast doubts on the 'cat rubbing equals affection' folklore, I felt I had to try to find out more about how our cats use their scent glands to see if my alternative theory was true. The first thing I must say is that, of all the times cats rub on objects, no one has ever seen another cat visibly back off when visiting a rubbed area. Clearly the scent message is not a warning or deterrent. However cats do obviously inspect and sample rubbed areas and, I suspect, can thus be presumed to be learning something about the previous visitor who wiped its glands on the spot.

A cat will furl the side of its lips and draw air into its mouth in addition to sniffing with its nose

Often a cat will pause by such a location, half close its eyes and then appear to grin as it turns the side of its mouth towards the scent mark. It will then furl up the side of its lips and, if you are close to the cat, you may also hear a soft sucking noise. This is a well recognised method that cats use for sniffing, in addition to the use of their nose. They have a special sense organ in the roof of their mouths which they use particularly to smell out the sex and reproductive state of another animal. So if, as commonly happens, a cat comes up to you and appears to be 'sniffing' at your leg, outstretched fingers or whatever through the sides of its mouth, and then rubs you, it is highly likely it is not simply showing affection! Dogs, by the way, also have this same sense organ in the roof of their palate but, unlike cats, the entrance to it is not via the side of the mouth. Instead they seem to use the nose as a duct. It may be even that the grooved front of a dog's nose and the familiar licking of the nose with the tongue are associated with getting the scent to the inside of the mouth. Again, no-one really knows.

However, we do know that a wide variety of creatures possess this sense organ. Human babies have it during their first few months of life and then it disappears. Horses and snakes as adults also have a comparable sense of smell located in the roof of the palate. This is why a horse will often furl its lips back and expose its teeth as it gently greets a stranger and why a snake flicks out its tongue to collect smells in the air which are then drawn in for sampling inside the roof of the mouth. It is notable that you don't hear of the snake's flicking tongue being in any way associated with affection!

Using the recent researches of some Dutch scientists for my inspiration, I set up a simple test for Chilly and Motley to observe how they would respond to various smells. Having noted that cats usually choose to rub on some projecting surface about nine inches off the ground, I arranged to have made a test-rig consisting of a series of chopped-down broom handles projecting horizontally from a central stub like a capstan. Each of the wooden rods was brand new and, presumably, all of them smelt the same. I fastened some clean towelling around the end of each one in case fabric held a smell for longer than plain wood, and I then treated each of the sticks differently. One I left alone as a control while another I held in a metal clamp and took to a neighbour's house. I watched until their cats (strangers to Chilly and Motley) rubbed their faces against it—thus, according to my theory, leaving an odour. A third sample rod was placed in the litter tray of a different neighbour's cat until it was wetted, thus giving a urine-soaked

sample, and to the fourth rod I attached a toy fabric mouse filled with the plant commonly called 'cat nip', which is especially
attractive to cats. By bringing all together at one time, I could
give my kittens a choice and see how they would respond.
While this test was clearly not rigorously controlled, the simple
technique is capable of being used to present all sorts of odours
that readers may like to test on their own cats. For my purpose
it worked well and provided a neat demonstration of a wide
range of cat responses to these objects.

Chilly would have none of it and would do little more than
walk right by my carefully assembled olfactory goodies.
Motley, however, came up trumps and gave the same performance repeatedly on different days. The 'blank' pole he would
ignore as he walked on by, though this may not be surprising
with so many other biologically interesting smells on offer close
at hand. The pole that had been rubbed by the strange cat was
carefully smelt, sometimes (but less often than I'd thought)
through the sides of the mouth, and then immediately treated
to an intensive bout of Motley's own rubbing using the side of
his head and neck. This resembled in function the behaviour of
one dog covering the scent mark of a previous dog by cocking
its leg and so when Motley came upon the urine-soaked pole, I
had my fears as to what might happen.

Mercifully, he didn't express his feelings by spraying but instead gave the sample long and careful attention by sniffing extensively through the sides of his mouth to the vomeronasal
organ in the palate. This confirmed the research findings that
cats, unlike dogs, do not use urine spraying to cover the
previously urine-marked areas of other cats. Instead they use
their urine smells as simple chemical messages which enable
them to communicate with each other even when one of the
parties has moved off elsewhere – an ideal scheme, you may
think, for a basically solitary animal. It has been found for certain that urine does carry definite information to both the male
and female cats that sniff it. For a start, they can tell how
recently another cat has been there before and this may well
help the cats to keep out of each other's way as they go off on
their hunting rounds (later on, we might look at how cats
parcel out a common area of ground among themselves). In ad-

dition, tom cats use it to tell the sexual condition of a female while, in contrast, females tend to give more of their attention to the scents rubbed off from the skin glands of other cats. We still don't know what additional information it carries from one cat to another and indeed this whole field leaves many questions for which we would love to have answers.

The cat nip-filled mouse? Well, most cat owners will already know that it can have a dramatic effect on some cats. They seem to get 'turned on' by it, involving much rolling, pawing and face rubbing. Some people have seen it as a cat aphrodisiac, for the rolling behaviours are somewhat similar to those exhibited by a female cat when ready to mate. I doubt that this is really true, but it certainly had something in it that perked up Motley. Maybe the explanation lies in the fact that cat nip has been found to contain a substance whose chemistry closely resembles marijuana! Quite likely we have been treating our cats to five to fifteen minutes of drug-induced nirvana to which they usually respond to by gazing into space and rolling around!

But, like many biological phenomena, not all animals respond alike. Thus while Motley was conspicuously excited by cat nip, Chilly never gave it any real attention at all. Having ignored my contraption completely, all she would do—as now—to demonstrate the rubbing behaviour was to keep pushing on my writing hand and standing on top of this paper. Why, Chilly, why?

*   *   *

Motley and Chilly had such contrasting temperaments that at times it was difficult to feature Chilly in the film at all. She was so aloof from proceedings and so bossed around by Motley that she could be relied upon to do absolutely nothing of interest for the film in sequences where the two cats were seen together. She would go to sleep, walk off or retreat behind the armchairs. Motley, in contrast, was a real bouncer: afraid of nothing, majestic in his splendidly conditioned coat, and delightfully outgoing. He performed most of the traditional cat behaviours that other owners will be familiar with and he seemed to enjoy teasing Snowy. He would march boldly up to him—but only when I was around to frustrate any retaliatory move by Snowy and prevent him from doing his room-mate any serious harm. Of the two cats, Motley became my personal favourite, I think because Chilly was causing me constant frustration in the film project while Motley was less demanding and less finicky, always behaving like a cheerful, carefree spirit. His ways were totally independent and with this came a sense of great self-assurance.

The problem that the essential character differences between the two cats presented was spotlighted very clearly by our experience in filming sequences of the hunting behaviour of a cat in woodland at night. Chilly was an obvious first choice to star because her Siamese colouring gave the camera a better chance to pick her out in the half-light. But equally relevant was the fact that she had done so little in the film up to that time that I was anxious to show her in action to maintain some balance in appearances by both cats.

We started filming with four people involved in operating the complicated and sophisticated 'worm's-eye view' equipment that Peter Parks at OSF has designed. Chilly would walk through the vegetation as per schedule but, try as we might, we couldn't get her to show interest in the rustling leaves that we pulled ahead of her on cotton, to demonstrate how her attention was attracted. After several days of filming with Chilly walking away from camera, across camera, towards camera and laying down to sleep under the leaves, we realised the situation was impossible. Reluctantly we decided that, once again, we would have to give Motley a try! Within minutes he was stalking and pouncing on our rustling leaves and shortly afterwards he came across a nocturnal moth. He stealthily lowered his head as he eyed it, trampled his back feet and then eagerly leapt on it and carried it away. Once again, Motley had delivered the goods while the camera was running and we were able to build up our sequence to demonstrate some of those ancestral hunting skills that are still so deep-seated in domestic cats and to show how, at night, most cats still revert to being totally at one with the wildlife world. This hunting sequence not only revealed some essential differences between the two cats but also showed most clearly how the skills of hunting and stalking developed from those many encounters that kittens

Motley stealthily lowered his head as he eyed a moth

experience in interaction with their litter mates and when playing on their own.

The kitten's preparation for independent life starts at the
nipple. Kittens, unlike young puppies, show a definite
preference for feeding from one particular teat on their
mother's belly. Immediately after the birth they will choose a
nipple to feed from and will then fight to dislodge any of their
siblings who attempt to feed from that teat. Thus you will find
that each kitten will usually return to its 'own' nipple when the
mother returns to the nest after a short period of absence. The
litter will not repeatedly squabble over which kitten gets what;
within a few days of birth each kitten has established its place.
In a way they resemble seasoned commuters settling contentedly into the same seat on the same train every day. Nevertheless, the biggest kitten often seems to feed from one of the
rearmost nipples which seem to supply the most milk.

However, if the kittens are separated from their mother for a
longer period, you will find that the established pattern is
forgotten as they struggle to get the best (furthest back) teats.

Starting from scratch

This early competitiveness is particularly important a little later on when kittens first encounter live prey. Rivalry between litter mates encourages them to approach and grab the prey before it has a chance to turn and bite them or run away.

As the kittens grow older they will start to play-hunt. If you give them, say, a toy mouse, one kitten will grab it and all the other kittens will stand aside and watch. The biggest doesn't necessarily get the play-food first. Most social mammals have a pecking order or dominance hierarchy so that the top animal will always take preference over ones lower down the status chain. Cats don't operate quite like that and, as kittens, will give way to the one actively at play. Another kitten won't take over until the original player gives up the toy.

Even in the early stages of life, kittens react differently depending on the texture and movement of the play object. If it moves or rolls, the kittens will chase it and push it with their paws. Only if it is soft or furry will the one that is playing with the object actually pick it up, throw it in the air and mouth it. In a way this shows that kittens have an instinctive predisposition to hunt and feed on small, soft or furry objects. The moth that attracted Motley during our night-hunting sequences, for instance, obviously lured him by its fluttering movements. In the event, Motley let it go, but not before having first carried it away and half-flattened it with his paw.

Later still, the mother cat will bring in live prey for the kittens. The first one to get it will grab it with its feet in the identical manner that the kittens have been using to grab each other during play. They have learnt in playing together how to limit the hardness of their bite, seeing just how far they can go before their litter-mate reacts violently. But now, with prey, their competitiveness ensures that they dash in and bite the prey at the back of the neck. Though awareness of the shape and texture that spells 'food' to a kitten is inborn, finding the place to bite is not. They have to learn during the play fights with each other how to restrain the prey and just where to bite at the back of the skull. The canine teeth of a cat are ideally designed to bite through the neck of a rodent and pierce the gaps in the neck vertebrae. Once there, the bones can be prized apart by the long pointed teeth and the spinal cord can then be severed.

Kittens learn how to handle prey in play fights with each other

The other teeth, particularly the main cheek teeth, are used to chew off flesh aided by the spiky 'teeth' on the flexible tongue which are used to rasp off all the remaining flesh from the bones. Seen in this light it becomes clear why the mother cat brings live mice to her kittens and allows them to 'play' with the small rodents. It is not cruel by nature's standards, for it is the way that the kittens must learn to become killers if they themselves are to survive. Ethical concepts such as 'cruelty' or 'right or wrong' cannot be applied to animals who may be acting simply on the basis of deeply programmed behaviours needed for their own survival.

Food capture is such a deep-seated drive in cats that they will break off and kill new prey when they are already feeding; often they kill more than they ever consume. They seem to enjoy the hunting more than the spoils, for cats tend not to gorge themselves from over-eating. Another apparently 'needless' behaviour of domestic cats is their tendency sometimes to play with and maim their prey, seemingly avoiding delivering the killing bite and so prolonging the agony. This can be seen where prey is tossed in the air repeatedly or clasped and pawed. The fact that the cat looks very casual and relaxed often makes cat owners think their animal is just 'playing' with its prey. I don't think science has a good explanation for this, though it does seem subjectively that the keyed-up, tense state that a cat displays prior to a pounce is totally different from its 'mood' once it has subdued or wounded its prey. I would imagine that the animal behaviour experts could readily identify different positions of ears, body and tail which differ greatly in the two situations. It is not helpful scientifically to say that some cats seem to 'enjoy' toying with a half-dead victim but it's certainly reasonable to suggest that they may undergo totally different emotions in these latter stages of food capture. Part of the answer may simply be that full or satiated cats are less interested in feeding than animals that haven't fed for some time. Careful record-keeping by scientists bears this out—in one way it is pretty obvious that a hungry cat is going to complete the killing of its prey more quickly—but there is more to it than that. For some unknown reason, the animals often repeat the taunting 'play' behaviour almost as if it gives them as much reward as feeding on their prey. And if this doesn't satisfy the enquiring mind, it may be just another example of how little we really know about our most familiar animals.

5

The 'Birth' Of Snowy

With our large indigenous cat populations, there are always more than enough kittens to go around, so most owners seem glad to give away their surplus kittens 'to a good home'—in fact most are glad to get rid of them to *any* home!

In the case of dogs, however, things are different. The demand for puppies, even cross-breeds and mongrels, outstrips supply and so they nearly all find homes quickly, even if three months later, a sizeable number of them have started to become disenchanted with their demands and three months more finds them becoming an expensive inconvenience to family holiday plans.

In America it has been calculated that 14% of the total dog population is turned over to dog shelters each year. The average age of dogs on entry is four years and before long most of them have to be put down. The owners must know that abandoning their animals is likely to be effectively a death sentence yet they presumably turn a blind eye to it and hope that the kindly attentions of the staff in the shelter will result in their ex-pet being found a new home. On this scale, however, it almost seems as if the dog is as much a sacrificial animal in society as a pampered pet.

It is puppies that are in demand, not adult dogs, and it seems a terrible shame that there is such a massive market for the youngsters when you remember the amount of publicity given to those poor animals which end up in homes for abandoned dogs. Think, too, of the recurring image of the 'dog pound' and the dog-catcher in all those Disney cartoons. It is as though there's a huge surplus in the canine population but the gratifying fact is that for every dog left to its fate on the streets there is a long waiting list for animals from breeding kennels and pet shops, to say nothing of private owners readily finding homes for surplus puppies.

Snowy of course was lucky. Not only was he wanted and treasured but also I (or whoever else would have been looking after him for his first year) was visited regularly by the Guide Dogs for the Blind Association so that his progress could be checked. Any problems the puppy walker has can then be ironed out and the dog's general development noted. In fact so helpful, tactful and perceptive are the Guide Dog supervisors that, as an American friend observed, 'Many kids in the States don't have such a thorough health-monitoring programme during their early development'.

From the time he came to me, Snowy was brought up under the watchful eye of the Association. But before he even arrived in my life and we had begun filming him, a lot of interesting behaviour on his part had, of course, already passed. Since our aim was to examine pets at all stages of their lives, I felt it would be appropriate also to study those early weeks. This obviously presented a problem. We had long since missed the boat as far as Snowy was concerned and so we set out to photograph the birth and first few weeks life of another white German shepherd. This would be useful in recapping in pictures the early development of Snowy himself.

So once again in my career as an animal photographer, I committed myself to the necessary preparations and the inevitable lengthy periods of waiting to be ready and on hand when a new generation of babies comes into the world. But this time, for a change, it would be easier. Instead of hanging about waiting for a wild creature like an inscrutable bullhead fish to spawn, all I had to bother about was a family pet. What could be simpler?

*　　　*　　　*

With a year of filming time stretching ahead of us, there were clearly going to be several possible chances—assuming we could get the right animals—of studying what goes on in those crucial and miraculous hours when a puppy makes the change from living in a sac of liquid within its mother's body to having to find all it needs to survive in the totally new environment of the outside world. In the film world, things very rarely happen the way you want them, so we were prepared to wait for the right opportunity and also to have to backtrack occasionally.

Although we had to get a somewhat exceptional puppy for the purpose of the film, there were several possible locations where white German shepherds could be found. For a start, there were the kennels of the Guide Dogs for the Blind Association from which Snowy himself had come. They choose and breed their dogs for temperament and aptitude alone but, unlike show breeders, they are perfectly happy with white dogs, whose increased visibility at dusk and in other conditions of poor light makes them in some ways preferable. What's more, the Association keeps detailed breeding records over many generations and so they can predict with a fair degree of accuracy those pairings of dogs which are likely to produce whites in their litters, even if both parents are in fact coloured.

As a second alternative, we found by chance that near to Oxford there lived one of the few breeders who, for personal reasons, defies the dictates of the rest of the dog-breeding world and deliberately produces white German shepherds by mating two 'pure-line' whites as parents. Admittedly her establishment lacked the sophistication of the clinically designed breeding quarters run by the Guide Dogs for the Blind Association but its existence did mean that our chances of witnessing the birth of a junior Snowy were considerably increased, particularly as it would happen within easy striking distance of our own base.

The wish to record all of the early stages in the life of a young puppy which could pass for Snowy was not simply in order to have highly appealing pictures of young puppies which would give continuity to our film, but for something of scientific importance as well. Man has controlled the breeding of dogs and cats for thousands of years and, as a result, has produced domesticated adult animals that now have an appearance and pattern of behaviour that are unlike those of their ancestors in the wild. Reproduction, however, is so crucial to the very survival of any animal that it is the part of our pet's behaviour that has been least altered by the process of domestication. In other words, when we watch the courtship, mating and birth of a domestic dog or cat, we are witnessing something basically unchanged from the experiences of their true wild ancestors hundreds of years before. A wildlife photographer could spend many months trying to record the reproductive behaviour of a wild dog and effectively finish up with the identical behaviour that a pet owner could observe at home from three feet away !

To show and interpret the behaviour leading to the birth of our white German shepherd would, I predicted, amaze even the people who have dogs of their own. 'Have you ever seen dogs mating?' I would ask people quite casually and go on to question how they thought the animals went about it. These apparently insensitive questions almost always produced a shocked, even embarassed, silence but when people realised I was serious the usual reply was, in fact, quite wrong!

'Why, it's obvious, isn't it?' they would say. 'The male dog jumps on the back of the female and in that position they mate'.

The truth is that most people have a totally mistaken impression of a dog's mating behaviour. To some people it is a source of embarrassment, to others it's an excuse for making cheap jokes, but an open-minded study of the subject reveals something of the delicate sensitivies and personal preferences that dogs show for each other. All too many people, seeing a pair of dogs taking a sexual interest in each other in the street, believe that adult dogs are always willing to couple if the female is in the right state. The truth is different. Breeders have told me that a female who doesn't want to be responsive simply will not let a male enter her. Derek Freeman, the expert in charge of the breeding of our British guide dogs, says that he knows of females who have mated with a particular male during a previous year who, if they smell that the same animal is in the kennels when they are again due to be mated, will not allow any other male to mate with her. In many cases, then, rather than being an indiscriminate brute process of grab and mate, the truth about dog courtship is that it can involve a high degree of selectivity about the choice of sexual partner.

The more I learnt about the courtship behaviour of dogs, the more I became aware of the personal and emotional dimensions that it held for the two animals involved. It left me with a hitherto unsuspected sense of regard for the individual preferences of dog courtship—something we are very respectful towards in humans. So what then are the essentials of dog breeding?

A male dog usually becomes sexually mature within his first year of life and from then on he is able to mate all the year round. An adult female, on the other hand, has one or two definite seasons per year when she is receptive to males. At these times, her behaviour changes and she becomes increasingly active and wanders over much greater distances depositing her powerful scent messages as she goes.

When she is ready to receive a male there is a well recognised series of behaviours which takes place. The bitch will typically run alternately towards and away from the male so that he is encouraged to chase her. Then, if she stops running away, the male is immediately brought to an appropriate position to start mating. When we filmed a white German shepherd courting a white female, it was a revelation to me how much bowing and invitation bouncing behaviours were performed. I cannot explain why I should have been so surprised to realise that some dogs seem to have feelings analogous to the lightheartedness of human love and courtship. It made me wonder at times whether I was losing some of my scientific objectivity and falling for a sentimental interpretation of what I was seeing.

Whatever the true explanation of the 'emotions' that courting dogs experience may be, the postures that they adopt are clear for all to see. First the couple investigate each other by sniffing. Then the male rests his chin over the female's back and mounts her from the rear. In this position the male's penis enters the female and this, in most people's view, is how dogs mate. In fact, it is only the position in which the animals first couple up. Once the male's penis is in place, it is held by the internal muscles of the female and he will then be held as he dismounts from the female, lifting one of his back legs over her back and standing side by side or back to back with his partner as mating takes place. Possibly, in this position, their wild ancestors could better protect themselves from any predators to which they might be vulnerable during the relatively long process of coupling. This 'tied' position may be maintained for anything up to half an hour and it is during this time that the female is fertilised. It is still not known why, biologically speaking, dogs need to perform this unusually lengthy locking in their mating behaviour. Scientists have found that the male's secretion has different components, which pass into the female at different times during mating. The male reproductive cells pass to the female first and the later secretions appear to activate the sperm. When mating is complete, the two animals simply separate and, if successful, the bitch will be ready to give birth about seventy days later.

When the time came to think about filming this, it turned out that the guide dogs did not have a suitable pair that were ready to mate. We turned instead to our obliging local breeder, who always seemed to have animals raring to mate. And so it was that a somewhat angular white bitch named Serena was allowed to romp around and finally seduce an apparently overwhelmed white male called Blinkhorn. We filmed the initial coupling and then the change in position of the male as he cocked one leg over his female's back while still coupled and turned to face away from her.

One other observation about this strange process is worthy of mention. While running the film of the dog's courtship behaviour back and forwards through the editing machine, I stopped at the point where Blinkhorn was just lifting his leg off Serena's back because it had suddenly struck me that this posture was *identical* to the 'leg-cocking' urination posture of dogs. Could it be simply chance that, firstly, only male dogs cock their legs to urinate and, secondly, that they only do it when they become sexually mature – the very time in their lives that they need the ability to dismount from their mates? Clearly there are other factors involved (such as males marking their territory positions by urination) but I can't help thinking that there may be some connection between the two activities which accounts for why only adult males cock their legs to urinate.

It doesn't take much observation to realise that the urine of all dogs and bitches is highly attractive to the noses of others and also that their urinating is often more concerned with leaving a chemical message than with the need to empty the bladder. Males are always going around 'covering' the urine scent of a previous male on some marking post and it could well be that among the messages coded in a single contribution is some indication of the approximate size of the animal that produced it, based on the height of the urine mark.

Females don't use marking posts as males do, although evidently their urine does give clues as to their reproductive state and when a bitch is on heat she greatly increases the frequency with which she leaves these small reminders of her availability. The squatting urination position of the female is evidently all she needs and it is interesting that young males adopt the same position before they reach maturity. In a way, it is comparable to males of the human species before they pass through puberty. They have high-pitched voices, unbearded faces and similar basically female features which change when they become mature males. Snowy himself demonstrated this well during his first few months, for his posture as a juvenile closely resembled that of an adult female.

Having recorded Serena being mated, we waited to film the birth of Snowy's stand-in. We knew in advance that the behaviour of the mother and newly-born infant is so distinctive and deep-seated that it was worth going to a lot of trouble to be able to film the event with great clarity. For this reason, we decided to move the white bitch, Serena, over to our film studios where we had built a special enclosure with a new whelping (breeding) box with sides that could be removed for maximum visibility.

We visited Serena on several occasions in her own home so that she could get to know us and wouldn't be upset by our presence when we finally attended the birth of her puppies. Then, with two weeks to go before she was due to give birth, we moved her to our film studios, and gradually accustomed her to our heat filters and lights by letting her sleep in her new box surrounded by all the filming gear that would be used on the great day.

Our experience as wildlife photographers has left us clear

about one thing in nature—never trust a female! Our patience has so often been stretched to the full by the need to watch and wait for a female to perform some simple piece of behaviour in front of the movie cameras. Whether the subject is a female salmon not laying her eggs or a one-ton female elephant seal not giving birth to her baby, a female squirrel not responding to a male or a female flea not reaching maturity, the lesson is the same. We probably spend more time waiting for females to respond in courtship, to give birth or feed their young than in any other part of our filming work. And nothing is worse than getting there too late, when the eggs have just been spawned or the babies have just been born. Being wise old hands, we followed our usual pattern and watched Serena in shifts day and night during the week the puppies were due to be born so that we wouldn't miss them. Every three hours during the night my alarm would go off and I'd stumble out of my bed, blearily throw on some clothes and go and take a peep at Serena. This process went on until, early in the evening of May 1st (Labour Day, appropriately) she started the birth process.

As it turned out, we had plenty of notice before the first of the babies was produced. Serena was kind to us: not only was she twelve hours ahead of her time but she obligingly gave us a clue by her refusal to take food during the previous six hours. Finally, she showed the characteristic pre-birth turning and restlessness as she lay below our lights on her bed of hessian-covered straw.

She behaved so co-operatively that I had time to call my colleague George Bernard, a specialist stills photographer, to the scene and to check and recheck all our gear and lights. We waited and watched as Serena started an intense bout of scratching at her bedding, a sure sign that birth would shortly begin. This vigorous and nowadays quite needless behaviour is though to be a relic of the actions of our dogs' wild ancestors, who would first seek solitude and then dig a hole in which to retire to produce their puppies. As it was, we had firmly secured the straw-filled hessian sacking to the base of the box so that Serena could demonstrate her instinctive behaviours yet not mess up our photogenically attractive fabric base to the whelping box.

S. & C.—C

After about thirty minutes, the scratching behaviour diminished as Serena lay down restlessly. After changing her position several times, her flanks started to contract. She began to lick her rear quarters as the first of the birth fluids began to flow out, showing that one of the membranes that had been protecting the puppies inside the mother's body had broken ready for birth. Serena lay on her side and reached back to lick up the fluids as her birth canal steadily expanded.

Soon a shiny black bulge distended her rear quarters and a neatly wrapped puppy slipped effortlessly onto the sacking. The transparent membrane tightly enveloped the puppy, like meat on a supermarket shelf. The new arrival, a black and white puppy, lay motionless as Serena licked and delicately chewed at the covering membrane until it could be freed, whereupon she ate up all the membrane. Still the puppy did not move. Over half a minute had passed since it had tumbled into the nest and the youngster simply lay there limp and damp, flopping around unresponsively under the action of Serena's tongue. Finally Serena began to chew on the umbilical cord which had attached the puppy to its mother while inside her body. Suddenly, with a squirm, the little body rocketed into action. Its little nostrils opened and closed and it twisted from its back on to its belly.

Serena continued to lick the pup and it, in turn, stumbled blindly towards its mother. Finding her belly, the youngster nuzzled into Serena's fur but was almost immediately knocked backwards by a renewed bout of licking. Once again, its head waving from side to side, the puppy dragged itself back to Serena's belly and pressed with her front paws into the fur. It moved around until it hit upon a nipple and, with no teaching from its parent and no trace of domestication, it did what thousands of wild mammals have done since they first appeared on earth—it bit on to a nipple and sucked its first mouthful of milk.

This apparently simple transition involves some of the most impressive biological processes that science has yet been able to evaluate. The moment a pup gulps its first lungful of air, there is a complete changeover to a new life-style and an abandonment of the previous one. Looked at most simply, the puppy would choke to death if it tried to breathe while still inside the fluid-filled bag in its mother's womb. Yet soon after it has been born, it must begin the entirely different process of sucking in air in order to maintain its oxygen supply. If the newly born puppy doesn't start the changeover to breathing air quickly enough, it will lack the essential oxygen it needs to survive. Research has shown that if a mature dog's brain is denied oxygen for only five or ten minutes, the animal will suffer permanent damage and may even die. New-born puppies, however, have an amazing ability to survive without oxygen for as much as half an hour. They do this by breaking down proteins in the body for their energy, an ability which keeps them alive as they change over to a mechanism of fuelling their body from carbohydrates and oxygen by feeding and breathing like all adult animals. This miracle of chemistry means that even in the cases of prolonged birth, the puppy has an inbuilt mechanism to avoid brain damage.

To add to these extraordinary protective powers, the newborn puppy's brain is able to compensate for damage and reorganise itself at this most demanding period of its life. If a major region of the brain, say the centre of vision, is removed or damaged in an adult dog or cat, it will be virtually blind. In a new-born animal, however, another part of the brain will very soon take over this function and the animal will be able to see normally in due course.

The more I learn about the brain of any animal, the more staggered and impressed I become. If you or I were to begin to try to make a brain (or body) based on the repeated dividing up of a single cell, we wouldn't know where to begin. Yet that is what happens in each and every animal. No wonder we find the world of nature so fascinating. It is a subject in which the more one knows, the more one wants to know. In the case of our pets' brains, they develop just those abilities that the animals need at a particular time. It is all controlled with the most incredible precision. Thus, at birth, the only parts of the brain which are already developed are those which control the essential abilities of breathing, heartbeat and the sense of balance (so it 'knows' the right way up). The best-developed sensing nerves of the newborn pup are those going to the face for touch, smell and temperature awareness. But at birth the centres in the brain of the young animal are only functioning poorly and so it quickly takes on the temperature of its surroundings. Its fur is short and it has a relatively big surface area so that, taken together, these factors would mean that many animals would die in cold conditions if nature did not take care of this by giving the animal a brain mechanism that can respond to unsuitable temperatures by motivating the animal to keep it crawling until it finds a suitably warm environment.

From the outset, puppies and kittens have the ability to learn. Although few people realise it, the very fact of a baby animal getting milk from its mother's breast is, of itself, a reward which will encourage the animal to repeat the behaviour and ensure its survival. It will reinforce those behaviours and physical conditions associated with feeding. Thus, if receiving the reward of feeding at the nipple is associated with a particular artificial smell the new arrival will, within a few days, come to follow that smell—even if it's only a trace put on to a cloth or tissue.

Just as some parts of the pup's brain are well developed at birth, many others are not, either because the nerves haven't been properly formed or because they have not yet joined up to the brain. It all depends upon what the animal needs to do at that stage. Thus the movement which is most important at the start for getting the animal to the breast is mainly developed in the front legs which are used in crawling towards and pummelling the mother's breast for milk. The back legs are basically just dragged around at this time. Another region of the brain, the reticular formation which is concerned with keeping the body alert and responsive, is so poorly developed at birth and for the first few days that the animal spends as much as 90% of its time asleep or in a semi-conscious state. Its mother, of course, will look out for its safety during this period so the young animal which has recently suffered the trauma of birth can develop its other mental faculties in peace. It doesn't need to be alert, and the brain mechanism will only develop fully when the time is right and it becomes necessary for survival.

This brief examination of a puppy's coordination of body

cameras ever closer to capture the details of the next puppy's birth—which, hopefully would be a white one. Serena was very tolerant of our presence—she was now accustomed to our lights and cameras—but I would warn prospective observers that some bitches and some breeds do not welcome the presence of humans when they give birth. By now Serena's first two puppies were suckling contentedly and some time elapsed before her flanks started to contract again, signifying that one more was on its way. This should be great, we thought. First the dark pups and then the big build-up as we await the birth of the first white one. George and I moved in even closer as Serena prepared to give birth again. At last we would have a surrogate young Snowy.

But sadly this was not to be. Serena was soon licking away at a well-endowed male which was quite unmistakably brown. It was clear that this would be the last of the litter, and George and I stared at each other in disbelief. Surely pure-line white dogs, mated together, should produce at least one white puppy? We switched off all the equipment and I went to phone Serena's owner.

Four healthy puppies for Serena—but all dark-coated

'It can't possibly be,' came the hesitant response. 'Blinkhorn and Serena are pure-bred whites. This sort of thing doesn't happen...'

We ummed and aahed for a moment or two. Then there came a strangled groan from the other end of the line. 'Oh, no, surely not,' she said, as the light dawned. 'There's another old dog in my kennels ... a coloured dog called Buck. His father was supreme champion at Cruft's and I bought him for breeding ten years ago ... but he's never managed to father any puppies.'

There was another pause and then she went on.

'We've always thought he's sterile so we put him in with Serena. Well, after all this time...'

So here was the father of our puppies! After nearly a month of planning, building sets, watching, waiting, feeding, shooting and editing several hundred pounds' worth of film, we still didn't have the 'birth' of our film star.

A day or two later, I returned Serena and her litter to her owner. Buck was pointed out to me and as I looked at him I could swear the old rogue was grinning!

6

More Problems — And A Solution

No wildlife photographer gives up easily when stalking his quarry, let alone when the animal concerned is no more wild than a pet dog! Serena's embarrassed owner offered to mate two more of her white adults so that we could have a second chance of filming the birth of our surrogate Snowy. This time Buck and all the other males were kept well away so that when we brought Tammy to our filming kennels, we knew that she must produce an all-white litter.

Again, we won her confidence and walked and fed her until, in good time, she settled comfortably in her new home surrounded by our camera equipment. We watched and waited and made regular checks at night. Very early one morning, three days in advance of schedule, the poor dog must have almost burst. I got in to find the kennels in chaos. Tammy had scratched the place to tatters and the whole area was a gory mess. I watched as the last of her litter was being born – seven all-white puppies but at that moment they were all red, nestled beside a crimson-streaked mother. It was her first birth and even if I had been there on time, it would have been impossible for aesthetic reasons to use the film. So once again we were denied Snowy's birth sequence.

However, we were relieved when the vet confirmed that mother and pups would definitely be all right in due course. The pups were fine once they had been cleaned but Tammy was going to take some time to heal and was in no condition to be filmed.

On phoning the news of this second frustration to our ever-helpful breeder, she suggested that now we had at last got our new-born white puppies, it might still be possible to film their development using another animal as their mother. Such a possibility had never crossed my mind but, when it was all explained to me, it seemed the idea might just work.

Our old friend Serena was still suckling her young, even though by now they could easily be fed by hand, and perhaps we could take advantage of Serena's docile nature to persuade her to adopt all of Tammy's white litter. Tammy, in turn, could then be nursed back to health without the burden of looking after her brood.

By now I was physically weary, frustrated and beginning to despair. On impulse I agreed to take our vehicle to collect Serena together with all her own pups so that she would take the return move with minimal upset. She and her family were to be housed in a separate room overnight and then on the next day, when she had settled down, I planned to have someone take Tammy out on a short walk and then bring in Serena to see if she would adopt Tammy's white litter.

Things didn't quite work out that way. When docile Serena reached the film studios, she heard the squeaks of Tammy's pups and possibly smelt what had been going on. She became very agitated, even though she was housed separately twenty feet or so away. An assistant at OSF, Georgina, was carrying Serena's own brown puppies inside to join their mother when the bitch suddenly turned aggressive and bit her fiercely. It was patently obvious that the idea wasn't going to work and so next morning Serena, Tammy and their respective litters were returned to their owner in separate vehicles. It was time to start again from scratch.

*   *   *

Our birth sequence was fast becoming one more example of how pets often turn out more difficult to film than we imagine. So once again, we turned to our friends at the Guide Dog Association for help.

Sure enough, Derek Freeman explained, they did occasionally get a white German shepherd in a litter, but they weren't prepared to breed for colour alone since their main concern was temperament. This was fair enough, I thought, but it still didn't help me with the film. However, because of their detailed breeding records it was possible for them to predict which pairing of animals was likely to produce a litter including whites.

We chose a white bitch and she was mated with a brown male so we had to repeat all the courtship filming again. This time, however, the two animals hardly paused for any play behaviour and so we were not going to be able to show the 'mood' of the animals in courtship. Nevertheless, we now had our fertilized bitch being looked after by the experts and it was just a matter of setting up all the camera gear in the Guide Dogs breeding block and waiting.

And waiting and waiting and waiting. In the end it was clear that our plump mother-to-be had aborted her litter so, as before, all our efforts (and those of the male dog) proved fruitless!

Two months later another white guide dog bitch came into season and this time a white male German shepherd was brought in to be her partner. We could, of course, have possibly used the sequence of two white animals courting that we already had in the can as an alternative. However the birth sequence had become such a chronicle of misadventures that we decided to refilm the whole lot from scratch. When advised of the appropriate time, we travelled up to the Guide Dog establishment and watched in the rain as the dog and the bitch walked around showing very little interest in each other. It seemed very unlikely that anything would happen there and then and so, as a bitch may be receptive for five days or so, we agreed to return in a couple of days to repeat the attempt.

This second time was scarcely more successful—and it seemed that the female simply didn't fancy the white male that was offered as her partner. It does, of course, happen that a bitch will simply not allow a particular male to mate with her, as I've already suggested. However, after about half an hour of encouragement, our two white animals did tie up in the mating position. At last, it seemed, we were almost home and dry.

We all stood around looking pretty pleased with each other. Derek Freeman went to note the successful pairing in his breeding records, only to return a minute or two later looking crestfallen. He'd just found that his assistant, doing voluntary overtime, had successfully mated the female to another, brown stud dog the evening before. No wonder she wasn't much interested in mating again! That litter, when they arrived, were all brown. To add insult to injury, there were two further pairings of guide dogs which were thought might produce our missing white puppy but in neither event did the resulting litters contain a suitable animal.

Failure! We had two sequences of a white male mating with a white female, one sequence of a white female giving birth to four brown puppies, and a few shots of a solitary day-old baby. The outlook was beginning to seem pretty gloomy—even Serena's brood was now grown up and so we had missed the chance of showing both the birth and the behaviour of the brown puppies in their first few weeks of life. Who would have believed it?

A partial solution to our problem came almost by chance. A lady living near Birmingham, the owner of a brown German shepherd, had phoned up the Guide Dog Association to say that—surprise, surprise – their bitch had just produced a litter with four browns and two whites!

'Oh no, no, no!' I gasped, head in hands, when the news was conveyed to me. If I got permission to follow the behaviour of the litter during its first few weeks of life, I would still lack sequences showing the mating of that particular brown mother and, of course, the birth. But at least I'd have managed to fit one more piece into the jigsaw puzzle. These problems of getting some kind of continuity into the film, I think, illustrate part of the frustration of making any wildlife film. With actors you can at least tell them what to do and thus assemble your film fairly coherently. Animal behaviour, on the other hand, is a fraction more difficult to control!

Hurried phone calls followed with both the owner of the new mother and with our BBC producer, Peter Jones. We agreed to make the best of a bad job and, despite all the technical problems, to use the Birmingham puppies to illustrate puppy behaviour. We did cheat in one small way, however, by showing only one of the white puppies in the litter to dramatise the rarity (the extreme, frustrating, unexpected, unbelieveable, annoying, embarrasing rarity) of a white German shepherd puppy!

Janice Evans, the owner, turned out to be a tall, slim student who was training to be a teacher at a college in Wolverhampton. She lived at home with her parents, her brother and her lovely brown German shepherd Ellie (whom we later discovered to be Snowy's half sister). She was also puppy-walking another dog, a Labrador, for the Guide Dogs but this animal had been boarded out for the time that Ellie was carrying her litter. All the family, like all the pet owners I worked with during the year, were most helpful and friendly. Here again, I set to wondering whether expressing an interest in pets is almost a guarantee of acceptance by pet owners, leading them to open their hearts and houses to meet one's needs. Perhaps any shared hobby or interest immediately opens doors and hearts, but with pets as the bond, I seemed to have an all-powerful password which would gain the maximum co-operation of any secret society.

'Snowy Junior' showed the appropriate stages of development for a one-week-old puppy. His eyes and ears were still closed, he struggled to feed at his mother's teat using mainly his front legs to progress with and he still relied on his mother's presence for warmth and for his excretory needs. As he had no functional muscles yet to control facial expressions or to wag his tail, he seemed fixed in a mask-like trance. At long last, it seemed, we had everything going for us, and we could begin the long process of filming the various stages of this young puppy's development during the crucial first few weeks of life.

At this time a puppy's development is effectively indistinguishable from that of a wolf cub. All this we were able to record faithfully as Snowy Junior passed through the various stages of development. For about the first ten days, the pup basically relies on its reflexes but from about twenty days onwards, the little animal becomes more reactive. It sleeps less and is conspicuously better co-ordinated; it starts to walk on four wobbly legs. By three and a half weeks the puppy begins to respond to loud bangs or its mother's barks. Its ear muscles start to react by pricking up and pointing to face the sound, and the eyes open.

It is tempting to think that they can now see or—more ac-

curately—perceive visually what is going on. But this skill requires an awareness of form, movement, distance and so on
and it is clear that they are not really up to this, at least when
the eyes are just opened. The textbooks describe an elegant test
which demonstrates that this is not so—or at least it's intended
to prove this. Called the 'visual cliff' experiment, it depends
upon observing the response when the young puppy is put at
the top edge of an apparent drop which is, in fact, an optical il-
lusion. By using clear glass over the visual precipice, it is totally
safe for the young animal to walk over the firmly supported
glass without falling.

If you try a three-week-old puppy with this test, say the textbooks, it will walk right over the glass, even though its eyes are
open. However, by the time it is five weeks old, the same puppy will not step off the 'edge' even if it has never fallen from
anything in its past experience. We decided to try it for
ourselves, so we made three giant checkerboards with red and
white squares, and duly made the pilgrimage from Oxford to
Birmingham with our gear. And what happened? The puppies
at three weeks stopped dead in their tracks once they reached
the edge. Two weeks later, they would cheerfully walk over it
without hesitation! So much for the textbooks!

We could, I suppose, have illustrated and supported the
'classical' behaviour by editing together shots from our film
which seem to fit the theory. But by the time we had gone into
the editing room and watched the film of all the puppies at five
weeks walking on the glass, it seemed absurd to pretend. Not
for the first time in my filming career, we found that the 'truth'
from textbooks is by no means reliably born out in real life!
This is one reason why I would encourage any watcher of
'tamelife' to observe and note down a pet's behaviour and then
come to his or her own conclusions about what is going on. No
book on animal behaviour, least of all this one, is going to be
100% correct. We could all learn by hearing and comparing as
many other people's views as possible.

By four weeks of age, Snowy Junior's ability to move around
in a coordinated way resulted in him developing the necessary
behaviour mechanism to be able to excrete outside his bed. As
a result, the mother's licking behaviour gradually diminished.

By five weeks, he was beginning to eat solid food and drink fluids. He was highly interactive with the other pups—they began to use their tails and faces in body-language expressions and they spent less time close to their mother. They explored everything in their environment using all their senses, commonly sniffing and biting at their surroundings.

When six weeks of age, suckling had almost finished, and the pup's inclinations to lick his mother (or humans) in the face had developed. This behaviour, when directed to humans, is seen as enjoyable 'kissing'—another example of the way some people like to view their animal's behaviour in human terms—and as a disgusting hazard by many others. Its significance to the puppy can be understood when it is realised

Licking behaviour is a relic of a puppy's demand for food

that the puppy will lick more insistently as more time elapses since it was last fed. If we humans didn't take over from the mother by feeding the pup solid food as she ceases to provide milk, we would readily see the prime function of this licking behaviour. If we weren't around, the mother would continue to feed her hungry babies by regurgitating food in response to their begging-licking.

When this licking behaviour is performed by an adult dog on a person, it is presumed to be an expression of a similar close

association between the two and is intended to elicit play or
friendly attention for the dog. In the same way that the 'shake-
a-paw' behaviour we looked at earlier is a remnant from puppyhood which has changed from its prime functions, so face-
licking is a relic of earlier behaviour patterns. For my part, I
avoided letting Snowy kiss me whenever I could. To my mind,
it debases the real thing!

One of the problems of persuading people to share my enthusiasm for looking at nature's amazing processes is that most
natural phenomena go on so subtly that their finesse usually
passes unappreciated by the untrained eye. In the case of pet
watching, it is easy to miss the significance of the changes in the
behaviour of the pups and their mother because they take place
so smoothly and gradually. But it is worth stopping to ask one
apparently trivial question. How is it that pups come to
recognise their own parent as being the centre of their family,
the one from whom they willingly accept leadership?

The question obviously has a bearing on how the wildlife 'instincts' of dogs can be successfully transferred so that a person,
instead of a dog, comes to assume the role of the dominant pack
leader in the mind of the growing puppy. The experience of
many dog breeders over the years has indicated that the best
time to take a puppy from its mother and to start to socialise it
is when it is between six and twelve weeks old. Pet scientists are
now able to explain why this should be.

Once again, it is all to do with the natural instincts of the
wild dog. Having gradually developed its brain, senses and
muscles during the first four weeks of life, the puppy will begin
by the fifth week actively to socialise with its litter mates and to
relate to its environment. From the sixth week onward, the
puppy enters a critical period of its life during which it learns to
recognise its parent as an individual distinct from everything
else it is experiencing. It has been found that whoever is with
the puppy and acting in a parental role during the next six
weeks (weeks eight to ten are the crucial ones) becomes fixed in
the puppy's mind as being its natural parent, whatever the real
case may be.

In the wild, of course, the real mother would still be with the
youngsters at this stage, and we would think it only natural

that they would adopt her as their mother. However, we create an unnatural situation by domestication and, if the pups were kept in the company of dogs alone for their first, say, fourteen weeks of their life, then it is unlikely that they would become trustful and friendly towards humans. Instead their instincts and loyalties would become too dog-orientated and they would forever view themselves as indelibly attuned to react with other dogs. They would never adapt well to life in a human family.

In theory, if a puppy was brought up by a warm black box that moved on wheels and delivered suitable food, then that too would be viewed by the pup as its mother. What's more, by extension, its brain would be predisposed to treat a population of similar small black boxes as its kind.

This crucial period, during which young mammals fix on to the concept of their 'mother', is used in artificial situations where one species of animal is fostered upon another. A few years ago, I had a wonderful experience of this when by chance I found myself with an orphaned baby grey squirrel that didn't stand much chance of survival unless I could get it to feed. Attempts to force-feed it with warmed cow's milk from a glass pipette were getting us nowhere when I had the audacious idea of trying to foster him on a cat who had just produced three kittens.

Amazingly our cautious moves to introduce the still-blind 'Sammy Squirrel' to Beauty, the cat, met with success and we were able to bring up the squirrel safely to adulthood among the kittens. The cat naturally tried to bring up Sammy as a kitten and, as he was with Beauty at the critical period, he identified her as his mother and a representative of his breed. From then on, we rechristened him 'Sammy Squitten'.

Though his adventures were happily recorded on a film and in a book, *Squirrel on My Shoulder*, a major danger with such an imprinted alien is that he would be likely to approach an unfriendly cat as 'family' once he was released—and quite likely get killed for his trouble. How he fared in truth, I will leave you to guess.

The rapid learning process at the 'imprinting' stage is irreversible. No amount of subsequent socialisation with dogs or humans can put right behavioural problems that have resulted from inappropriate associations at that critical period. Once the imprint of 'parent' has taken place, much of the youngster's behaviour is directed towards that parent. The best-adjusted family dogs are so well integrated into human households for the very reason that they have had close, caring contacts with humans over their critical period. That being the case, it is no wonder that they insist on continuing to perform and direct their natural dog languages like paw-pushing, licking, tail-wagging and mating clasps towards people. It is therefore in that light that the 'tamelife' watcher should try to interpret them.

If the pup is taken from its mother and kept in the company of humans before it is six weeks of age, it tends to become too well humanised and it has problems relating and behaving appropriately to other animals. At the other extreme, if a wild animal is captured as an adult and brought into captivity, where it may be encouraged to loose its timidity and seek food or shelter from humans, it will never react towards them as it would towards members of its own species.

Indeed, dogs that don't have the chance to imprint on humans at the appropriate time can sometimes cause serious problems later in life. It is said that many of the dogs that make vicious attacks on people have been denied the opportunity to be imprinted on humans in their youth. (Incidentally, this is not the only reason. The single most important cause of dogs attacking humans is thought to be lack of owner dominance during the animal's upbringing. The youngsters are naturally going to try to find a high position in the new, human, pack and if they get their way too much they will restore their dominant role by an uninhibited bite). It remains true however that the best situation for domestic animals is one in which the puppy is in contact with people as well as other dogs when they are between four and eight weeks old. Then the puppy can safely be moved away from other dogs and into a totally human household with little or no subsequent problems in relating to both people and animals in the future. Snowy came to me at nine weeks of age and had had the benefit of plenty of attention from the kennel maids at the Guide Dogs for the Blind Association before he joined me. He fitted in like a glove and could not have been better adjusted.

Were Snowy to have been born a wild hunting dog in Africa, he would have been associating with his kind alone during the critical bonding period and thus have become assimilated naturally and totally into the wild dog society. But as a domestic dog, bred for the time he would be paired to a sightless person, Snowy's natural instincts obviously needed to be channelled and imprinted on humans early in life. So it is all the more amazing to realise that the major details of birth and early behaviour of our most common pets remain the same as their totally wild relatives. For me at least, it made the whole process not just a source of wonderment but also a privileged opportunity to witness and so share some of the fundamental and moving chords of wildlife behaviour that still beat deep in every one of us.

7

A Lot To Learn

While we were busy filming the birth, the real-life Snowy was getting on with the important business of growing up.

Our first walks outside the garden were carefully arranged to introduce him to traffic progressively so that he would not be frightened. We started in Blenheim Palace estate right next door and then moved on to quiet roads. Always on his lead of course, Snowy never even seemed afraid or alarmed by the traffic even when it was eventually whizzing by only a yard away.

Having got over my initial impressions of him being much larger than I had originally anticipated, I now knew him as very much a youngster who could almost look lost at the end of his lead. He would still chase his tail on occasions and was alert to every new experience. An operatic soprano on television once caught his attention and he stared intently at the screen, cocking his ears from side to side. That was his sole interest in the medium that was to bring him fame.

He also started carrying and chewing things. He had a particular fascination for the cats' food bowl and he would eat any remaining food before marching round the house with the bowl in his mouth. Unless recovered quickly, the plastic bowl would be treated like a bone and turn up mangled and tooth-pocked inside his sleeping box.

He liked to chase Chilly and Motley when I wasn't around —or at least if he thought I wasn't! Several times my attention was drawn to flying gravel as white paws skidded across the

Snowy in hot pursuit of a streaking cat

path in hot pursuit of a streaking cream or tabby cat. When I
yelled my disapproval Snowy would sometimes suddenly veer
off in a different direction, as if he had been going that way all
along and it was pure coincidence that the cat had crossed his
path. More often, though, once the chase was on, he wouldn't
let matters rest until the cat was safely up a tree or inside the
sanctuary of the house! Clearly I couldn't allow this, not just
with the well-being of the çats in mind but also because a guide
dog which will chase after cats (or anything else) when he has a
blind person in tow isn't the slightest use to anyone, least of all
his owner.

Little by little Snowy had to learn the meaning of the word
'No', whatever circumstances it was used under. This was just

one of a string of instructions that he had to know and obey. Some of them were simply those commands which any householder would wish to teach the family pet, while others were specifically directed towards his future as a guide dog.

I started off with a major advantage over most other puppy owners in that Snowy, like all British guide dogs, has a long and carefully selected pedigree which has been designed to produce superb, easily trainable and well adjusted dogs. I cannot stress enough at this point how the fact that Snowy turned out to be such a willing and obedient dog was really a credit to the breeding programme rather than the few skills which I brought to bear on his development. I was aware that the breeding records of guide dogs are so carefully documented that the organisation can choose parents whose own parents were themselves produced by successful·and acceptable guide dogs, and so on into past generations. It's probably as sophisticated and successful a breeding programme as exists for the most highly bred racehorses and I, as a puppy walker, was one of the beneficiaries.

Snowy's 'vocabulary', to which anyone with an authoritative voice could make him respond, consisted of the commands 'Sit' , 'Stay', 'Stand', 'Down' (laying down on his belly), 'Dead' (laying down on his side, head resting on the floor), 'Heel' (a command he learnt later in the year at dog training classes but which I used to make him walk to the left and slightly ahead of me), 'Fetch', 'Carry', 'Give', and 'Busy'. This last word is used to encourage the dog to relieve himself in a socially acceptable place when he first goes out prior to setting off on a walk. Lord knows what would happen if someone used this as a general command at a guide dog jamboree by dashing through the assembled dogs yelling 'Busy' at the top of his voice. The resulting chaos can scarcely be imagined. More seriously, because of the understandable distaste that dog wastes in public places cause, it is essential that guide dogs are disciplined to 'perform' in approved places only. If guide dogs and police dogs can be trained to do this reliably, it may be reasonable to expect other dog owners to show more social responsibility in this regard too.

Much of Snowy's training was the result of the combination

'Stay!'

of a sharp 'No' and a warm 'That's a good boy, Snowy' applied with a measure of consistency to his daily life. Thus he
learned to walk neatly on his lead, not to jump up, sit on furniture, beg food, bark or threaten in any way. And when working on the lead, Snowy was not allowed to stop to sniff!

This latter was something very alien to him, for all dogs rely
very heavily upon their senses of smell for social information
about other dogs. You only have to study dogs as they walk

down a city street to see how theirs is a world of smell. Humans have their own greeting ceremonies based on words, facial expressions and contacts like hand-shakes or, if you're lucky, kissing. To some extent, dogs rely on gesture too. When they approach one another, they initially signify their mutual recognition by alert head postures and tail signals.

But once Snowy got close to a strange dog his 'instincts' were to sniff around and under the other's back end to sample the various smells. Left to their own devices, both animals would indulge in such a greeting, often causing mild embarrassment to onlookers as it is so alien and offensive to human sensibilities. But it's only our own conditioning which makes it seem so: with a dog, it is simply a different social system in operation. In man's society, there are many complicated and important social ceremonies surrounding drinking and the subsequent exchange of information: we frequently meet people to 'discuss things over a drink'. Our inevitable visits to the lavatory are irrelevant to us, but with dogs, it is the other way round. Their act of urination is the ceremony. Whereas we humans have our pubs and bars, dogs have their lamp posts and trees where they can communicate with each other.

Clearly dog urine conveys many social signals. Male dogs use it to mark their territories, females to leave scent cues about their sexual condition. When one male dog smells a marking post that another has sprayed, he will cock his leg up and cover the area with a personal squirt. It is hard for a guide dog to be taught to ignore such a deep-seated communications system when it comes to be leading a blind person. Incidentally I advise my readers to watch out for a long 'shaggy dog' story explaining how male dogs supposedly first learnt how to cock their legs. It involves a claim that male dogs used to squat like females, and still would except that one day a wall fell on one as he was performing. Ever since then, the story goes, they have been prepared, and keep their leg ready to act as a prop!

Snowy learnt quickly and I found myself being tempted to show him off because, like a child, he would frequently become an attention-stealer in public. This presented me with a nice compromise between my emotional and scientific leanings. Initially I felt that I should not allow myself to bask in the

Puppies and females squat to urinate, only adult male dogs cock their legs

reflected glory of all the oohs and ahs that Snowy elicited, particularly if he was behaving well by, for example, laying down obediently while I was being served in a shop. I used to pretend to ignore the other human responses, recalling how pretentious I used to find other proud owners showing off their pets. But it didn't really work and I found that my best solution was to accept the public doting and praise and to turn the encounter into a public relations chat for guide dogs or to quiz members of the public about their attitudes to their own pets in a way which would help me in my own investigations into how people react with their pets.

It did reveal some of the powerful social benefits that possessing a pet can bring to people, benefits that can easily be accepted once they are pointed out, yet which are rarely stated for what they are. Owning a pet serves as a major social lubricant. Far more strangers will stop and react with an owner out with his pet than would ever be the case if the same person wasn't accompanied by an animal — a phenomenon which extends equally to pet owners displaying snakes, falcons, stick insects or even toads in public. Dog owners being the most frequently seen category, it is easy to imagine the host of warm feelings they receive as a result of other people's personal response to them because they are with their pets. Lonely people are made less lonely. Shy people have introductions made for them, while isolated or elderly people are brought into the community. Though this social ice-breaking isn't a universal occurrence, it is clear that a pet exerts a powerful—if transient—attraction for many other people besides its particular owner. Anti-pet feelings, on the other hand, tend to be conspicuous by their absence. There are people who strongly dislike dogs or cats but, for the most part, pet-owners are simply ignored by pet-haters.

These social benefits are made more satisfying by the kind of social intechange that takes place with other members of the public. In general, the kind of person who will stop and talk to an owner out with his or her dog is someone who is relaxed and confident enough to break down the normal restraints which stop us approaching complete strangers. Probably pet-owners themselves—or at least a past or potential pet-owner—they invariably make supportive, friendly remarks based around the animal in question, but which cast the pet owner in a glow—however undeserved—of reflected glory. The ego is thus flattered by the attention that others give to something outside ourselves, but which indirectly passes credit on to us.

A lot to learn

It is easy to make this simple analysis and to follow it with the conclusion that pets provide psychological props for shy and introverted people who would be ignored by the rest of society were it not for their animals, and indeed there's some interesting new research on this line of thought which we will return to later.

As far as I was concerned, however, I was more aware of the enhanced interest and social contact that came my way simply because Snowy was with me. To be honest, I resented this somewhat at first, believing that person-to-person contacts were the most valuable relationships in our lives and feeling that I wanted and expected to be interesting as a person in my own right and not simply because of my dog. Perhaps the scientist overruled the pet owner in that regard.

Something else which I felt rather unusual about human relationships with dogs was the way many people react about the disciplining of animals. Just as a total outsider would view the strong loyalties of our species (humans) to another species (dogs or cats) as so very strange that it requires special scientific analysis or explanation, so too there is a quirkiness about the typical response to an owner smacking his or her dog. While some people believe that a dog should never be hit to enforce discipline, I confess that I would and did smack Snowy if he repeatedly did something that I believed he knew was inappropriate. Even as I say this, I am conscious that several readers will find their emotions turning against me for being 'cruel'.

But if members of the public see a pet owner smacking his or her dog, the first reaction is for their sympathies to go to the dog and for the person to be viewed with distaste. Perhaps this is because all pets bring out in us deep emotions of protection and so when the owner, the protector-in-chief if you like, is seen to hit his ward for whatever reason, it comes across like Father Christmas eating venison!

I know that this observation is sensed by people working for the Guide Dogs for the Blind who depend on public contributions to finance their organisations. Having such a strong image based on the wholesome ideal of a loving dog helping to give happiness to an unfortunate sightless person, they cannot afford to have such warm sentiments sullied by ever being seen to smack their dogs to help discipline. Yet clearly their dogs are as well trained as any.

Looked at in a biological context, I find no problems in justifying the occasional smack as being a parallel of what takes place in nature. All growing dogs must learn to accept their subordinate role in the pack and any puppy that persistently steps out of line will be nipped by the boss. In fact some shepherds still bite their dog's ear as a reprimand, in a similar way to what would occur in the wild.

To my mind, every domesticated dog that is to fit in to human society must learn to accept the dominance of its substitute pack leader. In order to stop it doing things that are considered unacceptable, the owner would obviously try to reprimand by voice or to reward more acceptable behaviour in some way. However there are some strong-willed dogs (of which Snowy by his size and sex was potentially one – I was not alone in thinking that) who on occasions will not accept vocal discipline or a mild tap. Then, forgive me if this is heresy to some, I believe you need to smack to force the owner's dominance especially when it comes to *stopping* a particular piece of behaviour. Making a dog *do* something is a different matter and my experience later with other working dogs convinced me that hitting a dog was totally unnecessary and indeed counter-productive for that purpose.

It still remains true that I was somewhat inconsistent about smacking Snowy. I confess that I would do it in private but, to avoid people's adverse reactions and my own subsequent guilt, I sometimes consciously resisted doing it in public. Snowy soon realised this of course and took advantage of being allowed to misbehave more when we were 'on show'. An ideal opportunity was our first TV appearance together.

*   *   *

Saturday mornings on BBC television are dominated by a regular children's magazine programme called *Multi-coloured Swap Shop*. On two occasions during the year, I made a brief appearance to talk about pets. The second programme was a major studio presentation in which it had been planned that young Snowy, then only 14 weeks old, would meet Hovis, the boxer puppy of host Noel Edmunds, while Noel and I would talk a bit about some aspects of pets' behaviour.

The night before the live broadcast was spent in a London hotel. Special dispensation was given for Snowy to share my hotel room. He was by now exceptionally well-disciplined for his tender age and I felt sure that he would not let me down in public. After a trouble-free night, I found myself walking Snowy around the streets of London for what seemed an age, waiting for him to perform 'busy' so that I could take him confidently into the television studio without fear of him disgracing himself (and me) on camera in front of millions of young viewers. The absence of familiar grass was a problem but finally necessity overtook any initial reluctance to use the gutter! We eventually arrived at the BBC Television Centre and were shown to a dressing room labelled 'Dr. John Paling and Alsatian'. There, in one corner, the BBC had thoughtfully provided a neatly folded cloth, presumably intended for me to clean up if Snowy had an accident. He doesn't need that, I thought, as I put down Snowy's rug together with a juicy bone and his water bowl to keep him happy until we were due on.

As I said, the show went on the air live. As soon as the cameras and sound engineers moved their equipment over to screen Snowy and Hovis, both dogs seemed to want to show that they wouldn't be disciplined in public. As we should have known, they started to sniff around each other's back ends, their leads got entangled with each other and around Noel and myself and the result was a totally chaotic scene which served well enough as a demonstration of good natural dog behaviour but which showed up bad owner control in no uncertain terms. Our discussion fizzled out as we made ineffective efforts to stop our pets doing things that were 'not nice', and then we abandoned the whole thing altogether. The result, as several friends told me later, was hilarious.

When the transmission was over and my cheeks had stopped burning, there remained the slim satisfaction of knowing that however badly Snowy had behaved in the studio, at least he hadn't let me down by making a mess in the dressing room! Even if, in the eyes of the rest of the world, he was as bad as bad could be, the dressing room cleaners would certainly ap-

Snowy and Hovis got their leads entangled around Noel

preciate that Snowy was a dog who, under normal circumstances, was reliable and had as far as they were concerned
blotted neither his copy book nor the studio carpet. At least,
that's what I thought until my girlfriend, Wendy, who had
flown in from America, came into the room. I turned and promptly trod in the water bowl, leaving a prominent puddle that
rapidly spread over BBC grade III standard issue carpet! It was

hard to give Wendy a warm greeting with one soaked foot and thoughts of Snowy's now totally shattered image in my mind! Snowy, of course, left the studio at a steady trot with his tail cheerfully in the air. I slunk out pretending to be invisible and if I'd had a tail it would have been tucked guiltily away between my legs.

*   *   *

Some of Snowy's other public appearances, I'm glad to say, were a good deal less fraught. In particular, he served as an introduction for me to meet experts working in the field of police dogs, military guard dogs and explosive- and drug-sensing dogs. Together we visited various dog-training establishments and I learnt much there not only about discipline but also about how professionals view the psychology of teaching dogs for special roles. I was particularly struck by the way that dogs which are trained by professionals with a special function in mind are virtually never smacked. The scent-sensing dogs especially are trained to work for the reward of playing and struggling for possession with their handlers after a find, rather than from a fear of discipline if they fail. I was incredibly impressed by the 'play-bows' that the dogs used to signal their wish to play with their masters after a hunt had been successful. It seemed, to my eyes, that the more time one gives to the training of a dog, the less is the need for physical discipline. Time, intuition and an awareness of dog psychology are in my book the key tools for successful trainers.

Although I probably took more from these meetings than I contributed, there were at least two new ideas that Snowy and I did have to offer. The first arose out of a novel filming technique that has possible applications with many sorts of animals.

While I was visiting Wendy in Washington DC (minus Snowy), I toured the splendid new Air and Space Museum of the Smithsonian Institution. There, amidst the gigantic rockets and the fragile man-powered flight machines, is a fascinating exhibition of historic aerial photographs. Some of the earliest of these incorporated an idea that was new to me. In the early 1900s the Germans had started to use pigeons to get their cameras aloft, fixing tiny remote-controlled stills cameras to the bird's breasts before releasing them into the air. They thus obtained some remarkable aerial pictures, many of them even being framed with blurred wing feathers.

As soon as I saw this, it crossed my mind that I could use Snowy to carry his own movie camera for the film. After all, he was going to be fitted with a harness at the end of the year and he would be accustomed to carrying things like the control handle on that. Once he was used to this it seemed a pretty simple job to strap a lightweight remote camera to Snowy so we could take shots as seen from his point of view. I thought such a splendid brainwave was well worth a try, imagining how it would add visual variety to the shots in the movie film, how it could be used to take close-up pictures of Snowy's head as he ran along, how it would help guide dog trainers see the world from the point of view of the young dog, and even how it would help military personnel survey a room or building into which it wasn't safe to send a man. All these applications and many more came flooding into my mind as I stood gazing at those small, time-browned photographs of city scenes in Germany viewed by a pigeon in flight.

We set out with enthusiasm. By taking slow motion pictures of Snowy running, we could see that his bone structure wobbled from side to side far more than we would have imagined, making it difficult to secure a stable base on which the camera could be mounted. The shoulders, not the head, seemed the most balanced point so my colleague at OSF, Ian Hendry, constructed a spring-mounted camera support system for a Super 8 Bolex movie camera which could be attached to the top of a standard guide harness. The weight of all this was less than 3% of Snowy's own weight and he soon learnt to carry it along without any sign of discomfort. The Guide Dog Association's assessor had categorized him as having 'low body sensitivity' and this helped him to bear the new equipment without adverse reactions. We consulted them of course and demonstrated how unperturbed Snowy was by his additional special effects equipment.

But the results were terribly disappointing. The amount of camera movement resulting even from unhurried walking by Snowy produced film so jerky that it was unusable. The scenes looked as if they had been taken during a violent earthquake.

Snowy's arrival at Christmas. Here he is practising his 'play-bite' with my neighbour's children. But such excitement eventually proves too much for the young puppy.

Snowy and Chilly are introduced to each other. Snowy first 'tramples' (actually a friendly gesture!) and sniffs the newcomer. Chilly initially stays her ground, but then tries to move her body away without actually shifting her feet. To try and make herself look bigger, she fluffs up her fur and tail. Then suddenly she leaps back, and I have to reprimand Snowy for being over-inquisitive.

Another arrival: this time that of Motley. Snowy is full of curiosity, but Chilly remains characteristically aloof.

Snowy in his element, playing with a black Labrador called Ben. Note how Ben gradually gains the ascendancy in this encounter until Snowy displays his submissiveness by rolling on to his back in an appeasement gesture. Finally he performs the classic 'play-bow'.

Chilly had a small patch of fur shaved away so she could be sterilised. The fur grew back darker in colour than the rest of her body. This was because that bare patch on her body was colder than the rest, the new growth produced a darker pigment which helped compensate for the heat loss until the fur was fully grown once more. It then resumed its normal colour.

High jinks at home: Motley and Chilly in the wreckage of my living room which they have just ransacked in company with Snowy.

More high jinks: Motley playing with a dead bird.

◁ Motley among the spring flowers.

The visual cliff experiment is designed to demonstrate the depth perception of puppies at various ages. Snowy Junior, after initial reluctance to venture over the 'cliff', seems to find nothing alarming about going to sleep seemingly in mid-air.

My three pets enjoying the fresh air and sunshine in the garden.

A pair of white German shepherds mating. The actual fertilisation occurs when the animals are standing back-to-back, contrary to popular opinion.

The birth of a litter of German shepherds. Note how Serena, the mother, uses her tongue repeatedly throughout the birth process. See also the transparent membrane in which the puppy is wrapped, and which Serena has to tear away so the puppy can begin to breathe in air normally.

Puppies use their front paws to 'pummel' their mother's breast while feeding. As they grow older, this behaviour remains as the characteristic 'shake-a-paw' gesture.

A dog drinks by furling its tongue into a backward-facing scoop. A cat's tongue, however, goes straight down into the liquid, which then adheres to its surface as it is drawn into the mouth.

Two versions of the 'dog's eye view' camera harness which we designed for Snowy.

Snowy with his parents Rebecca (left) and Tollmark. White German shepherds can be produced from coloured parents, while the mating of two whites will not necessarily produce offspring of a similar colour.

Motley walks
watchfully
through the
vegetation.

Motley showing
the fatal injuries
which he received
in a car accident.

Snowy and Motley as I will remember them, alert, confident and relaxed.

Virtually nothing was recognisable from the extreme waving around from frame to frame. A new support on the harness was designed, this time more rigidly strapped to Snowy's side. It was certainly an improvement but again the results were unusable. Clearly much more money needed to be spent on the camera suspension system before it could be of use.

We allowed a national newspaper to take pictures of the two harnesses in use, together with some of the pictures that could be obtained in purely static conditions. Our ulterior motive was to suggest that, though we hadn't quite made the idea work yet, we did have designs for new and better suspension systems based on the stability devices used to stabilize oil rigs at sea. To design and build this would cost perhaps a couple of thousand pounds and in view of its widespread applications we hoped that the story would touch the heart or pocket of some pioneering soul who might help us to make the idea work well.

It didn't happen. The newspaper's sub-editor chopped out our message from the text and no one was made fully aware of how far we still had to go. The article made it seem as if the whole thing was ready to go into production. I remained convinced, nevertheless, that it was a good idea with many applications both for filming larger wildlife in national parks as well as providing an extensive new range of possibilities employing trained dogs. Someone will do it soon in Russia, Japan or America, just you see.

The other small idea that came forward at this time resulted from my tremendous admiration for the work and training methods of the drug-sensing dogs used by customs men at international sea and airports. Taking advantage of the fact that dogs can smell chemicals at strengths many times less than the human nose can detect, experts can train dogs to detect and seek out drugs such as heroin, marijuana and the like. Undoubtedly the presence of these dogs serves as a deterrent to people trying to smuggle the stuff into the country. This being the case, I reasoned, why don't we train dogs to detect the presence of other dogs which have been hidden by their owners to avoid the quarantine period which is part of the strict rabies regulations that we have in Britain? At present there are posters galore warning against taking dogs into Britain without undergoing a proper quarantine period but searches inevitably are random and cursory, and some dogs do get into the country undetected by present methods. What better way to sniff out a potentially rabid dog than to give the task to another dog?

Inevitably there are times when such a dog-detector-dog will locate a space which has recently been occupied by another, whose scent still lingers. However, my advisors on a dog's sense of smell and their ability to discriminate support my view that dogs could be trained to pick out when a dog is actually there. It seems to me to be certainly worth trying and, if it works and we are serious about keeping rabies out of Britain, then the knowledge that dog-detector-dogs were operating would deter a good many ill-advised smugglers.

8

Pet Language

The notion of being able to talk to animals and to have them talk back can be found in the very earliest myths. Ever since, children from all parts of the world have been brought up with stories of mice that talk to each other and horses that speak to men. These fantasies seem to reflect a deep-seated longing in us to be able to speak to and understand our animal friends. We are still a long way from achieving our goal, but many significant attempts have already been made at communicating with animals in a responsive and structured way—in other words at finding a language between the species.

We humans are unlikely to learn to speak catese or dogese, a vocabulary of the animal's own sounds, in the near future but there seems no good reason why someone hasn't used a voice-analyzing machine to isolate—and so understand—how the different pet vocalisations are used in different situations. For without any doubt, all the dog and cat owners I have met would vehemently maintain that their pets do make distinctive calls under different circumstances and needs. We owners come to recognise intuitively the 'meaning' of our pets' calls, although for most people it would be difficult to say precisely what the distinguishing features are and even more difficult to imitate the different calls accurately. It is astonishing to realise that while scientists have analysed in detail the specific call notes—even dialects—of many wild birds, we have no more than a handful of sound spectrographs of the vocalistions of man's most familiar animal companions! Surely here is a prime subject for some scientific research. I'm sure the results would be as fascinating and instructive as those that have emerged from bird studies. Do all dogs whine in a particular pattern when they want to attract your attention, do all cats purr in a distinctive way when another cat approaches their food? And do Russian pets share a common language with American pets? There is so much that could be discovered relatively easily, given the funding and the research effort.

For my part, I soon learnt to recognise a whole range of sounds that Snowy would make under different situations. Many of them were distinctive and, even if I couldn't see Snowy, I came to know what he was 'meaning' solely by hearing the call. More importantly, when I went to him or otherwise confirmed visually what his situation was, I found my understanding of his call frequently matched the situation I found him in.

If ever I was in doubt about one dog's understanding of another dog's call, then my experiences with puppies removed all uncertainty. While filming the development of the litter including the white German shepherd puppy at Birmingham, I took our tape recorder to capture some of the sounds of five-week-old dogs simply to serve as appropriate background noises in the film. As I was using a long tape that already included pet noises necessary for other parts of the film, I quickly wound through to the approximate position and started the tape to find where to begin. As it happened, there emerged the calls of a one-day-old German shepherd from a totally different litter. The pup had been separated from its mother and its cries came over the loudspeaker plaintive and clear.

Ellie, the mother of the litter I was filming, immediately became agitated. She dashed in, looked around, her ears flicked back and forth and finally she cocked her head on one side quizzically. Seeing nothing to relate to the noise, she ran round and round the table on which the tape recorder was sitting. Her pups, by the way, showed no response to the calls though Snowy, later, also pricked up his ears and came to look, showing no sign of anxiety or tension.

Had I been involved in studying the effect of one dog's call on others that afternoon, I may have made more of this incident. As it was, the filming work was more important and I didn't follow it up. More immediate was the fact that Ellie became so greatly distressed on hearing the call that it just wasn't funny. It would have been cruel to have continued to have her so upset, for there was just no way of restraining her and I felt she might even have snapped at someone if we had tried. And all this was simply caused by the tape-recorded call of a baby dog that was not even hers. Dogs and cats evidently do have very effective vocal communications between members of the same species and we hardly know anything about it.

*   *   *

Through training we can reward our animal companions—dogs in particular—if they follow our commands and, in that way, we can effectively make verbal communication with them. In return, we can perceive certain responses from animals which lead many owners to feel that they understand the moods and signals of their pets. A look in the eye and a tilt of the head is readily interpreted as a sure sign that Bonzo wants to go 'walkies' or that Tibbles is expecting her food.

Unfortunately the scientific study of animal behaviour progresses more slowly than these human intuitions. So many checks and controls have to be applied to observed behaviours and so many measurements must be taken, that it is a long time before the scientist can proclaim that a particular piece of behaviour 'means' a particular thing. However, there are some clear-cut examples of pet body language that we do understand and which scientists are agreed about. Obviously, the more of these we understand the more chance we have of being able to simulate phrases of their language. As we were photographing my pets, we caught some of these instances of body language.

Like a mother with her new baby, I had taken a particularly deep delight in walking Snowy during his first weeks with me, and this feeling never left me in the months that followed. I derived much pleasure and pride from this bouncy scamp running by my side through the grounds of nearby Blenheim Palace on my morning jog. Like a flag, his tail seemed a good indicator of mood. In fact, all the dogs I've ever known seem to use it to help express their mood. This being the case, it is a great shame that our aesthetic preferences in dog breeds results

Tails and ears indicate mood and signal likely dominance

in so many of them having their tails chopped off. It's quite possible that such dogs can live happily with their owners and communicate effectively without a tail but—with my eyes so attuned to wild animals—it just seems to me to be a sad case of needless human interference.

When a dog is confident, up goes his tail. When he is feeling dominated and wants to demonstrate his submission, down it goes until, when experience or the degree of threat tells him he is likely to get verbal or physical punishment, it goes right down between his legs. Watch two strange dogs meeting in the street. Both may start with their tails high as they approach and begin to sniff at each other in exploratory greeting. Then, before any growling or changing facial expressions occur, you are likely to see one dog's tail drop slightly while the other's holds its place or goes up even higher. If and when a dominance contest such as a scuffle follows, these signals will

Pet language

have already indicated the probable winner. I have watched
this several times when Snowy meets another German
shepherd dog. You can almost predict what is going to happen.
Watch the height of the tails of two dogs when they meet and
picture them as flags waving each owner's self-confidence.
Snowy, as he became a relatively large and socially dominant
dog, would visibly lift his tail high over his back as he approached a new dog. Then, as the two animals moved closer to
interact, he would lower his tail (and ears) somewhat if the
newcomer showed comparable dominance.

Cats too use their tail for signalling. From the earliest ages, a
kitten following its mother around the room or approaching her
to feed will have its tail up high. You'll recall that when Chilly
met Snowy for the first time (never having seen a dog before)
she held her tail stiff and erect. When Snowy's reactions cause
her mood to change to one of intimidation, her tail initially
dropped as she lowered her body to the ground and then she
made the curious gesture of leaning as far back as possible
without actually moving her feet.

When Motley and Chilly walked through the spring flowers
they invariably held their tails high. Carrying such a signal,
they could never be thought of as hunting for, as soon as a cat's
attention is attracted to its prey, its tail—indeed its whole
body—drops down to a low profile. Clearly it would not help
the predator to advertise its presence by holding aloft this flag-
like signal.

Another response which we've seen before is the classical
bottle-brush fluffing of the tail which occurs with the sideways
arching of the body at times of extreme threat. This spon-
taneous reaction obviously gives the other animal a sense that
the threatened cat is larger than it really is and that it is ready
to spring. One foot is usually half lifted from the floor in
readiness to strike back.

I saw this threatening paw-up posture many times as Chilly
and Motley got to know each other. At first Chilly, the original
resident, stood her ground and retained dominance of all the
best locations but bit by bit Motley began to challenge. The
best sleeping basket (surprisingly the one on the floor, not the
one by the central heating boiler) became the chief prize which

was fought over as if it epitomised the relative dominance of the cats over the whole household.

As Chilly lay on her new blue blanket in her basket, Motley would make repeated runs and bounce on and off the side of the basket. Chilly would sit motionless and watch until Motley graduated to daringly holding his position actually on the edge of the contested territory. Then Chilly would tense and suddenly lunge towards Motley, who immediately bounced back on to the floor again. The next sally by Motley produced spitting and a two-footed stamp from Chilly. Then she held her position rigid and waited with one front paw off the ground. For some reason Motley misjudged his jump on the next occasion and, as he leapt, his rear legs swung over the edge of the basket and he suddenly found himself side by side with an equally surprised Chilly.

In a flash he scrambled on to the top edge of the basket, head facing away and licking his lips. Both of these actions serve as sign language: the head turned away completely avoids the act of staring at the adversary, which would be an aggresive signal, while the licking is a sign of tension resulting from the mouth and throat going dry under sudden stress – just like humans in fact.

A few moments later, Chilly jumped at Motley and, in a flurry of spitting, yeowls and clawing that particular contest was resolved by the tabby intruder being bundled out of the basket.

As I picked up Motley a few moments later I was struck by the distinct smell of his wetted fur. Although I have heard no one else mention it, I wondered if aggressive cats don't just spit saliva but add some other ingredient which might account for the curious extra tang. Although that particular encounter resulted in Chilly holding her own, it was one of many in which the balance of power was gradually shifted until Motley came to rule the roost.

The initial communication process between Chilly and Snowy, on the other hand, was made all the more interesting because both animals were using their own languages. There is one piece of dog language which we well understand and which we can easily reply to in like manner. All you need is to lose a

In a flash Motley scrambled to the edge of the basket

little of your dignity—something which most pet owners readily forego when they are playing with their pets. This is the mock 'bow' with which a dog invites play.

Snowy 'spoke' to me with this particular behavioural signal from the moment he arrived. I was able to confirm that it wasn't solely directed to people about a week later, when we had our first fall of snow and we used the occasion to film a scene of Snowy meeting Ben, a mild-mannered black Labrador belonging to David Thompson, a colleague at OSF.

The two dogs were let loose in the virgin expanses of crumbly snow and allowed to romp to their heart's content as our various cameras whirred. Snowy didn't know any better and bounded up to Ben with every confidence. Ben seemed to be more intent on scampering around in rings and hardly troubled to do more than dash by Snowy. Then, as we started the high-speed camera in an attempt to produce a lyrical slow-motion sequence of the dogs at play, Ben simply turned round and fled. There was something about the pitch of the camera motor that clearly no self-respecting Labrador could stand. We stopped the camera and tried again. But as soon as the dogs resumed play and the high-speed motor got up speed, Ben's tail dropped between his legs, his ears were pulled back and he charged off as if struck by lightning.

All these goings-on meant that we soon gave up trying to use that particular camera but also indicated that Ben had lost some of the natural self-confidence and dominance that he had been so ready to demonstrate a few minutes before. Snowy gambolled towards him, and as Ben stayed put, half-waiting for the camera whine that to him always seemed to accompany the puppy's approach, Snowy performed the most perfect 'play bow' that you could every wish to see. This is the one sign that everyone will have seen dogs perform but, like me at the beginning of this project, never properly understood.

It is a highly distinctive posture that involves the dog dropping down on its 'elbows' while keeping its rump in the air and, possibly, wagging its tail. The chin is commonly held on the ground too and the total effect clearly means, in sign language, 'Come on, let's play'. This simple sign is more impressive when you realise that the angle of the tilt is totally fixed whatever the breed or size of dog. It applies in identical form in every country across the world —a sort of 'doggesperanto'. Dog relatives like wolves and foxes use the very same posture, so the meaning (and presumably the biological importance to all these animals) is very widely understood. If you need further proof, try playing with your own dog and, if your back permits it, suddenly drop down to the play-bow posture and see what happens. Once you realise that this posture speaks so clearly to other canids (and is not simply dogerel), it is amazing how often and in what situations you see other dogs using it to people, other dogs and even cats—Motley and Chilly did not understand it!

There is another variation of this invitation-to-play signal

Pet language

Snowy performed the most perfect play bow

which I detected in Snowy and which I haven't seen recorded elsewhere. In a playful mood, Snowy would dash around and then come to an abrupt stop, directly facing me a small distance away. If I moved towards him or even if I stayed still, his next move would be a bound almost on the spot. When his front legs hit the ground, they would be spaced apart, so that his head could be lowered in a bobbing motion. This struck me immediately as being a shadow of the play-bow, i.e. dropping the front of the body in relation to the rear, and having the same implied meaning of 'This is all in play'. I filmed this action with the slow-motion camera so that I could check on my impression of this rapid movement. It clearly was just as I describe.

Although it may seem a trivial thing for a dog to spread its legs out sideways, a study of the bone structure of dogs will tell you that it has very little scope to do this. The dog skeleton doesn't permit much lateral movement of the legs, unlike animals like giraffes which frequently do the splits as they drink. However much it may impede the dog's flexibility, this disability has one practical advantage—at least as far as

107

humans are concerned—which I am glad to pass on to anyone who has the necessity to use it.

If you find yourself faced with a vicious guard dog leaping at you at 30 mph, one recommended way to protect yourself is to turn and face the dog, grab its front feet and force its legs apart. This is reputed to immobilise the dog because it stresses or breaks the skeletal limits of sideways motion. If I felt that this piece of sage advice would result in dogs being abused, I would not offer it, though I cannot vouch personally for its effectiveness because I fail to see how the average man or woman could develop the speed of reaction and coordination—to say nothing of the courage—to make it work. For my part, having worked with many military and police dog handlers, I would react to a charging guard dog with rigid panic. All that might save me as I passed out would be if I could somehow contrive to land on my back with all four limbs held upright and my throat and genitals exposed—in effect, reflecting the submissive posture of dogs! To be serious, it does seem as if dogs 'see' humans differently if you forsake your upright posture and fall to the ground. Lowering one's effective height in relation to a dog's does seem to alter the animal's response and there are many records of someone exciting a dog in play-fighting and then unintentionally falling over, at which point the dog attacks them for real.

I should, however, point out that British police dogs are trained *not* to attack if the person they are pursuing stops stock still. My rigid panic should save *me*, at any rate! Furthermore, the dogs have to be under control, so if you stopped running the police dog handler, if he were in earshot, would (or should!) be able to call to his animal to stop. A different situation, however, exists for military guard dogs, where there are special security requirements around aircraft hangers, ammunition stores and suchlike. Once these guard dogs are set to chase in earnest, they are specifically trained not to bite in any one place. When released, they aim for whatever takes their fancy, though they can still be called off when the job is done—and the intruder captured. I wouldn't care to use the high-speed cameras to film what would happen next—it would certainly put me off snooping around their installations.

Pet language

The slow-motion camera revealed one further play-mood signal which I had not properly observed at first sight using a normal-speed camera. When Snowy moved off after his initial front-legs-astride pounce, he ran with a pronounced bouncy stride, a gambolling action rather akin to a spring lamb. Although it is easier to pick out visually rather than in words, it can be seen as a springy run in which the body and legs are lifted higher than when the dog is making a direct dash from A to B. At the same time the front 'wrist' joint of the dog is flicked from bent to straight at the very last second before touching the ground and, as a consequence of the springy action, the legs don't extend forward during each stride as much as in non-play running.

Once again, this bounding behaviour is clearly apparent from an early puppy stage when the youngsters are learning to coordinate their leg muscles. Looking at puppies later, having identified this play mood in Snowy, it seems as if the puppies also use their bounce run during their play bouts.

Having made this recognition, I was amused the next day to see my colleague Sean Morris prancing around the car park, legs apart and bouncing up and down, trying to get Snowy to play with him. Sean's style of locomotion was clearly no practical or conventional way of getting from A to B—it simply paralleled Snowy's play bounce in a way that I'm sure he could recognise clearly. Perhaps men and dogs are not so dissimilar after all!

Such interpretations seem obvious when they are spelt out like this but, for me at least, they add greatly to my feeling of understanding and rapport with the animals I share my life with. When you realise that most of us simply 'get the feeling' that our dog or cat is meaning something specific from some transient look (in other words, we're acting on a hunch rather than concrete evidence), then it really is a major step forward to specify by peculiar movements of particular parts of the body what action always appears to be associated with a given social situation such as courtship, feeding, play or aggression.

Another dog behaviour that excited my curiosity was the guilty look that many dog owners will have witnessed if their pet has offended against some principle or property. During the first month, while the house was occupied solely by Snowy, Chilly, Motley and myself, I was so protective towards my pets that I would only let them out when I could keep an eye on them. I was always afraid that if they ran off, I would be left without a film star for the remainder of the year. My caution may seem crazy to most cat owners, who would naturally expect that, given an acre of garden and woodland in a quiet cul-de-sac, any ordinary cat would revel in its freedom and return home reliably for food and affection. However, having had to keep close tabs on wild animals so as to build up film sequences, my attitude to Snowy and the cats was equally zealous since, after all, they were no ordinary pets.

At times when all three film stars had to be left indoors together I would lock them in the kitchen. By now, I thought, I could trust them all together and, one memorable evening, I left them alone while I went to the theatre. On my return, the animals were nowhere to be seen. Instead the kitchen floor was decorated with the tatters of chewed-up towels and the cats' plastic feeding bowl! The door to the hall was ajar—it could not have been properly secured and had probably sprung open when I shut the other door to the kitchen as I went out. One of my slippers was chewed in the hallway and the sitting room door was invitingly wide open. As I entered, Snowy shot like a rocket through my legs, while inside the scene was a mixture of devastation and serenity.

A newly purchased chrysanthemum had been knocked out of its pot, scattering vegetation and soil across the floor. The back of a good pair of leather shoes had been used as practise for various gnawing techniques. A wine glass had been knocked over and smashed, its contents drenching a favourite art book whose pages had buckled as a result. Snowy had been caught red-pawed!

Casting my horror-stricken eyes around for signs of further destruction, I found two sleepy feline heads nestling against each other in the comfort of an armchair. Emitting a bellow of rage (which hardly disturbed the weary couple) I grabbed them, but as soon as they felt my grip their claws extended instinctively and they dragged up the cushion with them as well. The result was that the cushion was lifted from the chair and

A scene of devastation

dropped on the coffee table, breaking a second wine glass in the process. Wildlife photographers are often viewed as peaceable folk who are endowed with endless patience and tranquility, especially when they are around animals. I have to confess that there are occasionally exceptions to this golden rule, and at that moment I was less concerned with understanding their animal language than that they should understand mine.

I hauled the cats off to the kitchen, where I found Snowy already lying as flat as he could in the back of his box. As I stormed in he gazed unwaveringly up at me. His ears were down, his neck was held low and there was a lot of white showing in his eyes, making a nice biological contrast to mine which were red and reflecting a substantially different mood.

'You naughty dog,' I snapped at him. 'What the hell do you think you're doing?' Suddenly I became conscious of my own ludicrous posture: chin jutting forward, eyes wide and staring unblinkingly into the culprit's face. If Snowy was anything of an animal behaviourist, he would infallibly recognise these signs as human body language spelling out 'anger', for this gesture is also part of a dog's body language, accompanied by graduations of bristling back and furled lips. He couldn't hold my gaze and dropped his eyes. There was a whispered whine, a feeble wag of the cramped tail which, producing no softening of my stare, he quickly stopped. From a low starting position he muzzled upwards towards me again and opened wide those white-rimmed eyes. If ever I saw a dog look guilty, then Snowy's look said it all!

*   *   *

But did it really? I personally was oscillating between restraining my fury, trying like a good scientist to calmly analyse Snowy's body-language postures and keeping an open mind about assessing just who did all the damage. I paused, having

Snowy's look said it all

calmed down a little, while still retaining as best I could my attitude of anger so that I could study Snowy's stance. Is there really a 'guilty' look that dogs have? Before dog owners nod confidently in the affirmative, let me phrase that another way. Are there specific indentifiable physical postures that your dog adopts when you think he has a guilty look? Are the eyes wider than when he is simply frightened? Is the neck angle different from when he is being submissive? Or is your notion of a distinctly 'guilty' look just your human interpretation of what you think the dog feels? Perhaps the posture is not really reflecting guilt but rather some form of fear in anticipation of being reprimanded for the misdeed. I looked, lunged threateningly, studied Snowy's face, stared and frowned intently—and I confess I couldn't decide one way or another. I would be delighted to hear if anyone can identify a clearly distinct guilt expression. If so, then it has far-reaching implications on our attitudes and responsibilities to animals.

Some would say that if a dog really does feel 'guilt', it is because it has a 'conscience' about what is right or wrong. And if it has 'conscience' then it must have a 'spirit'—in the religious sense—independent of its sense of fear for what reprimand might follow. And if dogs could be shown to feel 'guilt' and hence have a 'spirit' with an inherent sense of right or wrong (developed through training) then our moral responsibility to these and all other creatures may seem to be of a higher order than many people at present would admit.

Surveying the whole field of man's associations with animals, I find that through the ages we have used (some would say abused) animals for our own purposes with no sense of respect for any spirit the animals might have and, therefore, for the animals' presumed rights. It is a thorny topic, for pets themselves are kept only because mankind wants them the way they are. The dog has been bred into many varieties purely to be, in different ways, at the service of man. Nevertheless, animal rights is an issue that pet keepers (and other interested parties like non-vegetarians, fishermen and horse jumpers) may like to face after they have confronted the greater priorities in their lives. I have tried to face it in my own life but I haven't reached a firm conclusion.

My present view? Well, for what it's worth, I'm not a vegetarian and I do value human life (with some possibly arbitrary exceptions of very early foetuses, serious social criminals and those who voluntarily wish for euthanasia) higher than animals and I am prepared to see animals used—even killed—by man. This is not to support needless, cruel or degrading treatments (defined in my terms) but having looked hard for a body language of guilt that would imply the existence of a spirit or sense of right or wrong, I have to conclude that I could find no objective evidence that animals have this property of conscience.

Nevertheless, even if the animals that man associates with can never be shown to have an independent spirit, then there are still compelling reasons why we should value and protect the sanctity of those living creatures who share this planet with us. What's more, most of the reasons relate to mankind's own best interests, let alone those of the 'lower' creatures. I could be wrong. Snowy may have fine feelings deeply ingrained in his doggy bosom. I always feel he does and my intuition tells me that Snowy, Motley and Chilly, somewhere about their being, each have a spirit allied to ours to which I can relate in a fundamental way. But my feeble attempts to explore this aspect of Snowy's behaviour scientifically left me floundering. And to make matters worse the Guide Dogs for the Blind Association —contriving, as ever, to help the animal—made it almost impossible for me.

9

Talking To Animals

The big problem with the Guide Dog Association was that they supervised me so thoroughly in the interests of the job that the dog was going to do that they reduced my ability to do the job I had set for myself. This was not intentional, of course, but without either them or I realising it at the time they got me to do something that from then on effectively made my own tasks twice as difficult.

Alison, who was the area supervisor for the organisation and who had delivered Snowy to me in the first place, made monthly visits to check that things were progressing all right, to advise on any problems and to make suggestions for how Snowy's development and training could best be directed to his ultimate role as a guide dog. At first I felt this visit was somewhat like returning to school, with me being corrected for unsuitable traits or procedures and being given instructions on basic things like how much food to give and ways to stop unacceptable habits like barking or lead chewing. I came to realise that the advice that was gently offered was in fact good sense, and was almost invariably an improvement on my own procedures, being based on the experience of bringing up thousands of dogs. My own role was somewhat ambiguous. As a director of a company whose job included farming out work for others to look after creatures like foxes, scorpions and salmon, it came as a salutory experience to be lectured by someone several years my junior on how to look after an ordinary dog. Much credit goes to Alison, however; she soon proved her considerably greater competence in this field and won my lasting respect and admiration.

So what then could possibly go wrong? Well, believe it or not, I found myself being given lessons on walking Snowy on the lead in the nearby town of Woodstock! I knew of course that all guide dogs are taught to keep on the left-hand side of the walker and that they must not be distracted from maintaining their steady forward walking pace. This means that they must not stop for smells (a difficult natural instinct to suppress) nor must they stop or deviate for enticing sights like cats, a flapping coat or the million and one sudden events that can occur in a crowded street. To be honest, I was rather proud of how well Snowy responded to my instructions and so, when walking him under Alison's supervision along the street, I made him sit and lie to demonstrate his skills. That clearly was an error. I should have kept him moving with the lead length—'So'—and holding it across my front—'Like that'—and so on. All very well, but I felt there was more confusion in my mind about what was requested than in the actions Snowy and I carried out. Was I too ready to be defensive? But then came the instructor's recommendation that from then on broke much of my ability to watch Snowy as a critical outside observer.

'Keep talking to him,' was the suggestion. 'By the tone of your voice—it doesn't matter what you say—he will be given constant feedback about whether he's doing right or wrong, whether he's too far forward or back. And by a jerk back on the lead, you can reinforce your order not to pull ahead.' But the most important new message for me was the need to keep up an endless stream of chatter, altering in tone according to how well Snowy was performing and thus meeting the Guide Dog requirements.

Well, it did seem strange. For the first few hours or days I felt like an archetypal grandmother who talks incessantly to her cats. It is difficult—it really is—to talk total gibberish, so one resorts to using natural human words to tell the dog his progress. 'OK Snowy—good dog—good boy that's right—now. Oh no. Slow down, slow down then. Hey! slow—off then—don't you hear me? Alison's told you you've got to listen

to what I tell you. Yes—you have. That's good now. Good
boy, good dog then. That's—a—good —dog—Snowy. OK
then now we're going to go into this shop. Yes—we—are.
Steady, steady, steady.' And so it goes on. Effectively most of
the words in the conversation represented me talking to myself.

I hadn't done all this before for two very good reasons. Firstly I found that Snowy already walked well in the approved
Guide Dog position (at least to my satisfaction) with the
minimum of words of instruction and also that when I took
Snowy for his walks I liked to walk in relative silence, enjoying
the countryside and turning totally different thoughts over in
my head. Our morning jogging period through the grounds of
Blenheim Palace helped reinforce Snowy's correct position in
relation to me. All dogs have to be kept on a lead there and so
as Snowy ran along on his lead beside me, he was already
maintaining the right position. As I puffed my geriatric torso
along, the last thing I had been concentrating on was indulging
in a non-stop monologue with Snowy. But from that time on,
our morning run became an incessant, one-sided narration
about not chasing the new-born lambs, minding the puddles at
the edge of the track and establishing the identity of any on-
coming dog walker—but mainly about how good a dog Snowy
was being and whether he should continue 'steady' or not pull
or keep up or whatever. And I confess that Snowy did become
even better as a result of all these additional verbal baths.

Have you ever stopped to analyse what happens to a person
when he or she develops a non-stop conversation with a pet?
Believe me, the effects on the person are staggering! The words
sound so trivial when you eavesdrop on someone speaking a
few sentences to their attentive dog or cat, but for me it made
such a massive difference to my objectivity that I discovered a
social factor of immense importance to anyone remotely interested in the human-animal bond. After a handful of days the
habit had become ingrained, and from then on my ability to
relate intuitively with Snowy shot up well above anything that
had existed previously. On the other hand, most of my ability
to step back mentally and observe Snowy's behaviour critically
and to analyse it in terms of postures, causes and effects went
out of the window.

I wondered hard and long about what we do to ourselves as we constantly repeat in warm and affectionate tones, 'Good doggy, that's a good dog, yes, good boy'. Is this the same as self-hypnosis? Is this self-generated, dog-motivated auto-suggestion? Are we not doing what psychologists train people to do to give them confidence to maintain an attitude of mind? Don't they tell people, 'Keep saying to yourself over and over again, yes I am successful, I am a winner, I can beat him.' And with this indoctrination, you will come to believe it and you will win/be successful/gain confidence or whatever. It really does work.

Suddenly it flashed into my mind that people who constantly talk to their pets *must* be indoctrinating themselves as well. They are doing all the necessary things. They are *repetitively* saying it—'Good dog, good boy....'—and they mentally mean and *believe* it. It isn't just a meaningless string of words, an insincere statement to convince the dog of an attitude you don't really hold (as people so often do with other people!) Our communication with pets is totally honest, sincere, straightforward and in no way devious. No wonder we can relax and feel good about such an uncomplicated relationship. There are very few human communications where there is no absolute possibility of a misunderstanding or a disagreement. It becomes increasingly clear that this 'good feeling' that we pet owners have about our totally trusting, totally honest, totally dedicated companionship with animals may come about in part as a result of us speeding up and reinforcing that bond by a process something like self-indoctrination as we talk to them.

I kept coming back to it. *I* had certainly been changed by the hours of constant talking to Snowy. As I re-examined just what I was doing and saying and thinking as I spoke to him it seemed more and more that I was unwittingly going through the mechanical and emotional procedures of brainwashing myself, reinforcing my feelings by routine, talking to Snowy as if he could understand my actual words.

When I got down to examining statistics, the whole extent of human-pet talking was stunning. In an American survey 98% of all pet owners admitted to talking to their animals and this is in a country where it is somewhat less fashionable and more prissy to be a pet keeper. In the U.K. I guess that figure would be 100%. Anyway, when questioned 80% of the pet owners reported that they talked to their pet 'as a person' and not 'as an animal'—a fact that must surely be revealing, though I don't know how the 20% spoke to their pet as an animal! Did they bark, meow or chirrup? The more I consider it, I reckon *everyone* not doing parrot impersonations or dog howls *must* have been talking to their pet 'as a person'. I wonder if, human nature being what it is, the 20% were not meowers and cluckers but really folks who didn't feel it was kosher to admit to the person doing the survey that they were stupid enough to talk to a dumb beast!

Perhaps more relevant is finding that 28%, or nearly one in three, agreed that they 'confided in their animal and talked about the events of the day'. Surely such verbal intimacy is not matched by our pet's understanding? Well, I personally doubt it. I would however go along with the 78% of those sampled who felt that their animals were 'sensitive to human moods and feelings'. But I would put an average dog's understanding of the number of actual words at about 15-20. Yet many people will claim with unshakeable conviction that their dog or cat has the ability to recognise many more words. Some seriously claim a recognition vocabulary of hundreds or even thousands of words.

So why then *do* we talk to our pets in the way we do? One answer could be that we know of no other way to talk; and talking to our pets in human language is the only way we know. That may well be, but it doesn't explain how most people not under instruction by Guide Dog supervisors will on occasion chatter incessantly to their pets. Does the establishment of a close and firm bond between any animal and a person require such lengthy small-talk from the human member of the pair? I noticed that the effect non-stop talking to Snowy had on me was really a common factor in all our close man-animal relationships. Had I pinpointed the social glue that *made* the bond so strong and deep and long lasting? Was it, at least in part, a process of self-suggestion when the owner was in a suitable mood?

I was convinced by now that there was something at the back

of all this talking to animals that was important, fascinating and at the same time seemingly pathetic and crazy. Fancy expecting a little kitten to understand the words of a grown man—yet we've all seen it and perhaps, just as surprisingly, never viewed it before as suggesting actual insanity!

Another small fact added to my theory of auto-suggestions. When we talk to our pets they don't show any of the comparable facial signs of a lack of understanding that humans are so sensitive to. We are typically relaxed and affectionate in manner when we babble on to them. This is just the best possible mood to have if a subject is to be willing to learn. As every good teacher knows, you never can teach anyone anything if they feel opposed to you or under attack or criticism. The compliance and uncritical attention of our pets, dogs in particular, leaves us with soft feelings of warmth and belonging. We ourselves are perhaps more in the mood to be affected by our words than the animals we have been pretending they are intended for.

Talking of moods brings us to the most obvious oddity of our talking to animals. Why all this 'baby talk'? The voice goes soft and the words are often almost sung, as if the speaker was cooing lovingly to a six-month-old baby. 'What is it then? Where's it gone? What then? Well, do you want your food?' The tonal qualities of pet-directed 'baby talk' are interesting for they are more commonly used by adults than children. Youngsters tend to treat their pets less like a baby and more like a slightly junior sister. At first sight, the fact that people do use styles of speech to pets that are reminiscent of a mother talking to her baby may suggest that pets are, after all, child substitutes. It is easy to call to mind images of elderly people who have lost or have never had children who seem to go as far as possible towards treating their pets as if they really were their babies. Some observers have suggested that many childless people turn to pets as a substitute upon which to lavish their caring instincts and that is why humans get so involved and become so absurdly infantile in their behaviour towards their pet. I later came to believe that this represents only a small minority of pet owners and the real reason why most people have pets is something different.

It certainly is true that many—perhaps most—people on occasions regress to a baby-language tone when they speak to their dog or cat. But if you listen to the words, it is by no means identical to a mother talking to her child. Students in America have pointed out that when a mother talks to her child she varies the language according to the age of the child, but in most cases she uses a simplified form of human language to help the youngsters to speak. This seems to involve repetitions of already familiar words and the conscious usage of new words identified with their meaning. So deeply rooted is this behaviour in parents that we are not usually aware of what we are doing. If next time there is a chance, you pause and listen, then it does seem that human 'mothercare' is a form of language apprenticeship. This being so, it seems obvious that the purpose and presumably the motivation of pet talk is different. Talking to pets thus must have a different function for the speaker for even the most nutty pet owner doesn't expect his (or her) dog to learn to quote Shakespeare!

I returned to these ruminations later in my year with Snowy. For the moment, it was enough to realise that I had joined the ranks of the intuitive, less objective pet-talking fraternity. From now on, I would have to work harder at viewing Snowy, Chilly and Motley dispassionately. With all the deep feelings involved in pets it is little wonder that most owners can no longer be dispassionate. It is almost a contradiction in terms and I began to see why most of the good pet scientists that I was reading about and starting to meet had no pets of their own. I know of more than one case where the scientist had to borrow a pet so that he could be photographed (with the right image) for the portrait on the dust jacket of his book.

The Guide Dogs for the Blind Association was right. The more I talked, the closer grew the bond between Snowy and me and the more responsive he was to my discipline—and not only during walks. He became a super-obedient dog, who could be trusted to obey all basic commands. He was astonishingly intelligent, a marvellous character. I couldn't possibly have had a better dog!

But just a minute. Was I now being objective? Don't all devoted owners think that? Perhaps I was falling back into the old trap. How good was he really, not just in my eyes but compared with other dogs? So it was that we joined that devoted band of enthusiasts, the Kidlington and District Dog Training Club. They met in a disused social club on a nearby airfield and they provided Snowy and me with some new experience and good friends. First impressions were that the best obedience-trained dogs were collies and German shepherds. Inevitably I compared him with the other pets and those were obviously better at their skills than he was. But, I thought, he *was* probably brighter—it was just that he hadn't been doing it for so long! In any case my mind was partly directed to using the dog-training scene as a laboratory to view owner-pet interactions. I actually watched to see if the most obedient dogs had owners that talked most to them, so matching my new theory about the great importance of owner-talk. It could not be considered a properly conducted investigation as I, as the observer, was often occupied walking in a ring following other dogs and responding to the leader's shouts of 'Turn', 'Leave your dog', and so on. However, for what it was worth, I could not see an obvious correlation between the amount of owner talk and dog obedience.

While we were sitting out, I could watch more intensively and then I thought I could see a definite link between the best-trained dogs and their handler's behaviour. It didn't relate to pet talking but to another common human response to our animal companions—petting. The owners of the most obedient dogs seemed to stroke and fondle their animals far more as they sat out waiting for their turns. Most commonly their attention was directed elsewhere but nevertheless their hand was caressing their pet in a distracted way. They seemed unaware of how they were responding to their dog but it was evident how deep-seated, habitual and mutually satisfying this expression of their bonding was.

My outstanding memory of our time at dog-training classes concerned not other dogs but Snowy himself. I had come to feel that Snowy was at least as good as (and potentially better than) most of the dogs there and everyone there could surely see how reliable he was in responding to all the training commands! Believe me, when an owner gets a little bit arrogant at indoor dog-obedience classes there is no better way to bring him down to size than for a dog to stop rigid in the middle of a walk round, despite all orders to keep moving on to heel. It's not so much the hold-up of the line of dogs and owners following on behind, rather the indignity of cleaning up the consequent pile of steaming wastes that are then deposited!

Snowy, I could have killed you!

10

One Good Turn

Motley was always fun. His coat was sleek and his reactions were rapid. On one occasion when my American friend, Wendy, visited me, she brought with her a wide variety of gimmicky toys of the sort that you could only expect to come from the States. A delightful—and tough—woolly mouse and some fluffy toy birds with feathered tails and bells on elastic were among the most popular. For Snowy there was a white plastic imitation newspaper called *The Daily Growl*, complete with a squeaker and printed text of 'dog news'. He gnawed through this successfully within two days and then turned his attention to one of the furry birds before it could be rescued.

The birds were suspended on elastic from door knobs so that Motley could spring up to catch the toy and then pull it down, before letting it go. As it shot up again, he would leap in the air, twisting along his length and seemingly changing positions in mid-air to make another capture.

Chilly? Well, she never seemed to want to play at all. Even if mouse or bird were dragged in front of her she would give it only casual interest. Meanwhile my sleep would be disturbed in the dead of night by Motley engaging in mortal combat with the toy bird against the kitchen door. I was so impressed by the kitten's aerial manoeuvres that I tried to film his leaps in slow motion to illustrate a cat's amazing flexibility. But whenever we tried to film it, we needed to set up about six powerful lights and run a rather noisy camera—and you can guess the result. Chilly was off like a flash and Motley quickly lost all interest in

Motley engaged in mortal combat with a toy bird

playing with the toy. So we waited and then tried to tease him into reacting, but his mind was always on other things. Six different days we tried it, always with the same negative result. It was hard convincing friends that our cats wouldn't play with a fluffy toy on elastic—at least so that we could film either of them with the high-speed camera.

There was another way we could demonstrate a cat's flexibility, however, and at the same time investigate a question that many people have argued over. How does a cat manage to turn over so rapidly enabling it always to land on its feet? It is a phenomenon that most people have witnessed. Owners will playfully hold their cat upside down a few feet over a soft chair, and marvel at the speed of reaction the cat displays as it rights itself in mid-air. To be impressed by it is one thing, but there is another aspect which is perhaps even more marvellous if you stop to analyse it. What does the cat use to push against to enable it to turn and right itself in mid-air?

Physicists had been aware of this apparent dilemma many years ago. The airborne cat seems to break a basic law of physics—namely, that every action produces an equal and opposite reaction. If something wants to move, it has to have something to push off against—the ground in the case of a walker, water for a swimmer or air in the case of a bird's wing. The cat in free fall doesn't use air resistance to push its body against to make the turn, so how does it do it?

For our film, we watched Motley hunting along a bedroom shelf attracted by a goldfish bowl. As he clambered around the smooth glass sides, he trod on an overhanging magazine and, in a flash, over he went on to the bed we had thoughtfully positioned about three feet below him.

The action was too quick for the naked eye to comprehend but the slow-motion camera enabled us to show the stages involved in the incredible turn. As he lost his footing and began to fall, he found himself on his back with all four feet facing upwards. Then he began to jack-knife his body by bending at the waist. Next, with a twist his head and front end began to turn downwards while the back end was still facing upwards. So flexible is a cat's backbone that it can twist its body almost halfway round, i.e. 180 degrees along its length. Finally, as Motley's head and front legs almost faced the ground, the back half now turned to follow with a flick of the tail which seemed to aid the action. He was now right way up, showing how in about 1/100th of a second a cat can spin its own body in mid-air so that it drops to the ground safely on all fours. The physics experts have compared its skills to those demonstrated by swimmers who have perfected the techniques of high-board diving. There too the body can turn itself well after it has left

One good turn

A cat can twist its own body in mid-air

contact with the diving board. In both cases, we can see that by jack-knifing the body it is possible to use the bend in the region of the waist to serve as fulcrum for one half of the body to push, pull and roll against the other.

The high-speed camera we used to film this runs at 500 frames per second (fps) instead of the usual 24 for normal-speed cameras. This means that when the high-speed film is projected on normal equipment running at 24 fps the resulting action on the screen is slowed down something like six times. We used this technique to shed new light on several common pet behaviours. For example, how did Snowy manage to dry himself after a splash in the local river? Obviously, like all dogs, he just shed water in every direction by shaking himself violently. But it is rare that anyone stays around for long enough to study this technique! Usually, when a dripping wet dog cheerfully approaches you, you will disappear like a shot for fear of getting drenched from the shower you know will follow. Here again there is a conflict between human and dog behaviours, for my own instincts in running away would suggest to Snowy that I was inviting him to play and he would follow on my heels with redoubled energy.

And then it would happen. Suddenly Snowy would stop abruptly and, with a movement that started slowly and then speeded up to a frenzied oscillation, the water would fly off in every conceivable direction. But the high-speed camera revealed once again that pets, just like all other animals, possess some amazing skills that largely pass unnoticed.

Some parts twist vigorously to the left while other parts are shaking to the right

The dog's shake starts up at the nose and gradually works its way back to the tail. The animal pushes forward his snout and begins to turn his head, then his neck, then his shoulders from side to side using his front legs as pivots—as if he's doing a rhumba, in fact. As different parts of the body start at different times it soon becomes clear that some parts are twisting vigorously to the left while other parts are shaking to the right, effectively doubling the relative speed of the different areas of loose skin as waves of shaking pass down the body. It all suddenly makes sense because, if all the body moved in the same direction at the same time, the animal would shake itself off its feet.

The skin of a dog is sufficiently loosely attached to the muscles below for it to get into quite a swing as it shakes. As the flapping fur, jowls and ears change their direction from right to left, the drops of water are flicked off with tremendous force. No wonder it feels to us more like an attack from a million water pistols! Finally, the animal slows down. The head stops first, followed by the shoulders, then the rump until finally the tail alone is circling like a baby pig's as the last of the droplets cascade into the air.

Once again, here was something so apparently simple and yet which became absolutely fascinating when slowed down by our specialist cameras. As a matter of interest, cats don't have this ability to dry themselves by vigorous shaking, which might explain their notorious dislike of getting wet! But the high-speed sequence that gave us most fun—and most headaches—was an investigation into the drinking techniques of dogs and cats. Have you ever stopped to think how a dog or cat manages to lap up liquids with its tongue while, if any human tried the same thing, he would succeed only in splashing the stuff all over the place? To demonstrate just how inferior our drinking abilities are, I again sought the co-operation of George Bernard. George is always game to try anything new and he agreed to be the guinea pig and allow me to film him with the high-speed camera while he tried in any way possible to sup up water from a clear glass vessel.

I don't think either of us had realised just how difficult, indeed almost impossible, it is to do. The stubby human tongue stabs into the water and tries in vain to scoop forward and lift the water into the throat. Our problem is that, as we push our tongue out as far as possible, the end becomes fairly rigid and we can't turn it upwards and forwards to make a suitable scoop. The harder George tried, the more water he splashed around. Then, sensing a more practical way, he improvised by furling his tongue into a tube and, keeping it still, used it to suck the water up. This method, though still very inefficient, did deliver more liquid than even the most vigorous attempts at lapping.

A further way for us to drink is to lower the whole mouth into the water so that we take a 'bite' of water and then, having got it in the throat, simply swallow it. But this technique, like sucking, is nothing like a lapping action so I was still left puzzled by how Snowy, Chilly and Motley were able to beat us at such an apparently simple task.

The answer, when it came, astonished me—even more so since, as it happened, none of my pets were originally involved in solving the mystery. Instead the honour went to a neighbour's German shepherd who happened to be around when I was using the high-speed camera away from our studios. It was a lovely sunny day and I asked the owner to take her dog for a run to make it thirsty while I filled a transparent dish with water and lined up the camera. On its return, the dog bounded up to the water and began to drink greedily, seemingly unconcerned by the noise of the high-speed camera as the drive mechanism roared a few feet from the animal's head.

Then, as is always the case with high-speed filming, we had to wait a day or two until the film had been sent away to a specialist laboratory and processed before seeing just what the technique had revealed. Looking with the naked eye had given me the clear impression that dogs have a much longer, more extensible tongue than man which, when extended, has a much broader and scoop-like tip. Whatever the technique used, one thing was evident; it was remarkably efficient. The dog had emptied the dish in no time at all.

So how did it do it? The processed film showed that it did use its long broad tongue as a scoop, but that this was only part of the story. In fact, the dog scooped up the water backwards. As the dog's tongue first enters the water, we saw that the tip was folded back like a backward-facing spoon. The tongue itself moves forward from the back of the lower jaw towards the nose but as it is pushed into the top few centimetres of water, a bow wave raises the level of water ahead of the tongue. As the wave is pushed along, it curves round and drops into the cup of the tongue. Then the tongue is lifted back up into the mouth with the tip still curled back so that it acts as a ladle. Once the jaw's

shut, the water is swallowed in just the same way as happens
with humans.

This drinking technique was so clear, neat and virtually
splash-free on the high-speed film sequence that it was obviously a 'must' to include in our film. This time, of course, we
would feature Snowy. It is very rare for a wildlife photographer
to find a sequence that he knows in advance will show dramatic
new facts as well as being simple and reliable to film. As much
of the filming had been somewhat disappointing up to that
point, I positively looked forward to the next fine day when my
colleague Philip Sharpe could take Snowy for a trot and then let
him have his drink in front of the high-speed camera. There
were a few minor refinements, however. To improve the
lighting, I added some front lights at ground level to reduce the
dark shadows from the sun and to give us a better view of what
exactly was going on.

Snowy performed perfectly. He was already familiar with all
our camera paraphernalia and it didn't bother him a bit. He
gulped up the water as the camera recorded his technique. He
seemed a bit messy but that didn't really matter, for the main
thing was simply to show how a dog manages to empty a water
bowl so efficiently.

Efficiently? Forget it! When the film came back it showed
that Snowy was a terrible performer. He faultlessly curled his
tongue back to make a ladle, but one second he would stick his
mouth so far into the water that he was almost gulping it directly, then the next he would withdraw his head so that only his
tongue was cupping up the water and, as he withdrew it, he
was catching it on his closing lower jaw and spilling it
everywhere! Far more water was being splashed out than was
going into his mouth. No wonder the bowl emptied quickly!

We had obviously made him so desperate for a drink after his
run that he was gulping impatiently and throwing water
everywhere. This was easy to rectify. The next time we filmed
it, we didn't even run him at all. He still was a willing performer in front of the camera, but once again the film showed
that, apart from the backwardly cupped tongue, his technique
was anything but exemplary. Perhaps he was still so young that
he hadn't yet properly learned the co-ordination between lower

jaw and tongue so that he could close his mouth the moment *after* the tongueful of water was in his mouth. He seemed to be a bad judge of distances, for he often put his head down so low that he was almost biting the water, and this caused him to choke and lift his head out with his mouth wide open.

Three times I tried before I was forced to face the disappointing conclusion that he couldn't make a neat job of drinking water. He splashed around so badly that instead of being impressed, a human observer could only be amused at his pathetic attempts to do the thing that every other dog around can seemingly do so readily.

The conclusion for me was obvious. I would have to film another white German shepherd's head and cut it into the film at the crucial place. It wasn't ideal but it had to be done. As it happened, I was able to go back to the same breeder who had furnished us with Serena when we were filming the birth sequences earlier. She had about eight dogs kept in a rural setting and used mainly for breeding. These dogs were only a part of her breeding stock, for she had terriers and other breeds as well, including coloured German shepherds.

Admitted the dogs were not as house-trained or accustomed to strict human discipline as one would have liked, but that hardly mattered. They were white and they must drink and I sorely needed some pictures of one of them for the film. So it was that before setting up the high-speed camera, Philip and I found ourselves mowing a lawn to make the background match the setting where the real Snowy had already been filmed running up to drink. Which animal should we try first? It didn't really matter. Serena was one we knew of old so we asked if she could be brought out. Much barking, the other dogs locked in, a lassoo trick with a slip collar and Serena was presented in front of the bowl. But by now she was muddied from the skirmishes inside her pen. She wouldn't pass as Snowy with that appearance, even if I only filmed her mouth and tongue. 'Never mind, let's try some film and treat the day as an audition session,' I decided. 'We'll try all the dogs, see which has the best technique and then return for a proper shoot.' Philip agreed. The sight of an unwilling grubby dog seemed a bad omen for getting a perfect sequence at that precise moment.

'O.K. let's try it,' I called as the sun broke through and I lay on my belly peering down the viewfinder.

It *is* a pity dogs don't speak human language! Serena seemed disinclined to drink. The owner bent down and wet Serena's lips and then pulled her so her head was over the bowl, making a heart-rending plea to the dog's finer sentiments so that I could film some action.

The sun went in. That meant insufficient light to film with but Serena now began to drink so I started the camera anyway and the motor revved into action. Immediately Serena stopped and turned and ran between the owner's legs. We tried again and again but Serena would not oblige. 'You can take a dog to water. . .' I began to think.

It was as well that there were another nine white dogs to try. It meant that we were able to have a whole day of futile efforts. None of them would slurp for more than a few seconds before stopping. In some cases the camera noise put them off completely but for the most part the dogs simply couldn't be persuaded to drink at all in the unfamiliar situation! However there were bits and pieces where the different dogs did drink while the camera was actually running and so, as we packed up our gear at the end of the day, we reflected that we might just have enough to cobble together to serve our purpose.

When the film came back from the processing labs four days later, there was no doubt about it. None of it would do! There were all sorts of problems which the film revealed, although they did all furl their tongue back and used the scoop to lift water towards their mouths. One of the dogs had a good technique but it flicked the water *at* its mouth with its backwards-folded tongue and the camera revealed that on every gulp a massive stream of water was sent upwards at either side of its mouth. Another must have been a reincarnated mermaid, for it tried to drink while most of its jaw, including the nose, was under water! The high-speed film showed it blowing copious bubbles from its nostrils as it gulped water into its mouth! For one reason or another, each dog seemed unlikely to provide what we were after. All was not lost, however, for one of the kennel ladies had three white German shepherds of her own, one of which was not only house-trained and obedient but also a 'good drinker', as she claimed (fancy having to ask owners that!). We were welcome to go and film it, and the fact that it was housed another hour's drive away seemed neither here nor there in the circumstances, particularly as there were two other possibles in the same stable.

One learns from past mistakes and traumas, however, so this time I took the precaution of asking the family who owned the dogs to try them out before I got there. I even loaned them a tape recording of our noisy high-speed camera so that we would not get involved in more false starts because its racket upset the animals.

A few days passed and we heard that all the tests seemed fine, so we again set out on a pilgrimage, this time to Aylesbury. On arrival I found that the head of the household was a security guard with about eight German shepherds as part of his stock. Once I got over being surrounded by so many large dogs in what had suddenly become a very small sitting room, it was time to go outside and try our luck—only to find that none of the dogs would do what we wanted. In any case it began to rain so we had to postpone our attempt until another day.

By the time we made our return trek, the kind and co-operative owners had found new stimuli which would help our task. The first secret weapon was home-made chicken soup. Apparently the dogs loved it and because of that drank more carefully. As it was almost colourless, we could dilute it a little yet still be able to see the tongue action through the liquid. It was a good idea but it didn't look right through the camera, being still too cloudy and rich. We tried a couple of times but by now the dogs were 'tweaked up' at the start of the camera run and didn't drink much before stopping.

The second weapon was the idea of the security man. He pulled from his pocket an almost empty bottle of Marakesh, a colourless liqueur, and poured some into a new container of clear water. The dogs, we were told, loved it but the mixture may have been made a little too potent for Sheena, Elsa and the gang, and in turn they took one sniff and refused to put their tongues into it. We diluted it but by now the familiar lesson was dawning on us. It wasn't going to work.

So we had to admit our failure with white German shepherds. The best we could do was to use the original dog and, in the film, simply show it as being a near neighbour of Snowy. That would have been fine were it not for the fact that the dog had sadly been killed before we could get back to film it properly! So much for a simple sequence. In the end, however, we were able to get what we wanted. All these other attempts had taken so long that by the time we came back to Snowy, he had grown and improved his own drinking technique. He was by no means perfect but he did well enough to allow us to show the essence of a dog's drinking technique.

So what about cats? How do they drink? By now you'll probably be able to predict how Chilly responded to the high speed camera. Motley, however, was different—as always—and gave us a good performance the very first time we ran the camera. We used milk this time which, though not transparent, was a great favourite with the cats—and this made me think that perhaps we should have tried the dogs on milk too. When the film came back, we could see that Motley and, presumably, all other cats have a drinking technique that differs from both dogs and humans.

What takes place is this. As the cat's tongue goes into the liquid, it seems to go almost straight down. It certainly doesn't scoop forward and, while the tip has a slight curl backwards as it withdraws into the mouth, the tongue doesn't appear to have the backwards scoop action so clearly visible in dogs. Instead the cat has a drinking action in which the milk appears to stick to the tongue as it is lifted out of the fluid. The mouth is then closed and when the tongue reappears it is pink and relatively milkless, ready to be submerged again.

Our pictures were clear enough yet it still was not evident why the milk stuck to the tongue. Our task of interpreting this wasn't made any easier by the white screen of milk. So to get another view I arranged to film what was going on when viewed from below the glass container. Again the high-speed camera was used and we were conscious that any results would have to be interpreted with caution because the drinking action could well be different as the last few drops were being lapped from the bottom of the vessel.

The visual results were impressive. What was at first an undisturbed layer of milk seen from below became blotted out by a large, spotty and spiky tongue. Motley's tongue in operation was revealed as an excellent sponge. The most prominent feature was the large 'teeth'—made of a horny material and projecting backwards on the tongue—that can easily be felt when any cat licks your hand but which obviously are also used when grooming. Behind each spikey tooth was a small recess that, when Motley licked the bottom of the vessel, simply soaked up large volumes of milk by absorbing it into the surface of the tongue. That seems to be the cat's secret. Using its tongue like a sponge, it can readily take up fluids without scooping one way or the other.

Having satisfied myself about how Snowy and Motley drank I can now invite you to lay by the side of your pets when they're drinking and see if you agree. If you happen to have a £12,000 high-speed camera, six months of time, some home-made chicken soup and a bottle of Marakesh, that may also help you make up your mind! And if all this fails, I suggest you pour the soup over the camera and drink the whole bottle of Marakesh yourself!

11

A Taste Of Freedom

As I've hinted before, there seems to be a strong polarisation in people's feelings about pets.

Those who share their homes, day in, day out with animals seem to enjoy their companionship—at least for a time—while others who can't for one reason or another have a pet of their own seem to derive great satisfaction from contact with other people's animals.

On the other hand, a substantial number of people undoubtedly have a strong antipathy towards pets. Some people have a lifelong aversion to any kind of domestic animal, some despise just one species or another, and some (as I suggested in an earlier chapter) became disillusioned after unfortunate experiences with animals of their own. The grounds for these attitudes vary. Some extend their disapproval to include pet owners as well—people whom they see as babyish pamperers of 'soft' animals. Another major group in the anti-pet lobby is formed of people who don't like to see animals which they view as being once proud and noble, degraded—in their opinion—by breeding and domestication into animated furry toys.

Since most of my own life has been spent in the study of wild animals, with a close association with domestic animals coming only relatively late in my career as a naturalist, I found myself reassessing just what man does to one-time wild animals during the process of domestication. For a start there are many levels of domestication. The elephant has remained virtually unaltered despite having been used in the service of man since the third millenium BC, while some ornamental goldfish have been altered almost out of recognition by the process. Simply taming an animal like a squirrel is not the same thing as domestication, for in the latter case there is the essential difference of man's gaining control over the animal's breeding, thus giving him the chance to select and develop characteristics better suited to his own needs and goals—more meat or milk for instance, a more placid temperament, greater speed or strength. Snowy himself, of course, is the end product of special breeding programmes by the Guide Dogs organisation and, before that of countless generations of dog breeders.

At the same time, man not only moulds the behaviours and anatomies of the creatures he keeps in captivity but also usually provides them with protection against most of their natural enemies. Thus, many features of behaviour and body build would cause these animals to be killed and picked off more quickly by their natural predators if they were put out into the wild again. Snowy's white colour—the result of breeding—would have the effect of making him less easily concealed when he was a vulnerable youngster and more easily spotted and avoided by his potential prey in later life.

And for that matter, man is in some ways domesticating himself. My own need for glasses or contact lenses, for instance, would be severely limiting to my chances of survival were I out in the wilds. But man's available technology protects me from facing the immediate consequences of my deficient eyes. (I'm also red/green colour blind, which gives me a good start as a photographer!)

Such features that would be deficiencies in the wild animal become perpetuated when the mechanisms of survival and breeding are taken away from nature and placed into the hands of man. In this way the purist is certainly correct in seeing pets as being in some ways degenerate, disfigured and simplistic animals. On the other hand, the domestic animal is potentially so well suited to life close by man that it provides unique possibilities for interactions and interdependence with humans on economic and social levels that would never be possible with wild animals. I was tempted to say 'with God's creatures' but in the case of pets they are now almost as much man-made creatures too!

Cats may be a partial exception. They have been bred so that, unlike wild animals, they are not afraid in the presence of humans but they certainly do seem to retain an unalterable independence and pattern of wild behaviours despite thousands of years of domestication. Cats are often described as having nine lives. Looked at another way, I think they definitely have two. One is the indoors cat curled up on the bed, the other is the outdoors cat on the prowl looking for mice, birds and other prey. Usually these are two sides of the same animal—very few domestic cats fail to display signs of wild behaviour such as the hunting instinct given half the chance.

When I first had the two cats, I had kept them indoors for nearly two months in case they ran off and left me, but from then on I began to give them an increasing taste of freedom. I soon found that my trust was rewarded by their fidelity in returning home after their forays. They still worried me because of a tendency to perch in the wheel arch of my parked car—a favourite haunt—but I soon learnt to check where they were before I started the vehicle. When left to their own devices outdoors, both cats would chase the brimstone butterflies amidst the flowers while the spring bulbs provided a new hunting ground for them. I occasionally sat with Snowy by my side and watched them simply as part of the wildlife of the garden. They would catch sight of birds flying overhead and the hunting instinct seemed to be sharpened by the frustration (in human terms) that this caused. I realised what was afoot and my worst fears were realised one Sunday morning as I was in the kitchen. I saw Chilly freeze as a blackbird flew by and landed on its nest at the top of a pile of cut-down branches. Only a few days previously, Motley and Chilly had found a young blackbird that had been killed by a car and returned to eat it on the doorstep. Since their appetites had been whetted by this, it wasn't long before the inevitable happened.

Chilly stalked towards the base of the pile and effortlessly and silently began to climb towards the nest. Within seconds, I was racing down the steps to the lawn, followed joyfully by Snowy who misread the signs and thought it was another of our chasing games. Mercifully all four baby blackbirds were still alive as I grabbed Chilly in the nick of time. After this episode, I locked her in the house for three days to keep her at bay until the birds had flown.

Although the killing of songbirds is what upsets most cat owners, it should be remembered that the natural diet of cats is mainly rodents. In fact the natural hunting behaviour of cats is such that birds are far less easily caught than mice. For a start, the cat really is a specialist at waiting, particularly outside a mouse hole. It delays its pounce until the rodent has strayed far enough away from its burrow and then the rapid jump and a bite behind the neck finishes the matter.

Birds, however, tend to be always on the move, hopping around as they feed. In order to keep close enough to pounce the cat is forced either to wait and hope the bird moves towards it or to try to follow it, in which case it will most likely be spotted and the bird will fly off. The scientist who is regarded as one of the top experts on cats, Leyhausen, believes that in practice cats mainly catch old, sick or infirm birds anyway. However, small birds do make up 4-18% of the diet of free-roaming cats so that's a fair number of birds taken overall.

The instinct for cats to hunt and kill is of course well known to have survived virtually unaltered by all the years of domestication. I don't think many cat owners derive much pleasure from finding their pets in the act of mauling a half-mangled mouse or standing on the doorstep proudly displaying a limp-necked bundle of feathers. Yet most seem simply to shrug their shoulders and accept it. I wonder if anyone has actually tried to control the breeding of cats so that they could selectively breed from those animals that displayed a reduced tendency to hurt and kill. This technique has worked with dogs in the past, so is it just that their behaviour is more easily moulded by breeding or is it that no one has felt sufficiently impelled to try it with cats? I guess that some enterprising American or Japanese cat-breeding company would be well towards it in fifty years—if the demand was there!

As it is, the most effective remedies I have heard of to keep cats away from things like bird tables are somewhat impracticable: orange skins, orange juice, or the dung of a large wild

Silently Chilly began to climb towards the nest

cat like a tiger spread near the base of the table are claimed to do the trick and keep potential hunters at bay...

*   *   *

As I watched Chilly and Motley in the woods and lawns around my home, I could see other ways that showed how the instincts of wild cats had remained basically unchanged despite domestication. Their use of scent marks on low branches and their general way of parcelling out territories still parallels wild cats.

Although cats, particularly toms, mark by urinating or rubbing glands on objects in their territory, these scents never seem to have intimidating effects on other cats that smell them. They do nonetheless give information about the previous visitor to the spot and presumably help to keep these basically solitary animals apart. Domestic cats are less repulsive to each other than are all their wild relatives. They can be made to share a home base, like Chilly and Motley, but even then they will separate from each other when out in the field.

Cats living together in a particular environment clearly overlap their territories. The situation is somewhat complicated because there isn't one single boss cat who always takes priority over all the others around and in any case there are no clearly guarded boundaries to any of their territories. Outside the home base, every detail of which is known to the resident cat, there are well-used paths leading away to other areas used for hunting, courting and so on. A female cat will typically restrict herself to an area of about a square kilometre while toms wander over areas several times this, especially during the breeding season.

The territories of domestic cats overlap but in general different animals have relative dominance over the others at different times of the day or night. Thus only one animal will have unchallenged use of an area at any one time. Later, another cat will come in and take over the unchallenged top position for hunting in that territory for an 'agreed' time, to be followed by another cat and so on. In other words, they have territories for common but not simultaneous use and a top cat at one time will not try to take over from another cat in the same area at a different time. It's a kind of shift system. Cat territoriality is based not just on a sense of place but also on a sense of time and for this system to work it is obvious that our feline friends need a good inbuilt clock. That, of course, is just what our cats possess.

You only have to check with a few owners to find examples of cats that display an incredible array of feats of timing. In my own experience I can point to cats that regularly wake their

Even cats which share a home base will separate from each other
when out in the field

owners a few minutes before the alarm goes off, cats that go
and sit by the door just a short time before their owner returns
home, and cats that seem to 'know' when some regular event is
going to take place, even if there are no time clues that we
humans can perceive. All this seems to confirm the incredible
accuracy of the cat's internal time clock which, in nature, is so

important if it wants to get to its territory during its own allotted time.

But there is something else that may be connected with a sense of timing which is far in excess of human abilities. Cats are remarkably good at finding their way back home—indeed they are famous for it. Once they had exhausted the garden's possibilities, Chilly and Motley soon extended their explorations into the neighbourhood—yet returned infallibly. Other cats, males particularly, are known to make regular patrols along routes three or more miles long and yet seem to have no trouble in keeping track of where they are. This is not surprising, perhaps, for many wild animals have even more extensive territory ranges. Most of us will have heard stories of cats that have been taken to a new area, have run away and found their way back over twenty or more miles. Could it be that, in one way, cats resemble birds in having a navigational ability based on a highly accurate internal time-clock? By comparing the apparent time of day with what their internal clocks tell them, many birds can find their way over vast distances. This could explain an old experiment (not repeated, I'm pleased to say) in which stray cats were rounded up, taken by car on a circuitous route to a spot outside town and then put in pens. The cats, it is said, tried to get out in the same compass direction they would have to take to get back to where they started. There may be nothing in it—certainly the experiment wasn't rigorously enough controlled to provide compelling evidence—but one never knows. The mystique of cats has already led to many claims as to their psychic powers. I like to think I'm open-minded about this but first I'd love to know more about those senses our pets possess that are capable of so much more discrimination than our own. Only then should we begin to look for psychic explanations—for one thing, sense organs are relatively easier to study!

As I watched the cats passing to and fro amid the garden plants and flowers, exploring all the regular marking spots where cats before them had rubbed or sprayed their personal scent, it was easy to sense that one was dealing with behaviour that hadn't been much modified by domestication. Yet, when you get down to it, all our pets are a big step away from their ancestors, and there are a number of observable alterations to their behaviour which have resulted from man's influence on their breeding.

The first thing—which sounds so obvious when you read it but isn't when you think of the transformation entailed—is losing the tendency to run away in the presence of humans. Progressively tamer, more docile wild animals are chosen for mating to produce a man-tolerant domesticated animal. The problem is that when mankind consciously alters the species by selective breeding to produce a new characteristic, all sorts of other new and possibly unstable characteristics arise too. For example, if an animal is no longer to show fear of humans, it is likely to lose its fear of predators as well and then it will reduce its instincts to fight and to protect its offspring.

To develop an emotionally stable, fully socialised animal must have taken many years, but now, hundreds of generations later, our pets are so well adapted for life with humans that they are in fact better suited to such a lifestyle than being back in the wilds. The behaviour of most domestic animals has been deliberately altered in some ways to suit man's needs. Sometimes detrimental anatomical features and behaviours have also come along with the newly developed species— fighting in cattle, feather picking in chickens and of course hip problems in many of Snowy's breed of German shepherd. Most impressive of all is the long long list of why different behaviours have been developed in different animals—cats for pest destruction, horses for transport, dogs for hunting, alarm calling by peacocks, hens for laying, bulls for fighting and so on.

Domestication is a constantly developing process. One clear-cut trend resulting from domestication is a tendency towards a persistence of juvenile features. Put another way, it seems that all pets develop somewhat like an overgrown baby animal. Thus the facial area is relatively shorter, the musculature often flabbier and weaker, especially in domesticated dogs. This revolutionary process is the result of breeding from animals which exhibit the desired 'pretty' features. Other side-factors of man-made animals are changes of colour from the wild conditions, changes in length of hair, horn or feathers, and frequently rounder body shapes.

No one is certain why mankind first domesticated animals. Possibly goats and sheep were the first to be herded together for food and milk. Dogs were some of the earliest animals to be bred by man and it is usually assumed that they were kept in order to help in hunting or to guard man's primitive communities. However, no one knows for sure and my own personal hunch is that some father once brought home a baby animal for his children—as a family pet in fact. My evidence for this comes from a recent archaeological finding dated 12,000 BC of a man's skeleton with its arms resting on a dog. This is now viewed as the oldest record of a domesticated dog and suggests that the human-animal companion bond was there from the earliest times.

Whatever the prime cause, it is clear that pets—and dogs in particular—have been made to look more appealing by breeding which accentuates their baby-like looks so that this can be carried over into adulthood. It isn't true of all breeds, of course:German shepherds, for one, are an exception to this. You only have to compare a picture of an adult with a pup to see how the latter's down-turned ears and flattened face (more characteristic of a labrador) gives such an appealing look, but which isn't carried through into adulthood.

The barking and yapping of modern-day dogs also seems to be a hangover from babyhood. No wild dog or wolf barks anywhere near as much as house dogs but puppies do vocalise far more frequently. This too seems to be a sideline of domestication. It's as though both facial features and some behaviours become frozen at a particular age.

Consider too the general 'sensitivity' of pets. What scientists label as 'increased response thresholds to stimulation' really means that domesticated animals will often respond with less provocation or stimulation than would wild animals: fighting cocks—for example—will scrap at the slightest opportunity, while some dogs have such a low threshold that they will bite as a response to threat far more readily than a wild animal will. I suspect that dogs are also more willing to show affection at the

A taste of freedom

The German shepherd puppy's down-turned ears and flattened face change as it grows up but in many dog breeds they are retained in adulthood

least provocation—a factor that must add to their endearing qualities.

There is another factor that should make the most ardent 'back-to-nature' animal lover pleased that we· do have pets. They have been with man so long that they don't exhibit those pathetic repetitive responses and stresses that you see in certain zoo animals pacing their cages or intently playing ritualised games. If modern man does still need to associate with animals in such huge numbers as the statistics reveal, then it is surely a good thing that there are animals like Snowy, Chilly, and Motley around to fill that need.

It comes as something of a shock to realise that our dearest pets are really man-made descendants of purely wild animals and a moment's thought will bear out the fact that the only reason pet animals are still around is that man wants them for one or other of his purposes—perhaps to work, perhaps as an emotional associate. So, since we choose to use animals in these ways, what responsibilities does this give us?

Sitting on the lawn that afternoon, the cats perched up in the weeping willow and Snowy laying on the lawn beside me, the animals seemed so much a part of my life, so welcome and so fulfilling, I couldn't countenance anything but a devoted response by me to anything that might befall them. Yet so many pets are badly treated, neglected and often unwanted after a few months or, in the case of cats, are born in numbers too great to match owner demand. To my mind, this gives owners the responsibility of having their cats sterilized. This I had done with Chilly and Motley; Snowy too was sterilized, not because we were afraid of him escaping and contributing to unwanted litters, but because all guide dogs are so treated to limit the chance of them dragging their blind handlers towards sexually attractive mates. Sterilization both terminates the animal's breeding ability and limits the sexual drive of the animal towards other dogs. More important still perhaps is the fact that city-dwelling guide-dogs will frequently have to pass through areas that other male dogs regard as their own personal territories. Unless they are sterilized the intruders may be attacked and driven off: sterilized dogs are allowed through undisturbed.

Snowy was taken away for a week to have the operation and to have a chance to recover under expert supervision. It was also part of the Guide Dog organisation's policy to have all their dogs back in kennels for short periods during the puppy-walking year to check on their progress and to keep them familiar with the life in kennels that would follow for three or four months as they were finally trained on detailed harness work.

When he returned, I couldn't help feeling gratified at the obvious intensity of emotion and affection that he showed towards me. Such unswerving and uncritical adoration, not often experienced from other humans, may contribute to the owner's reciprocal infatuation for his pet. All was not well, however. Snowy was fit and suffered no obvious after-effects from the operation, but there was a minor criticism of his weight and condition from Derek Freeman, the head of the puppy-rearing section. Snowy, it was thought, was a bit on the light side and possibly his coat didn't quite have the sheen it might! So I was asked what I was feeding him on and if he had all the cod-liver oil and bone meal supplements suggested for him.

To my mind, Snowy looked and behaved as if he were in the peak of condition, but I nevertheless sympathised with the concern and scrutiny of the puppy-walking centre. They were as aware as anyone that, with the film, Snowy would be an ambassador for the Guide Dog Association and it was especially important that he always looked good. But he *was* looking good, so why the question?

Well, I admitted, I had changed one of his two daily meals to special dog pellets (dry food moistened prior to eating) because I was convinced that it was every bit as nutritious as the most gourmet meat from tins or the butcher, but this view didn't gain support from the guide dog experts. Like most down-to-earth Englishmen with interests in the countryside, Derek was convinced that there was nothing as good as 'the real thing'.

This wasn't simply an inflexible conservative attitude to their dogs' diet for, over the years, they had tried many variations of foods including dry pellet formulae. In his opinion a diet purely of pellets and water produced in many dogs a 'fall-off in condition'. The developing puppies were thought to put on less flesh than those fed on raw (or tinned) meats. Another difference some other people have claimed is that pellet-fed dogs produce many more wastes (or 'motions' as they are politely if somewhat bizarrely called). The motions resulting from a pellet diet are much more messy, two to three times as frequent and of greater volume than for dogs fed on raw meat and meal. This of course would mean—so the story goes—that while it may be more convenient for the owner to feed pellets, society pays for it by the increase in mess the dogs make!

I knew of such claims, I must admit, but I still felt that it was more tradition than logic that makes the British prefer 'wet' food, tinned or fresh, rather than some synthetic combination of ingredients carefully mixed, measured and compressed into pellets.

Naturally, I gladly agreed to change back to a fresh or tinned meat diet, but I was interested enough in what Derek had said to follow it up with the pet food industry. Here again, my eyes were opened.

First, I became aware of the astonishingly high level of research and control that is exercised by the largest companies. The mass production of pet foods is now down to such a fine art that even the cheapest end of the dog food ranges provides good value. As long as a tin of dog or cat food is labelled as a complete balanced diet (most are) then technically that product alone will serve all the dietary requirements of any dog or cat throughout its life! That of course would be a tediously uniform diet and one which few animals—or their owners—would care to follow but it says a lot for the careful control of ingredients and additives to match the government-confirmed standards of what *is* a guaranteed adequate dog or cat diet.

So why pay more than the minimum for an own-brand supermarket pet food? Partly the answer is because the basic dietary ingredients can be derived from different basic raw materials. Some—turkey perhaps—are more expensive than cheaper food like liver and give the owner the scope to vary the diet and pamper the pet. Many animals, of course, become choosy and don't seem to relish the tinned food offered to them. In this familiar situation it doesn't impress an owner to know that the food contains adequate dollops of every vitamin and trace element known to man if the animal sniffs at it and turns aside. Sales are easily affected unless the food has high pet-appeal. I suspect that some companies add a brand X to the products with no benefit other than to titillate Fido or Pussy into lunging at the fodder and gobbling it enthusiastically. And why not? The human food industry has been doing this for years with additives like monosodium glutamate.

Another reason for the wide price range for pet-food products is that while the animals eat the food, they don't buy it! A loving and concerned owner will be anxious to do the best for his family friend and (just like me at Christmas) will buy what looks appetising to him (or her) almost irrespective of the recipient's personal tastes. Thus food moulded artificially into apparently meaty chunks with richly colourful gravy might almost make the owner's mouth water as much as or more than the pet's! It is *meant* to! This cosmetic treatment is purely for the owner's eyes and not surprisingly it adds to the production costs. Its function in the very competitive business of selling pet foods is to make the owner buy one product in preference to another but to the dog a simple mashed slurp of the blend might be just as appetising and equally nutritious.

So what did these whizz kids of the pet-food world tell me about the question of dry pellets versus wet food? Gratifyingly, they supported me. I'm told that there is no reason why specifically compounded dry foods, moistened with water before serving, cannot provide everything that your pet needs. Most farm animals are fed on dry pellet food and in these animals the lack of good condition reflects itself in a reduction of their economic value. Because there already exists a huge industry providing basic dry ingredients for cattle food, pigs, chickens, rats, monkeys and many other creatures, it is a relatively cheap extension of this trade to formulate mixtures especially suitable for dogs or cats. Not only should it be less expensive but also, when sold in the supermarket, it doesn't involve the purchase of an expensive throwaway tin which costs as much as the food inside it. Most important of all, in other countries, particularly America, basic dry pet foods are far and away the most common diets and their pets don't look any the worse for it.

And, to let you into a secret, British pet food scientists agree that it is just as good as their tinned stuff!

While talking of feeding, it may be worth tossing in here a notion that cats may hold clues to help us resolve how to keep slim. Given an unlimited and always available supply of food, only about 5% of cats will become obese. On the other hand, dogs, in similar circumstances, will eat to excess and 90% or more will become grossly overweight. How do cats do it?

I don't think that anyone is totally sure, but research on other animals may have pointed the way to the cat's secret. For a start, it is not simply that they eat less; many cats with relatively large appetites stay slim. Instead it seems that the mammalian body (humans included) has certain areas of 'brown fat'—different from our ordinary layers of fat—just below the skin. After eating a large meal, the brown fat layer uses up all the excess carbohydrates by burning them up in the body and producing heat. Temperature devices show that the brown fat gets much hotter after a meal as it consumes all the excess. It seems that in humans these are the sites of body weight control and they are concentrated above the breasts and across the shoulder blades. Little is known so far about the brown fat layers of cats, but as they are naturally better at keeping their weight down than humans or dogs, it may well be because they have a super-efficient brown fat system. Perhaps this has something to do with cats' strong preference for a warm spot to rest in—even at the expense of some apparent comfort. Maybe it is easier to burn off their excess foods if their body is already as warm as possible? Whatever the answer, there is a fascinating amount of research to be undertaken here.

As soon as anyone sits down and starts asking questions about the interpretations of pet behaviours it becomes immediately clear that there are many gaps in our knowledge. There is usually no shortage of intuitive 'opinions'—conveyed as 'facts' from fellow pet owners but it is a tantalising field to know more about. Doesn't the importance of pets in our lives merit some research institute being set up to test out some of these questions?

12

Around And About

Everyone who 'walks' a guide dog puppy for the first year of its life must undertake to give the dog as much experience as possible of the situations it is likely to encounter when it finally joins its blind owner. Thus trips to busy towns are important, as well as familiarity with most forms of public transport—except escalators. These machines have proved disastrous for dogs and so I repeatedly emphasised 'no' whenever Snowy encountered one of these tantalising, busy moving stairways.

Naturally, the process of familiarisation was built up little by little so that Snowy was never thrown in at the deep end as regards sudden exposure to possible frights. Of course, most of this is what any puppy owner would do. The only special thing about looking after a potential guide dog is that one is given a small card certifying that your dog is being trained to be a guide dog and requesting the co-operation of shopkeepers and others to allow the dog to accompany you even if, normally, dogs are not admitted. If you think about it, this is an essential privilege that the young dogs must enjoy so that they behave appropriately later when leading their blind owner through his or her day.

Snowy was always fun to take out. He was remarkably well behaved and because of his colour, and later his huge size, he was always the centre of attraction. He was so docile, obedient and patient that, through my eyes, he was the best ambassador that the Guide Dogs for the Blind could have had. There was one notable occasion when I was shopping for jeans and had placed him in 'down' under a table in the shop. It took some time getting served but Snowy lay quietly under the table throughout, unaffected by the various feet, ankles and skirts that were constantly moving a few inches from his nose. I appreciated more fully how quietly he lay about ten minutes later when I changed my grip on my heavy shopping bags, only to find that I had left Snowy in the store. When I returned, he was sitting in the same place as I had left him, the only difference being that he seemed particularly delighted to see me!

Obviously one used discretion in taking Snowy into places that other dogs were not permitted to enter. For example, I avoided food shops, not least because customers as well as management don't like to see dogs there—a situation with which I can sympathise. However, there was a wide variety of reactions from sales assistants and managers as I led Snowy into stores which had 'Dogs prohibited—except for guide dogs' notices on the doors. The Guide Dogs organisation hadn't been operating much in the Oxford area at that time so shopkeepers were unfamiliar with the habits and needs of puppy walkers. In a way, Snowy and I had to break new ground and explain to all and sundry why I, who was obviously not a blind man (despite any quips my colleagues may offer), was asking for their co-operation in allowing my dog to accompany me. With a polite and firm approach, accompanied by the authorisation card and Snowy's official Guide Dog medallion on his collar, we almost invariably *were* admitted and even welcomed.

Talking informally to other puppy walkers I have met, I found that one could draw up a national league of stores showing how well they treated requests for co-operation. Woolworths come out near the bottom whenever I've discussed this. My experiences in Oxford (well away from the food section) bear this out. I was rudely treated and ordered to get out as quickly as possible. Debenhams in Oxford were the most toffee-nosed, suggesting patronisingly that if I cared to write in advance they would consider allowing me in the store before the customers arrived 'for a familiarisation session'. Perhaps I looked as if I had time on my hands! In any case, this would have defeated one of the main purposes—to aquaint him with all the distractions of normal shopping conditions.

People seem fairly widely agreed on the best of Britain's national stores in this respect—Marks and Spencer. In Oxford, I was often stopped by new sales assistants and politely asked if I was aware that it was company policy ... etc. But on identifying Snowy's birthright, they were unfailingly helpful and allowed us the freedom of the store. I think it boiled down to a mixture of company policy and the temperament of the people concerned. Snowy came to be treated like a welcome visitor by the sales staff at M & S and we did most of the training to avoid escalators there. So, on behalf of both of us (and many other guide dog owners too) thank you for your civilised and caring concern, Marks and Spencer! Another memorable day out with Snowy was our visit to the annual jamboree held by Guide Dogs for the Blind for all puppy walkers. It was a delightfully British occasion—a sort of cross between dog show, garden party and open day of the breeding centre held in the pleasant rural setting of a large old country house, now modified and extended to be the breeding centre for all British Guide Dogs.

Georgina, one of OSF's ever-cheerful assistants, joined Philip and me in making it a day out with Snowy. As there was to be a fancy dress category, and we had gone to some trouble to design a camera harness for Snowy to wear, we decided to enter him as a 'dog TV reporter'. He would wear the real miniature movie camera on his back and carry in his mouth an imitation microphone—a piece of clever improvisation, comprising a stick, some coiled flex and a gauze put together by Philip.

We wandered around the grounds mingling with families and dogs and learning a little more about the organisation and the people who help it. What was particularly impressive was the obvious loyalty that all the participants displayed. In a way, this charity has a massive advantage over almost all others in that it has such a direct and immediate appeal to the public's hearts. What is more noble and emotionally charged than the concept of a trained dog looking after and patiently guiding a sightless person? For this reason it's probably an easier cause to 'sell' to the public than other, equally worthwhile charities like care for geriatrics and the mentally subnormal, which trigger quite a different response in many people.

Snowy & Co

I made another observation from encountering the wide range of people associated with the Guide Dogs for the Blind. Most of those looking after the dogs were absolutely delightful people—families usually and often with a few young children who were equally dedicated to the dogs. This admittedly subjective impression may not seem worth mentioning until you put it against the 'licensed loony' image gleaned from stories in the press of elderly people missing a dog or a cat as if it were a missing child, or a family with dozens of different pets that overrun the household. I think this occurs for the reason that, because so many people have pets, it is the abnormal extremes who get all the publicity. The very normality of a well-adjusted, charming family with their lively kids along with the dog and cat all passes unsung. I would go further and say that of all the people I met working with guide dogs, the closer they worked with the dogs, the warmer they were as people. There was no sign of these animal lovers turning to animals as a substitute because they didn't get along with people—rather the reverse. It seemed to me that the people at the guide dog gala were more outgoing, friendly, kind and sensitive human beings than you would get at most comparable gatherings of five hundred or so elsewhere. I may, of course, have been seeking a reflection of my own image of dog owners but I don't think so, because my views have been confirmed in the experience of others to whom I have spoken.

The jamboree gave us a happy chance to meet Snowy's mother and father. We put them all together for a family album picture. Snowy's mother, Rebecca, was a delightful bitch who was somewhat unwilling to pose for pictures. Snowy's ten-year-old father, Tollmark, was a wonderful specimen with an immaculate temperament, one of the organisation's best stud dogs in fact. He later won prizes for being in best condition in his class and as we watched him it was impossible not to be left wondering where Snowy would be when he was ten years old.

As we might have expected, Snowy didn't seem to recognise his parents, nor they him. After the picture-taking session, Philip walked Snowy in the ring with all the rest of the first-year dogs. It wasn't that we expected a prize (though you never know, do you?) but rather that it was part of the atmosphere of the day for everyone to enter everything.

Snowy was soon eliminated. It may have been because technically speaking, his hind quarters stand too high compared with the ideal for the breed. But no one tells you: with a wave he was out of the competition. Philip was visibly disappointed for; like me, he had spent long periods with Snowy and had kindly dog-sat for me on weekends that I had had to go away without my white footstool. Snowy was everyone's friend back at OSF for that matter. We were both lucky to be working with people whose one common bond is an admiration and respect for animals. I only had to cast my mind back to innumerable coffee times where we all took our break in the open air and Snowy would always be played with and made an active part of the group. But again it occurred to me that the people who made the most contact with Snowy were the most socially popular people in the group, so perhaps there is something in the theory that, in general, people who like dogs also like people.

Towards the end of our garden party the class for dog fancy-dress was called. The three of us snook away to our car and dressed Snowy up with his harness and microphone. We felt that Philip's efforts made a most original and stylish outfit and bearing BBC stickers (cut from film can labels) he looked to our eyes to have an excellent chance.

There was a little indecision between the three of us. Philip, with all the effort he had put in, had expected to walk Snowy but, shamefully pulling rank, I insisted that I enter him as, after all, it was my idea to make a dog-mounted camera in the first place and I was rather too pleased with myself for thinking it up! So I marched him off, a little embarrassed that I had disappointed my young colleague. My embarrassment was heightened by finding that the dog fancy-dress class was really intended for children and all the rest of the entrants were knee-high to a grasshopper and accompanied by the most outrageously decorated dogs. There were dogs in bonnets pushed in prams, there were dogs with football kits on, there were dogs with decorated owners too—the diminutive Sherlock

The rest of the entrants were knee-high to a grasshopper and accompanied by the most outrageously decorated dogs

Bones, I recall, wore a deerstalker and brandished a pipe in his tiny hand. All in all I stuck out like a sore thumb and it was clear that our dress for Snowy wasn't so appropriate after all. I seem to remember that a dog with a bra and two balloons won it!

If the day out with the guide dogs was one of the most delightful, the days I spent with the police and military dog trainers were the most interesting and impressive. My previous memory of police dog tracking takes me back to the time a borstal escapee broke into my colleague Gerald Thompson's home right next door to our film studios and tried foolishly to make a dash for safety on being disturbed. Although he only saw an elderly man (sorry, Gerald) as he fled, he hadn't gone half a mile before one of our ultra-fit cameramen had him lying in the nettles.

The breathless arrival of the local force some ten minutes later produced a splendid tracker dog that rushed around excitedly. Having partly recovered from the elation of catching the criminal red handed (or, remembering the nettles, red bottomed), we watched enthralled as the policeman chased around after the sniffing dog at the end of a long rope. This gives the dog an effectively free rein yet enables the handler to keep in contact. The law gradually became redder and more breathless as he kept appearing and disappearing like an actor in an old Whitehall farce. At last the handler stopped exhausted outside our studio and with a wry smile and a wink confided 'It only works in the movies you know'!

When I spent a day with police dog trainers, I came away astonished at the diversity of skills that their dogs must display. It is asking a great deal of a dog's character to be aggressive, friendly and to keep following a scent in different situations on the same day. One minute the dog might have to attack a violent and possibly armed suspect, the next it may be called on to perform a public relations function at a school. Later still the same dog may be used to follow the scent of a lost child, for instance, or any one of dozens of similar situations that are the day-to-day work of police dogs.

It is the dog's tracking skills that remain most clearly in my mind. Snowy was being trained to disregard any and all smells as being disruptive when he was collared and walking on the lead. Police dogs are rewarded for developing their sense of smell and, equally importantly, keeping their mind on the task in hand. I well remember laying a trail across three large fields with much twisting and back-tracking until I finished up deliberately dropping my car keys in the grass before returning to base. This exercise was simply to keep the police dog's nose in practice and to show me the technique. He crisscrossed the first field until he found my trail and then, as the rope was paid out, he hared off with nose to ground. He lost me once as I had repeatedly circled a large tree and then set off in the wrong direction, apparently with equal certainty. But suddenly he stopped, lifted his head and set off in another wrong direction but in such a way that he picked up my later course about fifty yards away. Then he was off at a gallop again, chased by his handler at the end of some twenty or so feet of rope. Finally he went past where I had dropped the keys and, after sniffing aimlessly around, seemed finally to have lost all sense of my further direction.

It wasn't a perfect performance by any means but it was enough to convince me of the amazing persistence and scent discrimination skills that German shepherds like Snowy have, if they are allowed to use them. Talking about the dog's problems afterwards, it became clear that the conditions were by no means good for tracking. For one thing, we learnt that part of the police cadet force had just done a circuit of physical fitness exercises across the same fields, so confusing my own delicate foot odour with many less savoury contributions from running shoes.

To be more accurate, it is thought that the dogs respond to the most recent track unless they are given a particular identification scent to pursue. The scent is probably complex and as much the result of the crushed vegetation as of sweaty human feet. Some years back an enthusiastic ex-army major performed some enterprising experiments with tracker dogs. By setting a trail—running across a field—he gave the dogs a good start but then, mid field, he took to the air. Having rigged two wooden hoists 100 yards or so apart with a rope and chair suspended between them, he could float just above the surface of the ground yet not trample on it. If, as it were, his smell could drop off his clothes and person on to the ground, you would expect the dogs to locate it and continue the chase. None of them did. This confirmed in his mind (and mine) that most tracking depends on trampling the vegetation, especially when you consider that police dogs are known to have much more difficulty in following a trail on hard road surfaces.

One complication that would not have occurred to me was this. As most trails a dog follows do not lead to a successful conclusion, it is impossible to reward him appropriately for his efforts. The dog may have diligently followed a criminal's trail for two miles only to find it disappears at the point he got into a car and drove off. The poor animal could not have done better, yet the handler cannot know whether to praise him or not. For all the handler knows, the dog may not have followed the trail properly at all, and may have given up simply because it came to harder road. What good would it do to reward a dog's behaviour if he was doing something that worked against good tracking practice? It really is a problem because the handler simply cannot know. In the end he must depend on the dog's enjoyment of achieving the successful track and find. There is no way he can make a dog follow a scent unless the animal itself can be persuaded to do so. It must all be done with patience and kindness.

Another illuminating natural phenomenon that I learnt about through following tracker dogs was that the earth 'breathes'. The very concept delights me. In many ways, we still live close to the earth, seeing it as the mother of the plants which in turn foster the lives of all animals so it somehow seems right to conceive of the earth itself as having the ability to breathe too. In truth, the phenomenon is less to do with the breath of life than the changes in temperature between land and air. On cold mornings the air temperature will be colder than the earth so, since hot air rises, the scent in the air close to the ground remains down and conditions are good for tracker dogs. Later as the air above warms in the morning sun, the conditions usually reverse so that the air near the ground gets dispersed as new air drops down to the dog's nose level as the earth breathes in. It is not difficult to surmise that the latter conditions make for less successful tracking, a fact borne out by experience.

The military dog training school provided new insights for me and left me overwhelmingly impressed by the outstanding enthusiasm that the dogs and handlers had for their work. My entrée was the Mark I model camera harness that we had built for Snowy. While the equipment wasn't perfect, it did have possibilities for development if sufficient funds were forthcoming. I had frankly run out of funds under the modest BBC film budget and I still saw that the idea had potential if only I could enthuse a backer. I didn't mind who, providing that the dog was not upset by wearing the gear and I could benefit from some genuine Snowy-eyed views in our film. 'Imagine a dog harness view of Snowy chasing a cat', I used to encourage my listeners, conveniently ignoring the fact that he would never be allowed to do that anyway.

My ideas for possible military uses were vague but included the thought that a video-equipped dog maybe could be sent ahead to survey a potentially dangerous area such as a suspect's garden in Belfast. Clearly the trained dog would be at risk but it is sadly common knowledge that, under the pressure to protect human lives, kamikazi animals have been enlisted to give military aid before.

What struck me most as I explained my thoughts to the officer in charge was his ill-concealed disgust at the concept of training a dog to put itself at risk by blowing itself up while exploring a booby trap. Later, seeing the depths of the bond between these men and their dogs which is reflected in the performance of the partnership, I could better understand how distasteful it would be for them to risk their dogs in a callous scheme such as mine. Although not openly criticised, I felt somewhat chastened by the reactions my ideas generated. Some parts of the military establishments *do* have a heart, it seems.

Nevertheless we examined both styles of harness that we had developed and my host made some notes for his colleagues. Then came the highlight of my trip, watching the top military dog trainers teaching a batch of customs officers how to get the best out of their drug-sensing dogs. In a disused hangar, a warehouse store had been put together with crates, drums and abandoned vehicles. Each dog was trained to identify one single type of drug. The trainer would hide the particular drug used as 'bait' and the trainee was then brought in with his dog to try to sniff it out.

The principle used in this work is to make the hunt into a simulated competition between handler and dog. To work, the whole thing must be a gigantic game, each apparently trying to beat the other to locate the 'prize'. When 'found' (usually by the dog!) the two play-wrestle with the find to increase the dog's determination to hold on to it and, more importantly, to be motivated to win the game of hide-and-seek next time. It takes weeks for the trainer to learn the skills giving the right level of encouragement and keeping just the right distance away so the dog is constantly teased into diving in first to try to beat the owner to the find. Success depends to some degree on the keen nose and competitive instincts of the dog but as much as anything else the key seemed to be a deep understanding and relationship between man and dog.

My departing memory was of a particular trainer chasing and playing with his dog amidst the old crates and cars. The dog had just got the prize in its mouth and was bounding around in jubilation, always out of reach of his trainer. There were grabs and tussles and dashes here and there. The dog was having a high old time and was demonstrating play-bow after play-bow after play-bow. He clearly thought he had done well, but more so had his master. The dog had been conned into finding the drug that the handler himself could not detect inside the distributor of an old car. And it had all been achieved by great guile, subtlety and most of all kindness. Seeing the classical play-bows said it all. Training at the highest level is all done by kindness.

*   *   *

There was one event to which we took Snowy which was not quite what it seemed. The village dog show in our film had to be arranged from scratch to give us a chance to bring in other pets and to say things in the commentary that couldn't be covered over pictures of Snowy, Chilly and Motley alone. Also, for the pace of the film, BBC producer Peter Jones and I decided that we needed to go out and about. We wanted to give our viewers a break from close shots of our three stars in and around my home and at the same time we felt that we could do with an English countryside sequence to give character to the film. Simply decided but, as ever, not so easily arranged.

We consulted the local rural community council and found which villages were having summer fetes. We wrote around,

The dog was demonstrating play bow after play bow

asking if they were also having a small dog show at the same time. None were—at least not until the harvest festival season, and we wanted to do our sequence well before then. So we advertised on local radio—anyone having a village fete and 'exemption' dog show in the near future do let us know. 'Exemption' meant that it would not be run according to Crufts' professional standards, so we could get all and sundry joining in.

Several kind and diligent secretaries of local parish councils wrote and phoned in and we began to find the ideal. There wasn't one that combined the convenience of fitting into our time-tables together with being in a picturesque setting. Our best bet seemed to be Great Tew, an idyllically quaint village of thatched cottages with a long established local horticultural show and whose organisers, we were told, would be willing to arrange a dog show to add to the general appeal. They would agree to let us film what went on so, having been charmed by the youthful lightheartedness of the organiser on the telephone, we arranged to meet in the village pub to look over the lie of the land and to talk over both sides' wishes. Wendy was over from America (she flies for an international airline company which in part explains her spasmodic appearance) and she joined me to go out twenty miles from Oxford and back fifty years in time. The village pub was an obvious haven for locals, who clearly knew each other well enough to leg-pull about any subject under the sun. Our collaborator/organiser turned out to be a gentleman with a dry sense of humour. An author and playwright who chose the sanity of the countryside in preference to the madness of commuter's London, he clearly was game to do his best to arrange a spot of impromptu chaos for our cameras.

Our aim was to have a wide variety of dogs so we could see how man has produced so many specialist and different breeds from the one species. We also aimed to allow a good deal of freedom so that the dogs could interact and allow our cameras to record some of the body language postures that would result. We made it clear that we would invite some dogs along specifically to make up the numbers and to guarantee us a spread of breeds. Snowy would be there but we only wanted him to serve as a continuity link, to be seen to go in but then to keep in the background so that we could concentrate on other things.

The day dawned bright and sunny. The BBC film crew arrived from Bristol and Snowy, my son Sean, Wendy and I met them outside the show ground. Friends from the dog-training club and neighbours with their own invited breeds were all arriving so it looked a bit like Noah's Ark as they piled into the freshly mown field. Inside were such irresistible temptations as bowling for a pig, tombola for a bottle of whisky, guess the weight of the cake and donkey rides—the traditional array of rural events on such occasions—as well as the cool marquee with its displays of the horticultural pride of Great and Little Tew. The eye could feast upon polished potatoes of huge size, morning-fresh flowers in vases and home-made wine with handwritten labels more alluring than any vintage from the most famous French chateaux. And, of course, a ring of straw bales where the canine gladiators were to compete.

We had agreed to have five classes, including one for the best child handler and one for the dog with the waggiest tail. These novelty events gave us the chance to have dogs unfamiliar with the show ring side-by-side ready for possible interactions. The BBC camera crew were as much the centre of attraction as the official entertainments. I reflected that, in the same way as pets seem to generate a disproportionate level of attention in the man in the street, so too do people with outside-broadcast television equipment. My guess was that the crew were enjoying their day out too, simply because the village show made a pleasant change from the surroundings they usually worked in—feelings just like those of most other people on the field that day.

Having filmed Snowy entering the show ground, the dog show began. We intended not to interfere with it in any way but simply to film what happened. It was meant to be an informal, unstructured amateur event and it turned out to be so much so that we soon realised that we weren't going to get the shots we had anticipated. My colleague David Thompson once summed it up in a classic, heartfelt remark made after waiting for days to film a perch spawning: 'With animals, nothing is easy—and the difficult things are often impossible!' (We *did* successfully film the spawning!)

We could get all the pictures we wanted of the different breeds of dogs but then, half-way through the show, we were approached by two distressed owners of pedigree show dogs who where there at our invitation. The amateur judge, they pointed out, had the dogs and owners parading the wrong way round! It made a mockery of the whole thing. Nowhere in the show circuit would such nonsense take place. If any properly qualified person *they* knew was to judge a dog show, he would obviously know that much or he wouldn't be there at all. They felt so insulted by the situation that they were reconsidering allowing their dogs to be filmed at all.

A hurried conference followed where we talked of reversing the film in the processing labs to produce a mirror-image but finally we decided that we'd have to continue as planned. For filming continuity, the editor of the final film might need to mix early shots with later ones and, if we changed the direction of the promenade now, then that couldn't be done.

Another problem was the inevitable attention-seeker who continued always to have her (it *was* a 'her' on this occasion) dog on hand wherever the camera was pointing. She entered every class and somehow managed to alter her position so that she could be seen in almost every inch of footage we shot. To make matters worse, none of the dogs seemed much interested in their fellows. One event followed another, the child handlers and the waggy tails all came and went without giving our cameras the expected interactions. On the tight lead all these entrants did themselves great credit.

So, in desperation, we had to restage it. When all the classes had finished we asked several of the owners and some of the crowd to stay on so we could see what traditional wildlife patience would bring. We put dogs side by side who seemed to have the urge to be assertive and we asked the owners to hold them looser on the lead.

Two terriers broke the ice. With mutual growls they suddenly leapt at each other. With the slow-motion camera I had been able to show on a previous occasion that the 'bites' that dogs direct to each other in dominance disputes are 'inhibited' – that is to say, they don't clamp their jaws so as to cause damage. Beagles often squabble over food and when filming them two years before, I observed that the actual 'bite' was little more than a nip accompanied by fearsome barks and growls. With this experience and knowledge, it was interesting to record the number of distinctive body language postures that the dogs demonstrated during their display of threat. The angle of the neck, the stance of the front legs, the ruffled fur on the neck, the tail position and the furl of the lips are among the most obvious. As terriers were bred for their aggressive skills, to attack foxes in their dens, they are understandably pugnacious by temperament.

Snowy and all German shepherds have a similar reputation, derived from their guard dog image. To add to it, their upright ears and long jaw also add to their threatening appearance when viewed by members of the human species for whom, instinctively, those wolf-like features spell danger.

In truth, German shepherds can and do have splendidly docile temperaments and they make admirable pets if, like all dogs, they are properly trained. My friends in the Guide Dog Association also encountered similar prejudice against these

The German shepherd simply kept lifting its head back and tried to keep out of the way

dogs when they came to place them with a blind person. Thus, aiming to redress the balance, I had hoped to show how docile and pleasant German shepherds can be. A lady from the dog-training class had brought her German shepherd with her and it was clearly not wanting to get involved with these frightful terriers. One of the terriers, however, was joined by a neighbour's mongrel and together they took to barking at the bigger dog. For quite a while, the latter simply kept lifting its head back and trying to keep out of the way, thus demonstrating that that German shepherd was not aggressive by nature even under noisy provocations. Only when the mongrel leapt forward did it retaliate, and even then its leap and snarl were directed vertically upward rather than at the diminutive aggressor!

The last scene we recorded was of a tiny tail-wagging dog that was anxious to appease all the other dogs it met. It would lie on its back, legs up, with tail constantly wagging submissively. It made a splendid contrast in our body language series that we felt we had just about covered all our efforts, and could go home reasonably well-satisfied.

Life, however, is full of surprises. I was reminded of that a few days later when, still thinking about the dog's non-aggression, I took my car for servicing at a nearby garage. As soon as I got out of the car a massive Doberman Pincher guard dog came running over and leapt at me. Mercifully, I twisted around and it sank it's teeth in my rear! My eyes watered and I was struck dumb with anger and pain as the dog ran off! So much for the 'inhibited bite'. I complained to the garage owner who seemed infuriatingly unconcerned and then my colleague Ian Hendry arrived in his car to drive me back to work while my car was being attended to. I got no sympathy from anyone—just laughs at my expense. I truly couldn't bear to sit down, so I wedged my body in the air between the back of the car seat with my feet on the front dash board. Ian's mind was very fertile. He couldn't stop laughing. 'It's that dog-tooth check,' he said, pointing to the pattern on my trousers. 'It's a good job you turned round quickly or you'd never be the same again.' Back at OSF I got no more sympathy. As I undressed in the washroom to examine in the mirror the extent of the wound, there was much banging on the door as mirth-ridden colleagues called for me to 'Turn the other cheek' and other encouragements. It wouldn't have been so bad but later I learnt that the dog had been bred by a former girl-friend of mine. The event would have given her even more pleasure!

13

Catastrophe

In August, Snowy had to go back again into the Guide Dog Kennels for a few days as one of his routine visits. This gave me as good a chance as any to take a brief holiday. The two cats would be willingly and most ably looked after by my colleague Joan Tompkins, who had always been a willing cat sitter from time to time. They had been boarded with her before on previous occasions and got on well with her own cats. Motley, in fact, was so strong-willed and self-confident that he soon dominated the two residents as well as Chilly.

On my return I was greeted effusively by Snowy. He came bounding across the lawn, tail wagging and ears half back. He had got into the habit of nipping quite hard during his spell in the kennels and, although it was done in greeting, it hurt enough for me to tell him off as he almost bowled me over in his enthusiasm. He was jumping up too—another behaviour disapproved of for guide dogs. But in the excitement of our re-union, it was not the time to be too bothered about the finer points of preferred obedience. He was soon circling and sniff-ing his old territory over the lawns. When Snowy was settled in, I went to collect Chilly and Motley. Once I reached Joan's home, however, I knew immediately something was wrong. Sure enough my distraught friend told me Motley had been hit by a car. I was stunned. How could this happen? Joan had been away for only three hours and when she returned Motley was still in the house yet came to greet her with a pronounced limp, his tail trailing lifeless like a piece of string and his rear quarters looking messy. He had obviously been out and met with an accident. Though it was just before midnight, the vet was roused and confirmed that he had probably been injured on the road and that that there was nothing immediately he could do. Rest was the best thing and so Motley was put in his basket and slept for a day. He wouldn't eat when he woke up and his body looked flabby and much deeper as if he had lost control of his muscles.

I kept him at home with Chilly and Snowy and for a time he began to limp less noticably. We were optimistic at first but soon Motley went downhill and our vet confirmed a paralysis of nerves in his internal rear quarters. He had no control of his bodily functions and had to be manually emptied twice a day. His leg muscles were clearly beginning to waste away. I persisted in nursing him for more than two weeks but by the end of the month I had to make a decision I had never envisaged in my year of filming.

I collected the cat basket from the garage but when I returned to find Motley he was hiding under the car. It took me some time to lure him out. He still looked sleek and fit at the front of his body but the rear was now swollen and weak. My hand around his rib cage picked up the pronounced and rapid heart beats. My heart was thumping too. It had to be done and, scientist or not, I felt the cat knew.

At the surgery I didn't fancy waiting. Knowing the practice by now I sought out the vet's assistant and in a tense and abrupt voice explained I wanted Motley 'euthanised'. She didn't understand my American term at first but a few seconds later we were in the back room of the surgery, the lid of Motley's cage was lifted, he hopped out and walked straight into the vet's reception cage. It was not the time for words. I stroked him briefly, the door was shut, and I walked stiffly out into the evening light carrying the empty cat basket.

*   *   *

When one loses an animal which is, after all, a close member of the family circle, much grief and heartache results. In my case, being in close contact with animals on a daily basis and being seen (in my view wrongly) as the appropriate person in the neighbourhood to take in any broken-winged birds, cat-mangled mice or half-dead ducks, I had seen more animals die than most. But it is all so different when it is an animal you know well, especially your own pet. The closer the human-animal companion bond, the more the anguish; the more time and love you give your pet, the more painful the experience of death.

The subject of mourning for pets has been studied in some detail in America. The experts found that people go through all the stages of grief conventionally associated with the death of a human member of the family: spasmodic outbursts of uncontrolled crying, temporary disruption of one's ability to carry on a normal life, remorse for undone things; it is all there. And just as some are never able to get over the death of a relative or friend, so too some people's lives are never the same again after a particular pet has died. On analysing the very worst case of pet mourning, the researchers found that while there was no absolute type of person or pet for whom this permanent grief was prevalent, it tended to occur with middle-aged and elderly ladies who had no other family. Dogs were, statistically, far and away the main causes of such permanent mourning, but cats featured as well and so too did birds.

My own reactions were mixed. I felt a deep sadness that Motley had had to be killed. He was always to have been my personal pet, as Snowy was going to leave me at the end of the year and I had promised Chilly to Joan to look after full-time after all the filming had finished, and she was being looked after more by Joan than by myself on a day-to-day basis. Joan was so kind that I knew, if I asked, that she would let me alter our plans and allow me to keep Chilly instead. But it wouldn't have been the same. Chilly, bless her heart, could never be a substitute for Motley and I wanted her to stay with Joan because she was so clearly happy and at home there. Like everyone else, I had to face up to Motley's fatal injury both personally and also because it was one of the year's events which we had filmed as they happened, like a diary. Either we could show the truth in the finalised film or we could call on our stand-by cat—Cleo—to use for the rest of the filming.

Cleo was now a grown-up lady looked after adoringly by my neighbours Tricia and James. Her markings were still a fairly good match to Motley's and though she was now of a lighter build than he had been, to most people she could easily be mistaken for him. But my loyalty to Motley was so great that it didn't take me long to make a decision. Motley was Motley and only he would fill the role in my film. Though we'd allowed for using our 'double' under certain circumstances in the past, I felt that this had to be a case for sticking to reality. But whether I would professionally have made such a decision if my emotions were not so bound up with Motley I leave you to guess.

Tricia and James understood. We had actually filmed a sequence of Cleo watching television pictures early in the year but it was never put into the final film, so the integrity of Motley's spirit was left intact.

In the sad course of events my decision proved to have been the correct one, for within two weeks Cleo had disappeared and was later found flattened on the main road. Seeing the effect it had on Tricia and James I realised I was not alone in my grief and from then on I looked with more compassion at the long, serious faces of owners waiting in the vet's surgeries to deliver their pets for a final time.

*   *   *

Vet's waiting rooms, in fact, can provide all sorts of insights about humans and their pets. In a recent experiment in America, a research student spent some time sitting in one with her dog, looking for all the world like a patient owner waiting to see the vet but in truth making observations about how the other people in the room actually behaved with their pets when they didn't realise they were being watched. It may be surprising, for instance, to realise that vetinary surgeons don't treat pets! More precisely, vets don't treat animals so much as human beings. If you take a statistical count of how many encounters the vet actually makes you'll find that he actually sees more people than pets! Why is it that when, say, a little boy is ill, he will usually be taken to the doctor by only one of the parents, even if both are available at the time? Yet when the family pet falls ill, all the family—mother, father and the kids—commonly troop along and all expect to go into the vet's consulting room. Here is an outstanding difference which might indicate that we really do view our pets as fundamentally different to our children. Can it mean that our devotion to and concern for our pets is greater than that for our own children? If not, there must be some other definite reason to explain why, in a typical case, more people come along to accompany the patient if it is a pet than a human being. I confess I'm not sure that I can offer a good explanation but I am convinced it does suggest that pets and children do play different and separate roles in our lives and that animals don't simply fill a child-substitute role. All this—and more—you can readily see for yourself as you sit in any vet's waiting room.

The disguised researcher with her 'cover dog' made detailed counts of the ways in which owners interacted with their pets in the waiting room. She noted where they touched them, how long for, whether they were talking or looking at the animals at the same time, the sort of pet involved and so on. When all these observations were put together and examined one fascinating fact stood out: men touched, fondled, patted and stroked their pets just as much as women. They did it just as often and in exactly the same way, and in every detail they were seen to show their affection for their animal companions just as women did. Here again is a strand of evidence contradicting the image of pets as child-substitutes. Men use touch in inter-human situations far less frequently than women. Fathers are less likely to touch their own children than are mothers and it is generally recognised that they have less need for physical contact with their loved ones, particularly when in public. So what, I wonder, is going on when we see men using touch just as much as women?

Does it mean that pets provide us with an outlet for physical intimacy which conditioning or tradition denies us in public with other human beings? I personally think this is only a part of the issue, though it may be worth pointing out that adolescent children who hate to be touched will still keep up touch contacts with the family pets.

This survey showed that there was no statistical difference in the response to different sizes of animals: big dogs got the same attention as the smaller ones. This further knocks on the head the sexist stereotype of a single woman sitting with a small lap-dog as a child substitute, for macho, hairy-chested young men are just as likely to be fondling, caressing, stroking and embracing their mongrels! Of course, different people respond to different kinds or breeds of animals, and the man who lavishes his attentions on a bulldog might think twice about being seen with a poodle. But once the pet is matched with the owner, common grounds of behaviour can be seen over and over again.

As we begin to reject our stereotype of the pet's place in society, we can consider another approach. What follows is to my mind the biggest revelation in all my studies of cats and dogs. It is based on the findings of Dr Aaron Katcher and his associates at the University of Pennsylvania, Philadelphia. They have revolutionised our concepts of interactions of people and their pets in a series of brilliant and perceptive studies. They started, surprisingly, by studying heart-attack victims. They knew that people who, relatively speaking, could be seen to lack companionship, like the single, divorced or widowed, tended to be more susceptible to diseases such as heart attacks, and that in comparing similar age groups a bigger proportion of 'loners' were liable to die off compared with the marrieds.

No one was sure exactly why this was but it seemed a reasonable guess that the loss of companionship and the resultant isolation led to a tendency towards depression, morbidity and subsequent stress. But lots of other factors are involved too. For example, bereaved people tend to increase smoking and drinking and reduce the amount of exercise they take. So the scientists set out to check into all the likely social factors that might possibly influence human survival in so far as it affected patients recovering from major heart surgery. Over a two-year period, they monitored the people entering the local coronary unit with a diagnosis of major heart problems (angina pectoratis and myocardial infarctions to be precise). They took down all their social details: age, sex, health, job, financial situation, where they lived, size of family and so on. And then, gruesomely, they checked one year later to see how many of the patients were still alive.

A total of 84% survived but their records could now be examined and their circumstances compared with those who had since died. What emerged could be summarised like this. Statistically speaking, the chances of your surviving a heart attack are not influenced by whether previously you were rich or poor, man or woman, old or young, a jogger or a health fanatic on a high-fibre diet. The best social predictor for survival was *whether or not you returned home to a pet!*

Only 6% of the patients who returned home to a pet died in the first year after the operation. Of those who went home to a life without a pet the figure was 28%. But be careful! These impressive results should not be taken as indicating the existence of a new miracle cure for heart-attack victims. Instead they should be used as the starting point for a series of essential questions about what deductions we can draw from these facts. Could, for instance, the fact that dog owners take exercise themselves when they walk their pets mean that these people are marginally fitter as a result? How did this balance with the results from people who had pets which didn't require exercising?

Again the numbers of the survey were examined and this time all the dog owners, those who may be thought to undergo most pet-induced exercise, were excluded, and the survival comparison was made between those who owned any animal except dogs and those who owned no pets at all. The same result emerged just as clearly as before. It seemed that pets produced a beneficial effect immaterial of whether they caused the patients to take exercise or not.

Another check was run to see if the pet owners were fitter when they went into hospital. There was no difference again. They wondered whether pet owners came from a better social status group. Again, this didn't explain it. So it seems as though, from this specialist study, we really are on the track of something very important and deep-seated in the psyche of pet owners.

The research workers who turned up these findings made all sorts of checks to avoid jumping to the wrong conclusion. They compared all the other variables of the group of patients studied—married or single, how many children they had, how much contact with other people—and none of these factors had anything like the influence of the 'dumb' family pet. There was no getting away from it. What mattered most for survival, more than any of all the factors considered, was whether they owned a companion animal or not.

So where does this lead us? Well, the image of pets being mainly child substitutes is finally disposed of. People with children didn't survive any better than those without. If the fact that they had *either* children *or* pets had turned out to give them a better chance of survival, then this would have supported the child-substitute notion. But the results of this study showed that pets have profound effects on the lives of humans that are independent of, different from and supplementary to what other people—adults or children—provide. Pets simply offer a kind of relationship which people can't provide. And any belief that it is the single person that gets the most from a pet is challenged by the realisation that the medical effect of pets revealed by the study was equally prevalent whether people lived alone or were married, or received a lot of or little social support from other human beings. Singles had no more beneficial effects from pets than anyone else.

So what is our conclusion? Keep a pet and live longer? Pets certainly did seem to make those heart patients live longer, so why all this scientific reluctance to shout the results loud and clear so everyone can benefit? I think the reason is that the pet scientists are on to something potentially so exciting that they don't want to blow it by jumping too quickly to the most likely, though totally unexpected conclusions.

Before we make heady generalisations about the medical benefits of pets in the community, it would be useful to try to explain how such possible benefit may come about. What could Snowy actually do to me to keep me healthier? How may Chilly actually influence my medical condition and even my survival?

We still don't know for sure the answers to these questions, but I now believe that many of the observations I have been making about human responses to pets were important clues that had been staring me in the face ever since I adopted my pets. Consider what all pet lovers do to their animals: we talk to them and we pet them. These two actions become such obsessive, irresistible urges for many of us that for the most part we are not even aware that we are performing them. The one-way conversation with the pet becomes so much second nature that most owners never give it a thought. The 'petting' is often carried out unconsciously in a trance-like, distracted reverie while the owner's attention is directed to something totally different, such as a book or a television programme.

Until recently no one seems to have thought of ways of trying to measure the effects that pets may have on their owners. To say they make you 'happy' or 'feel more secure' or 'give companionship for children' is all very well but it doesn't provide the sort of definite figures or measurements that scientists need if they are to make sound comparisons. Nowadays, however, it is recognised that our fluctuating emotions are reflected by definite measurable changes of various systems inside our bodies. Thus changes in heart rate, blood pressure and the proportion of various chemicals in our fluids have all been studied by doctors and can be recorded with delicate sensors as our emotional states change. So what would happen if we took measurements of these medical indicators on people with and without their pets?

That is what we are all now waiting for. It isn't as simple to perform these tests as it sounds but what results we do have strongly suggest that talking to and petting our animals brings down our blood pressures significantly, even to figures below our normal resting state. If this is borne out by further rigorous testing, it would explain how pet-owning heart patients in general survive better than their fellows. If you regularly relax with and relate to your pets it can produce this reduced state of arousal in you which, in its way, is comparable to the proven medical benefits of practising transcendental meditation. Pets may thus be seen as a therapeutic drug—no wonder owners are addicted to them! And no wonder there is such fierce loyalty—easily mocked as a pathetically illogical devotion—to the family pet. Many people get so much benefit—consciously or otherwise—from their pets that it's hardly surprising that they devote so much time, inconvenience and money to their particular animal.

Based upon this appraisal of pet's roles in society, all sorts of new perspectives suddenly become possible.

Repeatedly caressing pets helps to strengthen the bond as both parties benefit

First, it is reassuring to know that not only does the stroking of our pets bring down our blood pressure, it also lowers the blood pressure and heart rate of our furry friends. They enter a physiologically passive, relaxed state as we repeatedly caress and stroke them and this presumably helps to strengthen the bond as both parties benefit so significantly from it.

Secondly, I *don't* believe that prescribing a pet is, on its own, a sure way of increasing a heart-attack victim's chances of survival. I *am* convinced, however, that in the study we've examined it *was* the presence of a pet at home that made all the difference. However I think the distinction must be drawn between on the one hand merely having a pet around and on the other relating to it so that an easy, warm, two-way bond is established. For those people who don't get on with pets, who have no patience for their demands, their inconvenience and their mess, a companion animal could be literally lethal to a returning convalescent because of the additional stress it would cause. Thus the finding should be interpreted as relating to a pet being the factor which *may* produce a beneficial lowering of blood pressure and associated favourable internal conditions, helping the recovery process, but cannot be a guaranteed panacea.

Thirdly, once one identifies talking to and stroking pets as being crucial self-rewarding activities for us, it is possible to put new interpretations on other related aspects of human nature. Take the apparent conundrum of why pet owners talk to their pets and the typical mood they are in when they do it. We have already seen that the language is not true 'motherese' but it is clearly reflective of an affectionate and simplistic level of relationship. The style is distinctive and different from ordinary adult language. The blood pressure of people speaking out loud or reading to other people always increases immaterial of whether the subject is exciting or boring, or whether the other people are friends or strangers. When the person stops speaking, the blood pressure readings drop down again. It therefore seems that we normally find talking out loud a relatively stressful experience—possibly because experience tells us we are being judged or that our statements may be questioned in some way. For however much of a friend the listener may be, whenever we talk we are looking for things like understanding, agreement or advice from the listener and we may be upset if we get inattention, disagreement or criticism. So why should chatting to our pets be more relaxing than talking to another person?

The reason is not hard to find. Our pets simply don't judge us. They don't evaluate. And we know that we have their empathetic response to whatever we say almost on call. You only have to remember how over 80% of pet owners believe their pets are sensitive to their feelings for the special nature of our bond with our pets to become evident. We can relax when we speak to our pets in the assumption that our words are *not* being perceived as they would be if we were addressing them to another person. It is perhaps nearer to the restful state of laying on a couch and speaking to a trained psychiatrist who has learnt not to show any personal judgement on whatever the client says. But, as Katcher points out, dogs may well serve us better. They are cheaper; the client can also gain by stroking them and they show their apparent affection for the client by licking his hand or nose, something that the therapist is unlikely to do! The apparently total empathy of our pets makes all the difference when it comes to talking to them. Despite popular pet-lore I now believe people who enjoy talking to their pets know in their hearts that their animal does not have critical understanding of the words being spoken. They're just like those people who talk to their plants—and probably for the same reason.

When you consider our touching and stroking of domestic animals, we already have good evidence for how such actions may influence blood pressure of humans. Something as simple as a nurse taking a patient's pulse rate is known to alter the very measurement that is being recorded. So it is small wonder that all the owners' fondling, stroking, patting and petting is capable of having a major effect upon his or her blood pressure readings. Intuition and simple observation suggests that the idle, unaware state of fondling is probably most effective in producing a calming effect on the human involved in the association. Maybe stroking pets serves a similar physical function as worry beads or the rosary of the Catholic faith.

It is increasingly recognised that touch has a big part to play in human beings at all stages of their lives. When we are very young, our need for physical contact is evident, especially when we feel lonely or frightened. As adults, we can see how this may extend to sucking objects and clasping things even when the child is seemingly lost in far-away thoughts. The common companion for a child to take to bed is a teddy bear or some other cuddly toy or, failing that, a favourite cloth. Young children also happily allow themselves to be fussed over and embraced by their parents.

Yet when children grow to seven or eight, they become reluctant to be openly caressed or fondled by their parents and they themselves stop using external objects for touch comfort.

Catastrophe

It is then that, statistically speaking, parents most commonly decide to take a pet into the family. Coincidence perhaps, or might it be that the pet in part comes to fulfil the role of a substitute touch object for both parents and child? It's an often disregarded fact that most pets are found in a full family environment.

That brings us on to another consideration. If, as I believe, pets have a unique role both in the human family and with the individual—and consequently in society at large—then ought we not make better provision for them in our cities and towns? When, say, 20% of our population had cars, the civil authorities made roads and garages for them. So why, when 50% of our society has a pet, do we actively discourage them in most cities? They may even be the social lubricant that keeps many a family from flying apart, reduces stress in neglected children, and provides companionship and security for the lonely and yet we haven't got around to doing more than discourage them in general. It may be too far fetched to suggest that the state might even pay hard cash to encourage responsible pet ownership for those that want them, though it could conceivably mean considerable savings in the social costs of broken marriages, psychiatric wards and minor social disruptions of many kinds. Far fetched maybe, but it is certain that the last few years have seen evidence at last emerge for the social status of pets to be raised. All the early studies which proved the value of pets to people came from remedial or therapeutic work: with blind people and seeing-eye dogs, with withdrawn, introverted children who were brought out of themselves by doves or dogs, and with prisoners who gained a new respect for life—and themselves—from caring for caged birds and fishes. Now we can see that these are merely examples of how disadvantaged people have gained from empathising with an animal. The beauty of our present findings is that they potentially apply to anyone in society, and not just to the isolated or the afflicted.

It has always been easy to see guide dogs like Snowy as the animal embodiment of a noble concept—a dog who was to compensate for the loss of sight of a human being and so help add to the fulfilment of his owner. But in a very real way all closely bonded pets fulfil a noble role in their own families. They give their human companions far more than ever we realise and far more than society gives them credit for. It was Snowy who led me to this realisation and by doing so he may have done a service not just for me but for some of my readers too.

14

The End And A New Beginning

I seem to be suggesting that there are many people, not at present pet owners, who could benefit substantially from taking in a pet. I'm equally aware that many others would vehemently oppose such a notion.

'It's all very well you handing out pets left, right and centre,' they would say, 'just because they might bring their owners' blood pressure down. *My* blood will boil if I get any more cats and dogs messing up my garden and fouling the pavements. And what about all the diseases carried by your stinking animals?'

There are justifiable pros and cons to both sides of these arguments. A lot of people, worried about mess, road accidents, biting and worse, have very real concerns about bringing more and more pets into the world. They're quite right, of course, in so far as it is still almost ridiculously easy for anyone, no matter how incompetent an owner they might be, to acquire an animal and inflict God knows what hazards on their neighbours ever after. On the other hand, if official regulations about keeping pets were tightened up I am quite sure that conditions would improve for the majority, to say nothing of the benefits which might accrue to the kinds of people we've just been discussing.

Take the case of those semi-wild dogs which roam seemingly at will through many parts of our towns and cities, causing distress to many people. If the authorities put off all but the most determined would-be owners by charging a far more realistic licence fee than the pittance which is currently charged and extending this to include other animals such as cats, if they instigated a registration scheme and a system of tattooing animals so that they could be traced, if the money from the licence fees was put towards providing dog toilets in parks and other public places, then I think the world would be better for all concerned, not least because responsible pet ownership could thus be seen as being officially sanctioned.

Then again, it's no use pretending that pets are not going to foul the wrong places at some time, but it seems reasonable to enforce some degree of responsibility on the owner to clean it up. But who would police this? A fair point, but I've found that in many parts of America public feeling is a good stimulus. After Fido has relieved himself in the wrong place and the owner does nothing about it, it's not unusual for the owner, some minutes later, to answer a knock on the door and find a neighbour handing a shovelful of waste back to him for disposal. If this seems a rather embarrassing thing to have to do—after all, many people find it difficult to make overtly critical gestures to others—it's worth noting that non-smokers now feel freer to ask others not to smoke in their vicinity than they did even ten years ago, and the smokers themselves seem to take it in better part too. Social pressures and changing public opinion can remedy a lot of ills.

The idea of special dog wardens is a long-standing one but in an era of drastic cuts in spending on social services I'm afraid it's one. which will have to stand even longer. Nevertheless, cities like New York have already appointed specialists to develop ways of making more areas of cities suitable for the needs of pets and people. As ever, money talks and that is why an increased licence fee is basic to any action.

So I accept that, while it is not an easy or straightforward question, if we do agree that pets have a valuable place in our society, we should translate this into more effort to make it work. Most of all, the concept of responsible ownership should be paramount and only those who are judged suitable and able to exercise that responsibility should be allowed to have pets. The rest of society and the animals themselves have rights just as important as we pet owners.

The end—and a new beginning

I say 'we' pet owners but, as my year with Snowy drew to an end, it was increasingly evident that I was not going to be a pet owner much longer. Chilly was unsettled by Motley's departure and became increasingly timid and furtive. Out on her own in the garden or estate she would be the first to run back indoors if she saw another cat. The times she spent 'on holiday' with Joan's cats while I was away always seemed to make her more settled there and so in advance of the year's end, I let her join that happy cat family. I had finished filming Chilly apart from the final 'farewell to Snowy' sequence and we simply reimported Chilly for that.

Snowy and I continued to live closely, sharing our days together. He seemed not to miss either Motley or Chilly and I felt it had been a good experience for him to have been brought up with two cats. At least he had learnt not to chase cats and to be tolerant of their being around.

He seemed to be growing bigger and bigger. I took him by car to show the audiences who came to see OSF films and he got to know the routine of collecting Wendy from Heathrow Airport, where there was usually a new ball or a *'Daily Growl'* for him to chew up on the way back to Oxford.

Then the day for his departure was finally agreed. From then on my emotions tensed and we consciously went round doing the 'this is the last time we'll do this together' circuit. We chased around the garden, ran around the park, lay by the fire watching television, walked round Marks and Spencers and, all too soon, Alison had arrived for that final time.

Many weeks before, Alison and I had talked about people's reactions when a guide dog is taken away forever from the puppy walker and so I knew what to expect. 'Make it short and sweet' was the policy: no long farewells on the doorstep, just get the vet's health card, grab the collar and lead, into the van and away.

My friends at OSF were almost as sad to say goodbye to Snowy for the last time as I was. He was an exemplary dog, a marvellously intelligent, kind and sensible companion: the best dog I could ever wish to have.

My eyes glazed over as I felt the wrench that was about to happen. He had given me more than I could ever give him back. He had been my passport to many new friends and to new perspectives of the value of animal life in its widest sense. He had brought home to me a new and essential realisation: we all, surely, owe to future generations the responsibility to devise a harmonious and stable social structure in which a high regard is placed upon the value of life, both animal and human.

Knowing what we know now—something of which I hope I've been able to put across in the preceding pages—it would seem that pets might provide at least part of the solution to this more readily than by other means. And yet we are still so woefully ignorant of many aspects of the human-animal companion bond. Time and time again I had tried to explore interesting facets of dog and cat behaviour in a domestic setting, only to find that when I came to try and check out my findings with more authoritative sources, there was just no one who had all the answers. Surely now that we know how pets have such a crucial importance to the health and psychological well-being of the community in addition to the obvious sentimental pleasures they bring to their owners we ought to think of the setting up of a special research programme into these matters. Government bodies exist to study matters as diverse as weeds and white fish, so it seems to me not unreasonable to hope for some detailed research into an area which impinges on our daily lives equally as much as do these fields.

This need not be too dificult a matter to organise. After all, in the U.K. alone there are millions of potential helpers willing to add their views to market-research sampling. In my own television appearances with Snowy I had asked the mass audience to contribute some positive feedback about their own experiences with pets, and I was amazed not only by the extent of the response, but by the degree of perception and common sense that was thus called into play. By careful phrasing and presentation of the questions, huge samples of valuable new information literally came flooding in. Married to an increasing depth of scientific research, such a democratic survey could, I feel sure, yield very beneficial results—and be achieved without huge expense, for that matter.

This could be of inestimable benefit to many parties: the pet owners, the legislature, the scientific community, society at large, the animals themselves and, perhaps most of all, to the young who, in this impersonal and transient age, could well gain from the stablizing influences that pet ownership and a general awareness of wildlife is widely known to engender.

It would surely be inconceivable now that pets should be ever outlawed and banished from our families. The Chinese tried that during the Cultural Revolution. Whether they realised it or not, it could be expected to add to the social ferment that was being actively generated in those days of the Red Guards. So society must look anew and find a balanced social policy towards the integration of pets in our everyday lives.

*   *   *

Again it was Christmas. When Alison calls to take away a guide dog puppy after its year with a family, she normally takes along a new puppy so the process can be started all over again. It helps the Guide Dogs for the Blind and it also softens the blow of losing the year-old pet. In my case, however, there was no replacing Snowy. My plans for the next year were once again uncertain, changeable by the needs of my job and by the possibility of my no longer being based in England. So when Alison arrived, it was a simple, though strained departure.

Snowy didn't seem to know or mind. He jumped into the back of Alison's van, the door was shut and his wet nose pressed an imprint against mine on the glass. The next moment he was gone. Another phase of my life was complete. I would be sent a picture of him when he was finally trained and paired with a blind person but I would never see him again. That was the firm policy of the organisation.

For a long time I missed finding Snowy around when I got up, when I went for my run or came back in the car. All of a sudden it was very quiet—as if the dust was being allowed to settle again. The memory of Motley was with me too and I still felt sad at his passing. He would have been a good companion to occupy my time now that Snowy had departed, but it was not to be.

The third member of the trio, Chilly, has blossomed forth in Joan's cat-oriented household and now is the life and soul of the party. She romps around with the other four cats and seems to have got over all the traumas of sharing a home—and a film—with Snowy, Motley and me.

But in the end, I finished up with pets in the household again. On 29 November I got married to the year's regular visitor, Wendy, who, being previously single, matched the statistics by having two cats of her own ('my dear babies...') and no dog. It was clear from the start that there was no way I could have married her without her cherished cats! Such is life! I've joined the statistics as a married couple with cats. Snowy, I miss you. Come back and help me straighten out the balance!

Postscript

Six months after I had said farewell to Snowy, I received the following letter from the blind person with whom Snowy was eventually paired:

Dear Mr. Paling,

I am just writing to let you know that Snowy has settled down with us since returning home with me from the training centre, Leamington, just over two weeks ago. He has taken to our two children, Dawn aged seven, and Mark aged five, and enjoys playing with them. Although at first my wife's guide dog, Gina, was a bit offish with him, she now plays with him and they both play together with a puller toy.

While I am at work, Snowy has to go in a kennel but I am told that he is very good but he does make a fuss when he sees me coming to fetch him.

The first time we got on the bus coming home from work, Snowy jumped up and lay down on the seat; I soon made him get off and go under. Mr. Sanderson, his trainer, said that he probably thought it was my turn to lie on the floor.

We are going on holiday to Torquay in September and are looking forward to that. Our friend is also coming with us with her guide dog.

I am very pleased with Snowy's work and the way he has fitted in with us all, and before closing, I would like to thank you for looking after him as a puppy.

Yours sincerely,

Ken Bowen

MULTINATIONALS AND TECHNOLOGY TRANSFER

The Canadian Experience

Edited by
Alan M. Rugman

Library of Congress Cataloging in Publication Data

Main entry under title:

Multinationals and technology transfer.

    Bibliography: p.
    Includes indexes.
    1. International business enterprises—Canada—
Addresses, essays, lectures. 2. Technology transfer—
Canada—Addresses, essays, lectures. 3. Research,
Industrial—Canada—Addresses, essays, lectures.
4. Corporations, American—Canada—Addresses, essays,
lectures. I. Rugman, Alan M.
HD2809.M84 1983   338.91'73'071   82-24650
ISBN 0-03-062833-4

Published in 1983 by Praeger Publishers
CBS Educational and Professional Publishing
A Division of CBS, Inc.
521 Fifth Avenue, New York, New York 10175 U.S.A.

© 1983 by Praeger Publishers

3456789   052   987654321

Printed in the United States of America on acid-free paper.

Preface

Research support for the majority of the papers published in this book was provided by the Centre for International Business Studies of Dalhousie University. The Centre is one of four in Canada founded, and initially financed, by the federal government to promote international business studies. As part of its research program the Centre awards research grants and visiting research fellowships to scholars engaged in work in areas such as the theory of the multinational enterprise, technology transfer, and the effect of government on international business.

In addition to the papers supported in this manner, this book also includes several papers by Canadian scholars working on related topics, especially world product mandating and applications of technology transfer to developing nations. These papers were first presented at the annual meetings of the Administrative Sciences Associations of Canada in Ottawa, June 1982, in the program of the International Business division.

As both the director of the Dalhousie Centre for International Business Studies and the program chairman of the Ottawa conference, I am pleased to bring these papers together in this volume as a contribution to the modern literature on technology transfer.

Alan M. Rugman

To Pat

Table of Contents

List of Tables

Table

List of Figures

1

Introduction:
Technology Transfer and
the Canadian Experience

Alan M. Rugman and Jocelyn M. Bennett

This book consists of eleven original papers dealing with three related themes:

- The determinants of research and development (R and D) in Canada; three empirical papers which evaluate the key variables determining R and D in Canadian industries. Included is an assessment of the role of U.S. multinational enterprises in the transfer of technology to Canada.
- The current public policy interest in making multinational enterprises provide "world product mandates" to their Canadian subsidiaries. The subsidiaries would do R and D in new product lines and would market the new products internationally. In return the Canadian government would provide subsidies for the mandated R and D.
- The transfer of technology abroad by multinationals based in a small open economy such as Canada. Also explored is the relationship between exporting and technological activity as well as the effective diffusion of the technology of a multinational.

Each of these themes is applicable in a wide context since Canada is representative of many advanced host nations into which technology has been transferred. Yet in the Canadian case, there is now an outward flow of technology as Canadian based multinationals go abroad. These firms are particularly active in the resource sector and draw upon the nation's country specific advantage.

The book will be of interest to those involved in the following issues:

- technology transfer
- research and development

- multinational enterprises (MNEs)
- world product mandates (WPMs)
- management of knowledge and proprietary information
- Canadian public policy

In this introductory note we provide summaries of the papers published in this volume. This helps to synthesize the chapters and also relates them to the three themes identified above.

First, the determinants of R and D in Canada are examined in four papers: at the theoretical level by Komus and at an empirical level by Alexander, Hewitt and McMullen. Together, this set of papers provides valuable insights into the relationship between the modern theory of the multinational enterprise and its role as an engine for the transfer of technology to small open economies such as Canada.

Dr. David Komus relates the role of R and D to the theory of internalization. The MNE has an advantage, the use of which adds to net earnings in each of its markets. One method to acquire this firm-specific advantage is through ongoing R and D. The objective of the MNE is to maximize profits. The return (net revenue) in each market increases as the level of the advantage increases but does so at a decreasing rate. This leads to an optimal level of R and D by which the increased net revenue is just sufficient to offset the incremental cost of its R and D. The firm-specific advantage has the nature of a public good within the firm. It is used in many countries but the investment in the advantage is made only once.

In a theoretical two country model, Komus derives an equation to calculate the discounted stream of profits over time (Revenue–Costs). From the model he finds that:

the MNE uses the advantage in both countries (home and host);
the MNE invests more to develop a larger stock of advantage than it would as a one country firm;
the greater the return to any advantage, the more advantage the firm will wish to have.

The cost terms of the equation indicate that:

as interest rates rise, the investment in R and D is reduced;
as the rate of depreciation or dissipation of the advantage rises, there is a lower optimal level of advantage; and
a higher cost (price of) R and D will also result in a lower optimal advantage.

Komus shows that the optimal amount (stock) of advantage will change with the mode of entry a firm chooses. This is a result of the changing values of the coefficients of the net revenue function and cost function. In determining the best mode of entry into a foreign market, the MNE will choose the mode that maximizes the discounted flow of profits over time. In considering the point in time when the optimal gross investment in R and D is negative, Komus shows that the period of zero investment starts before the time when the lower advantage is optimal and should, therefore, be anticipated in order to keep the net gain to the last unit of positive investment equal to zero. During these periods, R and D expenditures cannot be recovered since the MNE cannot sell any part of the advantage.

In summary, the Komus paper uses a dynamic model to consider the optimal level of R and D for a profit maximizing MNE to undertake. R and D activity produces a stock of a firm-specific advantage, the use of which increases (at a decreasing rate) the net revenue of the MNE in each country in which it operates. The MNE is found to invest more in R and D than it would as a one country firm. The level of R and D is found to depend positively on the rate of return to the advantage and negatively on the costs of R and D, the rate of dissipation of the advantage, and the rate of interest.

Dr. Judy Alexander's econometric study is an attempt to isolate the determinants of R and D in Canada. Alexander defines R and D as any systematic and creative work undertaken in order to increase the stock of knowledge, and the use of this knowledge to devise new applications.

Alexander employs the following independent variables to explain variation in R and D for a sample of Canadian industries:

foreign control: percentage of sales of an industry made by firms which are foreign controlled;
technology: four subgroups of technologically advanced and less advanced industries;
R and D grants: government incentive subsidies;
concentration: percentage of the market controlled by the top four firms;
net profit: before taxes, an indicator of liquidity.

Regression analysis employing different combinations of independent variables shows that only R and D grants are a significant variable in every regression equation. All other variables specified were found to be insignificant. These results confirm the results of Globerman, Howe and McFetridge and Hewitt, who also found most variables to be insignificant.

Alexander's explanation for the poor explanatory power of the R and D determinants is that R and D may be determined conjointly with the specified variables so that a simultaneous equation model would provide better results.

Dr. Gary Hewitt's careful econometric work on the determinants of R and D is becoming increasingly well known, especially to those doing research in Canada on the effects of foreign ownership on Canadian secondary manufacturing industry. In the work reported in this volume, Dr. Hewitt makes use of a unique data set to test the variables determining the ratio of R and D undertaken in a Canadian subsidiary relative to the R and D undertaken by the parent (U.S.) multinational. Hewitt's work is therefore a test of the extent to which the MNE decentralizes its R and D effort in a host economy such as Canada.

The data set is unique since Hewitt had access to unpublished Statistics Canada data, at firm level, on the R and D undertaken by Canadian subsidiaries of MNEs over several years in the mid-seventies. This permitted him to do regression analysis on the cross firm variation in R and D by U.S. MNEs in several Canadian industries: electrical, machinery and chemicals (and a subgroup of it—pharmaceuticals).

Building upon earlier work, Hewitt specifies several key independent variables as the determinants of R and D in the Canadian subsidiary relative to the parent's overall worldwide R and D. He finds government grants to be a significant variable in the electrical industry but not in the others. In addition, the degree of foreign ownership of the equity in the MNE's Canadian subsidiary is significant in the electrical industry. The results are less than overwhelming; indeed, they are disappointing to those of us who believe that firm level testing of R and D is more important than industry level tests. Perhaps the results will improve in the future as data become publicly available to match the sophistication of the econometric techniques currently available but constrained by inadequate data on the subsidiary R and D variable.

As background to the study, Hewitt discusses the different types of R and D. Initially, a U.S. based firm will export abroad. The exports are thought to play a minor role in adding to the firm's revenues. When the export markets are threatened or the firm consciously alters its global strategy, foreign production will take place. Local, adaptive R and D will occur in the foreign subsidiaries as the parent's technology is geared toward the local market. The adaptive R and D will persist until it is either phased out or replaced with original R and D. In a *marketing intensive* MNE, local original R and D is expected to evolve from adaptive R and D as the parent firm establishes autonomous world divisions. This is in contrast to an *R and D intensive* MNE in which there is little foreign adaptation of technology; rather, the R and D is termed global-original. The MNE will centralize the R and D function if the United States is the largest and best test market and if economies of scale exist.

McMullen presents and tests a model to explain the length of lag between first world use of an innovation and the date of its first use in Canada. She defines innovation as a new or improved product or production process. New data on innovations adopted by firms in Canada in the 1960–1979 period are used to test the model.

McMullen describes two types of innovation—first, original innovation resulting from in–house R and D and second, imitative innovation that results from a process of diffusion of information. This adaptation of technology, already in use elsewhere, is the dominant form of innovation in Canada. This fact should not be discouraging since firms in all countries draw upon an international pool of technology. Internalization theory indicates that R and D tends to be centralized in the parent MNE; therefore, little R and D is done in the subsidiaries of host nations. The results of McMullen's work provide some confirmation of this since she finds (1) that foreign controlled firms in Canada do less original R and D than firms controlled domestically and (2) when acquiring technology externally, foreign controlled firms rely predominantly on intracorporate sources.

The model presented is unique in that it attempts to overcome the problem of simultaneity, that is, the problem that occurs when the dependent variable being tested influences the independent variables. The model consists of three equations that are analyzed by least squares regression. In the key equation, the dependent variable is the lag length in years.

Three variables are incorporated that influence risk: (1) level of capital investment required; (2) the degree of "radicalness" of the innovation; and (3) source of technology (intracorporate transfer versus in-house or arm's-length sources).

Three additional variables reflect the influence of rate of return, if risk is held constant: (1) payback period; (2) percentage of cost funded by the government; and (3) transaction costs, i.e., patents.

It is hypothesized that as the perceived rate of return increases the lag length should decrease. The author's premise is that the expected rate of return must be high enough to compensate for the level of risk that will be incurred.

McMullen's findings are that lag length is increased by the cost of the innovation relative to firms sales, that is, lag length increases because of the increased risk with a larger investment; and a technology that is new to the firm or an improvement. Lag length is shortened by an innovation with a short payback, government funding, and technology that is transferred intracorporately.

The author concludes that as the rate of return on an innovation investment increases, the technology will be adopted earlier. Applying her findings to Canadian policy issues, McMullen states that if the risk faced by the firm exceeds the risk faced by society, then a case can be made for government intervention to reduce risk. Furthermore, because foreign controlled subsidiaries play a positive role in technological change by contributing to a reduction in lags, a policy to reduce foreign direct investment (FDI) could have negative consequences for lag lengths and hence the rate of technological change in Canadian industry.

The second theme explored in this book is the relationship between multinational enterprises and host nations. In particular, these chapters examine a new policy initiative of the Canadian federal government. Subsidies for R and D are to be restricted to the subsidiaries of multinational enterprises that can demonstrate that they have secured a world product mandate (WPM) from their parents for the development of a new product line.

Chapters by Rugman, Wolf, and Etemad explore the complexities of Canada's world product mandate strategy and its implications for other host nations. Rugman explains the historical developments of Canada's WPM policy and then relates this to the modern theory of the MNE, namely, the theory of internalization. He then focuses on the issues of a WPM from the viewpoint of the MNE. Wolf relates the development of the WPM strategy to the more general topic of U.S.–Canadian free trade. He examines the special problems of tariffs, factor costs and scale economies as these constrain the use of both internalization theory and WPM strategy. Etemad puts the WPM issue in perspective by considering all its pros and cons from the viewpoints of host and home governments, as well as from the viewpoint of the MNE.

Rugman's work on the theory of internalization suggests that technology represents a firm-specific advantage (FSA) of the MNE. It is controlled by the internal market of the firm to safeguard against the risk of knowledge dissemination. In analyzing the decision making behavior of the MNE, Rugman points out that a WPM increases uncertainty for the MNE. It leads to a change in the MNE's internal organization and structure since the development of a new product line in a subsidiary increases the autonomy of the subsidiary. There is also a change in the external environment faced by the MNE after the host country grants a subsidy to the subsidiary of the MNE.

The mandate leads to a decentralized form of organization as the subsidiary becomes an expert in a new process. The subsidiary is more likely to become an independent profit center and perhaps, in time, a potential rival producer. This increases the costs of control to the MNE and leads to the risk of dissemination of its FSA in knowledge. Additional risks occur to the parent as the subsidiary is inclined to be more involved with government officials and politicians. Rugman finds that the WPM is a trade-off between control via the internal market and the potential loss of control through decentralized R and D. The decision made will depend upon the costs of private versus subsidized R and D and the risk of loss of control following the adoption of a decentralized R and D process.

Wolf presents many variations of a WPM. One example is a mandate limited to production rights only, with the R and D, finance, and marketing functions being retained by the parent. Another is a geographically limited mandate. Wolf assumes that a mandate will include some R and D work but not necessarily an international marketing function. Wolf suggests two major factors that influence the decision to implement a WPM strategy. First, the management of the parent MNE must be willing to implement a WPM, and the management of the subsidiary must demonstrate the depth and capability to carry it out. The second factor is the extent to which R and D can be decentralized, depending on scale economies present in the R and D function and firm size.

Wolf presents a simple cost–benefit model that summarizes the factors involved in the WPM decision. Briefly, the sum of costs less subsidies is compared to the cost of producing the product line in the cheapest alternative location.

In an interesting chapter, Etemad argues that the parent has little incentive to grant a WPM because, once done, the MNE and other subsidiaries become hostages to the mandate agreement. The parent becomes fully dependent on one source supply and must prevail upon other sister subsidiaries to honor the mandate. Etemad suggests that when the subsidiary enlists the support of the host country to obtain the WPM, it gains a sense of control and internal harmony with its host environment, an improvement from the previous adversarial position. Several features of the WPM are welcomed by the parent. These are the reduction of risk, sources commitment and responsibility and friction. The MNE, however, will also suffer a loss of bargaining power because of reliance on the mandate holder, suppliers, labor unions and host governments. A massive reallocation of power, authority, control and responsibility from the parent to the mandated subsidiary will occur.

The third theme of the book concerns the relationship between technology transfer and export marketing strategies. To what extent does an economy largely dependent upon technology transfer from abroad use this technology to stimulate exports? McGuinness addresses this issue from the viewpoint of an advanced nation such as Canada, while Kindra examines it from the perspective of less developed countries. In a related issue, Rugman considers the recent emergence of MNEs based in traditional host nations. He finds that Canadian based MNEs are increasing in importance and are concentrated in the resource sectors which reflect on the country specific advantage of Canada. The implications of these three papers for public policy are brought out by each of the authors.

Professor Norman McGuinness uses original data and tests the observation that firms with a high level of R and D tend to export a greater proportion of output than firms with a low level of R and D. Does this suggest that R and D leads to better products, with an international competitive lead, or could there be factors other than R and D intensity that have a greater impact on exports? In his study, McGuinness examines the firm, product and market characteristics to determine if there are more basic causative elements underlying the relationship between R and D and exports.

Data were collected in questionnaires distributed to Canadian industrial firms requesting information about firm characteristics, market structure, market conditions, product types and R and D intensity. Questionnaires employed a perceptual scale from 1 to 7. Using the principal components method, ten situational factors emerged with eigenvalues greater than 1.0. Using R and D intensity and foreign sales intensity as dependent variables, multiple regression analysis confirmed McGuinness' research model that both R and D intensity and situational factors affect foreign sales intensity—but that situational factors play a larger role.

Interestingly enough, McGuinness also finds that situational factors explain nearly 50 percent of the variation in R and D intensity and suggests that management may have less power than assumed to set levels of R and D. Certain market characteristics were found to have strong effects on R and D intensity. Very competitive markets characterized by price sensitive customers, even with a few large competitors, depressed R and D spending. Mature markets with stable technology promoted R and D as did youthful, rapidly changing markets.

Situational factors had an impact on foreign sales intensity that exceeded R and D impact considerably; in particular, the type of product manufactured was significant. Custom engineered and systems products had lower than average exports. The best export performers were found to be component type producers, followed by standard products.

In light of this study, McGuinness concludes that emphasis placed on R and D as a quick route to international competitiveness may be misplaced. He suggests that the comparative advantage approach should be followed. This places emphasis on the product types that perform best.

Kindra's paper is useful since it covers a vast amount of ground: the definition of technology transfer, the linkages between technology transfer and export marketing strategies and the relationship of technology transfer to economic development. Based on survey research, Kindra identifies four stages in the process of technology diffusion in LDC based firms. The author aims to provide a blueprint for export marketing strategies for firms at each stage by obtaining an answer to the question of when is a local firm able to take over certain functions? Kindra's four stages of technology assimilation are as follows:

Do-how: In this stage, the employees of the firm become familiar with basic skills. There are no exports, and the local producer is a seller of production capacity.

Do-why: In stage two, skills are further developed through learning-by-doing. There is an attempt to reduce dependence on imported technology and to use local suppliers. A basic marketing department may be established and the producer may try to export.

Know-how: This phase focuses on development from within. "Pull" based strategy in this stage results in a "marketer" of products. The firm will still have access to the parent's technology but undertakes its own product redesign, development and modifications. There is a sense of quality consciousness at this point.

Know-why: Transition to the fourth stage is the most difficult to achieve. Learning by research entails the ability to translate a concept into products and use the same product for different concepts or applications. Heavy financial requirements are necessary for the R and D investment and the firm must have the ability to face high risk and absorb losses.

Kindra states that evolution to the fourth stage is attractive, for then the firm can command high profits based on its unique skills. This phase is unnecessary when the product is low cost, standardized, has a stable technology, faces little competition, and marketing does not require strong brand positioning. In such cases, the firm is advised to remain in stage three. Kindra states that governments in less developed nations may be unwilling to commit grants for stage four that could be "better" spent on agricultural machinery. This may be an additional reason preventing a firm from reaching the last phase.

Using internalization theory as a seminal base in the final chapter, Rugman explores the extent of foreign activity of the largest 17 Canadian based multinational enterprises. Also examined are data on their performance in terms of mean profits and risk of earnings relative to other multinationals over the 1970–1979 period. The involvement of Canadian multinationals in less developed countries is analyzed next. It is found that Canadian multinationals are much more active in resource based sectors than are multinationals from other nations. This finding is consistent with the theory of internalization, since the firm specific advantages of our multinationals reflect Canada's country specific advantage in resource intensive products.

In summary three controversial aspects of technology transfer are addressed in this book: First, the variables determining research and development activity in Canada, a representative host country to foreign multinationals. Second, the prospects for an increase in R and D in Canada through the policy of world product mandating. Third, the relationship between exporting and R and D, especially the transfer of technology by multinationals to developing countries. For these reasons the chapters in this volume constitute an important contribution to the literature on multinationals and technology transfer.

2

The Level of Research
and Development Activity
of Multinationals

David W. Komus

INTRODUCTION

Research and development (R and D) activities are carried out by a large number of multinational enterprises (MNEs). In this chapter the optimal level of such activity is considered in the context of a simple dynamic model.

One explanation for the role of R and D within a MNE is given by the internalization or eclectic theories of foreign direct investment (FDI).[1] In these theories the MNE has a firm-specific advantage, the use of which contributes to its net earnings in each of the national markets in which it operates. For the multiple use to be most profitable, the advantage must have the nature of a public good within the firm; that is, its use by one affiliate must not diminish its use by any other affiliate of the firm. One way by which a MNE can acquire this type of advantage is to undertake R and D activity.

A firm-specific advantage of this type can be viewed as a stock possessed by the MNE. It is increased by investments that take the form of R and D expenditures. It depreciates or dissipates because of R and D activities of rival firms, the expiration of patents, and the loss of secrecy concerning R and D results.

The use of the advantage increases the net revenue of the MNE in each country in which it uses the advantage. Over the range of levels where the optimum will occur, the return (net revenue) increases as the stock of the advantage is increased; it does so, however, at a decreasing rate. If the net revenue is not increased for at least some level of the advantage, there will be no return to the investment and no R and D will take place. If the net return increases at an increasing rate, the model is explosive and an infinite level of R and D becomes optimum, although financial constraints may limit the rate of expansion of R and D activity.

NATURE OF R AND D ACTIVITY

R and D activities take place over time and produce a series of results, with each of these becoming commercially useful at a particular point in time. After a result is introduced other firms may try to copy or imitate it, either by undertaking R and D that enables them to avoid patent or other restrictions or by attempting to obtain information that is being kept secret by the originating firm. The methods used depend on how the particular R and D results are protected; thus, any R and D result gradually becomes available to other firms and ceases to confer an advantage to the originating firm. This loss of the exclusive use of a result is the dissipation or depreciation of the stock of the advantage.

To maintain a stock of firm-specific advantages a firm must continually undertake new R and D activity, thus obtaining new results to replace those that, by becoming public knowledge, are no longer specific to the firm.

R and D results are of a number of different types including: the development of new products or product lines; improving existing products; developing new or improved methods, techniques, or processes of production; and the adaptation of existing products or production processes to specific markets or countries. The first three of these are appropriate to the model presented here while the fourth, which does not have the required public good property, is not. The fourth involves a return from only a single market and will be used only to the extent that it has a high return in that market.

New products or product lines open up new markets and have associated revenues and costs which determine the return to the R and D. The pattern of the introduction of new products into a number of national markets and the location of the R and D and production activities has been considered by the product cycle model. (See Vernon, 1966 and 1979.) Improvements to existing products should result in increased sales and sales revenue by making the product better suited to the market or by moving the product to a different segment of the market. There could be cost changes associated with this. Changes in the production processes will usually result in greater efficiency or productivity and will lower unit costs. These three types of R and D results are not distinguished in the model developed here as the net revenue function used is not of sufficient detail to require or accommodate this.

STRUCTURE AND ASSUMPTIONS OF THE MODEL

The model presented here uses a general functional form to represent the net revenue of the MNE in each country in which it operates. Net revenue is a function of the stock of the advantage only, with the levels of sales, production, and trade not being specifically included. This requires the assumption that the levels of sales, production, and trade can be quickly varied by the MNE and that they are chosen by it at each point in time in order to maximize the net revenue earned in each country, given the level of firm-specific advantage possessed by the firm at that time. At each point in time the firm can do no better than to maximize its net revenue by taking its advantage as given. The choice of any other combination of levels of sales, production, and trade simply reduces the net revenue and reduces the funds available for possible investment in the advantage.[2]

Implicit in this is an assumption that the MNE can quickly vary the amount and type of labor and of capital equipment that it employs to suit its current requirements. This is not realistic for short time periods, particularly for specialized types of capital goods, but if it takes longer to adjust the stock of the firm-specific advantage than it does to adjust the amount of labor or capital equipment used, the results of the model presented here are still significant.

There are markets for labor and markets for many types of capital goods (both new and used). There is, according to the internalization and eclectic theories of FDI, no market for the firm-specific advantage of MNEs, and this is part of the reason for FDI. Thus, it is reasonable to assume that the stock in the firm-specific advantage will take longer to adjust than will the levels of labor and capital equipment used. The lack of a market for the firm-specific advantage also means that the MNE cannot sell its existing stock of advantage. Thus, negative investment in the advantage is not allowed.

In this chapter the objective attributed to the MNE is profit maximization which, in a dynamic context, is the maximization of the discounted flow of profits over time. This is consistent with the internalization and eclectic theories (though not exclusively so) and reflects the concern those theories attribute to the MNE to earn return to its advantage in several markets.[3]

It is further assumed that the exchange rate is fixed and known with certainty thus allowing all values to be expressed in the same currency, which can be assumed to be the home country currency. This simplifies the mathematics, but excludes consideration of the effect of changes in exchange rates and of the uncertainty because of fluctuating exchange rates. Although these are important for MNEs, they are not central to the issue being considered in this chapter.

MATHEMATICS OF THE MODEL

The profit function for the MNE can be set out as follows:[4]

$$\pi(t) = \int_{0}^{\infty} e^{-R(t)} NR_1(t)(A(t)) + NR_2(t)(A(t)) - q(t)I(t)d(t) \tag{1}$$

This reflects the case in which the advantage has the nature of a public good within the firm, with the same advantage being used in each country while the investment in it is made only once—not once for each country. In the equation the MNE is represented as a two country firm, and it will be assumed that one is the home country and two is the host country. As nothing further is specified about each country, this assumption does not limit the generality of the model. The extension to more host countries could be made by replacing $NR_2(A)$ with $\sum_{i=2}^{n} NR_i(A)$. This is not done in the mathematics of the model, but the extension to more countries is considered when the results are interpreted. The situation of the MNE can be compared to the position it would be in as a one country firm by removing the $NR_2(t)(A(t))$ term from equation (1). This comparison is considered below.

The terms in equation (1) are defined as follows:

π = the discounted stream of profits over time
$r(t)$ = the rate of interest at time t
$R(t)$ = $\int_{0}^{t} r(s)ds$, and is required to allow the rate of interest to vary over time
$NR_i(t)$ = the net revenue earned in country i at time t
$A(t)$ = the stock of the firm-specific advantage at time t
$q(t)$ = the cost of R and D at time t required to achieve a given level of increase in the stock of the advantage
$I(t)$ = the investment in the advantage at time t

The net revenue is the net revenue after taxes in each country, exclusive of any R and D expenses. The total revenue includes all sales in that country plus any exports made to other countries, including exports to other parts of the MNE. The costs deducted include all expenses for labor, capital, finance, and other inputs used, including imports from other parts of the MNE and also including any taxes paid. Expenditures on R and D are not counted here, but expenses to transfer the advantage to a specific host country are counted as costs in the net revenue for that country.

The costs of R and D are included in the model in a very specific way. The cost term $q(t)$ represents the costs after taxes of obtaining a given increment in the level of the advantage, where this increment is represented by the investment term, $I(t)$. The total expenditure at any time is represented by a number of units of $q(t)$. The R and D expenditures can take place in more than one country, but all contribute to the same stock of advantage and are all grouped in the one term $q(t)I(t)$.

The risk and uncertainty associated with R and D is not included in the model presented here. Treating $q(t)$ as an expected cost [or $I(t)$ as an expected increment] with an associated standard deviation would be one way of giving some consideration to this uncertainty. The effectiveness or degree of success with which R and D is carried out will vary across different firms. This can be reflected by allowing $q(t)$ to have different values for different firms or industries.

The depreciation of the stock of the advantage is represented by the loss of a proportion, $\delta(t)$, of this stock at each point in time. This is the simplest way to represent the depreciation and makes it independent of the other characteristics of the stock and of the current level of R and D expenditures. This could be modified, but the version used here does allow some consideration of how the rate of depreciation affects the level of R and D expenditures.

The change in the stock of the advantage is represented as follows:

$$\dot{A}(t) = I(t) - \delta(t)A(t) \tag{2}$$

where a dot over a variable represents its time derivative. The advantage existing at the initial time period is treated as a parameter. Thus,

$$A(0) = A_0 \tag{3}$$

A model with this structure can be analyzed using optimal control theory. The Hamiltonian for the problem is:

$$H = e^{-R(t)}\{NR_1(t)(A(t)) + NR_2(t)(A(t)) - q(t)I(t)\} + \lambda(t)\{I(t) - \delta(t)A(t)\} \quad (4)$$

The first order condition gives

$$\frac{\partial H}{\partial I} = e^{-R(t)}(-q(t)) + \lambda(t)(1) = 0 \quad (5)$$

The adjoint condition requires that

$$\frac{\partial \lambda}{\partial t} = -\frac{\partial H}{\partial A} \quad (6)$$

The transversality condition requires that

$$\lim_{t \to \infty} \lambda(t)A(t) = 0 \quad (7)$$

Then

$$\frac{\partial H}{\partial A} = e^{-R(t)}\left\{\frac{\partial NR_1(t)}{\partial A(t)} + \frac{\partial NR_2(t)}{\partial A(t)}\right\} + \lambda(t)(-\delta(t)) \quad (8)$$

and from (6)

$$\dot{\lambda}(t) = \lambda(t)\delta(t) - e^{-R(t)}\left\{\frac{\partial NR_1(t)}{\partial A(t)} + \frac{\partial NR_2(t)}{\partial A(t)}\right\} \quad (9)$$

This can be solved for λ. Using a standard formula (see Chiang 1967, pp. 436–438) gives

$$\lambda(t) = e^{-\int -\delta dt}\left\{B + \int -e^{-R(t)}\left[\frac{\partial NR_1(t)}{\partial A(t)} + \frac{\partial NR_2(t)}{\partial A(t)}\right]e^{\int -\delta dt}\,dt\right\} \quad (10)$$

where B represents a constant of integration. Using standard procedures (see Chiang 1967, pp. 440–441) this can be solved for B and the equation for λ(t) can be stated as

$$\lambda(t) = \int_t^\infty e^{-R(s)}e^{(-\delta(s-t))}\left\{\frac{\partial NR_1(s)}{\partial A(s)} + \frac{\partial NR_2(s)}{\partial A(s)}\right\}ds \quad (11)$$

Substituting (11) into (5) gives

$$\int_t^\infty e^{-R(s)}e^{(-\delta(s-t))}\left\{\frac{\partial NR_1(s)}{\partial A(s)} + \frac{\partial NR_2(s)}{\partial A(s)}\right\}ds - q(t)e^{-R(t)} = 0 \quad (12)$$

Taking a time derivative of (12) gives

$$\delta \int_t^\infty e^{-R(t)} e^{(-\delta(s-t))} \left\{ \frac{\partial NR_1(s)}{\partial A(s)} + \frac{\partial NR_2(s)}{\partial A(s)} \right\} ds + e^{-R(t)} \left\{ \frac{\partial NR_1(t)}{\partial A(t)} \right.$$

$$\left. + \frac{\partial NR_2(t)}{\partial A(t)} \right\} + q(t)r(t)e^{-R(t)} - \dot{q}(t)e^{-R(t)} = 0 \tag{13}$$

Substituting in for the integral from a rearranged (12) gives

$$\delta(t)(e^{-R(t)})q(t) - e^{-R(t)} \left\{ \frac{\partial NR_1(t)}{\partial A(t)} + \frac{\partial NR_2(t)}{\partial A(t)} \right\}$$

$$+ q(t)r(t)e^{-R(t)} - \dot{q}(t)e^{-R(t)} = 0 \tag{14}$$

Cancelling the $e^{-R(t)}$ terms and rearranging gives

$$\frac{\partial NR_1(t)}{\partial A(t)} + \frac{\partial NR_2(t)}{\partial A(t)} = q(t)(r(t) + \delta(t) - \dot{q}(t)/q(t)) \tag{15}$$

which is the main mathematical result of the model.

RESULTS OF THE MODEL

In equation (15) the right-hand term represents the costs of employing one unit of the advantage for one time period and can be considered as a flow price of the advantage. The term $q(t)r(t)$ is the interest charge on $q(t)$ for one period, $q(t)\delta(t)$ is the depreciation charge incurred, and $\dot{q}(t)$ is the rise in the cost of acquiring a unit of the stock of the advantage. It appears with a negative sign since a rise in the cost (or price) represents a gain to the owner and offsets the other elements of cost. It is a gain because, to the extent that it now costs other firms more to acquire a similar advantage, the existing advantage is worth more. The gain should be reflected in a higher return to the advantage, although it cannot be directly realized by the sale of the stock of the existing advantage. The right-hand term payment represents the sum of the marginal net revenues to the stock of the advantage in each country in which it is used.

Equation (15) states that the sum of these marginal revenues is set equal to the cost of the advantage at each point in time. This involves only current values because no constraints on the level of investment in the advantage have been considered to this point. It is similar to the marginal conditions that arise from many maximization models. The interesting point is that it involves a sum of the marginal revenues in both countries in which the MNE operates being set equal to a single cost term.

To consider this aspect of equation (15) further, a more specific functional form for the net revenue is required. This gives a more specific function for the derivative of the net revenue with respect to the advantage and allows additional mathematical results to be derived. The form used must meet the conditions already imposed on the net revenue function (increasing at a decreasing rate as the stock of the advantage increases) which requires a positive first derivative and a negative second derivative. Although a variety of functional forms meet these requirements, there are advantages to using one that allows the mathematics to be easily solved. The one used is:

$$NR = A^{\alpha} \qquad 0 < \alpha < 1$$

The time references have been omitted to simplify the notation and will be omitted in the equations that follow. The derivatives are:

$$\frac{\partial NR}{\partial A} = \alpha A^{(\alpha-1)}$$

and

$$\frac{\partial^2 NR}{\partial A^2} = \alpha(\alpha - 1)A^{(\alpha-2)}$$

which have the required signs. To distinguish the net revenue function for each country let

$$NR_1 = gA^{\alpha}$$

and

$$NR_2 = hA^{\alpha}$$

where g and h are both positive but can have different values. The α term is the same in both countries so that the mathematics can be solved.

Equation (15) now becomes

$$\alpha g A^{-1} + \alpha h A^{\alpha-1} = c \qquad (16)$$

where

$$c = q(t)(r(t) + \delta(t) - \dot{q}(t)/q(t))$$

For a one country firm equation (16) becomes

$$\alpha g A^{\alpha-1} = c \tag{17}$$

These two equations can be solved for A. Starting with (16),

$$2\alpha(g + h)(A^{\alpha-1}) = c$$

and

$$A^{\alpha-1} = \frac{c}{2\alpha(g + h)} \tag{18}$$

Since $(\alpha - 1) < 0$ the left-hand side of equation (18) can be rearranged to be $1/A^{-\alpha+1}$ and (18) can be stated as

$$\frac{1}{A} = \left(\frac{c}{2\alpha(g + h)}\right)^{(1/-\alpha+1)}$$

Noting that

$$\left(\frac{c}{2\alpha(g + h)}\right)^{(1/-\alpha+1)} = \frac{c\left(\frac{1}{-\alpha + 1}\right)}{2\alpha(g + h)^{(1/-\alpha+1)}}$$

and rearranging gives, for equation (16),

$$A = \left(\frac{2\alpha(g + h)}{c}\right)^{(1/-\alpha+1)} \tag{19}$$

and for equation (17),

$$A = \left(\frac{2\alpha g}{c}\right)^{(1/-\alpha+1)} \tag{20}$$

Given that $0 < \alpha < 1$, then $0 < -\alpha + 1 < 1$ and $(1/-\alpha + 1) > 1$. Also, $g + h > g$. Thus,

$$\left(\frac{2\alpha(g + h)}{c}\right)^{(1/-\alpha+1)} > \left(\frac{\alpha g}{c}\right)^{(1/-\alpha+1)}$$

This shows that the optimal stock of the advantage is larger for the two country firm. In the case considered here the situation in the home country is identical for both firms.

The result shows that the MNE not only uses its advantage in both countries but also invests more in order to develop a larger stock of the advantage than it would as a one country firm. Increasing the number of countries in which the MNE operates would change the $(g + h)$ term to include more coefficients and would increase the size of the optimal stock of the advantage. These results do not depend on the specific functional form used and are consistent with the basic net revenue function initially specified, whereby net revenue increases at a decreasing rate. The marginal revenue condition for the one country firm is $MR_1 = c$ whereas for the two country firm it is $MR_1 + MR_2 = c$. To maintain the equality with the same cost term, the marginal revenue in country one must be reduced. This is done by increasing the stock of the advantage.

A similar type of result applies to R and D that the MNE can make use of in only one country, such as that used to adapt a product to a particular national market. Such R and D is carried on to a lesser extent than it would be if the results were useful in more than one country.

Equations (19) and (20) show that the optimal stock of the advantage depends positively on the coefficients of the net revenue function and negatively on the cost term. Thus, the greater the return to any given stock of advantage, the larger the advantage the firm will wish to possess, provided that the costs are the same in both cases.

The cost term includes three elements: the interest rate, the rate of depreciation, and the cost or price of R and D. If the net revenue function remains the same, a higher interest rate will be associated with a lower optimal advantage. The structure of interest rates are economy wide and affect all firms and industries. A high interest rate reduces investment in R and D (similar to its effect on other investment), and this may have implications for macroeconomic policy. To explore this the model used would have to include both a more specific tax structure and a specification of the effects of R and D on future economic growth. The question of what interest rate the MNE should use for discounting is not considered here. If the home rate has more influence than the rates of other countries, a high interest rate in one country will lead to a lower level of R and D by the MNEs based in that country compared to other countries.

A higher rate of depreciation results in a lower optimal advantage if the other factors are the same in both cases. This rate will vary depending on the industry and the firm. If a firm is better at keeping its R and D results secret or in protecting them in other ways than are rival firms in the same industry, the first firm will have the larger optimal advantage. Similarly, a higher cost, or price, of R and D results in a lower optimal advantage, other factors remaining constant. If these costs vary across firms due to the efficiency with which they carry out R and D activities, the more efficient firms will have a higher optimal advantage.

There may be relations between the return to an advantage and its costs that offset some of the above results. The more difficult types of R and D may have a larger return than other types of R and D but will also have higher costs. These two conditions will have opposite influences on the optimal stock of the advantage. When the return to a particular type of R and D is high, competitive R and D by rival firms should increase the depreciation rate for any advantage gained. If some firms can switch the area in which they concentrate their R and D activities, the above types of considerations should result in the return to different types of R and D activity being equalized. This possibility cannot be explored by the model presented here. It would require an oligopoly model in which the level and type of R and D activity is one of the major elements of the competitive behavior of firms.

R AND D AND METHODS OF MARKET ENTRY

In the discussion of FDI three methods of obtaining a return to a firm-specific advantage from a foreign market have been noted: FDI, exporting, and licensing the advantage to a local firm. (See Rugman 1981a, pp. 53–74 for one discussion of this.) The works on this examine the costs and revenues associated with each alternative. Authors maintain that the rate of depreciation of the advantage is higher with licensing than with FDI or exporting, and they represent this by an additional cost term. The revenue and other costs also depend on the mode of entry. The alternative providing the highest net revenue is chosen by the MNE. Buckley and Casson (1981) represent the costs and revenues by discounted flows over time and look at the possibility of the firm switching from one method to another as market conditions change. These works did not look at the level of investment in R and D made by the MNE to obtain its advantage. This is the major item considered by the model presented here, and the level is shown to depend on the method of market entry.

In the model presented here, the changes in the depreciation rate and in the other costs and revenues would be represented by changes in the depreciation rate coefficient and by changes in either or both of the coefficients of the net revenue function. The MNE will choose the mode of entry that maximizes its discounted flow of profits over time, as given by equation (1), and this result corresponds with those obtained in the above mentioned works. The choice requires a comparison of the maximum attainable discounted profit stream under each alternative in order to determine the best mode of entry into the foreign market. The values of the coefficients of the net revenue function and of the cost function depend on the mode of entry. The optimal stock of the advantage depends on the same coefficients. Therefore, the optimal advantage will vary with the mode of entry.

The general nature of the functional forms used here limits the results that can be obtained on this topic. It can be noted, however, that the higher depreciation rate under licensing is an increased cost and must be offset by a higher net revenue if licensing is to be used. From equation (19) one can see that these two conditions will have opposite effects on the optimal stock of the advantage; thus, nothing further can be said about the level of the optimal stock. If exporting and FDI are associated with the same depreciation rate, the one chosen will have a higher net revenue and will therefore also have a higher optimal level of R and D.

ADDITIONAL RESULTS

An additional investment condition can be derived. To simplify the notation let $1/-\alpha + 1 = b$. Then equation (19) can be written as:

$$A = \frac{2^b \alpha^b (g + h)^b}{c^b}$$

Taking log time derivatives of this gives:

$$\frac{\dot{A}}{A} = b\frac{\dot{\alpha}}{\alpha} + b\frac{\dot{g} + \dot{h}}{g + h} - b\frac{\dot{c}}{c}$$

Recall that $\dot{A} = I - \delta A$, so

$$\frac{I}{A} = \delta + b\frac{\dot{\alpha}}{\alpha} + b\frac{\dot{g} + \dot{h}}{g + h} - b\frac{\dot{c}}{c} \tag{21}$$

Similarly, equation (20) gives:

$$\frac{I}{A} = \delta + b\frac{\dot{\alpha}}{\alpha} + b\frac{\dot{g}}{g} - b\frac{\dot{c}}{c} \tag{22}$$

These conditions indicate that gross investment as a proportion of the stock of the advantage depends positively on the rate of depreciation and on the rate of increase of the coefficients of the net revenue function and negatively on the rate of increase in the costs of R and D. These are different from that of the level of the advantage itself. A higher rate of depreciation lowers the optimal level of the advantage while increasing the level of R and D expenditures as a proportion of that advantage. The effect on the actual level of R and D expenditures is indeterminant unless precise values are assigned to the coefficients. The level of the advantage at any point in time depends on the value of the coefficients of the model, while the net investment in the advantage at any point in time depends on the value of the coefficients of the model, while the net investment in the advantage depends on the rate of change of the values of the coefficients.

If all the coefficients of the model remain constant so that the time derivatives equal zero, the R and D expenditure will be at the level required to offset the loss due to depreciation and net investment will be zero. If the multiplicative coefficient of the net revenue function remains constant, the proportion of gross investment to advantage for the MNE and the one country firm will be the same, although the actual levels of each will be different for the two firms. If the values of the coefficients depend on the mode of entry into the foreign market, the investment ratios for the MNE will depend on the mode of entry as will the level of the advantage.

RESTRICTION ON NEGATIVE INVESTMENT

The gross investment in the advantage—R and D expenditure— has been constrained to be non-negative. It remains to consider the effect of this constraint, when for some point in time the optimal gross investment is negative. The conditions under which the optimum will be negative can be seen from equation (21). Allowing all of the coefficients but α to be constant reduces the equation to:

$$\frac{I}{A} = \delta + b\frac{\dot{\alpha}}{\alpha}$$

Thus, for the optimal investment to be negative it must be that $-b(\dot{\alpha}/\alpha) > \delta$, when $\dot{\alpha}$ is negative. This says that the net revenue must be declining at such a rate that the optimal advantage is falling faster than the rate of depreciation. The other net revenue coefficients can give the same result or the cost term must increase at a sufficient rate, with a constant net revenue, to make the optimal advantage decline faster than the depreciation rate.

Equation (12) can be used to consider this further. It gives the gain in profits at time 0 to a unit increase in investment at time t and states that this equals zero on the optimal path. By discounting back to time t instead of time 0 and substituting the discounted flow price of the unit of investment over future time periods for its cost, equation (12) can be written as:

$$G(\tau) = \int_t^\infty e^{(-r+\delta)(t-\tau)} \left\{ \frac{NR_1(t)}{A(t)} + \frac{NR_2(t)}{A(t)} - c(t) \right\} dt$$

On the optimal time path, when investment is positive, this equals zero. If it were positive, increasing the investment would increase the return, and if it were negative, decreasing the investment would increase the return. For negative investment to be optimal it must be the case that $G(\tau) < 0$, when gross investment is zero. Representing the period of zero investment as that between times m and n, when $m < n$, it follows that $G(m) = 0$ and $G(n) = 0$ since these are the ends of positive investment periods. Thus, the following relations can be set out for the period of zero investment:

$$G(m) - G(\tau) > 0$$

and

$$G(m) - G(n) = 0$$

Subtracting the appropriate integrals and discounting back to time 0 gives

$$\int_m^\tau e^{(-(\delta+r)t)} \left\{ \frac{\partial NR_1}{\partial A} + \frac{\partial NR_2}{\partial A} - c \right\} dt \geq 0 \qquad (23)$$

and

$$\int_m^n e^{(-(\delta+r)t)} \left\{ \frac{\partial NR_1}{\partial A} + \frac{\partial NR_2}{\partial A} - c \right\} dt = 0 \qquad (24)$$

These two conditions state that over the first part of the period of zero investment the return to an additional unit of investment would be positive but that over the entire period it would be zero. Thus, the period of zero investment is not confined to the period when the lower advantage is optimal but starts sufficiently before that to keep the net gain to the last unit of positive investment equal to zero. Thus, it is optimal to anticipate the period when a reduced advantage is appropriate. During such periods previous R and D expenditures cannot be recovered by a sale of part of the stock of the advantage.

CONCLUSION

The model developed here has shown that the MNE not only uses its advantage in foreign markets in order to increase the return earned on its advantage, but also invests more in the advantage than it would as a one country firm. In addition, the optimal stock of the advantage depends on the mode of entry used to serve a foreign market through the effect this has on the net revenue earned in that market and the effect on the costs of R and D to the MNE. The non-saleability of the stock of the advantage makes it optimal for the MNE to anticipate any period during which a reduced advantage is optimal.

The model presented here may be open to a number of possible extensions. The first would be to consider the risk associated with R and D, probably by using some form of mean variance approach. Another would be to make the rate of depreciation a function of the level of R and D. Since R and D is a competitive activity, increases in the level at which all firms undertake it should result in a higher rate of depreciation of the advantage of each firm. This is one of the simplest ways of including some of the influences of the competition between firms in the model. For any possible extension, the mathematics used will make the solution of the model more difficult and in some cases may make an analytical solution impossible (see note 2).

NOTES

1. For a discussion of internalization theory see Rugman (1981a); for the eclectic theory see Dunning (1977) and (1979).

2. An optimal control theory model of a MNE that included sales and production functions and the level of exports was attempted in Komus (1981, pp. 192–210). The model included a capital stock in each country but could not be solved for an investment condition for each capital stock unless very restrictive assumptions about the form of the production functions were made.

3. Komus (1981, pp. 26–40) includes a discussion of the possible objectives that can be attributed to a MNE.

4. The basic model of the investment decision used was inspired by Nickell (1978, Chapter 2), who looked at investment in capital goods by a one country firm.

3

The Determinants of Research and Development Activity in Domestic and Foreign Controlled Industries

Judith A. Alexander

INTRODUCTION

Canada performs proportionately less Research and Development (R and D) than other developed nations, and the private business sector generates proportionately less R and D than in other countries.[2] This lack of R and D in Canada has been a matter of concern to Canadian policy makers. It is widely believed that the rate of technological change and innovation can be manipulated by the state, and this assumption underlies the discussion of a science policy for Canada in the sixties and also the senate inquiry into science policy in Canada in the seventies.[3] McFetridge (1977) states that an increase in the level of Canadian R and D has been suggested for reasons of national prestige—to prevent Canada from "becoming a second rate country" and from "falling behind in the technological race."

This paper has two objectives: to attempt, by regression analysis, to isolate the determinants of R and D and to compare our results with those of other researchers who have examined the question of the determinants of R and D and to compare our results with those of other researchers who have examined the question of the determinants of R and D in Canada, namely Globerman (1973), Howe and McFetridge (1976) and Frankl (1979). One problem with such a comparison is that the results of firm level and industry level studies may not be strictly comparable and, furthermore, the logic of choice for industry of firm level analysis is seldom articulated. For instance, Globerman (1973) cites the existing sample survey data as biased but fails to note that his use of industry data must mask many of the interesting facts of firm level behavior. In general, in empirical work at the industry level, the theory has simply been a pragmatic analog of the theory at the firm level.[4] There are some acknowledgments that, in fact, there may be differences; thus, Frankl (1979) finds that size is not a significant determinant of R and D, suggesting that, in fact, the use of industry level data will swamp any firm size effects.

Howe and McFetridge (1976) make explicit an economic theory of the first which shows that R and D will be continued to the point where the expected marginal return from that investment is just equal to its cost. They derive a reduced form equation from this model which they then test. Klein (1946) has shown that the first order conditions for maximization of individual units will also hold in the aggregate; thus, we can feel comfortable in using models or rationales such as theirs with industry level data.[5]

The definition of R and D that we shall use is that by Statistics Canada: "any systematic and creative work undertaken in order to increase the stock of knowledge . . . and the use of this knowledge to devise new applications." R and D will be further broken down into current and capital expenditures.

THEORY AND SPECIFICATION

This section of the chapter outlines the independent variables to be used in attempting to explain the variation in R and D for a sample of Canadian industries. We discuss the rationale for including these variables and compare our equations with those of Globerman (1973), Howe and McFetridge (1976), and Frankl (1979).

The phrases "foreign owned" and "foreign controlled" are used somewhat loosely and interchangeably in the literature. The concept of control and the form of the foreign ownership variable in a regression equation warrant careful discussion. Since we shall be using data from the Statistics Canada annual reports for the Corporations and Labour Unions Returns Act (CALURA), their Statistics Canada definition of control will be used: "in the absence of conclusive evidence to the contrary, a corporation is considered to be foreign controlled if 50 per cent or more of its voting rights are known to be held outside Canada or are held by one or more Canadian corporations that are themselves foreign controlled."[6] Thus a firm is either controlled by a foreign country or controlled domestically, a classic attribute variable. In this industry level study, the percentage of foreign owned assets will be used as an indication of the number of foreign controlled firms, and foreign ownership will be a continuous variable. We could expect that industries with 100 percent foreign owned assets would consist of firms that are foreign controlled and that the industries with about 2 percent foreign owned assets would be almost exclusively domestically controlled firms. High concentration ratios accompanied by high foreign ownership would virtually guarantee that firm control and industry ownership were similar.

The impact of size on R and D is ambiguous in the literature. At the industry level both the size of the industry and the level of concentration affect the size of the firm, and it is at the firm level that most discussion has taken place. Hamberg (1966) and Howe and McFetridge (1976) use a cubic function for size, but both are working at the firm level. The most emphatic in his inclusion of the size variable is Hamberg, who suggests that both sales and assets provide reasonable proxies for size, but that the addition of profits may lead to multicollinearity problems between sales and profits. However, Hamberg does note that if R and D is measured by employment, there is a strong positive correlation between R and D and size among large companies. At the industry level some cognizance must be taken of the relationship between the size and concentration of firms in a fixed size industry. The *a priori* arguments propounded for and against size as a determining variable are conflicting.[7] Daly (1979) reports on the empirical findings for the dependency of R and D on size. He suggests that the size of the market dictates a low level of R and D to Canadian firms, both Canadian and foreign owned. Furthermore, he reports on McFetridge's and Weatherby's (1977) results as showing that "there is no tendency for the proportion of expenditure on R and D to rise as firm size rises in Canada and that in general the size–progressiveness relation has little to commend" (McFetridge and Weatherby 1977, p. 241).

In this study preliminary regressions were run using size as an independent variable. Neither size nor size squared was significant and, in the light of the previous discussion, they were included as independent variables in the regressions reported in this paper.

Technology has been treated in a somewhat unsatisfactory manner in the literature. It is usually an attribute variable by which the sample can be broken up into subgroups of "technologically advanced" and "technologically less advanced" industries. Thus Globerman (1973) stratifies his sample into four groups and, with this grouping, finds his foreign ownership concentration index and growth variables insignificant. Only by partitioning his sample into two groups can he find significant results and then only for those industries that are technologically advanced. Frankl (1979) identifies technologically advanced industries as those whose R and D intensity in the U.S. is above the mean R and D intensity, without further explanation. Scherer (1965) provides some rationale for classifying industries as more or less advanced according to the relationship between patents filed and the level of sales. This, however, is not so much an indication of technological advance in an industry as it is technological opportunity or, in Scherer's words: "the vigorous scientific climate of those fields [which are advanced] has assured a continuous supply of new technical possibilities exploitable to satisfy existing or latent demands. In effect, science and technology exert a push on inventive output in these fields."[8]

An alternative approach to the measurement of R and D activity would be to use the "Probable Industry of Potential Use of Canadian Patented Inventions."[9] The rationale for this would be Scherer's argument that the number of patents filed provides a proxy for the level of R and D activity in an industry.

> In spite of their shortcomings, patent statistics seem to be a useful indicator of inventive activity. They should indicate in which industries the search for new or improved processes is most intense and how this intensity changes over time. They should indicate the relative effort devoted to R and D in different fields and the types of inventions developed.[10]

Unfortunately, these figures were not correlated with either the total or current R and D activity figures and this attempt to find an alternative measure of R and D was abandoned. We shall use Globerman's index of technology.

Government incentive grants commonly have been used as an independent variable, for example in Hamberg (1966), Globerman (1973), Howe and McFetridge (1976), and Hewitt (1980b). The argument for their inclusion is simply that, in Hamberg's words, "in an era in which the . . . government . . . finances some sixty percent of total private industry spending on R and D, government R and D contracts are an obvious candidate for inclusion in our regression model."[11] The figure is lower in Canada but the point is the same.

Since government grants would encourage R and D we expect a positive coefficient for this variable; but to the extent that the government grants finance work which would have been undertaken anyway, it is possible that a one dollar grant results in less than a one dollar increase in R and D. If variables in ratio form are used this would result in a negative coefficient for government grants. At the industry level we expect that the government would choose to support different industries at different levels.[12] The distribution of those grants among different firms in a given industry is not relevant to our discussion.

We had difficulty finding figures for government incentive grants broken down by industry. Figures are available for groups of industries but not disaggregated to the level that we require. Also, there were insufficient yearly observations to extrapolate figures satisfactorily. Since we are only concerned with the relatively short period 1974–77, we have used the same—1974—government grants data for each year. These figures could have been inflated each year by the increase in GNP, say, slightly changing our regression results. Since the significance of our regression coefficients is of interest, and not their sizes, this slight bias was not considered important.

The inclusion of concentration also originates with Schumpeter (1950), and this variable is expected to be positively correlated with R and D. Thus Howe and McFetridge and Globerman both use concentration as an explanatory variable, but neither finds a significant result. Rather than using the Herfindahl index, CALURA produces a concentration ratio of the 33 major industry groups. This value will range between 0 and 100.

THE DATA

There are no published data on R and D undertaken by subsidiaries of multinational firms in Canada. The data made generally available by Statistics Canada are at the industry level, although some researchers such as Hewitt, Frankl and Howe and McFetridge have had access to firm level data.

To my knowledge, no author has carefully examined the available industry level data and deduced the kind of firm behavior which would be consistent with that data. Some theoretical work has been done on the statistical properties of aggregation,[13] but it has not yet been applied in this area. There are some advantages in this approach over the sample survey method. The industry level data are readily and freely (for all intents and purposes) available and do not suffer from the possible bias of survey data admitted by the surveyors.[14] The statistics in future years should improve as the Statistics Canada statistics have longer runs. Finally, such an analysis will allow for better comparison between firm level and industry level studies and could even provide a check on the possible bias in survey results.

The data set was created by reconciling the Science Statistics and CALURA classifications of industries at the two-digit level. We have retained the appropriate numbering from CALURA. This consolidated list is almost identical with Globerman's. Of these seventeen classifications, numbers 15 and 17 are probably too diverse to be legitimately called "industries" but will be included because of the severe problem of limited degrees of freedom.

RESULTS AND DATA INTERPRETATION

Preliminary analysis suggests that over the four years 1974–77 all variables are highly serially correlated and, in fact, the best predictor of R and D is previous R and D. Initially, unscaled regressions were run using S and S^2 as independent variables; neither of these variables was significant in the scaled or unscaled regressions and hence were dropped from consideration. The impression gained from these

TABLE 3.1

Results for the Estimation of the Equation
$$CRD = B_0 + B_1 FC + B_2 CON + B_3 NP + B_4 GRT + \epsilon$$

Coefficient	Years			
	1974	1975	1976	1977
Constant	12.900	12.0	5.76	14.30
FC	0.065	6.6	0.03	0.39
	(0.26)	(0.44)	(0.12)	(1.20)
CON	-1.40	3.50	0.34	-1.14
	(-0.10)	(-0.22)	(0.85)	(-0.94)
NP	-0.00	0.01	0.00	-0.00
	(-0.03)	(0.98)	(-0.04)	(-0.24)
GRT	3.10*	3.30*	3.64*	4.14*
	(4.41)	(4.01)	(4.50)	(4.70)
R^2	65.70	63.90	67.60	75.30

*These coefficients are different from zero at the 1% significance level.

TABLE 3.2

Results for the Estimation of the Equation
$$CRD/S = B_0 + B_1 FC + B_2 CON + B_3 NP/EQ + B_4 GRT/S + \epsilon$$

Coefficient	Years			
	1974	1975	1976	1977
Constant	2.92	1.91	0.608	2.57
FC	0.01	0.03	0.010	0.02
	(0.31)	(0.54)	(0.22)	(0.59)
CON	-1.33	-1.32	0.02	0.00
	(-0.52)	(-0.50)	(0.34)	(0.03)
NP/EQ	-7.40	-6.10	-3.20	-13.70
	(-0.44)	(-0.38)	(-0.21)	(-0.83)
CRT/S	5.51*	6.26*	6.66*	7.40*
	(4.43)	(4.25)	(4.20)	(4.69)
R^2	64.6	62.7	64.2	73.7

*These coefficients are different from zero at the 1% significance level.

regressions is that the government grants for R and D variable (GRT/S) is the only robust independent variable in the group. Given that only the one variable is consistently significant, the R^2 values are surprisingly high. The technology variable is the Globerman index of technological progressivity which we have used as a dummy variable. The technology variable is not significant, while in Globerman's study only one set of industries (the technologically progressive ones) gave significant results. We repeated Globerman's experiment with eleven "technologically superior" industries for the 1977 data. It led to no improvement in our results. The variables for these eleven industries are denoted by a star. Omitting the size variables and regressing R and D on foreign control, concentration, net profit, and government grants for each of the four years produced one significant coefficient. Furthermore, scaling the variables and regressing the ratio of R and D to sales on foreign control, concentration, the ratio of net profit to equity, and the ratio of government grants to sales produced similar results. These results are produced in the accompanying tables. The conclusion to be drawn from these regressions is that government spending alone is a positive determinant of R and D expenditure at the industry level.

The significance of R and D grants in every permutation of the regression equations supports the results of Globerman for nine industries and (at firm level) of Howe and McFetridge and Hewitt for the electrical industry. We find that R and D will be higher in industries where government grants are higher. This result is not obscured by any competitive interfirm effects which may be the cause of the poor results of Howe and McFetridge and Hewitt. In our case the policy decision is to provide R and D grants to industries, and the distribution of those grants to individual firms is not a point of issue.

Globerman's equation (1) has only one significant coefficient, that of the G variable. Globerman's results are consistent with any of our equations in Tables 3.1 and 3.2. Only by deleting "technologically poor" industries does Globerman achieve a significant (positive) coefficient for foreign control. Running the regression equivalent to Globerman's for 1977 does not produce any outstanding improvement in the foreign control coefficient so again, this path was not explored. It is difficult to compare industry level results with Howe and McFetridge's firm level results.

CONCLUSIONS

The major finding in this chapter is that only the amount of federal government grants for R and D is significant and positively related to R and D expenditures. All other variables specified according to theory are found to be insignificant. In particular, R and D is not affected by foreign control or by the concentration ratio.

Although these results are less than satisfactory, a closer examination of the related literature in this field shows similarly weak results. Here one variable (grants) has been found to be significant across seventeen industries. No other empirical work on R and D has done as well.

Why do the econometric studies of the determinants of R and D have such poor explanatory power? The answer may well be that R and D is not causally determined by the variables specified but, instead, is determined conjointly with them. A simultaneous equation model could be developed in which R and D and profitability are jointly determined by variables such as foreign control, concentration, grants, size, and so on. The specification of such a model is outside the terms of reference of this study, but it presents a challenge for future work on R and D in Canada.

APPENDIX 3.1

List of Symbols Used

TRD   Total R and D, including capital expenditures

CRD   Current R and D

IRD   An index of R and D—the percentage of patents which might be potentially used in an industry

CON   Concentration—the percentage of the market controlled by the top four firms

DCON   A dummy variable for concentration where "1" indicates a concentration of at least 45 percent and "0" less than 45 percent

FC   Foreign control—the percentage of the sales of an industry made by firms which are foreign controlled, i.e., have more than 50 percent foreign ownership

S   Sales

GRT   The level of government grants for intramural R and D, excluding grants received under IRDIA

NP   Net profit before taxes

ASS   Total assets

EQ   Total equity

TEC   A dummy variable to indicate high (1) and low (0) technological opportunity in an industry

All regressions were run using the MINITAB Statistical package copyrighted by Pennsylvania State University, 1980.

NOTES

1. The research assistance of Roland Ghamen and the comments of Alan M. Rugman, Y. B. Yalawar and P. J. Rosson are gratefully acknowledged.
2. See Alan M. Rugman who cites an MOSST Background Paper from 1977 in *Internalization and the Transfer of Technology to Canada*, Centre for International Business Studies, Dalhousie University, 1980, published in Rugman (1981a). Mimeograph. Many others have made the same observation. See, among others, S. Globerman, "Market Structure and R and D in Canadian Manufacturing

Industries," *Quarterly Review of Economics and Business*, Vol. 13 (1973), p. 59.

3. See *A Science Policy for Canada*, the Report of the Special Committee on Science Policy, Ottawa: Queen's Printer, Vol. 1 (1970), pp. 1–37 for a brief review of the development of science policy in Canada.

4. See, for example, G. K. Hewitt, "A thorough testing of this study's model would require enough *firm* level data . . . but . . . industries must be treated as if they were firms. Despite these problems, it remains true that the empirical test was inspired by the study's scenario and offers some indication of the latter's plausibility." In "Research and Development Performed Abroad by U.S. Manufacturing Multinationals," *Kyklos*, Vol. 33 (June 1980), p. 311.

5. See L. R. Klein, "Macroeconomics and the Theory of Rationale Behaviour," *Econometrica*, Vol. 14 (1946), pp. 93–108.

6. Canada, Statistics Canada, *Corporations and Labour Unions Returns Act Report for 1977, Part 1 – Corporations* (Ottawa: Queen's Printer, 1980): 97.

7. For theoretical discussions see H. H. Villard, "Competition, Oligopoly and Research," *Journal of Political Economy*, Vol. 66 (1958), pp. 483–97; J. Schmookler, "Bigness, Fewness and Progress," *Journal of Political Economy*, Vol. 67 (1959), pp. 628–32; F. M. Scherer, "Firm Size, Market Structure, Opportunity and the Output of Patented Inventions," *American Economic Review*, Vol. 55 (1965), pp. 1097–1125; and A. E. Safarian, *Foreign Ownership of Canadian Industry*, 1966. 2nd ed. (Toronto: University of Toronto Press, 1973). Empirical work is reported by Safarian, Villard, Globerman and Howe and McFetridge.

8. F. M. Scherer, "Firm Size, Market Structure, Opportunity and the Output of Patented Inventions," *American Economic Review*, Vol. 55 (December 1965), p. 1100.

9. Canada, Statistics Canada, *Annual Review of Science Statistics 1977* (Ottawa: Queen's Printers, 1979), p. 49.

10. F. M. Scherer, "Firm Size, Market Structure, Opportunity and the Output of Patented Inventions," *American Economic Review*, Vol. 55 (December 1965), p. 1098.

11. D. Hamberg, *op. cit.*, p. 123.

12. See J. D. Howe and D. G. McFetridge, "The Determinants of R and D Expenditures," *Canadian Journal of Economics*, Vol. IX (February 1976), p. 62, and also for a list of incentive programs and a source for their description.

13. See H. Theil, *Linear Aggregation of Economic Relations* (Amsterdam: North Holland, 1965); H. A. John Green, *Aggregation in Economic Analysis* (Princeton: Princeton University Press, 1964); W. D. Fisher, *Clustering and Aggregation in Economic Analysis* (Baltimore: Johns Hopkins, 1969); L. R. Klein, "Macroeconomics and the Theory of Rational Behaviour," *Econometrica*, Vol. 14 (1946), pp. 93–108; and the discussion generated by Klein's article in the rest of volume 14.

14. See *ex gratia* A. E. Safarian, *Foreign Ownership of Canadian Industry*, 1966. 2nd ed. (Toronto: University of Toronto Press, 1973), pp. 29–49.

4

Research and Development Performed in Canada by American Manufacturing Multinationals

Gary K. Hewitt

INTRODUCTION

The research and development function is not one that can be easily decentralized. In spite of their desire to make maximum use of the capabilities of their foreign units, most companies cooperating in the survey make limited use of them for R & D. In spite of pressures to decentralize research activity, most companies carry out the bulk of it in the United States.

M. G. Duerr, "R & D in the Multinational Company—A Survey"[1]

Duerr's finding about the centralization of research and development (R & D) within U.S. parent companies certainly should have surprised no one in Canada. Four years before Duerr's extensive survey, A. E. Safarian took a close look at 280 foreign owned multinational enterprises operating in Canada. Of these, 227 were controlled in the United States. Safarian discovered that on a relative basis, most of the 227 Canadian subsidiaries spent considerably less on R & D than did their parent companies.[2]

The research reported here was supported by a grant from the Centre for International Business Studies, Dalhousie University and was first discussed in Gary K. Hewitt, "Research and Development Performed in Canada by American Manufacturing Multinationals," mimeograph. Dalhousie Discussion Paper in International Business, No. 3 (1980b). The author wishes to thank Alan Rugman, Director of the Centre for International Business Studies, and Humphrey Stead, Mickey Robinson and Ruth McDougall, all of Statistics Canada, for their help and cooperation. Useful editorial comments were made by Jocelyn Bennett.

In a more recent study, the Canadian Ministry of State for Science and Technology (MOSST) compared the R & D expenditures and total technology related payments of domestic and foreign owned groups of firms in six high and medium research intensive industries. MOSST found that the foreign owned groups performed less R & D but still managed to record higher technology related payments (including R & D expenditures) than did the domestically owned groups.[3] This result supports the hypothesis that R & D is centralized within the parent companies of foreign owned multinationals.

MOSST has apparently been convinced by its own research, for without offering a supporting reference, a subsequent MOSST background paper stated: "It is doubtful that the R & D target (1.5 percent of GNP by 1985) can be reached unless the impact of foreign ownership on the amount of industrial R & D carried out in Canada is reversed."[4]

If the Canadian government becomes serious about changing "the impact of foreign ownership" it will need to understand the reasons behind R & D centralization within foreign owned multinationals. One way to explore and test those reasons is to perform multivariate regression analysis, designed to explain cross firm variation in the percent of R & D located outside the parent company of a sample of multinational enterprises. This was attempted in an earlier paper that focused on the worldwide R & D activities of American multinational manufacturing companies (AMMCs).[5] Unfortunately, because of a lack of appropriate firm level data, the study's regression work treated whole industries as single companies. The present chapter's regressions do away with that assumption by restricting attention to the percent of worldwide R & D located *in Canada* by AMMCs belonging to the electrical, machinery and chemical industries.

The Canadian R & D data used in this chapter's regressions were taken from Statistics Canada's biennial survey of all known or suspected R & D performers.[6] To preserve confidentiality, all the equations were run in Ottawa by Statistics Canada personnel. Obviously, this study could not have proceeded without the full cooperation of Statistics Canada.

The exact samples used in the regressions were initially composed of all the Canadian subsidiaries of U.S. manufacturing companies in the electrical, machinery and chemical (including pharmaceutical) industries who: filed R & D questionnaires with Statistics Canada (Education, Science and Culture Division) in 1973, 1975 and 1977; did some R & D in at least one of those three years; and made sales in all three years. The samples were then pruned to their final dimensions by excluding subsidiaries whose parents were not included in the *Business Week* 1975 and 1977 R & D surveys and in the Harvard University's Multinational Enterprise Project.

PREVIOUS WORK LINKED WITH THE NEW

At the heart of the earlier study was R. C. Ronstadt's discovery that foreign R & D within a typical AMMC will tend to grow once established and that rapid growth depends on a change in the purpose of foreign R & D.[7] Such a change depends on the firm consciously altering its worldwide business strategy and structure and advancing, in sequence, through the stages of: autonomous subsidiary, international division (ID) and global organization. Foreign R & D typically will commence during the autonomous subsidiary phase when U.S. product and process technologies are adapted to better suit foreign conditions. By the time the firm reaches the global stage, adaptive R & D conducted abroad will have either evolved into "local original" (i.e., country or region specific) R & D or been replaced with "global original" R & D. Both these R & D types are concerned with world first (i.e., original) product development rather than mere alterations of products or processes initially conceived for the U.S. market.

J. M. Stopford and L. T. Wells, Jr. have identified two basic types of global structure. The first, preferred by marketing oriented firms, is based on dividing the world into equally emphasized but separate area divisions. Each area would have its own regionally focused *local* original R & D. Within the more R & D intensive firms, global organization usually takes the form of worldwide product divisions, each conducting its own *global* original R & D.[8] We hypothesized that the percent of R & D located abroad should continue to grow during the global stage in marketing oriented firms but not necessarily do the same in R & D intensive multinationals. This is because the latter's foreign subsidiaries must win a part of the company's global R & D programs, or their R & D capability will wither away as adaptive work becomes more and more superfluous.

In a previous study, the evolutionary scenario sketched above was crudely tested with regressions explaining cross industry variation in *PFRD*—the percent of worldwide R & D located abroad by the multinational corporations belonging to twenty, two-digit American manufacturing industries. The regressions' ten independent variables accounted for 82 percent of the observed variation in *PFRD*. This excellent performance was obtained despite the absence of an explanatory variable reflecting cross industry differences in the cost advantage of a U.S. versus "rest of the world" R & D location. That omission plus its apparent unimportance would have been upsetting and surprising if the scenario had been built on the assumption that firms behave as fully informed profit maximizers. The scenario instead took a less traditional approach and modeled the companies as imperfectly informed, slow learning, "satisficers."[9] Encouraged by good empirical results, the present chapter leans heavily on the previous paper's scenario and its underlying satisficing approach.

Five of the nine independent variables used in the *PFRD* regressions obtained statistically significant coefficients. Three of the significant five have close parallels in this chapter's regressions. They are:

1. *GLOBE*—a dummy variable equal to unity for firms whose parents had, *in 1970*, global organization structures and equal to zero for firms having international divisions (the pertinent data were supplied by W. H. Davidson of the Amos Tuck School of Business Administration, Dartmouth College, and formerly connected with the Harvard University Multinational Enterprise Project— HMEP);

2. *LAGE*—the log of the years elapsed since the Canadian subsidiary was acquired or set up [this is based primarily on unpublished data collected in the HMEP. Whenever possible, the data were corrected to conform with information found in Marshall, Southard, and Taylor (1936)];

3. *LWRDI*—the log of the total company financed R & D conducted either by the Canadian subsidiary's parent or any of its worldwide subsidiaries divided by the group's worldwide sales [the data were taken from *Business Week* (1976, 62-76; 1977, 62-84; and 1978, 58-77)].

In addition to the three overlapping variables, there are another two appearing exclusively in the present study's regressions. They are:

1. *PGSUP*—the percent of a Canadian subsidiary's total current R & D accounted for by Canadian Federal Government R & D incentive grants made under the DIP, DIR, PAIT, and IRAP programs (the data were contained in the RDCI Historical File maintained by the Education, Science and Culture Division of Statistics Canada);[10] and

2. *POWN*—the percent of the Canadian subsidiary's shares owned by the controlling U.S. parent company [the data were published in Canada, Statistics Canada (1978 and 1979)].

There are two dependent variables used in this chapter's regressions. The first is *RC/RW*—the Canadian subsidiary's current (as opposed to capital) R & D divided by the *company financed* current R & D performed worldwide by the multinational enterprise that the subsidiary is a part of. Notice that the denominator is confined to self-financed current R & D while the numerator contains *all* current R & D however financed. In an attempt to eliminate this inconsistency, a new dependent variable, *ERC/RW*, was created by subtracting from *RC/RW*'s numerator all R & D financed by government grants or performed under contract. This was probably an over correction since a small part of the grants and a still smaller fraction of the contract support could have been earmarked for capital R & D.

Although it is certain that *RC/RW*'s numerator contains only current R & D, the same could be deduced only about the denominator. This deduction was based on the statement that: "*Business Week*'s survey drawn from 10-K data indicates that companies are now filing much the same data to both the Census Bureau and the SEC."[11] Since the Census Bureau conducts the National Science Foundation's (NSF's) annual R & D survey, it can be assumed that the R & D data it collects will conform to the definition laid down by the NSF. The NSF's 1975 *R & D in Industry* report indicated that R & D costs were factored into: wages, materials and supplies, and other costs (defined in the questionnaire to include service and supporting costs, depreciation, and share of overhead).[12] These are the separate components of current R & D. We conclude, therefore, that what the NSF (and the Census Bureau) refers to as R & D can be more accurately described as *current* R & D.

PREDICTED REGRESSION COEFFICIENTS

Before discussing the probable relation of *GLOBE* to *RC/RW* and *ERC/RW*, it is necessary to elaborate on what *GLOBE* measures. The Harvard Multinational Enterprise project classified AMMCs as having either: autonomous subsidiaries with domestic functional divisions, the same, but with domestic product divisions, international activities coordinated through an international division (*ID*), or a global structure wherein the world market is divided into either area or worldwide product divisions, whose top managers enjoy equal access to the AMMC's president.[13] All firms included in our study's regressions had parents possessing either *ID* or global structure. In practice, then, *GLOBE* will measure the impact of a firm's parent having global instead of *ID* organization.

Ranked by R & D as a percent of sales, the electrical, machinery and chemical industries respectively held first (tied with transportation equipment), fourth and fifth places among the fourteen approximately two-digit classifications reported in the American National Science Foundation's 1975 *R & D in Industry* report.[14] It follows that the AMMCs belonging to these industries should fall into the R & D intensive rather than marketing intensive classification. If this is true, then *GLOBE*'s regression coefficient could be positive or negative since R & D intensive firms do not systematically increase or decrease their R & D when they switch from *ID* to global organization structures.

The log of the number of years elapsed since a subsidiary was acquired or set up, *LAGE*, is expected to obtain a positive regression coefficient in all three industries. This prediction is based on the assumption that sample subsidiaries did little or no R & D when they initially began manufacturing in Canada. As time passed, however, firms became better informed about Canadian R & D costs and opportunities and responded by curtailing or expanding their Canadian R & D facilities. There is no upper limit to the expansion option, but contracting an already small R & D operation usually means eliminating it entirely.

The next independent variable, *LWRDI*, was included in the earlier cross industry study because in concert with *LAI* (the log of advertising divided by sales), it was supposed to reflect the R & D versus marketing intensity of the firm. As such, *LWRDI* was expected to have a negative coefficient and *LAI* a positive one, because at all organization stages the marketing intensive firms should be more willing to decentralize R & D than are their R & D intensive cousins. As things turned out, *LAI*'s coefficient was statistically insignificant but *LWRDI*'s was significant and negative as expected. This led to a reconsideration of exactly what *LWRDI* was measuring.

It is now hypothesized that, other things equal, a firm's *LWRDI* should be greater the larger the proportion of its total R & D composed of original as opposed to adaptive work. As an inverse index of adaptive R & D intensity, *LWRDI* should be negatively related to the percent of worldwide R & D located in a Canadian subsidiary since it is easier and more necessary to decentralize adaptive as compared with original R & D.

Despite the new and hopefully superior motivation for running *LWRDI* in the regressions, curiosity alone would have provided sufficient reason to include *LAI* as well. Nonetheless, *LAI* was omitted because it was only available for 1975 and for just eight of the fourteen electrical firms, five of the eleven machinery companies and twenty-three of the twenty-six chemical firms in our regression samples.

LAGE and *LWRDI* are run as logarithms because they are *theoretically* unbounded whereas the dependent variables are upper bounded at unity.[15] This immediately creates the possibility of a nonlinear relationship which log forms can accommodate but linear specifications cannot.

PGSUP is the only independent variable which reflects the cost advantages or disadvantages of a Canadian R & D site. To the extent that the Canadian government is willing to subsidize R & D performed in Canada, firms should respond by increasing the share of total R & D located there. The same does not necessarily apply to the share of *self-financed* R & D located in Canada.[16] A positive regression coefficient is expected for *PGSUP* in the regressions having *RC/RW* as the dependent variable, but no clear prediction can be made vis-a-vis the *ERC/RW* counterpart equations.

Ideally *PGSUP* should have been divided by the percent of the relevant parent's non-Canadian R & D paid for by grants from non-Canadian governments. Such data are unavailable. In running an undeflated *PGSUP*, we are assuming an equal degree of non-Canadian government support enjoyed by all firms. Though perhaps unrealistic regarding any one non-Canadian government, this assumption is a good deal more plausible considering all such governments taken together.

For the last independent variable, *POWN*, a good case can be made for expecting either a positive or negative regression coefficient. On the one hand, an AMMC will discourage subsidiary R & D performance if this risks *unnecessary* sharing of worldwide monopoly rents with Canadian minority owners (i.e., *POWN* should have a positive coefficient). Such sharing will be unnecessary unless the Canadian shareholders provide an otherwise unavailable or prohibitively expensive R & D resource. On the other hand, if the R & D results promise to be sufficiently subsidiary specific, an AMMC might encourage subsidiary performance when this provides a low cost means to ensure that minority owners bear a share of the R & D costs (i.e., *POWN* should have a negative coefficient).

Some readers may wonder why Canadian sales as a percent of the enterprise's worldwide total (*PSALE*) was excluded from this study's regressions. There are two reasons for that. First, the scenario lying behind the empirical work provided no role for *PSALE*; and second, when *PSALE* was tried at an earlier stage in the work it consistently failed to obtain a statistically significant regression coefficient.

REGRESSION RESULTS

In an effort to increase effective sample sizes, each regression was first run pooling the data from 1975 and 1977 (i.e., the same firm in 1975 and 1977 was treated as two separate firms). Each equation was then rerun using dummy variables to allow all the independent variables (including the constant) to obtain different coefficients according to whether the underlying data were from 1975 or 1977. Whenever an "F" test found no statistically significant difference in the sum of squared residuals between the pooled and fully dummied regressions, only the pooled results will be displayed.

Tables 4.1 and 4.2 contain the results obtained using *RC/RW* and *ERC/RW* respectively as dependent variables.

In terms of statistically significant coefficients, only in the 1975 electrical industry does a change in dependent variable make any real difference. The *ERC/RW* version of that industry's regressions shows statistically significant coefficients for the constant, *LWRDI* and *POWN*; but none of these was statistically significant in the *RC/RW* variant. Except for the 1975 electrical industry, Table 4.2 will be ignored in the analysis to follow.

The results overall were somewhat disappointing since there was just one case in which *GLOBE* attained statistical significance, three instances of a significant coefficient for *LWRDI*, and one each for *PGSUP* and *POWN*. *LAGE* failed to reach statistical significance in any industry.

Weakness in *GLOBE* and *POWN* is not particularly embarrassing since both were included more as a backdrop to the other independent variables (i.e., to maintain *ceteris paribus* conditions) than as a direct test of the study's underlying "scenario." This is certainly not true though for *LAGE, LWRDI* and *PGSUP*.

The best and most enigmatic single performance was made by *LWRDI* because it was significant in three out of the four industries

TABLE 4.1

Dependent Variable—RC/RW

Independent Variables	Electrical 1975	Electrical 1977	Machinery	Chemical
C	.093859 (1.222)	-.63224 (-3.051)†	-.259202 (-2.057)*	-.029602 (-1.256)
GLOBE	-.006588 (-.573)	.070515 (2.571)†	.005463 (.281)	.004519 (.625)
LAGE	.005804 (.993)	-.002414 (-.1556)	.008489 (1.076)	.006059 (1.502)
LWRDI	.030241 (1.840)	-.148662 (-3.189)†	-.050534 (-2.914)†	-.006184 (-1.385)
PGSUP	.130457 (2.935)†	-.153978 (-1.798)	-.023220 (-.350)	-.013442 (-.429)
POWN	.022078 (.773)	.019997 (.200)	.080316 (.772)	.000586 (.230)
R^2	.75	—‡	.44	.08
Number of observations	14	14	22	52
F	4.8938†	—‡	2.5401*	.7868

*Significant at the 90% level (two tailed test).
†Significant at the 95% level (two tailed test).
‡The pertinent R^2 and F statistics are unavailable because time and money were exhausted before this regression could be run entirely separately.

but had a positive instead of negative sign in the 1975 electrical industry. We can think of no good reason for that unexpected sign or for the considerable difference observed overall between the 1975 and 1977 electrical results.

The chemical industry won the distinction of being the only one with an insignificant "F" statistic. This prompted a more in-depth look which led to separate regressions being run for its largest three-digit component. Table 4.3 shows the results when the regressions were run separately for the pharmaceutical and nonpharmaceutical parts of the chemical industry.

The findings for the pharmaceutical industry were quite pleasing because both *LWRDI* and *PGSUP* registered statistically significant coefficients having the predicted signs. Insignificance, however, remained complete in the nonpharmaceutical subpart.

TABLE 4.2

Dependent Variable—ERC/RW

Independent Variables	Electrical 1975	Electrical 1977	Machinery	Chemical
C	.095042	-.589683	-.241352	-.027220
	(1.930)*	(-3.001)†	(-1.943)*	(-1.188)
GLOBE	-.004373	.059623	.006613	.004935
	(-.594)	(2.293)*	(.345)	(.702)
LAGE	.000483	.001395	.007426	.005677
	(.129)	(.095)	(.954)	(1.448)
LWRDI	.031237	-.144592	-.049433	-.005711
	(2.965)†	(-3.272)†	(-2.891)†	(-1.316)
PGSUP	.063038	-.091601	-.048709	-.019546
	(2.212)*	(-1.128)	(-.745)	(-.641)
POWN	.042640	-.018457	.070004	.000532
	(2.329)†	(-.194)	(.682)	(.214)
R^2	.78	—‡	.47	.08
Number of observations	14	14	22	52
F	5.7084†	—‡	2.7950*	.7636

*Significant at the 90% level (two tailed test).
†Significant at the 95% level (two tailed test).
‡The pertinent R^2 and F statistics are unavailable because time and money were exhausted before this regression could be run entirely separately.

TABLE 4.3

Independent Variables	Dependent Variable— RC/RW		Dependent Variable— ERC/RW	
	Pharma-ceuticals	Nonpharma-ceutical Chemicals	Pharma-ceuticals	Nonpharma-ceutical Chemicals
C	-.112400 (-2.235)*	-.012577 (-.709)	-.114247 (-2.247)*	-.015049 (-.791)
GLOBE	.006115 (.489)	-.000114 (-.022)	.006388 (.505)	-.000996 (-.179)
LAGE	.003026 (.370)	.004015 (1.528)	.002936 (.355)	.004485 (1.590)
LWRDI	-.035981 (-2.573)*	-.003502 (-1.078)	-.036598 (-2.589)*	-.004004 (-1.148)
PGSUP	1.00562 (2.205)*	-.001804 (-.687)	1.06758 (2.315)*	-.005480 (-.297)
R^2	.45	.13	.46	.13
No. of obser-vations	22	30	22	30
F	3.4883*	.9258	3.6543*	.943

*Significant at the 95% level (two tailed test).

CONCLUSIONS

The most obvious point to note about the present study is its weakness in terms of confirming the previous paper's findings. There are four general explanations that can be offered for this:

1. Differences in dependent variables. It is possible that Canada constitutes a special case in the sense that the reasons for locating R & D in Canada are different from the reasons for placing it anywhere else outside the United States. Data pertinent to assessing Canada's comparative advantage as an R & D location would have to be found to further pursue this line of questioning.

2. Differences in independent variables. We are thinking especially of *DTINT* and *XUSI* which performed well in the industry level work but have no counterparts in the present study's regressions. *DTINT* reflected the technical intensity of each U.S. industry and *XUSI* was the industry level percent of majority owned affiliate sales accounted for by exports to the United States.

3. The three industries examined in this study are fundamentally different from the other industries included in the earlier work. Chow tests were employed to thoroughly investigate this possibility. At the 99 percent confidence level, we could *not* reject the hypothesis that the three electrical industries found in the original industry level study were drawn from a different universe than the other seventeen industries. This also applied, at the 95 percent confidence level, to the previous paper's five chemical industries. In contrast, even at the very liberal 90 percent confidence level, the same hypothesis was *rejected* for the three machinery industries included earlier. It follows that the electrical and chemical industries might indeed be special cases but the machinery industry probably is not.

4. There are some variables omitted from both the firm and industry level work that could have a serious effect on the former but not on the latter. This refers to any relevant characteristic which varies greatly from company to company but little from industry to industry. A good example of this is country of residence preferences on the part of key scientists and engineers. As another example consider subsidiaries acquired by takeover who had an R & D capability at the time of takeover. Such subsidiaries are, *ceteris paribus*, much more likely to retain R & D functions than are other subsidiaries to acquire them later. This would account for a significant part of the interfirm variation in *RC/RW*. The same would not be true for cross industry variation in *RC/RW* unless there is considerable difference across industries in the propensity to take control of subsidiaries already having R & D activities.

Canadian government policy makers should perhaps take a close look at this chapter's findings. In particular they might be persuaded by *PGSUP*'s dismal empirical performance to re-think whether direct government grants are an effective way to encourage Canadian R & D within AMMCs, especially for firms belonging to the machinery and chemical (excluding pharmaceuticals) industries. The *POWN* results could also stimulate a policy review of the attempts to encourage Canadian equity participation in foreign owned firms.[17]

POWN's regression coefficients indicate that increased Canadian shareholdings in U.S. controlled subsidiaries will at best have no effect on their R & D spendings and might even reduce them. It should be remembered that R & D is a prime example of what firms seek to internalize in order to avoid the high costs of using open markets.[18] The cost savings of internalizing R & D transactions are immediately reduced when minority shareholders can insist on an accurate and fair accounting for all inter-company sales of technology to their particular subsidiary.

There are four practical ways in which this study's empirical work could be improved:

extend to other industries;

restrict attention to what is happening within three-digit rather than two-digit industry aggregations (this will almost certainly require pooling data from different years in order to obtain respectable sample sizes);

include among the independent variables a simple count of the number of countries each AMMC is active in (this will provide a rough index of how well informed the firm is about R & D outside the United States and Canada); and

employ a dummy variable in the regressions to account for whether or not each company has ever acquired a Canadian subsidiary with an established R & D program.

NOTES

1. Michael G. Duerr, *R&D in the Multinational Company* (The Conference Board, 1970), p. 2.

2. A. E. Safarian, *Foreign Ownership of Canadian Industry* (University of Toronto Press, 2nd ed., 1973), pp. 182-88.

3. Canada, Ministry of State for Science and Technology, *R & D in Canadian and Foreign-controlled Manufacturing Firms*, MOSST Background Paper #9 (Ottawa: Department of Supply and Services, 1979), p. 2.

4. Canada, Ministry of State for Science and Technology, *R & D Policies, Planning and Programming*, MOSST Background Paper #13 (Ottawa: Department of Supply and Services, 1981), p. 24.

5. Gary K. Hewitt, "Research and Development Performed Abroad by U.S. Manufacturing Multinationals," *Kyklos* 33(2) (1980a): 308-27.

6. For a description of the survey and the firms included, see Canada, Statistics Canada, *Industrial Research and Development Expenditures in Canada* (Ottawa: Information Canada, 1976), Cat. No. 13-203, p. 9.

7. R. C. Ronstadt, "International R&D: The Establishment and Evolution of Research and Development Abroad by Seven U.S. Multinational Enterprises," *Journal of International Business* 8 (1978): 7-24.

8. J. M. Stopford and L. T. Wells, Jr., *Managing the Multinational Enterprise/ Organization of the Firm and Ownership of the Subsidiary* (New York: Basic Books, 1972), pp. 54-58.

9. For an introduction to what is involved in the "satisficing" approach, see H. A. Simon, *Administrative Behavior* (New York: Macmillan, 1957), or

R. M. Cyert and J. G. March, *A Behavioral Theory of the Firm* (Englewood Cliffs, N.J.: Prentice-Hall, 1963).

10. For descriptions of the Defense Industry Productivity program, the Defense Industry Research program, the Program for the Advancement of Industrial Technology and the Industrial Research Assistance Program, see respectively: Canada, Department of Industry, Trade and Commerce, *Defense Industry Productivity Program* (Ottawa: Information Canada, 1973a); Canada, Defense Research Board, *The Defense Industrial Research Program* (Ottawa: Defense Research Board, 1968); Canada, Department of Industry, Trade and Commerce, *Program for the Advancement of Industrial Technology* (Ottawa: Information Canada, 1973b); and National Research Council, *Industrial Research Assistance Program, Information for Applicants* (Ottawa: Department of Supply and Services, 1978).

11. *Business Week*, "Survey of Corporate Research and Development Spending: 1975," June (1976): 63.

12. See National Science Foundation, *Research and Development in Industry, 1975* (Washington: U.S. Government Printing Office, 1977): 46 and 82.

13. For further details and sources pertinent to the organization classifications, see J. P. Curhan and J. W. Vaupel, *The Making of Multinational Enterprise— A Sourcebook of Tables Based on a Study of 187 Major U.S. Manufacturing Corporations* (Boston: Graduate School of Business Administration, Harvard University, 1969): 5.

14. See National Science Foundation, *Research and Development in Industry, 1975* (Washington: U.S. Government Printing Office, 1977): 59.

15. Strictly speaking, to avoid problems associated with running a limited dependent variable, RC/RW should have been replaced by $RC/(RW - RC)$. This was avoided here because RC/RW is directly motivated by this chapter's theorizing, and in regressions run for the previous industry level study, the two analogous dependent variables obtained practically identical results. See Gary K. Hewitt, "Research and Devleopment Performed Abroad by U.S. Manufacturing Multinationals," *Kyklos* 33(2) (1980a): 318.

16. Interested readers are directed to J. D. Howe and D. G. McFetridge, "The Determinants of R & D Expenditures," *The Canadian Journal of Economics* 9(1) (1976): 61–62 for a brief discussion of the effects of government R & D grants on the performance of self-financed R & D.

17. In the 1977 taxation year, foreign owned companies having 25 percent or more Canadian ownership paid a 20 percent instead of 25 percent withholding tax on remittances to their parent firms. See the Canadian Income Tax Act sections 212(3) and 257(1) cited in Canada, Foreign Investment Review Agency, *Selected Readings in Canadian Legislation Affecting Foreign Investment in Canada*, Part 1: Federal Laws and Regulations as of October 1977, FIRA Papers, No. 2 December (Ottawa: Department of Supply and Services, 1977): 39–41. Further evidence of a policy to encourage Canadian equity participation in foreign owned firms can be found in the so-called "Gillespie Guidelines." See Canada, Department of Industry, Trade and Commerce, *New Principles of International Business Conduct* (Ottawa: Department of Industry, Trade and Commerce, 1975).

18. For a survey of internalization literature, see Alan M. Rugman, "Internalization as a General Theory of Foreign Direct Investment," *Weltwirtschaftliches Archiv* 116(2) (1980): 365–79.

5

Lags in Product and Process Innovation Adoption by Canadian Firms

Kathryn E. McMullen

INTRODUCTION

The application of knowledge and insight in novel ways by firms results in the development of original innovations. These are the product of in-house R & D. Imitative innovations result from a process of diffusion of information and adoption of technologies already in use elsewhere by firms that recognize the application to themselves of technologies being employed by others. Imitative technologies can be developed through either in-house R & D or can be acquired from outside sources via intracorporate transfer, licensing arrangements, joint ventures, contracting of consultants, or other transfer arrangements.

Although both the development of original innovations and the adoption of imitative innovations are important, innovation adoption is dominant in Canada. Canada is not unique in this respect; firms in all countries draw upon an international pool of technology. It would be unrealistic to expect that any one country could consistently surpass all others in the innovative application of new and existing knowledge in all fields—the world technological system is an interdependent one.

The support of the Economic Council of Canada is gratefully acknowledged. Thanks are due to a number of people who were helpful during the course of the research, particularly Dr. Neil Swan for his comments and Peter Sinclair for his programming assistance. Any errors or omissions are, of course, the full responsibility of the author.

For every technology, each firm in an industry can be placed somewhere along the diffusion curve corresponding to that technology. For each firm and technology, therefore, there is a lag length measured from the date of first world use of a technology to the date of first use by any given firm. Adoption by a firm of a technology not previously used by that firm constitutes, from the perspective of that firm, adoption of an innovation. It is these—lags in innovation adoption—which form the units of analysis in this chapter. The purpose is to outline a model of innovation adoption lag lengths which identifies the factors that determine the place taken by Canadian firms in the innovation diffusion cycle. The data are drawn from the Economic Council of Canada Survey of Innovation which was conducted during 1979–80. It is briefly described in a later section.

The chapter is organized into five sections. The first section consists of a discussion and assessment of the relevant innovation diffusion literature. In the next section, a model of innovation adoption lag lengths based on, but more comprehensive than, existing lag length models found in the literature is outlined. This is followed by a brief description of the Economic Council of Canada Survey of Innovation from which the data for the analysis are taken. In the fourth section, the lag length model is expressed as a three-equation simultaneous system, the parameters of which are estimated using a three-stage least squares (3SLS) procedure. The fifth and final section consists of the conclusions and recommendations.

INNOVATION DIFFUSION: THE LITERATURE

Two complementary theories are useful in illustrating both the nature of changes that take place over time in the characteristics of innovations and innovation adopters and the reason why the efficient operation of the diffusion process is important from an industrial policy point of view. These are product life cycle theory and innovation diffusion theory.

According to product life cycle theory as outlined by Vernon (1966) and Wells (1972), in the early stage of a new product technology, price elasticity is comparatively low, unit profit margins and levels of risk are high, product changes are frequent and rapid, and production is skilled labor, rather than capital, intensive (see also Utterback 1979b). Over time, the demand curve becomes increasingly elastic, unit profit and risk levels decline, and product standardization occurs. Emphasis shifts from unique product characteristics to a reduction in production, particularly labor, costs, and an increase in capital intensity.

Empirical findings regarding the shape of the innovation diffusion curve show that, typically, the curve is logistic (Mansfield 1968). Early in the diffusion process there are relatively few firms in an industry which are willing (and able) to accept the risk involved in applying a new technology. Over time, uncertainty levels decrease as demand grows and more firms adopt the innovation. Near the end of the cycle, saturation levels are approached that result in a leveling off in the rate of innovation adoption.

An integration of product life cycle theory and innovation diffusion theory, as shown in Figure 5.1, demonstrates the benefits to be gained by early adoption. Implicit in this representation of the innovation diffusion process and the changing nature of innovations and innovation adopters over time is that innovation adoption is successful. At each stage, some firms attempt adoption but fail, with greater chances of failure early in the diffusion process. Firms that are successful early adopters are rewarded by high unit profits. Price elasticity is low, there are relatively few competitors, and production runs are short since frequent product changes are made in response to market signals. Capital intensity is low; instead, skilled labor is required. Since there are few, if any, foreign producers, exportability of the innovation is high. Over time, both market size and the number of producers increase. Increased competition reduces unit profit margins and the emphasis shifts to efficiency in production. As a result, production runs lengthen, capital intensity increases and the requirement is for cheap labor. Foreign competition increases, an important factor being abundant supplies of cheap labor in developing countries.

Some of the early studies of innovation diffusion examined the factors affecting the diffusion of agricultural innovations, as for example, that by Grilliches (1957). Spatial patterns of innovation diffusion were studied by geographers. Berry (1972) traced the diffusion of television stations and Hägerstrand (1972) used Markov chain analysis to model the pattern of information diffusion throughout a sample population. In these studies, evidence was found for two patterns of diffusion: (urban) hierarchical filtering and neighborhood (contagion) effects. More recently, economists' attention has shifted to the analysis of the diffusion of industrial innovations as it has become increasingly realized that both the development of new technologies as a result of research and development and the spread of

FIGURE 5.1

The Typical Diffusion Path of Innovations and Changes
in Product Life Cycle Characteristics Through Time

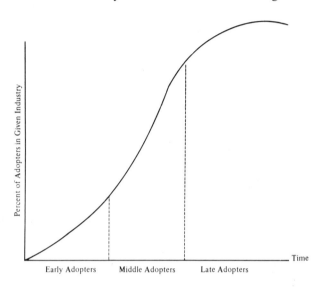

	Early	Growth	Mature
Risk	High	Decreasing	Low
Price elasticity	Low	Increasing	High
Unit profit margins	High	Decreasing	Low
Competition	On basis of product performance	Increasing standardization	On basis of product differentiation/price
Production runs	Short	Lengthening	Mass production
Factors of production	Skilled labor intensive; low capital intensity	Increasing capital intensity	Unskilled labor; capital intensive
Export potential	High	Growing investment abroad	Increasing import competition

Source: See L. T. Wells (ed.), *The Product Life Cycle and International Trade* (Cambridge, Mass.: Harvard University Press, 1972), pp. 3–33.

these new technologies throughout a population of potential adopters are important to industrial competitiveness.

Innovation can occur in several forms. It includes new and improved products, production processes, and organizational methods and structures. Often, innovation adoption by a firm involves changes of all three types. The study of innovation diffusion has commonly taken the form of determining, over time, the changing proportion of users among a potential population of adopters and has been measured by the proportion of firms (or output) in a given industry that uses (or is produced by) a given innovation.

Since it is the firm that is the adopting unit, we can ask: What factors affect the firm's decision *whether* to adopt a given innovation and what factors affect *when* actual adoption takes place? The growing body of industrial innovation diffusion literature represents the attempts of several researchers to answer these questions. Throughout this literature there are several common threads in terms of specific hypotheses tested and accepted (or rejected).

Several factors have been found to affect the rate of diffusion of innovations. Empirical work by Bernhardt (1970) and Sutton (1975) examined the impact of uncertainty on the rate of diffusion of catalytic cracking and computers, respectively. High levels of uncertainty retarded the rate of diffusion and uncertainty tended to decrease as an increasing proportion of potential users adopted the innovation.

Generally, although there are exceptions, profitability of the innovation has been found to have a positive influence on the diffusion rate (Mansfield 1968; Bernhardt 1970; Mansfield et al. 1971; Tilton 1971; Davies 1979). According to Mansfield (1968), cost of the innovation tends to be inversely related to the rate of its diffusion, a reflection of the higher risk attached to larger investments. Davies (1979), however, found no tendency for more costly innovations to diffuse more slowly. East of access to capital, particularly the availability of internally generated funds, acts to speed up innovation diffusion (Nabseth and Ray 1974).

Globerman (1974) discussed innovation diffusion rates in Canada relative to those in foreign countries and the factors affecting the rate of diffusion. Adoption proceeded at a slower rate in Canada than in other developed countries for which comparable data were available. Larger, more specialized firms in Canada were found to adopt innovations more quickly than smaller, more diversified firms as a result of scale economies and the benefits of "learning-by-doing." The probability of innovation adoption was found to be greater for firms investing explicitly in formal R & D activities (see also Nabseth and Ray 1974).

In another case study, Baumann (1973) found diffusion rates to be faster in Canada than in the United States. He concluded that in this case, use of the new process resulted in greater cost saving at a smaller scale of operation. Since the Canadian industry consisted of smaller firms than in the United States, the process diffused more rapidly in Canada. When these results are compared to those of Globerman (1974), it becomes apparent that diffusion rates are conditioned by the particular technology under study, particularly its scale relative to that of firms.

Davies (1979) examined the influence that concentration has on rates of innovation diffusion. His results gave no clear evidence on the nature of the relationship. He concluded that a problem lies in the fact that the concept of industry concentration incorporates characteristics that exert opposing forces on the speed of diffusion. Davies argues that on the one hand, the relationship between the number of firms in an industry and diffusion speed is positive. On the other hand, an increase in size inequalities exerts a negative influence on diffusion speed. He concluded that the optimal industry structure is one of a few equally sized firms.

Similarly, Adams and Dirlam (1966) concluded that the United States lagged behind other countries in the adoption of the basic oxygen process because the oligopolistic U.S. steel industry had a vested interest in maintaining the status quo and so retained existing processes despite the cost advantages offered by the new basic oxygen process. Not only did Canadian steel producers adopt the basic oxygen process before U.S. producers, but the rate of diffusion of the technology throughout the Canadian steel industry also was higher until the late 1960s.

Globerman (1974) provides a synthesis of the different empirical findings with respect to size of firms and competitive pressure. The financial and risk advantages enjoyed by larger firm size encourage the faster spread of innovations in industries characterized by significant economies of scale. However, these advantages might be of little significance unless larger firms experience competitive pressure to adopt as, for example, from the entry or threat of entry of new firms into the industry or external competition in the form of imports.

Finally, in nearly all studies, managerial attitudes have been put forward as influencing innovation diffusion rates; however, results have not been strong, primarily, it is suspected, because of the difficulties involved in measuring individual behavioral characteristics.

A factor which has been recognized as important (Nabseth and Ray 1974; Globerman 1974) but not dealt with explicitly in the innovation diffusion literature is the role of access to information. Allen (1977) studied the sources of information used by Irish firms in adopting technology. Personal contacts, particularly with foreign firms, were found to be important sources of information and of new technology. Foreign controlled subsidiaries tended to acquire information and technology from their parent firms whereas Irish firms relied more heavily upon universities, research institutes, government agencies, and industry associations, all of which substituted for the lack of a parent. Allen (1977, p. 32) concluded that "parent firms serve as a rich source of technology for their subsidiaries, and may have a generally positive effect on domestic technological development." Furthermore, through the movement of personnel between foreign and Irish controlled firms, there was further potential for technology transfer beyond the subsidiary. Von Hippel (1978) stressed the often crucial role played by customers in terms of idea generation and sources of information used in technical problem solving. In other studies, equipment suppliers have been found to be important to the innovation diffusion process. Globerman (1974), for example, pointed out that the earlier diffusion of tufting equipment in the United States than in Canada was partially a result of the fact that the equipment was produced and marketed by U.S.-based firms. Geographical proximity to suppliers can offer advantages in terms of servicing, technical expertise, and equipment improvements, and so act as a spur to innovation diffusion.

Innovation diffusion research has been strongly criticized. Rosenberg (1972) and Gold (1981) have questioned the definition of an innovation as a clearly defined, essentially unchanging product or process to be adopted by firms. Instead, improvements and modifications, by making an innovation valuable to a wider range of users, cause an increase in the number of potential adopters, the effect of which is to slow the measured rate of innovation diffusion. The learning period necessary for skills to develop to use the innovation will vary depending upon the complexity of the innovation and the extent to which the technology is novel or amenable to the utilization of skills already available or transferable from other industries. This applies to mechanical skills, facilities, and design or engineering capabilities. Often, the rate of innovation diffusion in a user industry will be governed by the capital goods sector which supplies the requisite machinery.

Rosenberg (1972) discussed the role of complementarities, the obverse of which is bottlenecks. A given innovation may be slow in diffusing if other innovations which allow the relaxing or bypassing of constraints are not available. Also, just as new technologies are continually improved, so are existing ones. The relative advantage of existing technologies may, therefore, remain strong for some time, thus retarding the rate of diffusion of new technologies. In addition, there are social, legal and institutional factors affecting diffusion rates, for example, regulation, availability of labor force skills, licensing/patent policies, and so on.

Gold (1981) criticized the value of some of the commonly tested explanatory variables. For example, he pointed out that although profitability has been found to exert a strong influence on diffusion rates, it really explains little and, in fact, is tautological in the sense that one can conclude only that profitable innovations are adopted because they are profitable. Like most other innovation diffusion researchers, Gold stressed the need for an understanding of the actual decision making process involved in innovation adoption, that is, the role of managerial characteristics. More attention should also be given to the impacts of innovation adoption on skill mixes, input and output prices, and other qualitative characteristics.

Innovation Diffusion Literature and Simultaneity

Although the innovation diffusion literature has generated several hypotheses, there is no consensus regarding a single innovation diffusion model that satisfactorily explains observed patterns and rates of innovation diffusion across different industries and innovations. In our first attempt to explain lags in adoption by firms in our sample, we drew upon this literature. Following tradition, we adopted a fairly simplistic approach at first in that an attempt was made to incorporate (when permitted by data availability) most hypotheses tested in the literature in a single ordinary least square (OLS) regression model having as its dependent variable lag lengths (in years) for innovations adopted by firms included in the Economic Council Survey of Innovation. This approach did not work well, however, and it became apparent that such an all-encompassing OLS model suffered from problems of simultaneity resulting in unreliable and biased parameter estimates. Indeed, the failure to allow for simultaneity is a problem in much of the literature.

In light of the simultaneity problem, it became necessary to develop a more fully integrated model of innovation adoption based upon managerial decision making. The model, described in the next section, simultaneously explains lag lengths and two other endogenous variables: the cost of the innovation and the sources of technology used by adopting firms. The model is crude but the results suggest that it is a fruitful line of research which, if pursued further, could lead to the development of a richer model of innovation diffusion.

A MODEL OF INNOVATION LAG RATES

A central hypothesis of the model is that the decision to adopt consists of trading off the level of risk perceived to be associated with a given innovation with the expected rate of return from that innovation. Risk is an *ex ante* concept involving uncertainty about future events (Wetzel 1981); it is the chance that expected returns will not materialize. Financial risk is generally defined as the variance or standard deviation of returns (Malkiel 1981). In order for innovation adoption to occur, the expected rate of return must be sufficiently high to compensate for the level of risk perceived to be incurred; as perceived risk increases, so too will the expected rate of return required for adoption to take place increase. Other factors to consider are the time taken for potential adopters to become aware of the existence of the innovation and any barriers to adoption that might exist.

Bearing in mind the limited variables available in the survey for measuring these characteristics, we arrive at the first (and key) equation:

$$LC_{ij} = a - b_1 X1_{ij} + b_2 X2_{ij} - b_3 X3_{ij} - b_4 X4_{ij} + b_5 X5_{ij} + b_{E1} E1_{ij} - b_{E3} E3_{ij} \qquad (1)$$

where

$LC_{ij} = \ln \dfrac{\text{lag length ij}}{\text{mean lag length}}$ [1] for the ith innovation adopted by the jth firm

$X1_{ij}$ = dummy variable equal to one if the ith innovation adopted by the jth firm showed a pay-back period of less than 3 years, zero if its pay-back period was 3 years or more

$X2_{ij}$ = dummy variable equal to one if the ith innovation adopted by the jth firm was new to the firm, zero if it represented an improvement over existing operations

$X3_{ij}$ = R & D/sales ratio in the year of innovation commercialization of the jth firm adopting the ith innovation[2]

$X4_{ij}$ = percent of cost of the ith innovation adopted by the jth firm funded by government

$X5_{ij}$ = dummy variable equal to one if the ith innovation adopted by the jth firm was patented by an unaffiliated firm or individual, zero if the innovation was not patented or if it was patented by a parent or affiliate

$E1_{ij}$ = ratio of the total cost of the ith innovation, jth firm, to the total firm sales of products of the industry to which the innovation is classified; the sales are those made in the year of innovation commercialization

$E3_{ij}$ = dummy variable equal to one if the technology for the ith innovation adopted by the jth firm was acquired by intracorporate transfer, zero if the technology was developed in-house or acquired from an arm's-length source.

The expected signs on the coefficients are given in Equation 1 and are rationalized as follows.

There is a negative sign on $X3_{ij}$ since lag lengths increase as the length of time taken for a firm to become aware of the existence and possible utility of an innovation increases. Time to innovation awareness is, to a certain extent, under the firm's control; it depends upon the acquisition of information, a costly activity in terms of both capital and human resources. Technologically oriented firms will expend resources on searches of a number of information sources, and active information searchers should become aware of potentially useful technological opportunities more quickly than passive information acquirers. One measure of research intensity is the R & D/sales ratio (Grabowski 1968). Firms that spend large proportions of their sales on R & D activities are more likely to have the resources necessary to scan the literature and to make contact with other researchers, other firms, and so on in order to gather information regarding new technologies in place elsewhere. Therefore, as firms' R & D/sales ratios increase, the time taken to become aware of new technologies and hence lag lengths should decrease.

A second variable designed to capture the phenomenon of "innovation awareness" is $E3_{ij}$. This is a dummy variable equal to unity if the technology was acquired through intracorporate transfer. One of the competitive advantages associated with multiplant firms is economies of scale in research activities. By maintaining large, centralized research facilities, technological developments in a number of fields and countries can be monitored. Also, large, diversified corporations develop many innovative technologies in-house. Awareness information and technological information and assistance required for innovation adoption are diffused throughout the multiplant organization through both formal and informal channels of personal contact.[3] Such centralized corporation research facilities and resources augment and sometimes replace local R & D resources, certainly at the plant level and not infrequently at the firm level. Hence, information and technology acquired through intracorporate channels should also show shorter lag lengths through shorter time to awareness than information and technology acquired through in-house or arms'-length sources alone. The adopting firm can also take advantage of sophisticated intrafirm capabilities for assessing the risk/rate of return relationship.

Consider now the influence of risk on lag lengths, holding rate of return constant. Lag lengths will tend to increase as perceived levels of risk associated with an innovation increase since firms will delay innovation adoption until such time that risk levels decrease to a point where they will be compensated by the anticipated rate of return. The effect of risk is captured by the two variables $X2_{ij}$ and $E1_{ij}$.

First, the perceived risk of the innovation will be a function of the "radicalness" of the innovation. An indication of how radical an innovation is, from the viewpoint of the firm in question, is whether it represents a new or an improved product or process (Leroy 1976). Hence, the variable $X2_{ij}$. It is expected to have a positive coefficient since levels of uncertainty, and so lags, associated with the introduction of a technology that represents an improvement over products or processes currently in place in the firm should be lower than in the case of a new, unfamiliar technology since the former should be easier for a firm to understand, assess and incorporate into current operations (Cooper and Little 1977).

The variable $E1_{ij}$ captures another aspect of riskiness. As the level of capital investment required for adoption to take place increases relative to firm size, the perceived level of risk associated with innovation adoption also will increase since a greater proportion of the firm's financial resources will be tied up in a single risky venture. As this proportion increases, the consequences of failure increase in severity so that the coefficient of $E1_{ij}$ is expected to be positive.

Next, consider the influence of rate of return, with risk held constant. Perceived rate of return is expected to show a negative relationship to lag lengths, i.e., as perceived rate of return increases, the length of time from first world introduction of an innovation to adoption by firms should decrease (Mansfield 1968; Wilson et al.

1980). The variable $X1_{ij}$, equal to one if the innovation showed a pay-back period of less than 3 years, is one measure of rate of return. Its coefficient is expected to be negative.

Another variable capturing the rate of return influence is $X4_{ij}$. Its coefficient also is expected to be negative. By lowering the proportion of innovation cost incurred by the adopting firm, the proportional contribution made by government programs[4] will increase the rate of return on the innovation as perceived by the adopting firm and hence should contribute to a reduction in lag lengths.

The final component of the lag length model is the existence of institutional barriers to adoption, particularly patent protection. One aim of patent laws is to confer upon the patent holder a short-term monopoly over a particular product or production process. Imitation by other firms is not permitted without the consent of the patent owner. Hence, in order for innovation adoption to occur, contractual negotiations and transfer agreements must be entered into by potential users of the patented technology. Such transaction costs are significant (McFetridge 1981) and will have the effect of reducing the expected rate of return to the technology purchaser. This factor is captured by the variable $X5_{ij}$, the sign of whose coefficient is expected to be positive.

To resume the problem of simultaneity identified earlier, a second equation is estimated to recognize the endogeneity of the cost of the innovation relative to firm size as measured by sales ($E1_{ij}$). It is:

$$E1_{ij} = a + b_{LC}LC_{ij} - b_2 X2_{ij} + b_6 X6_{ij} - b_7 X7_{ij} + b_4 X4_{ij} \tag{2}$$

where the two variables not previously defined are:

$X6_{ij}$ = dummy variable equal to one if the ith innovation adopted by the jth firm was a process, zero if it was a product

$X7_{ij}$ = ratio of R & D costs to total innovation costs of the ith innovation adopted by the jth firm [5]

Consider first the influence of lag length (LC_{ij}) on the cost of the innovation. Early in the life cycle of a product, production is small-scale and highly specialized. Production runs are short and are skilled labor, rather than capital, intensive. Over time price competition increases, production runs lengthen and capital intensity increases. Emphasis shifts from product to process innovation. Therefore, the cost to firms of adopting older technologies, that is, those showing longer lag lengths should be higher since investment in plant and equipment will be greater in scale than if the technology is young. Hence, a positive sign on LC_{ij} is expected.

A second factor expected to influence relative cost of the innovation to the firm is whether the innovation represents, from the perspective of the firm, a new or an improved product or process. Drawing from the discussion above, the level of risk attached to technologies new to the firm, and hence unfamiliar, will be higher than for technologies representing an improvement over existing products and processes. Firms will be less willing to invest large amounts of capital in risky or highly uncertain ventures. Therefore, firms will invest relatively less of their resources in innovations that represent significant departures from current methods of operation than in the case of the less risky improved type of innovation, yielding an expected negative sign for the coefficient of $X2_{ij}$.

Third, it is expected that product innovations will be relatively less costly to adopt than process innovations (Utterback 1979a). The variable $X6_{ij}$ is therefore included, with a positive sign expected. Due to indivisibilities, the introduction of new or improved processes frequently must take place on a large scale whereas in the case of product innovations, small-scale trial production frequently is possible.

Fourth, it is expected that innovations, whether product or process, that require relatively large investments in plant and equipment will also be large in proportion to firm size; therefore, as manufacturing start-up costs increase as a proportion of total innovation costs, so also should the total cost of the innovation increase relative to firm size, yielding an expected negative sign on $X7_{ij}$.

The final factor affecting the relative cost of the innovation is the proportion of innovation cost covered by government subsidization. Firms will spend what they perceive to be a reasonable amount on innovations and, theoretically, innovations receiving some government funding would not occur without that government aid. If this is the case, government contributions should come after business contributions and so be added to the firm's investment, thus increasing the total investment in the innovation relative to firm size (see Howe and McFetridge 1976). The sign on $X4_{ij}$ should therefore be positive.

A third equation recognizes the endogeneity of $E3_{ij}$ which distinguishes between innovations for which the source of the technology was intracorporate as opposed to in-house or arm's-length. The equation is:

$$E3_{ij} = a + b_8 X8_{ij} + b_{E1} E1_{ij} - b_3 X3_{ij} - b_9 X9_{ij} - b_{10} X10_{ij} \qquad (3)$$

where the as yet undefined variables are:

$X8_{ij}$ = dummy variable equal to one if the jth firm adopting the ith innovation was foreign controlled, zero if it was domestically controlled

$X9_{ij}$ = ratio of sales in the field of the jth firm introducing the ith innovation to average sales in the field of firms in that industry in the year of innovation commercialization

$X10_{ij}$ = age in the year of innovation commercialization of the jth firm adopting the ith innovation

What are the factors determining the choice between intracorporate sources of technology and other sources, i.e., in-house R & D and arm's-length purchases of technology? In recent years, increasing attention has been focused on the R & D and technology transfer behavior of firms. Of particular relevance to this study is a paper by Davidson and McFetridge (1980) which examined, in detail, the factors determining the relative costs of intrafirm and market technology transactions. Davidson and McFetridge conclude that internalization, i.e., intracorporate transfers, will be more advantageous if some of the associated costs are "sunk," that if, if a parent–subsidiary relationship has already been established. By definition, all foreign controlled firms in Canada have parent firms elsewhere and are components of larger multinational enterprises. It is expected that foreign controlled subsidiaries located in Canada will be more likely to acquire their technology from parent and affiliated firms, yielding an expected positive sign on the coefficient of $X8_{ij}$.

Several other factors will influence the incidence of intracorporate transfers. First, the larger the innovation involved, that is, the greater the cost of the innovation, the more likely will a subsidiary acquire the innovation intracorporately since one advantage of MNEs is the ability to spread R & D expenses across a number of subsidiaries (Davidson and McFetridge 1980). Thus, we enter $E1_{ij}$ and expect a positive sign on its coefficient.

Not all subsidiaries in the sample are dependent on their parent companies for technology, however; in fact, while 81 percent of the innovations introduced by domestically controlled firms were developed in-house, 54 percent of the innovations by foreign controlled firms were also developed using in-house R & D resources. It is expected that as the R & D intensity of firms, as measured by R & D/sales ratios in the year of introduction of the innovation, increases, the incidence of intracorporate technology transfers will decrease. A negative sign for the coefficient of $X3_{ij}$ is expected.

FIGURE 5.2

Schematic Outline of the Lag Length System of Equations

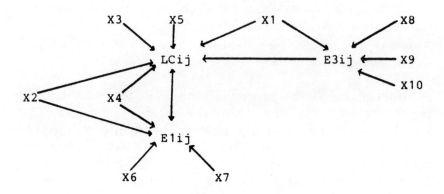

Two other firm characteristics are considered to be important: size and age of the firm. Young subsidiaries and those that are small relative to other firms in the industry should be less able to undertake sophisticated and intensive R & D activities (Terpstra 1976). Hence, they should be more dependent on their parent companies for technology and show greater reliance on intracorporate sources of technology. The signs of both $X9_{ij}$ and $X10_{ij}$ should therefore be negative.

To summarize thus far, the model to be tested consists of three endogenously determined variables: lag rates (LC_{ij}), the cost of the innovation (relative to firm size) ($E1_{ij}$), and the source of the technology for the innovation ($E3_{ij}$). Several exogenous variables (designated X in Figure 5.2) are expected to determine each endogenous variable and, in some cases, the same variable simultaneously determines two endogenous variables. The model as outlined is shown schematically in Figure 5.2.

Before discussing parameter estimates, the data upon which the analysis is based are briefly described. The advantage of the data base is that it contains data on a wide range of innovation and firm characteristics and on several industries. Therefore, unlike most previous researchers in the field, we are not constrained as seriously by the problem of a small number of observations. On the other hand, the survey data do contain some weaknesses, as discussed in the following section.

DATA: THE ECONOMIC COUNCIL SURVEY
OF INNOVATION

During 1979–80, the Economic Council of Canada conducted a survey of innovation and technological change in five Canadian industries.[6] Usable questionnaires were returned by 170 firms which reported on 283 product and process innovations successfully adopted in the 1960–79 period which had most contributed to their profitability. Innovation and firm characteristics are described in detail in De Melto, McMullen and Wills (1980).

Of the 283 reported innovations, 111 were imitative in nature, that is, they were first launched or used elsewhere in the world by other firms. Product innovations number 77 or 69 percent of the imitative innovations while process innovations number 34 or 31 percent. The industry breakdown is: telecommunications equipment and components, 32 percent; electrical industrial equipment, 25 percent; plastics compounds and synthetic resins, 19 percent; smelting and refining, 14 percent; and crude petroleum exploration and production, 9 percent. These innovations form the sample of innovations to which lag lengths are attached. However, as a result of missing values on some variables for some innovations, the analysis reported on is based on a total of 73 innovations. The distribution of lag lengths is very skewed: the average lag is 8 years and the median is 5 years with 27 innovations showing lags of 10 years or more.

There are two important characteristics of the innovation data base that set the present study apart from most other studies of innovation lag lengths. First, lag lengths, the key dependent variable in the analysis, are estimated by the respondent firms. As a result, they are subject to inaccuracy introduced by human error in recall and in awareness of the true first date of innovation commercialization elsewhere in the world.

The degree of inaccuracy introduced by recall and awareness error is unknown and could not realistically be checked because of the second distinguishing characteristic of the innovation survey data base: it consists of 283 discrete innovations. In contrast, the studies reviewed above are based upon analysis of a few pre-defined innovations.[7] By focusing upon a small number of selected innovations, the first world use could be determined accurately and the diffusion path traced. It was not possible to check the accuracy of the estimate of first world use of the innovations by the respondent firms since, on balance, the gain in accuracy would not be sufficient to justify the time and effort required.

RESULTS AND INTERPRETATION

Before estimating the 3-equation system using three stage least squares,[8] all observations were weighted by the total cost of the innovation (1971 dollars) for two reasons: to adjust for the wide variation observed in the size of innovation investments and to take account of the fact that it is the larger innovations which will elicit rather more formalized decision making procedures in taking the decision to adopt.

The results are reported in Table 5.1. In general, they confirm the theory. The coefficients on most of the variables are significant as tested by the t-ratios and, with only a few exceptions, signs on hypothesized relationships are in the expected directions. Yet, it turns out on close investigation that the magnitudes of the impacts of most of the variables on lag lengths are quite small.

Taking first equation 1 which has LC_{ij} as the dependent variable, it can be seen in Table 5.1 that the two risk related variables—$E1_{ij}$ and $X2_{ij}$—are significant. Lag lengths tend to increase as the cost of the innovation increases relative to firm size ($E1_{ij}$). This reflects the higher levels of risk associated by firms with large-scale investments. At the mean, total innovation costs represent 19 percent of the firm's sales in the year of innovation commercialization. A 20 percent increase in this ratio would result in a 5.5 percent increase in the lag length at the mean, an increase of three months. Similarly, $X2_{ij}$ is significant and positive; firms take longer to adopt innovations representing new products and processes than innovations representing improvements over technologies already in place. A 20 percent increase in the proportion of new innovations such that, at the mean, new innovations represented 72 percent rather than 60 percent of all innovations would result in a 6.2 percent increase in the lag length at the mean, again an increase of three months.

The acquisition of the technology for the innovation from an intracorporate source rather than through in-house R & D or from an arm's-length source contributes to a reduction in lag lengths, the coefficient on $E3_{ij}$ showing a negative sign as expected and statistical significance at the 5 percent level. One-third of the innovations were based upon technology acquired from an intracorporate source (primarily foreign based parent companies). A 20 percent increase in this proportion such that 40 percent of the innovations were acquired from an intracorporate source would result in a reduction in lag lengths of 3.7 percent at the mean, that is, two months. No statistical evidence was found that the length of the adoption lag is affected

TABLE 5.1

Parameter Estimates for the Lag Length System of Equations

Variable	b-Coefficient	Standard Error	t-Ratio
A. Dependent variable: LC_{ij}			
Constant	-.46	.29	
$X1_{ij}$	-.40	.21	-1.92*
$X2_{ij}$	.50	.18	2.74‡
$X3_{ij}$	-1.46	1.57	-.93
$X4_{ij}$	-.01	.01	-1.67*
$X5_{ij}$	.28	.29	.95
$E1_{ij}$	1.42	.28	5.04‡
$E3_{ij}$	-.57	.29	-2.01†
B. Dependent variable: $E1_{ij}$			
Constant	.66	.14	
LC_{ij}	.37	.13	2.90‡
$X2_{ij}$	-.33	.10	-3.31‡
$X6_{ij}$	.06	.10	.64
$X7_{ij}$	-.24	.16	-1.49
$X4_{ij}$	.003	.004	.81
C. Dependent variable: $E3_{ij}$			
Constant	-1.18	.35	
$X8_{ij}$	1.38	.33	4.15‡
$E1_{ij}$	1.61	.46	3.49‡
$X1_{ij}$	.44	1.14	.38
$X9_{ij}$	.01	.04	.19
$X10_{ij}$	.002	.004	.49

* Denotes significant at the 10 percent level.
† Denotes significant at the 5 percent level.
‡ Denotes significant at the 1 percent level.

by firms' R & D/sales ratios ($X3_{ij}$). It appears, therefore, that firms that acquire the technology for their innovations from foreign based parent companies have a lag length edge over firms relying upon in-house R & D for the development of the technology for their innovations.

The impact on lag lengths of perceived rate of return is captured by $X1_{ij}$ and $X4_{ij}$ both of which are marginally significant at the 10 percent level and show the hypothesized signs. As the realized payback period becomes shorter, lag lengths decrease. Similarly, as the level of government funding of the innovation increases, lag lengths decrease, though, again, the size of the impact is relatively small. An increase in the average level of government funding of innovations from 8 percent to 10 percent, a 20 percent increase, would reduce lag lengths by only 1.5 percent at the mean or by about one month. It can be safely concluded, however, that as rates of return on innovation investments increase, technologies are adopted earlier. By reducing the cost to the firm, government subsidization of innovation investment acts somewhat as a spur to innovation adoption. It is very likely that the impact of government funding of innovation investment would have been even greater were it not for the fact that, in many cases, firms merely substitute government funds for their own funds (Howe and McFetridge 1976). In other words, not all firms spend more on innovation adoption by the amount of the government contribution. If government funds were truly additive in all cases, it is probable that the size of the impact of government funding on lag lengths would be greater.

When the results of the $E1_{ij}$ model (equation 2) are examined, it can be seen in Table 5.1 that fewer of the hypothesized relationships are supported statistically, though all relationships are in the expected directions.

Both $X2_{ij}$ and LC_{ij} are significant determinants of the size of the innovation investment relative to the size of the firm. New innovations ($X2_{ij}$) are perceived as being relatively more risky investments than improved innovations; firms are less willing to invest large amounts in unfamiliar technologies. On the other hand, by adopting improved innovations, firms can apply the benefits of learning-by-doing gained from previous, related methods of operation and hence are less averse to investing relatively large amounts of capital.

The relationship between LC_{ij} and $E1_{ij}$ is positive and significant. This result lends added support to the attitude toward the risk component of the model. As technologies age and progress along learning curves, firms regard those technologies as increasingly less risky investments. As a result, larger proportions of firms' resources are allocated to innovation adoption when the technologies involved are older. The remaining three variables ($X6_{ij}$, $X7_{ij}$ and $X4_{ij}$) used to explain the relative size of innovation investment, though not significant, do show relationships in the expected directions.

Turning finally to the $E3_{ij}$ equation (equation 3), the results listed in Table 5.1 show that $X8_{ij}$ and $E1_{ij}$ are significant, positive factors determining intracorporate technology transfers, as hypothesized. None of the remaining variables ($X3_{ij}$, $X9_{ij}$ and $X10_{ij}$) is significant and the sign on each is opposite to that expected.

The variable for foreign or domestic control ($X8_{ij}$) is a strong determinant of the source of the technology for innovations. Intracorporate sources of technology are used by foreign controlled firms. Domestically controlled firms, on the other hand, tend to rely upon in-house R & D resources to develop technologies for innovations and, to a lesser extent, upon arm's-length sources. To some extent, this reflects the fact that the majority of domestically controlled firms are autonomous and so do not have the option of acquiring technology intracorporately. Several domestically controlled firms are, however, controlled by other Canadian controlled firms. Despite this, essentially no intracorporate technology transfer activity occurred.

To determine the impact of foreign control ($X8_{ij}$) on lag lengths, the reduced form of equation 1 was obtained. The sign on the coefficient of $X8_{ij}$ is negative as expected, i.e., the impact of foreign control is to cause a decrease in lag lengths. At the mean, 66 percent of the imitative innovations analyzed were introduced by foreign controlled firms. A 20 percent increase is this ratio such that 79 percent of the imitative innovations were introduced by foreign controlled firms would reduce lag lengths at the mean by 9.9 percent, that is, by five months. Conversely, if the mean level of innovations introduced by foreign controlled firms was reduced by 20 percent to 53 percent, lag lengths would increase by 16.4 percent at the mean, or by eight months. Thus, the impact of $X8_{ij}$ on lag lengths exceeds in magnitude the impacts exerted by any one of the other variables in the key (lag length) equation.

The results show that age, size and R & D intensity characteristics of firms have no significant effect on technology sourcing behavior. A significant variable is relative cost of the innovation ($E1_{ij}$). When the investment involved is relatively large, firms tend to rely on intracorporate sources of technology. This behavior can be interpreted as a type of risk reduction: it is unlikely that parent companies will release to their subsidiaries technologies that will fail. It also reflects the greater R & D resources of centralized corporate R & D units to which subsidiaries have access.

SUMMARY AND CONCLUSIONS

In this chapter, a model of lag lengths in innovation adoption has been developed and tested. The model implies that risk and rate of return considerations play key roles in determining the length of the lag between first world use of a product or process innovation and use of those innovations by firms in Canada. Furthermore, a trade-off occurs between the two: by accepting only innovations with lower levels of risk, firms also accept lower rates of return. On a more positive note, (successful) risk takers are rewarded by higher rates of return.

More specifically, it was found that the length of lags in adoption are affected by the cost of the innovation relative to firm sales and whether the technology is new to the firm or an improvement in technology currently in use by the firm, both of which measure risk. Innovations with short pay-back periods and thus high rates of return are adopted sooner, and government funding of some innovation costs, by increasing the rate of return to firms, contributes to shorter lag lengths. Shorter lag lengths also result when the technology for innovations is transferred intracorporately. The reduced form results indicate, first, that an increase in levels of foreign control would contribute to a small reduction in lag lengths for innovations adopted by firms in Canada and second, that a decrease of equal magnitude in the proportion of innovations introduced by foreign controlled firms would result in an even larger *increase* in lag lengths.

Overall, the statistical significance of the model and its constituent variables is strong. The impacts of the variables are small, suggesting a lack of clear-cut, decisive policy measures. From a more theoretical point of view, however, it is clear that simultaneous methods of analysis should be used when examining the process of innovation diffusion.

 ꞏ In terms of policy, what can be done with the risk component of the model? We know that a reduction in risk would contribute to shorter lags, but is there a case for government to reduce the risk faced by firms? The analysis in this chapter is not very helpful on this question. A strong argument for such government intervention exists only if the risk faced by firms exceeds the risk faced by society.

If efforts are made to reduce private risk, for example, by scaling down technology so that the cost to firms is relatively lower or by introducing more improvement innovations and fewer technologies that are completely new to firms, it is quite possible that the rate of technological change or its quality would be less than if the system were left to operate without such official interference. The question of the level of risk faced by firms and the level faced by society and the case for intervention is really an argument beyond the scope of this chapter.

Risk, however, is traded off by firms against rate of return, so perhaps a more fruitful approach would be to consider only the rate of return component. An increase in the rate of return realized by firms would contribute to shorter adoption lags. But would the short decrease in lag lengths justify the costs to government of directly, through funding of innovation activity, or indirectly, by tax and other measures, improving the rate of return to firms from innovation adoption? This, too, is a question which cannot be answered satisfactorily without careful additional research.

Problems in arguing strongly for or against intervention in either the risk or rate of return component of the model are encountered because the socially optimum rate of innovation diffusion has not been identified. A similar problem is encountered concerning the identification of the socially optimum level of research and development spending for countries (see Palda and Pazderka 1982). Further research on both of these questions is required.

Last, there is evidence that policies toward MNEs in Canada could have an impact on the length of adoption lags at a given level of risk and rate of return. Caution in the treatment of foreign controlled firms is advisable since these results indicate that MNEs play a positive role in the process of technological change in Canadian industry by contributing to a reduction in lags associated with adoption of product and process innovations first introduced abroad. A reduction in levels of foreign control or at least in the rate at which foreign controlled firms adopt technologies developed by parent and affiliated firms could have negative consequences for lag lengths.

NOTES

1. This transformation is applied to lag lengths in order to adjust for the marked skewness in their distribution.
2. Firms were asked to provide data on sales, R & D spending, and employment at both the overall firm level and in the "field," i.e., in the industry to which

the innovation is classified. As a result, measures of firm size and level of R & D spending can relate to either total firm activity or to activity in the field, the choice between the two being somewhat arbitrary. Through this chapter, firm activity in the *field* is used as recommended by Utterback (1979b). Similarly, all measures apply to the year in which the innovation was introduced by the respondent firm rather than to 1978.

3. Examples of formal intracorporate information channels given by firm interviewees are information newsletters, regularly scheduled meetings between head office and subsidiary management, and so on.

4. Programs specifically referred to by respondent firms are the Program for the Advancement of Industrial Technology (PAIT), the Defence Industry Productivity Program (DIPP), the Industrial Research Assistance Program (IRAP), and the Industrial Research and Development Incentives Act (IRDIA). Howe and McFetridge (1976) examined the impact of PAIT, DIPP, IRAP and the Defence Industrial Research Program on the level of R & D spending in a sample of firms and found that R & D spending levels increased by the amount of the grant in the electrical industry for Canadian controlled firms and by less than the amount of the grant for foreign controlled firms. In the case of the chemical and machinery industries, firms receiving grants did not show increases in R & D spending.

5. This is the inverse of the variable as expressed in the text. As manufacturing startup costs increase as a proportion of total innovation cost, the proportion represented by R & D costs decrease.

6. The survey response rate is 41 percent. In addition, interviews designed to elicit general information with respect to firms' R & D and innovation behavior were conducted with the chief executive officers of 53 firms.

7. For example, Mansfield (1968) studied the diffusion of the shuttle car, the continuous wide-strip mill, the pallet-loading machine and the diesel locomotive; the diffusion of catalytic cracking and of computers were studied by Bernhardt (1970) and Sutton (1975), respectively; and Globerman (1974) examined the diffusion characteristics of tufting machinery and NC machine tools, to name just a few.

8. The three-stage least squares estimation procedure is taken from the *SAS* (Statistical Analysis System) *User's Guide*, Raleigh, N.C.: SAS Institute Inc., 1979 edition.

6

Multinational Enterprises and World Product Mandates

Alan M. Rugman

INTRODUCTION

The multinational enterprise (MNE) is one of the most remarkable institutions of the postwar era, operating across many national boundaries to produce and distribute goods and services on a worldwide basis. One of the first host nations to experience such foreign direct investment in its economy was Canada. Today its manufacturing industry is over 50 percent foreign (U.S.) owned. The upsurge in Canadian nationalism over the last decade is representative of a more critical attitude toward MNEs displayed by many countries, especially some less developed nations, in recent years.

A common concern expressed in such host nations is the desire to increase control over some of the technology owned by the MNEs. This is essentially a distributional argument, which may well conflict with efficient management of technology by the MNE. However, it has led to the propagation of host government policies designed to stimulate the amount of research and development (R and D) undertaken in the host nation, including, in many cases, more R and D in the subsidiaries of the MNEs. In Canada, subsidies for R and D are available to all firms, on a nondiscriminatory basis. However, a new proposal being debated in Canada today is to restrict government grants for R and D to those subsidiaries of MNEs that can secure a world product mandate (WPM). This chapter explores some of the theoretical and practical problems of a world product mandate strategy, using Canada as a representative case study.

The developing public interest in the subject of world product mandate strategy for Canada has reached a stage where a precise statement of the meaning of a WPM is required. This paper attempts to draw out explicitly the many diverse strands of public policy, economics, trade, and marketing that make up the concept of a WPM strategy. It is shown that a model of WPMs can be developed and that the analytics of a WPM strategy can be simplified into relatively predictive statements.

It is also shown that the theory of WPMs can be reconciled with the modern theory of the multinational enterprise. In fact, elements of the WPM issue are anticipated in recent work on the theory of internal markets by Casson (1979), Dunning (1979), and Rugman (1980, 1981a). Although it is not the purpose of this work to propagate the theory of internalization per se, a reconciliation of the key elements of WPMs with those of the theory of internalization will be helpful.

In the first part of this chapter Canada's WPM strategy is reviewed so that a theory of WPMs can be developed later. The simple model developed can be applied to the underlying public policy issues of WPMs. The centrally organized internal markets of the multinationals are contrasted with the more autonomous organization required by WPMs. The perceived relationships of the multinationals and their subsidiaries with the host nation are specifically incorporated into the analysis in order to evaluate the costs and risks to the firm of a nationalist policy to subsidize technological development in the host nation.

CANADA'S WORLD PRODUCT MANDATE STRATEGY

This section of the chapter investigates the viability of a WPM strategy for Canada. In terms of public policy we need to know if a WPM strategy should be adopted and, if so, what form it should take. Although there are many unresolved technical and conceptual issues in the concept of a WPM strategy, it is rapidly becoming a major topic of public policy discussion.

The adoption of a WPM strategy in Canda will have a profound implication for the future direction, viability, performance and growth potential of much of Canadian secondary manufacturing industry. It is one of the most important public policy initiatives in Canada today. Its repercussions go beyond the basic issue of technological development and affect the structure of Canadian industry in general. It is relevant for international business in Canada and with the concern for the generation of an efficient industrial strategy for Canada.

Yet there are both advantages and hidden costs in a WPM strategy. There are potential costs in the sense that public funds to support the development of technologies for WPMs have an opportunity cost, that is, they might be better spent elsewhere. To make an optimal allocation of public funds it is essential to have available as much evidence as possible on the costs and benefits of the WPM option.

There are several reasons advanced by advocates of a WPM strategy:

First, the economic environment in Canada is moving away from the protection which encouraged MNEs to enter and establish miniature replicas (branch plants) of the U.S. parent firm (see Rugman 1980).

Second, the reduction of tariff and nontariff trade barriers is increasing the exposure of Canadian industry to international competition. Increased access to technology is necessary for survival in the global marketplace. There is a possibility that the federal government may start to implement recommendations of the Hatch report and introduce subsidies for exporting firms, whether they are domestic or foreign owned.

Third, for Canadian manufacturing industry to make good use of foreign subsidiaries the latter should be encouraged to seek WPMs. These permit the subsidiary to be responsible for the development and worldwide marketing of a specific innovation. The subsidiary needs to bargain with its parent to secure a potentially profitable mandate, but once it has one the subsidiary can use the internal market of the multinational organization to distribute and control the new process.

Unfortunately, such decentralized mandating may be in conflict with the desire of the parent firm to use its internal market to avoid the risk of dissipation of a home country technological advantage. Internalization theory predicts that most R and D will be undertaken by parent firms and that control of the R and D function is centralized [see Rugman (1981a) for greater detail on this point]. This conflicts with the premises of the WPM strategy. A reconciliation is necessary.

THE LITERATURE ON MNEs AND WPMs

Already a substantial literature has accumulated on the public policy option for Canada of a WPM strategy. The first serious exposition of WPMs is found in work by the Science Council of Canada

(1980), summarized in Witten (1980). Bourgault and Crookell (1979), Crookell and Caliendo (1980), and Rutenberg (1981) add some academic substance to the proposal. Recent papers by Wolf (1981) and Etemad (1982) explore some of the implications of WPMs.

As argued by Crookell and Caliendo (1980), at least three key attributes of Canadian industry are relevant to an understanding of the current interest in a WPM strategy.

First, Canadian industry is perceived by both federal and provincial governments as producing insufficient technology. Consequently, there is observed to be a deficit in the technological balance of payments. Management fees and royalties are paid by the subsidiaries of multinationals, licensees and partners in joint ventures for imported technology, but there are insufficient exports of technological products to match these imports.

Second, the apparent lack of technological output by Canadian industry is related to the large degree of foreign ownership in the manufacturing and resource sectors. It is frequently alleged that subsidiaries of multinationals on the average do less R and D than their parents. It is also hypothesized that the R and D output of independent Canadian firms is not the same as that of foreign owned firms. The relative R and D performance of foreign and domestic firms is the subject of several studies, analyzed in Rugman (1981a).

Third, the protected nature of Canadian industry is being challenged by the latest GATT agreements to reduce tariff and some nontariff barriers. Greater international competition raises the possibility of increased pressure on technologically deficient Canadian firms. It also raises the prospect of incentives for greater effort in R and D in order to survive. Clearly there are changes in the environment of international business in Canada that raise the prospects for new policies toward technology. One such policy is the WPM strategy.

The work of Rugman (1980, 1981a) on the internal markets of multinationals can be extended to draw out implications for a new theory of WPMs. One substantive point is that technology represents the firm-specific advantage of the multinational which it goes to great lengths to protect. The risk of dissipating firm-specific advantage is the main reason for the relative neglect of licensing because it does not permit the same degree of control as direct investment. Another crucial theoretical issue to be examined is the degree to which the R and D function of a multinational is centralized. The WPM strategy requires a decentralized R and D capacity. To what extent is the control of R and D centralized, and can the product innovation and development strategy of the MNE be decentralized?

Remember that innovations are being considered, not product improvements or adaptations for which no R and D is required.

Spence (1975) has suggested that the internal markets of a firm are responsive to conditions of imperfect information and that firms are hierarchical and centralized. He states: "... resource allocation processes that are internalized are those which are not efficiently carried out in a centralized manner ..." (p. 171). He states that the papers of Arrow (1975) on the vertical integration, and others on the organization of internal markets, all develop the point that centralized decision making is made by the firm. Thus the theory of internalization is a theory of centralization in decision making including applications to the R and D function of the MNE.

Although Williamson (1975), Chandler (1977) and others, such as Porter and Zannetos (1978), discuss the complexities that result when internal decisions of the firm are centralized, they are more concerned about the difficulties of running an administered market within a firm rather than the R and D function itself. If anything, their analysis would tend to support the need for a centralized R and D function, as the costs of communication and information transfer within a firm are perceived as major obstacles to the achievement of an efficiently administered internal market.

Fischer and Behrman (1979) recently studied the centralization of the management of foreign based R and D of 35 U.S. and 18 European MNEs. They found that the more successful MNEs followed a centralized R and D strategy and that the loosely coordinated companies were less efficient in their use of R and D done by the foreign affiliates of the MNE. The internal advantage of the MNE in knowledge or technology was better allocated on a worldwide basis when the MNE followed a centralized corporate plan. The centralized firms have superior communication and control systems. The "less tightly coordinated firms ... appear to invite problems of omission and redundancy in the management of their R and D activities."

Killing (1975) has examined the transfer of technology via the licensing modality to Canadian owned secondary manufacturing firms. Based on original data of licensing agreements collected from fifty Canadian manufacturing establishments, Killing finds that licensing is not a viable long run growth option for (Canadian) firms lacking their own R and D base. Licensing of technology will breed dependence upon the foreign (U.S.) licensor unless the Canadian licensee uses the knowledge acquired to build up its own in-house R and D capacity.

An interesting theoretical explanation is advanced by Killing to explain this, namely that the Canadian licensees lack the managerial core skills to incorporate the new technology within the long range plans of the firm. The concept of core skills limiting the growth of the firm was first introduced by Wrigley (1970) in terms of the strategy and structure of business enterprises. However, a similar agreement was made earlier in economic theory terms by Penrose (1959) who demonstrated that the growth of the first is limited by the extent to which the management team or group can be expanded in an efficient manner.

Killing also found that 60 percent of the completed licensing agreements in his study restricted the firm from exporting. This is similar to a finding on proposed licensing agreements in the Gray Report (1972) which indicated that 58 percent faced export restrictions. Both of these studies conflict with a Statistics Canada survey of 510 licensing agreements for 1972, of which only 24 percent had export restrictions. Killing suggests that this is explained by the inclusion of licensing agreements relating to minor process details in the Statistics Canada survey which usually ignore export restrictions. Such minor agreements were excluded in Killing's study.

The work is important since nonequity contractual agreements are likely to increase if FIRA is given the authority to review the performance of existing multinationals in Canada as is proposed. Such expanded government intervention will affect the foreign investment decision of multinationals. Essentially, giving greater power to review agencies such as FIRA serves to raise the cost of foreign direct investment relative to other potential options such as licensing or exporting. The latter modality has traditionally not been viable because of the Canadian tariff, and even if this is reduced, there remain substantial nontariff barriers to entry.

In future years foreign firms will be under increasing pressure to seek out new contractual arrangements such as joint ventures, licensing, and so on. One of the paradoxes of Canadian policy is that the WPM strategy is being proposed at the very time when the role of multinationals in Canada is diminishing, as the servicing of the Canadian market moves toward nonequity forms of involvement.

Despite the questionable nature of Canada's WPM strategy, it is apparent that it is an issue of serious concern to the makers of public policy in Canada. To investigate further the analytics of the WPM strategy in the next section of the study it is now assumed that the Canadian federal government is in the process of implementing a new support program to promote WPMs. This permits the impact of a

WPM strategy upon the MNE to be examined in greater detail. Since the WPM is imposed by governments it can be modeled as an exogenous parametric change imposed upon the decision making structure of the MNE. This internal administrative structure of the MNE is examined in more detail in the section "Toward a Theory of WPMs," and the strategic response of the MNE to a WPM is considered. In turn, the perceived actions of the MNE will presumably have some future impact upon Canadian policy in this area.

THE COMPLEXITY OF A WPM STRATEGY

This section investigates some of the complexities of a WPM strategy for Canadian public policy. As discussed above much of the writing on WPMs has been imprecise, leading to the potential misuse of the WPM concept. Therefore I begin by a precise definition of a WPM, followed by an explanation of this definition.

The concept of a WPM needs to be defined carefully. For example does it mean a mandate for the actual research and innovation of new products, or can it be used to explain the mere development of a process? The latter (process innovation) is mistakenly included by advocates of WPMs yet it clearly does not qualify for R and D support since control of the R and D function can be retained by the parent with the process innovation in the subsidiary being of little independent value. Such process innovation should be of no interest to the Canadian government as no true technological innovation will occur in Canada.

One of the major problems in current discussion of WPMs is that *new* product lines are not always considered; indeed, the product cycle model has been invoked (Rutenberg 1981) to argue for the granting of mandates in maturing or even standardized products. Clearly, only brand new product cycles themselves qualify for consideration as WPMs. The stated goal of the WPM is not simply to increase host nation employment and production in any old factory being closed down as the MNE retreats from sunset industries. Instead, it is to increase Canada's technological capacity and help improve the balance of technological payments.

For these reasons, in this chapter a world product mandate is defined as the full development and production of a new product line in a subsidiary of a multinational enterprise. To understand the precise nature of this definition more clearly, reference can be made to Figure 6.1.

FIGURE 6.1

Parties Involved in the WPM Decision

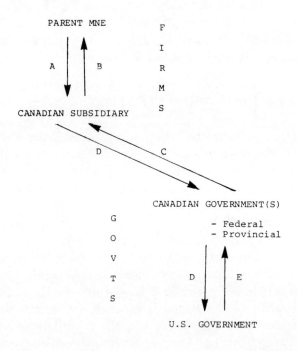

Key to variables: (A) Mandate; (B) profits; (C) subsidy for R and D; (D) exports of technology; (E) nontariff barrier.

In Figure 6.1 the interactions of the two key groups involved in the WPM are illustrated. These groups are:

First, the multinational enterprise (MNE), consisting of the parent firm and its subsidiary in Canada.

Second, the governments involved, namely the Canadian federal and relevant provincial governments and also various agencies of the U.S. government (ignoring for simplicity the complexities of the U.S. political system with its potential conflicts between the executive branch and Congress).

For a WPM to fly it is necessary to consider five factors, labeled A to E in Figure 6.1. These factors involve at least three sets of inter-related agreements: those that (a) the parent MNE and its subsidiary; (b) the subsidiary and the Canadian government; and (c) the Canadian and foreign (especially U.S.) governments. These points are now explained in more detail.

The first set of agreements involves the parent MNE and its subsidiary:

A is the award of the mandate by the parent MNE to its subsidiary. This decision involves an evaluation by the MNE of the relative costs and benefits of the WPM in comparison to its other options. This problem is discussed in more detail below in the section "Toward a Theory of WPMs."

B is the price paid by the subsidiary to the parent MNE for the mandate. Normally this will be in the form of profits from the subsidiary repatriated to the parent. These profits arise from the WPM. It will be difficult, however, to separate the general performance of the subsidiary from its specific performance on the WPM, so the mere evaluation of this return is difficult. Moreover, the performance of the subsidiary cannot be judged independently of its contribution to the total MNE. Rugman (1979) discusses the advantages to the MNE of international diversification. An implication of this work is that subsidiaries contribute to stability of earnings by protecting the worldwide market share of the MNE, even on occasions when their independent operations may not be profitable.

The second set of agreements concerns the subsidiary of the MNE and the Canadian governments involved in granting R and D subsidies.

C is the subsidy for R and D given by the Canadian government to the subsidiary once the latter proves it has secured a WPM. The grants for R and D are budgeted on the premise that Canada needs to subsidize technological innovation in order to achieve macroeconomic goals of productivity growth and high technology exports to help the balance of payments. The extent to which these policy objectives themselves are confused or inconsistent cannot be discussed here because of lack of space and time for this wide issue.

D represents the payoff to Canada for its R and D grants to the subsidiaries of the MNEs. The explicit payoff is in the form of increased exports of technologically intensive goods. Indirect payoffs occur in the form of jobs for scientists and researchers involved in the development of the new product line and also the potential white and blue collar jobs created by a successful product line. Harold Crookell has identified the need for a changeover of foreign owned secondary manufacturing industry in southern Ontario from factories to businesses. The WPM is clearly only one element in this process, so the impact on jobs should not be exaggerated. A partial policy of

R and D subsidies cannot solve the underlying problems of foreign ownership of Canadian industry. Either a comprehensive industrial strategy or a policy of free trade needs to be introduced to address this substantial issue. The WPM is a small and specific policy but one with some surprising complications.

The third set of relationships involves Canadian and foreign governments. As discussed above, D represents mainly the exports of technologically intensive goods resulting from a successful WPM. This now invites difficulties in Canada's international relations.

E is the potential retaliation by foreign governments to Canada's WPM strategy. If R and D subsidies are used by subsidiaries to produce and market internationally a new product line, then these exports will be regarded as benefiting from nontariff barriers to trade, namely, an indirect export subsidy.

Although Canada may earn a one shot trading advantage by being the first host nation to use such a nontariff barrier, it will not be able to continue to exploit such an advantage over time. Foreign governments will soon retaliate against Canadian exports and will either place taxes on them or introduce WPMs of their own. Pressure on the U.S. (home) government and on other host nations will arise because of the perceived job losses by workers in these nations and by competing firms aware of the international marketing advantage of the Canadian exporter.

These political and trading repercussions of Canada's WPM strategy have been ignored. Yet an analysis of the potential costs and benefits of the WPM should incorporate these repercussions. In the next section the WPM is analyzed in more detail. This analysis focuses upon the WPM from the viewpoint of the MNE.

TOWARD A THEORY OF WPMs

It has become apparent that a WPM strategy by the host nation will have a major impact on the strategic choice of a MNE. The WPM changes the relative benefits and costs of the R and D decisions being made in the internal market of the MNE. Although the MNE may still desire a centralized type of R and D function to meter and control the use of its firm-specific advantage in knowledge, there are now extra risks in such a strategy. The parameters change and the internal market of the MNE has to adapt to this uncertainty. The reaction of the MNE to a WPM is therefore more complex than has been assumed in the policy literature. This section now develops these points in a systematic manner.

Two variables are assumed to capture the major elements in the decision making of multinational firms. These are:

X = internal factors under certainty
Y = external factors under certainty

If uncertainty is introduced, we define the variables as:

X^1 = internal factors under uncertainty
Y^1 = external factors under uncertainty

A further theoretical assumption is that the managers of firms tend to be risk averse, so that the X^1 and Y^1 uncertainty situations are not as preferable as X and Y.

The characteristics of X include the so-called firm-specific advantage of knowledge identified in work on the theory of the MNE by Dunning (1979) and Rugman (1981a). The knowledge advantage of the multinational has usually been generated by ongoing expenditures on R and D which have given the firm a special technological capability. Indeed, a genuine firm-specific advantage means that the multinational holds a monopoly position in the use of its own technological knowledge.

The firm-specific advantage of the multinational firm need not necessarily have developed solely from its R and D expenditures for technology. Instead, there may be a unique advantage to the firm from its management organization, i.e., the manner in which it uses its management team and skills to administer the internal market of the firm.

The attributes of Y include the country specific factors that make up the outside environment within which the firm has to operate. The Y variable includes all of the economic, political, social and cultural factors that make up the environment of international business. All of these factors are assumed to be external to the multinational firm. Another dimension of this assumption is the realization that governments change the firm's external environment, for example when taxes, tariffs or regulations on international trade and investments are imposed or varied. In short, the Y factors are assumed exogenous to the firm.

The following cases can now be identified:

X + Y   = perfect certainty
$X^1 + Y^1$ = perfect uncertainty

$X + Y^1$ = external uncertainty
$X^1 + Y$ = internal uncertainty

The question is: where does the WPM strategy proposed by the Canadian government fit into this matrix of variables that affect the decision making behavior of the MNE? The first point to note is that as the WPM strategy involves the development of a new product in a subsidiary, there is a change in the multinational firm's internal structure, so X^1 is now the relevant variable instead of X. Second, it is now apparent that the host nation's government changes the environment (i.e., gives a subsidy to the subsidiary), so the external environment Y^1 is now the relevant variable. Therefore a WPM yields a model situation of case $X^1 + Y^1$.

Some of the complexities of the WPM model now become apparent. To secure a mandate the subsidiary needs to convince the parent firm that there will be overall gains in the MNE by the offshore development of a new product and its processing. These gains must be greater than any possible savings in logistics costs as a result of improved inventory control and lower cost of internal communication for a modern MNE. Such reduced logistics costs apply to already existing products and are not relevant to the WPM decision when innovation is concerned. Yet a new development involves uncertainty to the firm, as captured by the summary indicator X^1. Does the higher risk now require a greater than normal rate of return? Or does the offshore development serve to reduce risk by international diversification? At the firm level, these issues have not yet been considered, much less resolved, in the context of a WPM strategy.

Again, from the viewpoint of the parent firm, there is a greater probability of mandates being granted to subsidiaries in which the parent has confidence. Such confidence (the converse of uncertainty) is dependent upon evidence of solid economic performance and perceptions of sound management and reliable behavior on the part of the subsidiary. The similar cultural values and business ethics of the executives of U.S. and Canadian multinationals may work toward this reduction of X^1 and thereby increase the possibility of chartering Canadian subsidiaries with special mandates.

Perhaps one method for the host nation government to follow is to attempt to reduce the perceived risk of the multinational when it undertakes new offshore investments. This means that Y^1 can be reduced by policies that reduce the external uncertainty facing the multinational. In general, Y^1 falls when changes in government policies are minimized. Indeed, when policies of governments are harmonized there is the least uncertainty. This implies that a WPM strategy in Canada should be developed in close cooperation with both parents and subsidiaries and also with the home nation government.

Once a WPM is explained as case $X^1 + Y^1$ then an important prediction of the model can be made: The combined uncertainty of the internal product change and external environment resulting from the introduction of a WPM will lead to a more decentralized form of organization for the multinational firm involved. The reasons for decentralization are twofold.

First, the parent has to agree to give a mandate to the subsidiary. By definition the subsidiary now has an independent R and D capacity, although some elements of coordination of the R and D function may still be required by the parent firm. The new difficulty for the parent in preserving meaningful control of its internal market should not be underestimated. With a mandate for new R and D the subsidiary becomes a monopolist in the new process. It is not at all clear that the parent can secure sufficient relevant information to control the rents of its subsidiary. It is also apparent that such intelligence is now more expensive for the parent to acquire. Management fees and transfer prices cannot be set precisely any more, and the value of the internal market of the multinational is reduced.

Furthermore, the mandate gives the subsidiary the right to become an independent profit center. In time, it may even become a potential rival producer, threatening the dissipation of the worldwide firm-specific advantage in technology of its parent. The autonomy of the subsidiary resulting from a WPM is thus a significant risk to the MNE. These internal costs mean that X^1 is high for genuine WPMs but not as high if more mature or nearly standardized products are being mandated. Of course, the mature (or sunset) products are not technological leaders and will not appeal to Canadian policy makers.

Second, the introduction of more host nation political risk (which is part and parcel of a WPM strategy) will generate uncertainty, as reflected in Y^1. The more unpredictable host nation policy is, then the higher the costs of uncertainty in the external environment. Many elements may influence Y^1; for example, changes in public policy toward science and technology by provincial as well as the federal government, changes in political leadership at election time, the attitude of the media, and so on. Since the WPM strategy rests ultimately on the infant technology argument to justify public grants for R and D in private industry, it is a strategy based on nationalism which is an emotional issue at the best of times. Consequently WPMs have a high external risk, reflected in Y^1.

There is also a risk that the management team of the subsidiary will become more involved with the government officials and politicians of the host nation, since they are dependent upon them for continuing government grants to finance ongoing R and D expenditures. In time, the subsidiary may become more closely identified with the goals of technological independence of the host nation than with the objectives of its parent MNE.

Thus the risks of Y^1 arise from the decentralized form of organization required by the multinational firm to give WPMs. The greater autonomy of the subsidiary permits it to become a better corporate citizen for the host nation. With a WPM secured from the parent and subsidized by the federal (and probably some provincial) governments, the independent subsidiary is freed to make political alliances with influential politicians, civil servants, and opinion and media leaders in the host nation. It can tie itself into the nationalist network the more decentralized it is and the more autonomous it is perceived to be. Of course, a Canadian owned firm will always have an advantage with nationalists over a multinational, but at least the decentralized nature of a WPM permits the subsidiary to claim autonomy while retaining the flow of the firm-specific advantage to the parent.

In time an independent subsidiary may develop new core skills in its relationship with the host country government. Although a foreign subsidiary can never have the benefit of being Canadian, it can develop a stable and effective relationship with the host nation if it performs well and pays attention to its profile in the host nation. In short, the WPM offers long-run advantages to the subsidiaries of multinational firms in the form of closer political contacts in the host nation. Unfortunately, this process of a successful WPM will keep the risks of Y^1 high for the parent firm since the autonomy of the subsidiary increases the costs of internal coordination of the overall global strategy of the MNE once the external political environment is altered in such a manner.

Evaluation of political risk is one of the key problems facing the MNEs. They have to be aware of the microrisks that affect their specific sectors and also take as exogenous constraints the macrorisks that affect all MNEs together. The distinction between these types of risk is discussed by Kobrin (1979), building upon earlier work by Steve Robock.

To some extent the MNEs can treat microrisks as decision variables, and in this case the WPM can be modeled as a variable within the control of the MNEs. However, there are aspects of the

FIGURE 6.2

Functional Divisions of the MNE in an International Context

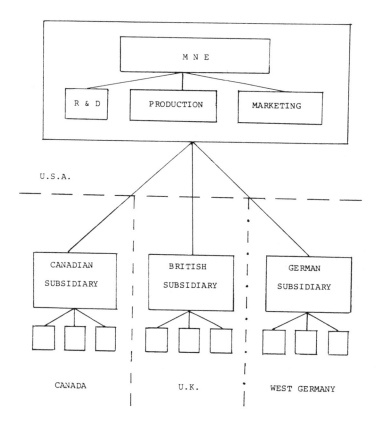

WPM which affect all foreign MNEs operating in Canada as a group: namely, the additional uncertainty stemming from the change in host nation policy. The manner in which MNEs react to the WPM strategy will depend upon their assessment of the relative weights of the microrisks versus the macrorisks.

As an example of the problems of the WPM it is useful to focus on the international marketing problems of an MNE when a WPM is introduced into its network. Figure 6.2 illustrates some of these problems.

In Figure 6.2 it is assumed, for simplicity, that the MNE has three functional areas: R and D, production, and marketing. Again, for simplicity, it is assumed that each of its three subsidiaries has these three functions, shown by their respective boxes.

The WPM involves the Canadian subsidiary and its box for R and D. The R and D subsidy increases the firm's R and D. In turn, this increases its output, thereby affecting the production box. In passing it can be noted that control of the R and D box of the parent MNE is also affected (adversely) by the WPM, as the previous discussion of the difficulty of decentralizing R and D brought out. Presumably, the production box of the parent MNE is not affected directly by a WPM, although there is some long-run danger if the firm-specific advantage of the MNE is dissipated.

The most interesting relationship to explore at this stage is the marketing box. In order to keep the Canadian government happy the subsidiary needs the payoff of increased exports (having produced the new product line in Canada). This may involve the creation of a new marketing department (one with international skills) in the subsidiary, which previously relied upon the international marketing division of the parent MNE. Most of the exports will go to the United States (like 70 percent of all Canada's exports) but some will go to other nations where the MNE has subsidiaries, for example Britain and West Germany in Figure 6.2.

The subsidiaries in these other nations will now object to the placement of the new product line in their own markets. As jobs will be lost and performance reduced in these subsidiaries, rival host governments will be lobbied for support in banning the Canadian goods. The parent MNE will be sympathetic to these grievances since most subsidiaries exist to capture a limited national market for the MNE.

To prevent this opposition within the internal organization of the MNE pressures will be brought on the Canadian subsidiary to downplay its international marketing department (if it ever starts one). Instead, the parent MNE will prefer to control the new product line through its own headquarters' international marketing division. In this manner the MNE can push the product to its other subsidiaries. Control of the marketing function is a crucial weapon that the parent MNE is very unwilling to surrender, especially if it has already lost control of the R and D function.

Now the Canadian subsidiary is in a dilemma. To satisfy its parent it cannot be an aggressive independent international marketer. Yet to pay off the Canadian government it needs to export. The resulting pressures on the management team of the subsidiary will be interesting to observe.

CONCLUSIONS

The essence of the WPM decision from the viewpoint of the multinational is the tradeoff between (a) control via its internal market with a centralized organization and (b) potential loss of control through decentralized R and D subsidized by the host nation. The choice made by the multinational will depend upon an evaluation of

- relative costs of private R and D versus subsidized R and D
- the risk of loss of control by decentralization of the R and D function
- the long-run prospects for the performance of an autonomous subsidiary and its probable contribution to the profits of the multinational

All of these costs are uncertain, so both X^1 and Y^1 are the essence of a WPM.

In terms of the internal factors (X^1), it was shown here that a WPM strategy has positive costs to the MNE rather than the zero costs assumed by its advocates. The WPM strategy in Canada appears to have been based on the premise that the MNE can award a charter to a Canadian subsidiary without any repercussions being felt in the firm or other nations. It has assumed that decentralization of the MNE's R and D function is possible and that a new product line in the Canadian subsidiary offers no problem to the parent. These premises are incorrect.

Since the decision by the MNE to award a charter for offshore R and D is not costless, the parent firm now faces extra costs in running the internal market of the MNE. All other things constant the WPM is more risky, so it is not an attractive option to the MNE unless it can be compensated by higher returns. The new elements of uncertainty facing the MNE include the difficulty in securing full intelligence from its subsidiary about the new product line. By definition the subsidiary is now a monopoly owner of a new product. The parent finds that decentralization makes it more expensive to acquire information about the correct internal pricing to be used for management fees and other internal transfers. These higher costs are partially offset by the R and D grants from the host nation to the subsidiary, yet over time a dependence on this grant develops.

In terms of external factors (Y^1), the subsidiary may now be more responsive to the political realities of the host nation (since it is dependent on the grants from the government) and may become more autonomous in its goals. While the parent firm can ultimately fire the management of its subsidiary there are clearly extra costs in letting its subsidiary get into such a possible situation. There are unexpected repercussions on foreign nations if Canada's exports of subsidized R and D intensive products are increased, since the WPM may be regarded as a nontariff barrier to trade. The effects of such external factors on the internal market of the MNE need to be recognized, and future work on WPMs might usefully address itself to these repercussions in more detail than was possible here.

7

World Product Mandates and Freer Canada-United States Trade

Bernard M. Wolf

INTRODUCTION

The concept of global or world product mandating has gained increasing attention in Canada among government officials and managers of Canadian subsidiaries of multinational enterprises (MNEs). The Canadian government's Export Promotion Committee (which produced the Hatch Report), the Ontario government's Advisory Committee on Global Product Manadating, and the Canadian Science Council have all advocated some form of world product mandating.[1] In its pure form, a global product mandating strategy involves assigning to a subsidiary total responsibility for all aspects of research and development (R & D), production, and international marketing on a worldwide basis with respect to a product or group of products. In practice, however, some functions are often retained by the parent or given to sister subsidiaries located in various parts of the world. The mandate can also be limited to a particular group of countries.

The concept of world product mandating is seen as a way to restructure the Canadian operations of MNEs in manufacturing, who control over 50 percent of assets in that sector. Many of these MNEs

The author benefited greatly from speaking to corporate executives involved in world product mandating at a conference sponsored by the *Financial Times* and Corpus Information Services on "World Product Mandating: Survival in the Post-GATT Environment," Toronto, October 5–6, 1981. Alan Rugman provided useful comments on an earlier draft of this paper.

originally established manufacturing facilities in Canada in order to serve the Canadian domestic market behind tariff walls. Typically, these Canadian branch plants produce a fairly wide array of products, each in relatively small quantity, thereby failing to achieve sufficient product specific economies of scale (and sometimes quality control) to be internationally competitive.[2] The small size of the Canadian market and trade barriers abroad have prevented the subsidiaries from obtaining the necessary scale. The import substitute nature of Canadian manufacturing (involving products similar to those produced elsewhere and often introduced into the Canadian market with a lag) has also meant that the subsidiaries have had little need to engage in R & D in Canada.

FREER TRADE AND WORLD PRODUCT MANDATES

As a result of the GATT Tokyo Round in which tariffs are reduced in eight annual steps ending on January 1, 1987, tariff protection on many products entering Canada will be substantially eroded (cuts in tariffs average 40 percent) and some nontariff barriers will be eliminated. A negotiated free trade area between the United States and Canada, as advocated by the Economic Council in its 1975 report, *Looking Outward: A New Trade Strategy for Canada*[3] and the Canadian Standing Senate Committee on Foreign Relations,[4] as well as by political figures in the United States, would go even further in this direction by not only reducing tariffs to zero but also by removing more nontariff barriers.

In a study for the Economic Council, which served as a background for its *Looking Outward* proposals, Ronald J. Wonnacott suggested that free trade would lead to a gain in the order of 7 to 9 percent of Canadian gross national product.[5,6] The argument is basically as follows. No longer limited to the small Canadian market with its demand for differentiated products, Canadian plants will cease producing a much more diverse mix of output than U.S. plants in the same industry. The increased production runs accompanying specialization are seen as reducing the gap between U.S. and Canadian productivity levels.[7] Specialization may also induce more R & D in Canada.

Faced with substantial loss of protection, either from complete free trade or from the less extreme case of reduced protection due to the Tokyo Round, the MNE will have to alter the structure of its Canadian subsidiary. (Of course, this is assuming that these losses are not replaced by other forms of protection.) Freer trade involves a change in the "rules of the game"; the firm must reevaluate how its resources can be best employed given a new environment. Essentially, two possibilities exist for the Canadian subsidiary. First, the operation can be severely curtailed or even be closed down. Such retrenchment would mean that the Canadian market would be serviced from another of the MNE's plants, especially one in the United States if it contained excess capacity. Second, the plant can be restructured or rationalized. The most complete form of rationalization is world product mandating. It appeals to Canadian subsidiary managers and Canadian government officials because it not only keeps the Canadian plant open, but it should make the plant internationally competititve and provide at least some additional research and development capability within Canada.[8]

An Ontario government advisory committee has reported that the pure form of world product mandating is unlikely to be the usual practice; less comprehensive variations will be more customary.[9] The chairman of the Committee, Lorne K. Lodge (Chairman and President of IBM Canada) has indicated that ". . . differences in operating style, organizational structure, manufacturing technology, even the nature of the product itself, all contributed to our conclusion that there is no one model or blueprint which works universally."[10]

A world product mandate received by a subsidiary can be limited either geographically or functionally. The geographical limitation would be in the form of granting the product mandate for only a portion of the world market such as only the United States and Canada. Functionally, the mandate could be limited to R & D and production rights only. Marketing would be retained by the parent or done by sister subsidiaries. The sister subsidiaries located in various countries would carry out the marketing in their own areas. In this case, the subsidiary will utilize the ". . . prepositioned knowledgeable foreign sales outlets"[11] of the firm. Having these marketing subsidiaries in a number of markets is one of the strengths of the MNE. Moreover, if the subsidiary is not producing an end product, the output may find its way as an input into another subsidiary's final product. In this case a sister organization of the subsidiary becomes the buyer.[12] An even more extreme example of mandating in which geographical and strict functional limitations apply is the Canada–United States Auto Pact by which only production rights are given to the Canadian subsidiaries. In fact, the mandating aspects are so limited that it is misleading to cite the Auto Pact as a case of world product mandating. The Auto Pact is a much more limited case of rationalization.

For a WPM to be successful, some R & D must be done by the subsidiary; otherwise, it is difficult for it to maintain its competitive position as the nature of the product evolves. However, even within a functional area such as R & D, there is scope for giving the subsidiary only partial responsibility. R & D can be divided in a number of ways such as basic research, applied research, and development. Lodge points out that ". . . generally speaking, few affiliates perform all the R & D related to their manufacturing mandate. They continue to draw . . . to some extent . . . on the enormous pool of technology which is typically available from their parent firms or from their sister organizations in other countries."[13]

Given that such a wide range of possibilities exists, the *Report of the Advisory Committee on Global Product Mandating*, prepared for the Ontario government, suggested that the term "product mandating" be replaced by "specialized mission."[14] For purposes of this chapter, the term world product mandating will continue to be used since it is widely accepted, and the assumption is made here that the mandate will include some R & D work but not necessarily any foreign marketing function. United States based firms like Black and Decker, Control Data, Garrett, General Electric, IBM, Litton, Phillips, Westinghouse, and Xerox are examples of firms whose Canadian subsidiaries have one or more WPMs.[15] In Europe, the process has been spurred by the formation of the European Economic Community and the free trade agreements made by the EEC with other European countries.[16]

The rest of this chapter is divided into four parts. The first and major section deals with circumstances under which a parent MNE will grant a WPM to its subsidiary. Following this section a simple model is formulated. The third part asks the question: what are the costs and benefits to Canada of establishing WPMs? The last section deals with the impact of WPMs on international trade.

FACTORS INFLUENCING THE DECISION TO IMPLEMENT A WORLD PRODUCT MANDATING STRATEGY

In interviews, managers of Canadian subsidiaries that have been awarded a WPM stress that the parent firm rarely initiates the idea of introducing the WPM to the subsidiary. Rather it is the subsidiary's management who must convince the parent of the feasibility of the

WPM. The WPM ". . . must be identified, justified and earned by the affiliate. . . ."[17] The subsidiary, through the internal market of the firm, must prove that granting the Canadian subsidiary the WPM is (and will remain) the most cost effective way of servicing markets for that product line; the subsidiary is competing with sister operations for the WPM. In other words, the subsidiary's management must engage in a ". . . goodly amount of 'internal selling' and persuasion"[18] proving that the WPM route is the best use of the existing Canadian subsidiary. There are quite a number of variables relevant to the decision.

Management

Both the management of the subsidiary and that of the corporate parent must be able and willing to implement the world product mandating strategy. As indicated earlier, the task of proving that the Canadian plant is best suited for a particular WPM falls on the local management. First, and perhaps foremost, the subsidiary must demonstrate that it has the managerial depth to carry out a world product mandating strategy requiring the export of internationally competitive goods. The type of management previously needed for a branch plant producing import substitutes similar to those made by the parent may be quite different. Of course, the parent may elect to strengthen the subsidiary's existing management to make it capable of implementing the required changes. Ultimately, however, unless the subsidiary's management is up to the task, the WPM will flounder even if other factors are favorable.

With respect to the corporate headquarters' management, there are three requirements to fulfill the WPM strategy. Initially, the management must be receptive to the notion of WPMs; otherwise, even the strongest case presented by the Canadian subsidiary will get nowhere. The corporate headquarters' management must also be able to separate out a viable product line so that the Canadian subsidiary obtains an exclusive role for which the parent has no ready backup. Finally, once the product line demarcation is established, sufficient autonomy must be given to the subsidiary to allow it to implement its task, but some control system must be used to monitor the subsidiary. Some control over a phase of its operation is given up by the parent in return for what it hopes will be an enhancement of its assets embodied in the subsidiary.

According to David Rutenberg, a professor of management, "Among U.S. corporations it has long been corporate practice to spread product divisional managements around the country, rather than insisting that they be adjacent to the company headquarters. . . . Given the precedent of operating autonomy, it is a small step to move the management of a product division from the United States to another safe and comfortable nation."[19]

The increased autonomy of the subsidiary and its new technical capability should provide incentive for the subsidiary's management to seek the mandate. Once a first mandate is successfully introduced, the subsidiary should have an easier time convincing headquarters to assign it further mandates.

Of course, both the subsidiary and parent management must also be aware that even with good management, the mandate may fail. First, R & D is always somewhat risky and the product could fail to evolve. Second, the market demand could decline before the subsidiary can establish follow-on products. Third, costs may become unfavorable for the subsidiary. Fourth, competition from foreign suppliers could intensify.

Decentralization of R & D

Since world product mandating means more than restructuring production, the feasibility of doing research and development in the Canadian subsidiary is of paramount consideration. Whether or not such R & D is likely to be done in Canada hinges upon two factors. There is, first, the issue of whether R & D can successfully be decentralized in a large country such as the United States, the home base of the majority of Canadian subsidiaries. Only if the answer is yes is it worthwhile asking the second questions: whether having some of the decentralized R & D done in a foreign country is a further serious obstacle.

In general, the case for decentralization depends to some degree on the extent of scale economies prevalent in doing R & D; the greater the importance of these, the less likely the decentralization. Related to these scale economies is firm size. Even if large firms do not do proportionately more R & D than some medium size firms, the larger absolute size of the R & D effort may allow decentralization when R & D scale economies are important. Thus, size of firm may be a relevant consideration.[20]

Work by Fischer and Behrman suggests that successful decentralization of the R & D function depends upon the way R & D activities are coordinated. The key is in establishing the correct mix between granting the R & D unit sufficient autonomy and exercising control by corporate headquarters so that the ". . . creative output will be in areas of corporate interest or in support of corporate policies."[21]

To see in which industries R & D can be feasibly decentralized, a useful clue could be provided by examining the extent to which R & D is decentralized among the operations of multiplant firms in the United States. However, the evidence would not be conclusive since not all potential decentralization may have been realized and some actual decentralization may be nonviable in the long run.

When part of the R & D is to be done abroad, the problem as seen by Fischer and Behrman is still essentially that of keeping the proper balance between autonomy and control. Nevertheless,

> A decision by the firm to internationalize R & D activities further complicates the nature of the control relationship existing between corporate headquarters and R & D. One reason for this is the introduction of geographic distance, market variations, and language and cultural differences of personnel. These amplify the problems which would be associated with even a straightforward coordination and control relationship.[22]

In their study of 34 American and 16 European MNEs they found that "firms with tightly coordinated R & D practices are better able to deal with international situations in the efficient allocation ot R & D resources than are loosely coordinated companies."[23] Furthermore, they note that the choice of a particular R & D coordination style by an MNE appears to be influenced critically by the scientific nature of the firm's industry.[24]

Rutenberg also makes the point that the very initial stages of a research and development project may not be suitable for world product mandating but later stages are compatible.

> Early in the life of a new product family there is no good information on which to base business decisions. Essentially, the idea of product development is to find all sorts of ideas, continuing the negative cash flow until the project has yielded just enough to justify cancelling it. This need to have the power to cut off funding requires a closeness that seems incompatible with global product mandating.[25]

Aside from the issue of coordination and decision making, there is the contention that doing R & D in a foreign country is likely to lead to a dissipation of the firm's knowledge base. In a recent article in *Canadian Public Policy*, Alan Rugman suggests that centralized R & D by the parent at home is required by the theory of internalization, an important explanatory theory of foreign direct investment. He points out that the "MNE prefers to control the rate of use of its knowledge advantage, and it is afraid of dissipation."[26] He further argues that "Unless R & D is centralized in the parent, its firm specific advantage is at risk."[27] Thus, Rugman believes that internalization leads to a centralization of R & D in the MNE.

Rugman is quite correct that the theory of internalization postulates that the firm will try to bypass the market in order to avoid uncertainties in the transfer of knowledge between parties and thereby generally seek to maintain its knowledge base for its own use. However, in spite of the firm's desire to keep its knowledge within its internal structure, the firm has been known to give up some control over its knowledge and use the market by licensing its know-how or by participating in joint ventures where the conditions are profitable enough or no alternative exists.[28] By the same token, other factors such as subsidies may overwhelm the parent firm's reluctance to do R & D even when there are hazards to knowledge dissipation.[29]

Moreover, there is the question of to what extent decentralization of R & D among subsidiaries does, in fact, dissipate know-how. If the Canadian subsidiary is wholly owned by the MNE and not considered to be in a sensitive industry as defined by the Canadian federal or provincial governments, the risks of dissipation should not be unduly large. Only when there is minority ownership or the threat thereof or the threat of nationalization should the MNE feel that its knowledge base is threatened by moving R & D to a foreign country. One might also note that regardless of where the R & D is done (even at the headquarters of the parent), there is always the chance that there will be a knowledge drain created by key R & D personnel leaving the firm.

Peter Buckley, one of the leading proponents of the internalization theory in fact regards it as a mistake ". . . to equate the internalization of activities with the centralization of those activities."[30] He finds internalization compatible with decentralization in some situations.

In summary, I would argue that (a) decentralization of R & D has differing costs depending upon the particular circumstances and (b) even when these costs are not nil, in some cases they can be counterbalanced by other positive factors. This view is borne out in empirical work done by Edwin Mansfield:

In many important industries, like pharmaceuticals, international technology transfer is being promoted by the fact that companies have been
carrying on increasing shares of their R & D overseas. Over ten percent
of the R & D carried out in 1980 by the (US-based) firms in our sample
was performed outside the United States. In some industries like pharmaceuticals, this percentage is much larger.[31]

We now turn to a brief look at the other factors which influence
the decision to implement a world product mandating strategy. These
can be dealt with more briefly.

Investment to Restructure the Subsidiary

Transforming the Canadian facility from an import substitution
operation to one carrying out a world mandating strategy may involve
considerable investment. The lower the costs of such a reorganization,
the more likely the WPM will be granted.

Subsidiary Closing Costs

If the alternative to world product mandating is closing the
existing Canadian operations, the costs associated with such a closing
will be relevant; they may be seen as an offset to the costs of implementing the WPM.

Costs of Production

The costs of production in Canada compared to other sourcing
locations is certainly a vital element. Wage rates, capital costs, raw
material prices and taxes are important. Obviously, the exchange rate
plays a leading role in influencing these costs. The recent fall in the
Canadian dollar relative to the U.S. dollar makes production in
Canada more attractive though this must be tempered by persistent
Canadian inflation in excess of that in the United States and by the
resistance of Canadian unions to grant the wage concessions made by
some American unions.

Transportation and Communication Costs

Since a WPM involves heavy exporting and importing, transportation costs are a consideration. The lower the transport costs, the more

favorable the climate for world product mandating. Communication costs are also worth noting. Both transportation and communication costs are influenced by the degree of government regulation.

Trade Impediments

If the subsidiary moves from import substitutes to a WPM, it must have assurances that previously domestically produced goods that have been displaced by the mandate now can be imported without heavy border duties. If tariffs continue to exist, a tariff remission scheme on imports similar to the one recently granted to Volkswagen could be implemented. In terms of the product line for which the WPM is granted, it is necessary that trade barriers in other countries (especially the United States) not be onerous. World product mandating makes sense only in a world with low trade barriers.[32] For the small number of products for which the Canadian market itself is large, this constraint will be less operative.

A high probability of reverting to steep international tariffs is also incompatible with world product mandating. Finally, it is useful to indicate that the chances of world product mandating are improved if the subsidiary has access to the entire Canadian market for its products which means that provincial trade barriers need to be eliminated.

Government Assistance

The conditions for achieving a WPM can be increased by the Canadian federal and/or provincial governments providing various forms of assistance. These may include R & D or employment subsidies, favorable terms for borrowing, tax relief or favored government procurement status. In the latter case, the government or its agencies can agree to give goods produced under the WPM special treatment or, more likely, give other goods produced by the firm, including some imports, favored status in return for the MNE establishing its mandate. Many of these devices have been used to lure existing mandates. The governments can also stipulate in large contracts for imports that "offset" work be done within Canada, and that could involve establishing a WPM for the Canadian subsidiary. This is how Westinghouse established its first mandate which involved large industrial turbines.

Government Attitude

In addition to providing monetary incentives to the MNEs in return for establishing a mandate, the attitude of the government toward foreign direct investment is important. MNEs are more likely to feel welcome when performance rather than ownership is the criterion by which firms are judged. The Canadian National Energy Policy (NEP) and controversy over enlarging the powers of FIRA[33] obviously do not encourage the granting of WPMs to Canadian subsidiaries of MNEs.

Special Conditions in Canada

A number of special conditions may serve as an inducement to world product mandating. First, although the aggregate Canadian market is small overall, it has some sectors in the area of natural resource extraction that are large on an international scale. These are the areas in which subsidiaries are likely to make the most convincing cases to their parent firms for establishing a WPM. Second, such benefits as the applicability of Commonwealth preferences may still be relevant even with the changes brought about by British entry into the European Economic Community. Third, the possibility of doing business with Libya or other countries with which the parent MNE is reluctant to trade for political reasons may make Canada an attractive base.

A MODEL TO EVALUATE THE FEASIBILITY OF WORLD PRODUCT MANDATING

The above items can be presented in the form of a simple model. The sum of costs less subsidies (or favored treatment) is compared with the cost of producing the product line (involved in the WPM) in the cheapest alternative location owned by the parent firm. All sums represent present discounted values over the chosen time span. The management factor (item 1) is assumed to be included in the relevant costs. A world product mandate is feasible in Canada when

$$C_{RA} + C_{RD} + C_{PR} + C_{TP} + C_{TB} - C_{CL} - S_G - A_S < T$$

where:

C_{RA} = cost of transforming or rationalizing the subsidiary from import substitution production to world product mandating

C_{RD} = cost of doing the R & D in Canada

C_{PR} = cost of Canadian production

C_{TP} = cost of transportation

C_{TB} = cost of trade barriers

C_{CL} = cost of closing the subsidiary (the sum is subtracted since these costs will be saved if the plant is rationalized rather than closed)

S_G = Canadian government inducements provided

A_S = special advantages of producing in Canada

T = total cost of carrying out the WPM from the cheapest alternative source

COSTS AND BENEFITS OF WORLD PRODUCT MANDATING TO THE HOST COUNTRY

The costs and benefits to Canada of attracting world product mandates must be seen in the context of alternative industrial strategy proposals which cannot be discussed in this chapter. However, a number of points still can be made. Obviously, a WPM is an attractive alternative that not only can save a Canadian subsidiary and the associated jobs but also carries with it R & D work that can be used as a basis for enhancing Canada's factor endowment. However, a WPM is not feasible in all manufacturing industries. The mandate overcomes the problem of a small Canadian market but it still must fit in with Canada's comparative advantage.

One disadvantage of freer trade which is often cited is that small indigenous Canadian companies will not be able to take advantage of markets outside Canada because they lack marketing resources.[34] In the case of WPMs, this disadvantage is somewhat mitigated because these firms can become suppliers to the MNEs carrying out the WPMs.[35] This will provide them with the opportunity to reach sufficient economies of scale without having to do the foreign selling.[36]

With all the virtues associated with world product mandating, there is the danger that the Canadian federal or provincial governments will embrace the strategy too extensively. Such documents as the Canadian Science Council's *Multinationals and Industrial Strategy: The Role of World Product Mandates* tend to extol the virtues of world product mandating without sufficiently emphasizing the risks involved.[37] If the governments become too uncritical about WPMs they may oversubsidize the strategy through the devices mentioned above. Particularly serious is the notion of turning government procurement policies into a form of industrial aid. The problem is essentially similar to what economists refer to as the infant industry tariff question. A subsidy is in order if the costs of the inducements are smaller than the social benefits that accrue to the nation (all properly discounted). If countries around the world playing host to subsidiaries of MNEs get into a bidding contest over who can provide the most enticements for WPMs, the host countries will all be losers. There is also the possibility that other governments may retaliate against Canadian exports benefiting from government assistance provided to facilitate the implementation of a WPM.

WORLD PRODUCT MANDATING
AND INTERNATIONAL TRADE

When a subsidiary of a MNE moves from an import substitution orientation to world product mandating, there are a number of implications for international trade. Obviously, international trade is increased. Also, intrafirm trade as a percentage of international trade rises. Using conventional industry definitions, the chances of increased intraindustry trade is high since a number of world product mandates sanctioned by a parent MNE are likely to be in the same industry.[38] This industry is probably also one that is relatively "footloose." Moreover, the distribution of WPMs is usually among industrial countries thereby increasing trade among these higher income countries.

In terms of the basis for trade, the role of various economies of scale becomes more important. In addition, if governments provide inducements for WPMs, then the proportion of trade partially dependent on the role of governments is enhanced. Since WPMs require low tariffs, the constituency for freer trade becomes larger, except in those instances when world product mandating involves government aids, especially government procurement policies that are often protectionist. Finally, given that R & D decentralization accompanies product rationalization in a WPM, the factor endowment of the country where the WPM is located will change over time; comparative advantage is thus altered by the WPM. Hence, it is quite evident that world product mandating strategy puts further distance between the simple Heckscher–Ohlin factor endowment theory and the realities of international trade in the world.

Whitman, viewing "the growing importance of intraindustry trade and of overseas production and investment in automotive parts" suggests that:

These developments represent phenomena based less on classical determinants of international trade—differences between nations in factor
endowments or production functions—than on the characteristics of
firms operating in an environment of imperfect competition and attempting to maximise the flow of benefit from their particular constel-
lation of advantages as conditions change over time.[39]

CONCLUSION

A world product mandating strategy provides the potential for
the government to achieve some of its national goals (employment,
investment, and level of technology in manufacturing) without unduly
sacrificing efficient allocation of resources. It is a very appealing
approach to restructuring Canadian manufacturing under conditions
of freer trade. Already it has been implemented in an impressive
number of MNEs but cannot be applied to all industries. To what
extent it can be implemented depends upon industry characteristics
(especially with respect to the possibility of decentralizing R & D),
size of firm, management attitudes and strengths, general economic
and political climate in Canada, inducements provided by the various
levels of Canadian government and alternative inducements provided
by other foreign governments. A simple model was developed to
illustrate the decision making involved in assessing the feasibility of a
world product mandating strategy on the part of an MNE.

NOTES

1. Export Promotion Review Committee, *Strengthening Canada Abroad*
(The Hatch Report) (Ottawa: Department of Industry, Trade and Commerce,
November 1979). Ontario Ministry of Industry and Tourism, *The Report of the
Advisory Committee on Global Product Mandating* (Toronto, December 1980);
Science Council of Canada, *Multinationals and Industrial Strategy: The Role of
World Product Mandates* (Ottawa: Ministry of Supply and Services, 1980).

2. See Richard E. Caves, *Diversification, Foreign Investment and Scale in
North American Manufacturing Industries* (Ottawa: Information Canada for the
Economic Council of Canada, 1975).

3. Economic Council of Canada, *Looking Outward: A New Trade Strategy
for Canada* (Ottawa: Information Canada, 1975), p. 108. The report advocated a
multilateral free trade area as Canada's best industrial strategy but considered
Canada–United States free trade as an attractive alternative.

4. Canadian Senate Committee on Foreign Affairs, *Canada–United States
Relations* (Ottawa: Queen's Printer, 1978), p. 121.

5. Ronald J. Wonnacott, *Canadian Trade Options* (Ottawa: Information
Canada for the Economic Council of Canada, 1975), p. 177.

6. However, critics of Wonnacott such as Roma Dauphin and Bruce W. Wilkinson doubt that a free trade area between the United States and Canada would be favorable to Canada. See Roma Dauphin, *The Impact of Free Trade in Canada* (Ottawa: Information Canada for the Economic Council of Canada, 1978), and Bruce W. Wilkinson, *Canada in the Changing World Economy* (Montreal: C. D. Howe Research Institute, Canada–U.S. Prospects Series, 1980), Appendix D.

7. Donald J. Daly, a close observer of Canada–U.S. productivity differences, states that ". . . it is my opinion that this [product specific scale economies] is the most important single source of the differences in costs and productivity [in manufacturing] between the two countries." Donald J. Daly, *Canada's Comparative Advantage* (Ottawa: Economic Council of Canada Discussion Paper, August 1979), p. 28.

8. The plant will have to be internationally competitive from the point of view of the firm in order to survive, but the competitiveness may be artificial if the government has provided assistance to attract the mandate.

9. Ontario Ministry of Industry and Tourism, *The Report*.

10. Lorne J. Lodge, "Global Product Mandating: A Business Perspective," speech prepared for a *Financial Times*/Corpus Conference on "World Product Mandating: Survival in the Post-GATT Environment" (Toronto, October 5–6, 1981), p. 7.

11. George J. Hubbs, Chairman and President of Control Data Canada, "Global Product Mandating: Does it Pay?", speech prepared for the *Financial Times*/Corpus Conference, p. 6.

12. In this case the rationalization can be classified as vertical rather than horizontal since the subsidiary is essentially producing a component which is being assembled with other components elsewhere.

13. Lorne J. Lodge, "Global Product Mandating: A Business Perspective," p. 8.

14. Ontario Ministry of Industry and Tourism, *The Report*, p. 3.

15. For a description of the world product mandates awarded to Black and Decker Canada, Westinghouse Canada, Garrett Manufacturing and Litton Systems, see Science Council of Canada, *Multinationals*. In the various cases of world product mandating if it is not clear what percentage of the Canadian subsidiary's output is accounted for by the WPM.

16. See Bernard M. Wolf, "Canada–United States Free Trade: Lessons from the European Experience" (Toronto: mimeographed, 1981).

17. Lorne J. Lodge, "Global Product Mandating: A Business Perspective," p. 20.

18. George J. Hubbs, "Global Product Mandating: Does it Pay?", p. 4.

19. David P. Rutenberg, "Global Product Mandating," in *International Business: A Canadian Perspective*, edited by K. C. Dhawan, Hamid Etemad and Richard W. Wright (Don Mills, Ontario: Addison-Wesley, 1981), p. 589.

20. See F. M. Scherer, *Industrial Market Structure and Economic Performance*, second edition (Chicago: Rand McNally, 1980), Chapter 15, pp. 407–38.

21. William A. Fischer and Jack N. Behrman, "The Coordination of Foreign R & D Activities by Transnational Corporations," *Journal of International Business Studies* 10 (Winter 1979), p. 28.

22. *Ibid.*, pp. 28–29.

23. *Ibid.*, p. 34.

24. *Ibid.*, p. 31.

25. David P. Rutenberg, "Global Product Mandating," speech prepared for the *Financial Times*/Corpus Conference, p. 4.

26. Alan M. Rugman, "Research and Development by Multinational and Domestic Firms in Canada," *Canadian Public Policy* 7 (Autumn 1981), p. 606.

27. *Ibid.*

28. For example, Western MNEs often license Japanese firms and establish joint ventures where it is otherwise difficult to penetrate the Japanese market.

29. Rugman readily acknowledges this point in "Multinational Enterprises and World Product Mandates" (mimeographed, presented at a seminar of the Economic Council of Canada, Ottawa, May 18, 1982). See Chapter 6 of this volume.

30. Peter J. Buckley, "New Theories of International Business: Some Unresolved Issues" (mimeographed, presented at a Conference on Strategic Factors in the Growth of International Business, Reading, England, March 20, 1982), p. 14.

31. Edwin Mansfield, "International Technology Transfers: Rates, Benefits, Costs and Public Policy" (mimeographed, presented at the Allied Social Sciences Meetings, Washington, D.C., December 1981), p. 3.

32. However, trade barriers attributable to government procurement policies may assist in the implementation of a world product mandating strategy.

33. Suggested by the Canadian government in a speech from the throne but later withdrawn.

34. See Wilkinson, *Canada in the Changing World Economy*, p. 165. However, some evidence to the contrary is provided by Daly, MacCharles and Altwasser. They cite a significant number of smaller Canadian owned companies that have secured a 'niche' in world markets. Donald J. Daly, Donald C. MacCharles and Wendy Altwasser, *The Canadian Business Review* (September 1982).

35. Lorne J. Lodge, "Global Product Mandating: A Business Perspective," p. 12, points out that ". . . for every Ford, Westinghouse or IBM, there are literally hundreds of smaller business, most of them Canadian owned, which supply an enormous range of products and services to our companies."

36. Currently, Canadian subsidiaries of U.S. based MNEs have an incentive to use the same U.S. suppliers as their parents (rather than local Canadian firms) since by producing similar end products they require essentially the same inputs. Such an arrangement cuts down on search behavior on the part of the subsidiary and generally assures low costs because of long production runs. Under world product mandating Canadian firms will have a better change of securing input contracts since the Canadian subsidiaries will be producing unique products. See Donald C. MacCharles and Bernard M. Wolf, "Statistics Canada's Flirtation with Mercantilism" (*Canadian Public Policy*, forthcoming).

37. Science Council, *Multinationals*, p. 11. For example, the Science Council mentions the positive employment effects of switching from a branch plant operation to a world product mandating strategy without adequately discussing the negative aspects. A rationalized plant might be much more capital intensive thereby requiring less labor which would have to be absorbed elsewhere.

38. For a discussion of the intraindustry trade phenomenon, see Herbert Giersch, editor, *On the Economics of Intra-Industry Trade* (Tuebingen:

J. B. Mohr, 1979). The link between intraindustry and intrafirm trade is discussed by Gerald K. Helleiner, "Transnational Corporations and Trade Structures: The Role of Intra-Firm Trade," pp. 159–181, and by several other conference participants in the Giersch volume. See also, Paul R. Krugman, "Intra-Industry Specialization and the Gains from Trade," *Journal of Political Economy* 89 (October 1981), pp. 959–73.

39. Marina von Neumann Whitman, "International Trade and Investment Two Perspectives," *Essays in International Finance*, no. 143 (Princeton, N.J., July 1981), p. 23.

8

World Product Mandating in Perspective

Hamid G. Etemad

SUMMARY

This chapter examines the concept of a world product mandate (WPM) from the perspectives of the host country, the subsidiary, and the multinational enterprise (MNE). A WPM has related, but different and generally positive, effects on host country–subsidiary/multinational enterprise relations. Mandated operations enjoy more efficiency than those of miniature and truncated plants and experience more cooperation between the host country, subsidiary, and MNE parent. This chapter presents a detailed discussion of a WPM's features, advantages and cost-benefits in three separate sections—from the viewpoint of the host, subsidiary and parent company (MNE).

BACKGROUND

The host country–subsidiary relationship is one of mutual interdependence causing conflict and cooperation. Multinational enterprises operate across country boundaries and are not necessarily dependent on any *one* operation or country. They possess technolgy, know-how, and expertise to transform resources into end products; but, they need the resources, location(s) for transforming them into end products, and finally, markets for selling those products. In this process, MNEs utilize resources, generate income and employment, and satisfy consumer and industrial needs. Smooth management of this process requires control (Alsegg, 1971, pp. 7–8; Robinson, 1978, pp. 24–30 and 643–49). It is not, of course,

necessary to do all these activities at one location. Different parts of
the process can be carried out in different locations (Robinson, 1978,
p. 143).[1] As operating conditions change, a function or a part of an
operation may be *shifted* from one location—where resources are
constrained (or cost of doing business is high or rising)—to another
location where such activities are welcome or can be carried out on
more competitive terms (Kujawa, 1972). If shifts are allowed to proceed unimpeded, MNEs can develop perfect *control* and be very
mobile (Etemad, 1980). Control may also require parallel operations,
multiple sourcing, and certain flexibility and freedom in action.

Host countries are sovereign entities. They possess and control
both the markets and resources that MNEs need. To generate employment and promote growth and development, host countries need to
have access to technology and expertise to utilize their resources
and accomplish their goals. By virtue of their sovereignty and regulatory powers, however, they claim full control over all activities
within their borders, including the subsidiary operation of MNEs,
and are very reluctant to relinquish it (for example see Delupis,
1973, pp. 49–64).[2]

In summary then, although MNEs and host countries can complement each other very well, which requires cooperation, the MNE's
need for control of its subsidiary operations, including mobility, and
the host country's sovereignty—and hence regulatory controls—over
her resources, markets and operations within its jurisdiction come
into conflict and tarnish their otherwise cooperative relationship.
This summary characterizes the nature of the business atmosphere in
which a subsidiary must conduct its operations (for examples of
conflict-cooperation cases see Vernon, 1976; Ringbakk, 1976;
Searby, 1976; Wells, 1977).

Given the above atmosphere, subsidiary managers find themselves
at the center of conflict. On one hand, they find themselves to be:
(1) dependent on their parent companies; (2) under the parent's administrative control; (3) expected to be loyal to the parent organization (Science Council of Canada, 1980); and (4) representatives of the
global interests of MNEs in the host country. On the other hand,
they are: (1) required to be good corporate citizens of the host country, and (2) expected to match or better the performance of their
host country indigenous counterparts. These are incompatible, especially in conflict situations. The WPM is a recent international business development which can promote further cooperation and offers
great potential in resolving a major portion of the conflict.

The balance of this chapter will examine the concept of a WPM from three different perspectives. First, it will study a WPM from the host country's viewpoint in terms of its advantages and potential costs as compared to a typical state of host country–subsidiary relations under other arrangements. Second, it will look at the effect of a WPM on the subsidiary's internal operation. Finally, it will examine the WPM's potential effect on the parent company's (MNE) global operations.

WPM FROM THE HOST COUNTRY'S PERSPECTIVE

Contrary to the notion of the nation state's sovereignty and regulatory powers, a host country's perceived lack of control is one of the major difficulties in the host country–subsidiary/MNE's operation. Host countries are not content with the fact that the locus of some decisions are not within their jurisdiction. Most of their *specific* complaints or concerns are directly attributable to the "miniature" or "truncated" nature of MNE operations in their countries. Some of these complaints are listed below:

- Absence of or insufficient R and D at the subsidiary level, especially when the market size is small
- Insufficient transfer or diffusion of technology
- Employment of obsolete technology
- Inefficient subsidiary operation/no economies of scale
- High transfer pricing for goods imported from other sister subsidiaries
- Downward pressure on the host's currency and drain on foreign exchange
- Low local content ratio
- Low or no exports
- Negative or neutral effect on economic growth and development
- Low or no adherence to host country's national goals

Most of the above difficulties are the consequences of the host government's own policies. Miniature and truncated operation is a typical MNE response to high tariff, nontariff barriers (NTB) and other regulatory restrictions (in the case of Canada, see Economic Council of Canada, 1975, pp. 34–47; Ontario Ministry of Industry & Tourism, 1980; Beigie, 1981; Rutenberg, 1981). When free access to the market is ruled out (by tariffs, quotas and NTBs), servicing of a country's need from the most economical location becomes unfeasible. Specifically, when importing is prohibitively expensive (because of the cost of protection), MNEs see no alternative but to jump the

trade barriers by establishing small and naturally inefficient operations in the host countries (*Business Week*, Jan. 24, 1976, p. 34;
Daniels, Ogram, and Radebaugh, 1979, pp. 139–42).

Also, when restrictive regulations increase operating costs or
reinforce inefficiencies, the scale of operation is expected to match
or be smaller than local demand. It should be clear that a protected
and inefficient operation is not—nor does it have the incentive to be—
competitive on the open world markets and hence exports from the
host country to other markets, especially for undifferentiated products, stand a very slim chance. This being the case, the subsidiary's
direct contribution to the country's economic development and to
the balance of payment *cannot* be significant. In addition to restrictions, infrastructural deficiencies (Mitchell, 1979) also force MNEs to
import components and/or subassemblies from abroad. In summary,
the size of the market, the stage of the host country's development
and, above all, their restrictive and regulatory trade practices, have
not been conducive to large, efficient and fully or semiautonomous
subsidiary operations.

The asymmetry of risk absorption in host country–MNE relations
is an added dimension. This includes commercial as well as country
and political risk (Kobrin, 1979 and 1981). The argument is that
developing a new technology, market, or investment involves very
substantial risks. MNEs have traditionally absorbed this risk. Once
the technology or investment is successfully developed, MNEs still
face a substantial "environmental risk" (Etemad, 1981), "regulatory
and sovereign risk" (Robinson, 1981) and "transfer risk" (*Business
Latin America*, July 25, 1979, p. 231). These risks are often present
and MNEs have little choice but to absorb them. From the host
country's viewpoint, however, the risk dimension is nonexistent or at
best insignificant since it traditionally has not been forced to bear
the costs. Host countries, for the most part, have refused to bear a
proportional share of the cost or risk of developing technology, a
product or a market.[3] Furthermore, they have been the primary
source of environmental, sovereign and political risk.

In addition to the above macro aspects of host country–subsidiary
relationships, Table 8.1 illustrates some detailed micro features of
miniature and truncated operations.

In addition to the tangible dimensions listed in Table 8.1, host
country–subsidiary relations under truncated operations suffer from
some intangible dimensions as well. For example, the host government often remains suspicious about the sincerity of the subsidiary's
effort to export. From the government's viewpoint, lack of "mandate"

TABLE 8.1

Main Features of Truncated and Miniature Operations

---

1 Scale of operations is smaller than optimum scale (small batches, small plant sizes)
2 Unit costs are higher than those of optimum scale
3 It does not provide as much employment
4 Local content ratio remains low
5 Buy/make decision of components or subassemblies is usually in favor of buying from cheaper sources (i.e., from abroad) than making it locally and, as a result, related industries (i.e., subcontractors) remain underdeveloped
6 Purchasing of components (especially from sister subsidiaries) allows for transfer pricing and its related disadvantages to the host country
7 High import of components from sister subsidiaries, transfer pricing and low or no exports apply negative pressure on balance of payments
8 There is little incentive to institute extensive R and D to improve production processes, develop locally originated technology, goods, and/or services, especially when the costs and risks are to be borne by the MNEs
9 There is little or no incentive to transfer new technology, unless forced to by competition or regulation
10 The local market remains isolated from international markets by virtue of its noncompetitiveness, protection, and/or regulatory restrictions
11 Locally produced products (for local markets) are not usually competitive on the world markets; there is usually another sister subsidiary that can produce and supply the international markets at lower prices and, therefore, the chance of exporting remains rather slim
12 1, 2, 6, 9, and 10 can be the potential sources for upward pressure on prices; widespread trade barriers may have sustained inflationary effects across the board
13 In multiproduct MNEs, local subsidiary produces a broad range of products without much concentration on any single one
14 When exports are low and/or imports are high, the host country government and subsidiary/ MNE management disagree about the cause; the government usually attributes it lack of "mandate," while the management blames it on noncompetitiveness and cost inefficiency, mainly as a result of restrictions

---

to export, as opposed to lack of competitiveness in the international marketplace, is the cause of low or no exports. This is sometimes combined with high import of components and subassemblies. This dimension of subsidiary–host country relations is not conducive to cooperation; instead, it leads to prolonged suspicion, distrust and friction. For countries with acute balance of payment problems, the above dimension may stop the government from improving the operating conditions or changing its behavior or outlook that led to truncated operations in the beginning. In fact, because of this implicit distrust, indigenous companies receive preferential treatment and incentives which improve their operating conditions to better compete in the export markets. Application of double standards—one for locally owned and another for subsidiary operations—may further tarnish MNE/subsidiary–host government relations. In the middle, of course, is the subsidiary's management. From the host government's viewpoint they are more loyal to their parent company (MNE) than to the host country and hence not the best corporate citizens to receive preferential treatment. Failure to receive preferential or at least equal treatment from the host country can be interpreted by the MNE headquarters as either managerial failure (on the part of the subsidiary) in securing a more preferred position in the host country or reinforcement of the old conflicts and possibly renewed friction. Neither of the interpretations is healthy or helpful to smooth and enhance subsidiary operations. WPM, however, eliminates or reduces some of these difficulties.

The WPM is an arrangement by which the MNE allows the subsidiary to transcend the restrictions of miniature or truncated operations by enlarging the subsidiary's mandate—the authority and hence its associated responsibilities—above and beyond the geographical or political boundaries of the host country. The sphere of the new mandate's activity and coverage depends on the interactions between the costs and benefits of the mandate in terms of economies of scale and learning, transportation charges, added cost of logistics, cost of tariffs and NTBs, and other charges associated with other intangible dimensions. For example, when economies of scale are reached at relatively low volumes or economies of learning are realized in comparatively short periods of time, the mandate is expected to be more limited in geographical scope than the global coverage implied in WPM. It is possible to have regional product mandates (RPM) especially when the demand of the contiguous reason is as large as or larger than the optimum plant size. In that case, instead of a real WPM, a more limited mandate in terms of authority and responsibility with respect

TABLE 8.2

Main Features of a Mature World Product Mandate in the Host Country

WPM allows for economies of scale, economies of learning and optimum scale (optimum batch sizes or economical plant sizes)[4]

WPM provides for more efficient operations resulting in lower unit costs that enhance competitiveness

WPM maximally creates employment which is not dependent on local trade barrier or local protection

WPM may have local content ratio (or local value added) as high as 100 percent

Given the optimal scale of operation, buy/make decisions are expected to be in favor of equally efficient operation which is an incentive for local related industries to follow suit and gear up to supply components or subassemblies to the WPM

Possibility of transfer pricing disputes due to purchasing of such components from abroad will be minimized

High exports combined with low imports will have a positive effect on the host country's balance of payments

There will be every incentive to support the continual viability of the mandate by extensive R and D at the subsidiary level

Given the benefits to the host and the need for ongoing R and D to support the mandate, R and D's high costs and risks are expected to be partially borne by the host country and indeed the mandate holder may become a future exporter of technology as well as the mandated product

Through other sister subsidiaries, the mandate holder develops access to international markets and by virtue of the open market competition, it will be constantly forced to remain competitive on the world basis

Due to economies of scale and learning, the mandate holder is supposed to become a competitive supplier of mandated product on the world market

There is no logical reason for the mandated product to apply any upward cost and price pressure on its industry or the market. Indeed, there will be some downward pressure

There will be a concentration of effort on the manufacturing, marketing and improvement of the mandated product

Since the efficiency of mandate is based on extensive exporting, the fear and suspicion about lack of exporting effort disappears

As opposed to disagreement between the host government and the subsidiary on intention or ability to export, both will cooperatively try to enhance the subsidiary's substantial competitiveness to be able to export continually

The adversarial relations causing disagreement, friction and conflict between the host government and the MNE/subsidiary is bound to be replaced by more supportive and cooperative relationships to at least one product is given to the subsidiary. A subsidiary may have to earn or win this mandate (the right to compete and possibly the authority to cover the region exclusively) on a competitive basis at least on the economic dimension and sometimes in terms of reduced risk, improved operating conditions (sociopolitical and economic) and the possibility of accelerated growth which would be impossible otherwise.

In contrast to all the disadvantages of truncated and miniature operations, a mature or fully developed WPM will have numerous potential advantages. A corresponding list of benefits is shown in Table 8.2.

In addition to the primary advantages listed in Table 8.2, a WPM provides the host country with the following secondary but important benefits:

the mandated product can become a source of national pride;

the secondary and tertiary employment, diffusion of technology, and competitiveness in the related products/components industries may help to overhaul the whole industry;

spillover effect in the related industries can contribute positively to balance of payments and economic development;

it encourages internationally oriented management philosophy and managerial practices (which are primarily concerned with longer ranges and strategic decisions) as opposed to that of provincially oriented ones which must address themselves to the day-to-day and tactical operational problems;

it is capable of cultivating a sense of trust, pride, and accomplishment between: employees and the employer; the subsidiary management and the host government authorities; and the subsidiary and its suppliers and customers. These qualities are usually absent in the local operations of MNEs and subsidiaries which have traditionally suffered from poor industrial and public relations.

From the host country's viewpoint, a fully developed WPM is a very good option.[5] It offers the country the advantages of having relatively autonomous and internally directed institutions that are operating on a worldwide basis without much of the actual costs associated with developing such institutions. The option of developing its own MNEs is, of course, a much better alternative for the host country; but that cannot be done without readily available technical and managerial help, expertise and through the worldwide network of existing MNE subsidiaries.

From a different perspective, a WPM operation based on sustained dynamic comparative advantage is bound to apply extreme competitive pressures on its industry, on the associated suppliers in the host country, and also on the international markets. It should not be difficult to envision how such pressures could cause a total overhaul in the worldwide industry and result in the majority of world market participants following suit or risking a loss of a substantial portion of their global markets. It is difficult, however, to forecast whether several WPMs in the same industry will be located in one country or scattered in several countries as the components of dynamic comparative advantage (e.g., location–specific advantages, firm–specific advantages, etc.) are different for all MNEs and change over time. In fact, where large-scale governmental support (economic and/or political) is one of the necessary ingredients of a WPM's success (e.g., in large industrial products like power plants, gas turbines, etc.), it is not to the advantage of two competitors to operate similar WPMs out of one country, as the local government can actively support only one of them.

Since the success of a WPM is heavily hinged upon extensive exports to other countries, the long-run industrial strategy in the host country must eventually adopt a "free trade" orientation; for import of other countries (from the WPM country) must be financed by their exports in the long run.

In summary, the WPM is an advantageous strategy which allows the host country to utilize its dynamic and long-run comparative advantage to harvest the benefits of trade, and to reorganize its industrial structure on the basis of free trade and comparative advantage strategies while capitalizing on a cooperative venture with the MNE and its sister subsidiary network and internal markets.

WPM FROM THE SUBSIDIARY'S PERSPECTIVE

The WPM can have profound effects on a subsidiary's operation. These effects can be divided and then studied under four separate categories: effects on the subsidiary's business relations; effect on management and organization; effect on the locus and composition of decision; and, finally, effect on risk and resource commitment.

Effect on Business Relations

Subsidiary's business relations refers to those relations with: (1) the host country or host government, (2) the parent company, and (3) its own employees and suppliers.[6] From a host country viewpoint, MNE–subsidiary is a very strong and indestructible coalition, for the subsidiary is under direct administrative, technical, at times financial and often indirect controls of the MNE (Weichman, 1974). The coalition is expected to take an adversarial position when it comes to dealing with the host country or the host government (Gunnemann, 1975, pp. 4–26), even to the extent that the relationship is characterized as zero sum games (Heller and Willat, 1975, pp. 19–29; Etemad, 1980). In short, suspicion, distrust and anxiety symbolize the host country–subsidiary relations while strength, confidence, trust and subordination characterize that of subsidiary and parent company relations.

The parent company has very little incentive to grant a WPM to any subsidiary. Doing so defeats the very basic feature of MNEs–that is, flexibility and freedom of choice with regard to source and location of supplies. Insofar as worldwide procurement of the mandated product is concerned, a fully developed or natural WPM implies that the parent enterprise gives up this privilege and commits itself to the mandated subsidiary as the sole source in control of supplies for its worldwide markets.[7] In other words, it agrees to be fully dependent on one subsidiary. This could be too great a burden for the MNE. In addition, the parent must prevail on other subsidiaries to honor the mandate. Also, the parent (and the mandate holder) must make sure that subsidiaries do everything in their power to make the mandate a successful one. In other words, the MNE and its sister subsidiary system may become the implicit hostages of the mandate agreement, insofar as the mandated product is concerned, unless a subsidiary earns its mandate.[8] MNEs are not in favor of such a position and hence would not grant a mandate to a subsidiary voluntarily.

In order to receive a mandate, a subsidiary must become highly competitive or find other sources of support. As a result of a mandate, the host country receives substantial benefits. Indeed, there is such a great deal at stake for the host country that it cannot remain indifferent. It finds itself obliged to lend active support to the subsidiary to bid for and finally secure a mandate. Given the profound future benefits to the subsidiary (because of the mandate), a subsidiary finds it difficult not to accept the help and support from an old adversary in fighting for the mandate. In this process, a new coalition (i.e., subsidiary–host country) is formed and the old coalition (i.e., subsidiary–parent) is weakened. As a result, in order to receive, operate and continue with the mandate successfully, the subsidiary will need the host government's continued active and substantial support for some time, at least in the beginning. This need changes the previous business arrangement or relation. The subsidiary–host government relations are forced to become more cooperative, which the local managers of the subsidiary welcome very much. A subsidiary gains a sense of internal harmony and control of its environment (e.g., subsidiary–host government adversary relations subside) and the host country–subsidiary relations undergo a profound change toward more cooperation.

Subsidiary–MNE relations cannot suffer very much because the success of the mandate is highly dependent upon the marketing and supportive effort of all other sister subsidiaries in trying to sell the mandated product in their own market(s), at least at the beginning when the subsidiary is incapable of selling to international markets independently. In reality, the success of even survival of the mandated operation is in the hands of the MNE's internal market, though the subsidiary network, which are all in turn under the administrative control of the MNE's headquarters. In a sense, the fate of the mandate is a hostage of the MNE's external control.

Subsidiary's industrial relations are bound to improve as the result of the mandate. MNEs have traditionally suffered from poor industrial relations, as they have been accused of playing off one subsidiary's labor force against another's. This situation changes with the mandate. The mandated subsidiary becomes an internally directed entity in control of its labor force and industrial relations and the fear of manipulation subsides. The set of operating forces and pressures change as well. The subsidiary will still be under constant pressure to contain wage settlements and control productivity. The pressure, however, is not caused by the parent directing them to do so but is a self-created pressure to remain competitive on the open international market to preserve the mandate's vitality and viability.

The relationship between the subsidiary and its suppliers is also expected to improve. As operations and sales grow and become steady, suppliers can rely on the long range horizon, capitalize on the economies of scale and learning in their own operation, and even invest in process R and D to improve upon their costs, design or quality. Improvements in quality, cost and competitiveness of the mandated product are to their advantage, as increased scales and success of the product on international markets gives the suppliers the benefits of these markets while it spares them from direct involvement in international marketing and its high associated costs.

In summary then, as the result of the mandate, the subsidiary gains more internal control as it becomes totally dependent on the parent for external markets. Also, as the MNE agrees to be more dependent on the mandated subsidiary, it implicitly increases its control of the mandate's ultimate fate (success or failure). It is evident that their interdependencies increase substantially and profoundly unless the host country, the subsidiary and the MNE decide jointly that the subsidiary should evolve into a natural WPM over time. Short of natural WPM arrangements, one should be able to see that the subsidiary becomes more dependent on the host country than ever before. Both subsidiary and host nation must rely on the MNE for its marketing and technical support just as the MNE becomes dependent on the subsidiary as the main supplier of the mandated product

Other changes in the subsidiary's relations are summarized in Table 8.3.

Effect on Management and Organization

Under a truncated or miniature arrangement, the management is primarily concerned with day-to-day and local issues. They are, for example, concerned with local production and local marketing problems. In other words, their orientation is local and their horizon short. This is mainly a result of the fact that most strategic decisions are made at the headquarters and by its highly qualified staff members who are only loaned to the subsidiary as needed for short periods because the scale of operation cannot support a full complement of permanent staff functions.

Once the subsidiary receives its mandate, it must prepare itself to deal with all aspects of the mandated product on a global basis, anywhere from dealing with total production to the international marketing of the product. The mandate transforms the subsidiary from its limited role to one somewhat closer to that of headquarters for the mandated product.[9] In that capacity, it is expected to perform all related line and staff functions globally, if necessary. To illustrate, the marketing staff should be able to handle truly international marketing problems. Likewise, the finance staff must meet the challenge of many new problems that did not exist before. They must, for example, be able to deal with several different foreign currencies as opposed to only that of the parent. Exposure risk management for the subsidiary assumes a complexity similar to that of the parent although its magnitude may be much smaller. In terms of distribution, a new function or position with worldwide responsibility must be established to deal with the logistics of exporting, shipping and

TABLE 8.3

A Summary of WPM Related Changes in the Subsidiary's Operation

Subsidiary's dependence on local markets decreases substantially, while its reliance on international markets increases greatly

The sales, employment and other activities of the subsidiary are not expected to fluctuate with the host country's level of economic activity as it diversifies its sales and activities geographically, as much as it would with that of international markets

A worldwide information collection and retrieval system is required to manage production and sales of the product on a worldwide basis; the information may originate from the sister subsidiaries; this is not required under truncated operations

The subsidiary must be ready to provide the sister subsidiaries with all product-related staff support (mainly production, shipping and sales) that headquarters usually provides to its subsidiaries

The subsidiary should be prepared to interact extensively with the host country government from the very beginning to gain their continued help and support; this may require a different kind of expertise than is normally present in the subsidiary operation

The subsidiary should be prepared to show the host country government that the host country will be much better off with the mandate than without it (e.g., cost and benefits related to Tables 8.1 and 8.2, respectively) to start the process and continue on with it

Since the management of the subsidiary must undergo a massive upgrading in terms of their capabilities and scope, the subsidiary can claim that it will have a much stronger management team which is to the advantage of both the host country and the MNE

The subsidiary, at very little or no cost to the parent, becomes a center for the mandated product's R and D on a continual basis, relieving the parent's staff from that task on the one hand and bringing much desired technology and product-related R and D to the host country with the technical support of the parent on the other hand

The subsidiary should also be able to show the parent that the benefits associated with WPM—economies of scale, concentration on one product, host country's involvement, risk reduction, etc.—by far outweigh the costs of increased dependency delivery to all corners of the world. It will suffice to say that all the simple and locally oriented functions of the premandate period will be forced to assume their much more complex and internationally oriented counterparts. Some of the other required changes are listed in Table 8.3.

Effect of WPM on the Locus and Composition of Decisions

As the scale of operations increases and the scope broadens, the mandated subsidiary is required to make more and more decisions. These are the types of decisions that previously were made by the parent and/or other subsidiaries. Therefore, the locus of decision making starts to shift away from the parent in favor of the mandated company. As mentioned earlier, in contrast to the premandate period, the nature of decisions is also more complex and much more substantial. To illustrate, the process of change in product design in pre- and postmandate periods can be compared. In premandate and under truncated or miniature operations, marketing staff only had to be concerned with the effect of design change vis-a-vis (1) local customer taste and acceptance, (2) local legal standards and requirements or vice versa, (3) local distribution, (4) local competition, and finally (5) local market share. However, in the postmandate the counterparts of any of the above effects is a complex problem or decision in itself. For example, the marketing research function for assuring that the product matches or exceeds the technical standards, the taste and legal requirements of all international points of sale (i.e., number of sister subsidiaries) is a rather difficult and complex problem. To solve this problem one may need to solve the corresponding but equally difficult problems of information collection, manufacturing, design and their associated costs.

Hence, in short, the mandated subsidiary will be facing more numerous and much more complex decisions. As the subsidiary makes and executes these decisions, it increases its control over more and more complex functions and broadens its scope over areas that it had no jurisdiction over before. Finally, to execute the mandate efficiently, the management and the organization of the subsidiary will undergo a maturing process by which they address long-run and strategic as well as short-run and logistic problems.

Effect of WPM on Risk and Resource Commitment

To receive the mandate, the host government must help and support the subsidiary in different ways. It can, for example, offer a grant for R and D, share in absorbing part of the risk and give different packages of incentives. In this process resource commitment and, as a result, risk to the host country increases. Conversely, resource commitment and risk to the MNE, if it were to grant the mandate on its own, are reduced. This seems to be the central reason and motivation for justifying the granting of a mandate to a subsidiary and hence increasing the MNE's dependence on the coalition of subsidiary–host country. Other risk and commitment related issues are shown in Table 8.3.

WPM FROM THE PARENT COMPANY'S VIEWPOINT

Certain features of the WPM should be welcomed by the parent. These are the features that lead to reduction of: (1) risk, (2) resources commitment, (3) responsibility, and (4) friction and conflict. As the subsidiary starts seeking the host country government's support to expand its operations by receiving and executing the mandate, the host country's level of resource commitment and risks associated with them increases. These are the resources that are required for the subsidiary's expansion and that the MNE is expected to provide under normal circumstances. From the MNE's viewpoint, the host government's implicit involvement in the mandate also reduces political, regulatory, sovereign and transfer risk(s) related to the mandate on one hand and also cultivates a more harmonious relationship between the host country–subsidiary or the MNE on the other hand. Therefore, as a result of the mandate, the subsidiary achieves its expansion goals at a lower level of resources and risk to MNE. These are beneficial features that MNEs have not been able to cultivate on their own under other international business strategies in operation currently.

There are, however, other dimensions that MNEs would rather avoid. Loss of bargaining power as a result of reduced sourcing flexibility and substantial, if not total, reliance on the mandate holder, suppliers, labor unions and, at times, the host government are among the somewhat troublesome features. Although increased external control of the parent can partially compensate for the loss of bargaining power and its associated disadvantages in the longer run,

TABLE 8.4

WPM Features that MNE Must Consider

The MNE must be prepared to delegate a massive reallocation of power, authority, control and responsibility from the headquarters or other subsidiaries to the mandated subsidiary

The MNE loses its mobility and hence loses some of its bargaining power related to that

The MNE is restricted to only one source of supply under the natural mandate arrangement and regional sourcing under regional mandates

The HQ will be forced to intervene on behalf of the subsidiary with mandate in other subsidiaries to avoid duplication, possible inefficiencies and finally to protect the mandate when granted

Unless adequate precautions are devised to guarantee absolute competitiveness and efficiency in the mandated location, the entire MNE family will suffer from noncompetitiveness because of its mandate agreement unless the mandate is earned on a competitive basis and is subject to review periodically

Special safeguards must be raised to assure compatibility, acceptance and fit of the product(s) produced by the mandated subsidiary with that of other subsidiaries, especially in industrial products

The MNE must require the mandated subsidiary to keep track of and be informed about the local needs, developments, and changes either by the governments or local industry members; this will increase information requirements and hence the flow of communication, with possible side effects of overloading the overall MNE/subsidiary communications

The MNE must ask all subsidiaries to cooperate with the mandated subsidiary in informing it about the product's successes or failures and provide adequate information and feedback to guarantee the success of the mandate in the international markets

The MNE must be prepared to accept and deal with the increased bargaining power of the mandated subsidiary, its government, and even its suppliers (including labor unions)

Sister subsidiaries must devise ways to deal with the mandated subsidiary as the headquarters with respect to the mandated product(s) and as a regular subsidiary with respect to others

The MNE must require a more intense planning, coordination and integration globally to cope with potential contingencies as its option are reduced and dependencies are increased

The MNE must be prepared to act as adjudicator with respect to disputes and violations of mandates between the mandate holder and other subsidiaries unless the mandate is an implicit one[10]

there is no substitute for this loss in the short run. Other features of a WPM that can have potential effects or require direct attention of the headquarters are listed in Table 8.4.

In summary, the WPM appears to be a more economically efficient organization than the truncated subsidiary it replaces. However, the implicit cost of some of its features should not be ignored.

CONCLUSION AND SUMMARY

World product mandating as a new international business strategy is capable of promoting far more cooperation between the host country, the subsidiary and the parent company than any other vehicle currently in use. It gives the highest possible degree of internal autonomy to the subsidiary while increasing the parent's external control. It shifts the locus of most product related decisions (and hence responsibilities) from the parent or other subsidiaries to the mandate holder and at the same time forces the mandated subsidiary to seek other subsidiaries' cooperation, without which WPM would not succeed in the long run. WPM restores a sense of power and accomplishment to the newly formed subsidiary–host country coalition, while it increases their interdependence on the rest of the MNE's system simultaneously.

In summary, WPM cultivates an environment that is highly conducive to efficient, complete and cooperative operation for all the participants—the host country, the subsidiary, and its parent company.

NOTES

1. Lee A. Iacocca, president of Ford Motor Company, in his 1976 address to the National Foreign Trade Convention (November 16, 1976) is quoted as having said "Today, Ford engineers in Germany may work on bodies and British engineers on engines of basically the same automobile for assembly in both countries or in a third country." Source: Robinson, p. 143.

2. Indeed, some countries extend their "sovereignty" beyond their borders. For example, see Davidow, 1976.

3. This has been a shortsighted view on the part of host countries, for the ultimate bearers of all the costs and risks are the consuming nations.

4. Optimum scale refers to the size of an operation with the most efficient production and management organization. The magnitude of size depends on the combination of cost and composition of input factors, technology, and actual economies of scale and learning involved. Theoretically, it corresponds with the lowest point on long-run total cost curve. The size is expected to be larger than local demand but may be much smaller than total world demand. Therefore,

depending upon the optimum scale, the number of plants involved in supplying world mandated product may vary from single to multiple plant/production sites.

5. Fully developed WPM is defined as an operation that has reached its optimum scale. Reaching optimum scale may take time and depends upon the rate at which other sister subsidiaries adopt the mandated product and/or the mandate holder exports to international markets independently.

6. A typical headquarters-subsidiary relation has been characterized in the literature as one of semiautonomy to complete subordination mainly due to "corporate acculturation," "system transfer," and/or "people transfers" (see Weichman, 1974).

7. A fully developed natural mandate is defined as an operation in which the mandated subsidiary naturally and gradually controls all aspects of mandated products on a global basis. Stated differently, the WPM subsidiary acts as the true headquarters for the product mainly because of its comparatively superior technological and expertise position. Therefore, the MNE's role with respect to the product is reduced to a holding company.

8. A subsidiary earns a mandate (explicit or implicit) when it outbids other sister subsidiaries consistently and over a long period of time. In response to this, the headquarters may rationalize their resources by restricting the less competitive subsidiaries from continuing on with the product and in favor of the most competitive (implicit mandate). Implicit mandate eventually can be transformed to explicit and pure mandate.

9. As a product headquarters, the new organization is neither a pure product division nor is it a pure international division. But it must certainly have elements of both, for it has to perform a substantial number of their functions combined.

10. An implicit mandate is a *de facto* one whereby the most efficient and competitive subsidiary consistently outbids others and earns an implicit mandate to compete with any other subsidiary even in their own local market.

9

The Influence of Research and Development on Foreign Sales Performance

Norman W. McGuinness

INTRODUCTION

There is now an almost overwhelming amount of empirical evidence that consistently shows that those countries, industries, and firms that spend more intensively on R & D also export more intensively. Since the first studies by Gruber, Mehta and Vernon (1967) many others have encountered the same result (Wilkinson 1968; Gruber and Vernon 1970; Baldwin 1971; Branson 1971; Horst 1972; Lowinger 1975). The same relationship has even been found to apply at the level of specific new products in individual firms (McGuinness and Little 1981a).

Just how technology is connected to trade is still an open question. Does R & D effort simply result in products that have an international competitive lead as is theorized in product life cycle thinking? Or does technology have an impact that relates more to the neo-factors view of trade? This latter view treats R & D effort as part of the capitalized human skills of a firm or an industry so that the impact of R & D on trade could manifest itself in many ways beyond just product advantage. A firm's ability to provide technical sales and service assistance, superior technical understanding on the part of management, greater flexibility in responding to customer needs, and many other aspects could reflect technically derived trade advantages.

The author wishes to acknowledge financial assistance for this research from the technology branch of the Department of Industry, Trade and Commerce, Ottawa.

Some of the problems in determining the exact role played by R & D are illustrated in a recent study by McGuinness and Little (1981a, 1981b). Although this research found that new industrial products representing incremental engineering advances had considerably higher export performance than more established products, it was difficult to understand the impact of R & D itself. Product life cycle reasoning would suggest that the intensity of R & D spent on developing the new product should correlate with the product's ultimate export performance. It did, but surprisingly the effect of product specific R & D was small enough to be pragmatically unimportant. Such a result implies that other inputs such as marketing expertise may have been more important than R & D to the export success of the new products.

Some reinforcement for this view was provided by another finding. Contrary to expectations, the overall R & D intensity of the firm had a stronger effect on the export performance of a new product than the R & D spent directly on the new product. This result poses a host of questions about the relationship of R & D to exports. Does overall R & D intensity create general firm advantages that affect the export performance of all the firm's products? Could R & D be acting as a proxy for more fundamental factors that cause trade, such as enterprising management or the export prone characteristics of the whole industry?

More questions are provoked by the characteristics of new products that are related to export performance. As expected, the relative advantage a product had over its competition yielded strong exports. But so too did products that represented a large important purchase as well as standard products produced by high technology firms. Could certain types of products enjoy a comparative advantage for

FIGURE 9.1

Research Model

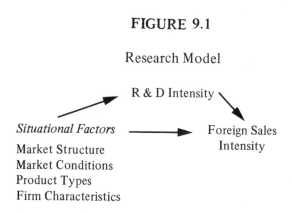

reasons other than superior functional performance? Is it possible that R & D is connected to exports, in part, by product type?

The purpose of this study, therefore, is to try to untangle the impact of R & D on exports from a variety of situational factors. The research model in Figure 9.1 hypothesizes that situational factors pertaining to the market, product or firm may influence exports directly or may act indirectly by causing a firm to increase its intensity of R & D effort. For example, a market which is changing rapidly could encourage both R & D and export activity. R & D could be motivated by the desire to keep pace with changing needs. Exports could be motivated by the need to find new markets for products that are becoming obsolete.

R & D AND EXPORT VARIABLES

Foreign Sales Intensity

The dependent variable in the study, foreign sales intensity, was measured by the foreign sales of the firm in 1977 expressed as a percentage of total sales in 1977. Foreign sales themselves were defined to include those from overseas licensing and manufacture in addition to sales which resulted from direct exporting. This is the same measure used earlier by McGuinness and Little (1981a, 1981b), who defined it to be broad enough to capture foreign sales from all modes of penetrating foreign markets.

An intensity measure was used as an indicator of how well a firm was performing in foreign markets in spite of certain shortcomings. Other measures such as a firm's share of its international markets or the rate of growth of that share are certainly more precise and more meaningful indicators of performance. Unfortunately, accurate data on the international market shares of specific firms are almost impossible to collect. Data for an intensity measure, on the other hand, are easily obtainable. Hence, it was used even though it makes the somewhat shaky assumption that the size of each firm's overseas opportunities are in proportion to its domestic sales.

R & D Intensity

The technological effort exerted by a firm was measured by the money spent on R & D in 1977 as a percentage of total sales in 1977.

R & D expenses were defined to include everything associated with technical research, development, engineering and designing. Prototype expenses were included as well, but capital equipment for plant modification and expansions associated with new developments were not.

This, again, is a fairly easy measure to collect. It does give a broad indication of how much effort a firm devotes to technology even though other aspects of R & D effort such as how advanced, new, or complex the technology is are not considered.

SITUATIONAL VARIABLES

Table 9.1 lists 29 measures used to capture the situational aspects of interest to this study. All except two are seven point perceptual scales responded to by a knowledgeable manager in each firm. The two nonperceptual scales contain data on the firm's sales in dollars and whether or not it is foreign owned. The 29 measures themselves are grouped into four categories: firm characteristics, market structure, market conditions, and product types, all of which are hypothesized to affect both exports and R & D effort.

Firm Characteristics

Firm size may affect both R & D and exports in similar ways. In an extremely thorough review of the literature on how environmental factors are connected to R & D activities, Kamien and Schwartz (1975) note that beyond a certain size, organizations have been found to spend proportionately less on R & D. A very similar observation is made by Hirsch (1971) concerning exports. Although his data are far from conclusive, Hirsch interpreted them to mean that export performance seemed to level off after firms reached a certain size. He also believed there was a threshold below which firms were too small to be involved in exporting. McGuinness and Little (1981a) on the other hand, found the effect of firm size on exports to be insignificant. To capture the effect of firm size, two measures were used: the total sales of the firm and its relative size in its industry.

The other measures in the firm characteristic category indicate the degree to which a firm is connected to an international manufacturing system, is free to export, and whether it is foreign owned. All these facets have fairly clear and well known implications for both R & D and exports.

TABLE 9.1

Situational Measures

Measure	
Firm characteristics:	Size (total sales) Relative size in industry Foreign owned Free to enter U.S. market with most products Free to enter other foreign markets with most products Products manufactured by affiliated firms elsewhere
Market structure:	Competition consists of a few large, dominant firms Competition consists of many small firms Competitors foreign owned Difficult to enter industry Small number of customers Sales made through agents and distributors
Market conditions:	Canadian market is very competitive Customers are very price sensitive Much price competition in Canada Very little difference between competitive products Most new products in industry originate elsewhere Needs of customers are changing rapidly New technology is changing industry New regulations causing changes Most technical change is predictable Demand in Canada is very stable
Product types:	Products similar to ours are manufactured in other countries Our products are similar to competitors' Our products are sold mostly as components to other manufacturers Our products usually represent a large purchase Our products must be engineered to application Our products are not purchased often Our products are purchased for plant expansion, modification, replacement programs

Note: All measures, except size in total sales and foreign ownership, are perceptual scales having a minimum of 1 and a maximum of 7.

Market Structure and Market Conditions

These two categories contain measures intended to capture the nature of the industry. Some of the scales relate to the degree of concentration and monopoly power that may exist. According to Kamien and Schwartz (1975) a full review of the evidence connecting market concentration to R & D intensity revealed "little consensus" in spite of strong positions taken by various researchers. Theoretically, firms do R & D to capture market power and continue to spend on technology to maintain a strong position once it is attained. On the other hand it is possible that firms with market power become complacent, rigid, overly concerned with maintaining the status quo, and might let their technological efforts decline.

The remaining scales in market structure and market condition categories can be easily related to stages of the product life cycle. These include measures of how competitive the industry is, how fast it is changing, and how differentiated competitive products are from each other. Stages of the life cycle, of course, have clear implications for R & D activity (Utterback and Abernathy 1975) and also for export development (Vernon 1967; Hirsch 1967).

Product Types

To capture the general nature of the main products manufactured by a company a variety of dimensions were measured. These included scales relating to the size of purchase, frequency of purchase, and the degree of standardization or custom engineering or system work involved. That certain types of products are more R & D intensive than others is fairly obvious. But whether some products are easier to export than others is not at all clear. Evidence that large purchase items and standard items if produced by high technology firms tend to have above average export performance (McGuinness and Little 1981b) is suggestive but far from conclusive.

DATA COLLECTION

Using the 1977 Directory of Scientific and Technological Capabilities in Canadian Industry (Canada 1977) a mailing list of about 285 industrial firms was prepared. Processors of primary materials and service oriented firms were omitted so that the final mailing list consisted entirely of secondary manufacturers operating in Canada.

The president or the top executive responsible for industrial operations in each company was mailed two questionnaires requesting a large amount of information. Of interest to this chapter is the second questionnaire which contained questions about R & D activities, foreign sales, and the environment in which the firm operated, and was not necessarily to be filled out by the president. The instructions asked only that it be completed by a manager who was knowledgeable about the industrial product operations in the company.

After follow-up by letter and telephone 64 completed questionnaires were received representing a relatively low response rate of 22.5 percent. Of the nonresponders 37 replied by letter and many others explained during follow-up telephone calls why they did not participate. A major reason was the length of the questionnaires. Since the overall study was somewhat exploratory a decision was made to collect a rather large amount of information from each respondent knowing that the response rate would suffer accordingly. The response rate also suffered because some respondents questioned the benefits of the research to industry, and others declined to respond because they had no formal R & D activities.

The responding firms operated in many different manufacturing industries. Exactly half the sample or 32 firms were foreign owned, 28 of them by the United States and 4 by other nations. The proportion of foreign control is somewhat less than its typical incidence in manufacturing in Canada but is a strong enough representation to capture its effect. The size of the firms in the sample covered a broad range. The smallest firm had sales of only $150,000 annually while the largest sold $1,100 million. Average annual sales of the firms was $79 million which, when compared to the sample median of $9 million, indicates that there were many more small than large firms in the sample.

The main bias in the sample seems to be its weighting toward big technological spenders. On average firms in the sample spent 3.84 percent of sales on R & D in 1977 which is well above the total Canadian business average of 0.6 percent in that year. Many firms in the sample, however, had fairly low intensities of R & D spending as indicated by the median R & D intensity of 1.06 percent.

FACTOR ANALYSIS RESULTS

Fairly high correlations existed among the situational measures, and factor analysis was used to condense the data to a more manageable set of variables. Using the principal components method, ten

TABLE 9.2

Situational Factors

Factor Name (Percent of Variance Explained)	Situational Measure	Loading
1. Market— competitive (13.7%)	Much price competition in Canada	.93
	Canadian market is very competitive	.81
	Customers are very price sensitive	.79
	Competition are few, large, dominant	.51
	Our products similar to competitors	.40
	Similar products manufactured in other countries	.32
	New regulations causing changes	.32
2. Market— changing technology and needs (11.7%)	New technology is changing industry	.93
	Needs of customers changing	.88
	New regulations causing change	.64
	Similar products manufactured elsewhere	.39
	Our products similar to competitors	-.30
3. Products— capital equipment (8.6%)	Our products purchased for plant expansion, etc.	.85
	Our products are not purchased often	.75
	Demand in Canada very stable	-.54
	Our products sold as components	-.39
	Very little difference between competitive products	-.29
	Firm size (total sales)	-.26
4. Firm— free to export (7.5%)	Free to enter U.S. market with most products	.80
	Free to enter other markets with most products	.75
	Products manufactured by affiliated firms elsewhere	-.51
	Difficult to enter industry	.27
	Most new products originate elsewhere	-.24
	Competition mostly foreign owned	.22
5. Market— oligopolistic (6.9%)	Competition consists of many small firms	-.79
	Competitors are a few large dominants	.59
	Demand is very stable	-.46
	Competitors mostly foreign owned	.38
	Difficult to enter industry	.37
6. Firm— foreign controlled (6.8%)	Foreign owned	.85
	Product manufactured by affiliated firms elsewhere	.64
	Difficult to enter industry	.37

(continued)

TABLE 9.2 (continued)

Factor Name (Percent of Variance Explained)	Situational Measure	Loading
7. Product—standard (5.3%)	Products are similar to competitors	.66
	Firm size	−.63
	Similar products manufactured in other countries	.48
	Demand in Canada is very stable	.43
	Very little difference between company products	.30
	Customers are very price sensitive	.27
	Customers mostly foreign owned	.26
8. Product—system (4.8%)	Products represent a large purchase	.74
	Products require system design	.65
	Products sold as components	−.37
	New regulations causing change	.35
	Similar products manufactured elsewhere	−.26
9. Product—component (4.0%)	Small number of customers	.83
	Product sold mostly as a component	.58
	Very little difference between competitive products	.31
	Most new products originate elsewhere	.30
	Canadian market is very competitive	−.30
	Products require system design	−.28
	Products are similar to competitors	.25
10. Market—predictable technology (3.4%)	Most technical change is predictable	.86
	Difficult to enter industry	.55
	Very little difference between competitive products	.54
11. Product—custom engineered (3.2%)	Products engineered to application	.85
	Competitors mostly foreign owned	.51
	Products require us to design system	.37
	Product similar to ours manufactured in other countries	.35
	Products not purchased often	−.26
12. Market—new products originate elsewhere (2.9%)	Most new products originate elsewhere	.76
	Sales in Canada are through agents and distributors	.76
	Size (total sales)	−.29
	Competitors mostly foreign owned	.24
13. Firm—size in industry (2.7%)	Firm is one of the largest in industry	.89
	Most technical change is predictable	.26

factors emerged with eigenvalues exceeding 1.0. Experimentation with different numbers of factors resulted in 13 factors being forced in the analysis. Not only was there a discontinuity in the eigenvalue curve between 13 and 14, but 13 factors yielded dimensions that were easier to identify.

The resulting factors in Table 9.2 contain three that describe characteristics of the firm:

Factor number	Factor name
13	Size of firm in its industry
6	Foreign control
4	Freedom to export

Of interest is the distinction between foreign control and freedom to export. The loadings on these two factors indicate that freedom to export is related more to whether a firm's products are manufactured by affiliates elsewhere than to whether the firm is controlled by Canadians.

Another five factors describe market characteristics:

Factor number	Factor name
1	Competitive
2	Changing technology and needs
5	Oligopolistic
10	Predictable technology
12	New products originate elsewhere

Three of these factors seem to describe aspects of mature markets. The "market competitiveness" factor indicates the degree of price competition that prevails. It seems to occur in markets where the competitors are large and where there is little differentiation between product lines. Another dimension of mature markets is captured by the "oligopolistic" factor. Characterized by a few, large competitors, these markets are regarded as difficult to enter and tend to be dominated by foreign owned firms. The final characteristic of mature markets is "predictable technology" where although there is little difference between competitive products the barriers to entry are high.

A youthful market dimension is portrayed by only one factor, "changing technology and needs." Changing technology and changing customer needs seem to go hand in hand and, to a lesser degree, so does regulatory change. There is a much larger degree of product uniqueness in such markets.

The final market characteristic, "new products originate else-where" seems to describe industries in which small firms act as importers and resell in Canada through agents and distributors.

The remaining five factors describe easily recognizable types of products and are self-explanatory:

Factor number	Factor name
3	Capital equipment
8	System design
11	Custom engineered
7	Standard product
9	Component product

MULTIPLE REGRESSION RESULTS

A variety of multiple regression analyses were performed using both R & D intensity and foreign sales intensity as the dependent variables (Table 9.3). The overall results confirm the research model in Figure 9.1. Both R & D intensity and situational factors affected foreign sales intensity but the situational factors played a larger role. The situational factors also explained nearly 50 percent ($R^2 = .47$) of the variation in R & D intensity but this relationship did not seriously dampen the influence of R & D itself on foreign sales.

Situational Factors and R & D Intensity

That nearly 50 percent of the variation in R & D intensity can be attributed to situational causes is an important finding. Management may have far less scope than is often assumed in setting their own preferred levels of technological effort. To some extent they may be free to choose the kind of environment in which they will operate. But having done so the level of R & D exerted may be determined largely by factors such as market prices.

Only one firm characteristic, foreign ownership, affected R & D intensity. Not surprisingly, foreign subsidiaries tended to be less R & D intensive which reflects the well known tendency for parent firms to do most of their technological work at home. As pressures

TABLE 9.3

Multiple Regression Results

	Dependent Variable			
	R & D Intensity	Foreign Sales Intensity		
Dependent Variables	With all situational variables[e]	With R & D intensity only	With situational variables only[e]	With R & D and situational variables[e]
Firm				
R & D intensity		1.29^a		1.04^b
Size in industry			5.50^c	5.56^c
Foreign control	-1.94^a		-4.56	
Freedom to export			5.88^c	5.39^d
Market				
Competitiveness	-3.42^a		-10.45^a	-6.81^c
Oligopolistic				
Changing technology and needs	2.30^a			
Predictable technology	2.01^a			
New products originate elsewhere				
Products				
Capital equipment			4.84^d	5.54^c
Systems design	1.32^c			-4.48
Custom engineered			-3.37	
Standard	-1.87^b			
Component			11.48^a	11.57^a
Constant	3.96^a	21.93^a	26.45^a	22.49^a
R^2	.52	.11	.38	.41
Adjusted R^2	.47	.09	.30	.33
F (sig.)	9.91(.000)	7.09(.010)	4.71(.000)	5.29(.000)

[a]Sig. .01. [b]Sig. .05. [c]Sig. .10. [d]Sig. .15. [e]Results for stepwise model yielding the highest adjusted R^2.

grow in industrialized host countries for subsidiaries to undertake more independent R & D effort, product mandates are often proposed as a solution. For the parent company, however, assigning a product mandate to a subsidiary usually entails a loss of direct control that seldom seems desirable unless the subsidiary has developed special capabilities that allow it to compete more effectively on the product line than the parent. The subsidiary, in effect, must entrepreneurially key in on market niches and demonstrate superiority in spite of general company policy that may not encourage such initiative. It is a very slow process in even the most aggressive of subsidiaries. But it may still be the most effective long-term strategy to make subsidiary operations competitive in international markets.

Even more important than firm characteristics in determining R & D intensities, however, were qualities of the market. Product life cycle thinking would predict that R & D effort would be lower in mature markets. This seems to be borne out by the much below average R & D intensities in markets that were preceived to be intensely competitive. Competitive products in these markets were perceived to be very similar to one another, and even though the competitors were large they did not have much market power.

Paradoxically, however, another type of mature market seemed to encourage R & D effort. These were markets characterized by stable technology. Again, competitive products were very similar which is an odd feature of markets where R & D intensities were high. Possibly these markets represent a stage of development that succeeds the chaotic early phases of new technologies. Firms in such markets may now have large engineering capabilities that make barriers to entry high. But the technologies themselves may be relatively slow changing and predictable.

Youthful markets, characterized by rapidly changing technology and needs, of course, prodded above average R & D intensities. Competitive products in these markets tended to be quite dissimilar which is in keeping with product life cycle thinking.

R & D Foreign Sales

When run alone against foreign sales intensity, R & D intensity had a small but significant impact. This impact continued at about the same level of magnitude when the situational variables were entered. Hence R & D intensity seems to have an independent effect of its own on foreign sales intensity.

What is curious, however, is the relatively small influence that R & D intensity exerted. It accounted for only 11 percent of the variance when run alone against foreign sales intensity. Moreover, its coefficient of 1.29 indicates that a 1 percent change in R & D intensity would, on average, raise foreign sales intensity only 1.29 percent, a trivial amount. Since the median R & D intensity of the sample was 1.06 percent an additional 1 percent would have represented a doubling or a very major change to over half the firms in the sample. Yet the corresponding addition to foreign sales intensity of 1.29 percent to either its median performance of 13.1 percent or mean of 27.2 percent is hardly an important shift.

R & D effort by itself, then, does not appear to be a particularly efficient way of increasing exports. Certainly, on the basis of these results, it would be very difficult to persuade managers to increase R & D spending if the only rewards are the rather skimpy and uncertain increases in foreign sales that this study reveals. This study, of course, like an earlier one with a similar finding (McGuinness and Little 1981a) cuts across many industries and hence presents an average view. It is possible that there are specific industries in which the impact of R & D on exports is more dramatic. If so, those industries would be the exception rather than the rule.

Situational Factors and Foreign Sales

Situational factors, on the other hand, had an impact on foreign sales intensity which far exceeded that of R & D. Regression runs (Table 9.3) yielded adjusted R^2 of .30 for the situational characteristics by themselves and .33 when R & D intensity was included.

The firm characteristics generally behaved as expected. Being free to export was important in encouraging strong performance. Foreign ownership, on the other hand, depressed foreign performance by dampening innovative activity. Both these findings confirm generally accepted views.

More interesting was the positive influence of relative firm size on foreign sales intensities. Normally, firm size is measured in more absolute terms such as total sales or total number of employees. Although theorists believe that larger firms should tend to have stronger exports, the empirical results have been mixed. McGuinness and Little (1981a), for instance, found firm size to be an insignificant variable. But here where firm size was measured relative to direct competition it emerged as an important positive influence. In fact, some of the firms rated as large in relative terms were actually quite small by absolute standards. This underscores the point that it is the stronger and more established firms in particular markets that develop exports. Firms that are large in absolute terms may not be strong exporters unless they also dominate their industry.

Product types also had a significant influence on exports for reasons other than their R & D content. Two product types, capital equipment and components, were strong performers for reasons that are hard to understand. It is tempting to speculate that Canada may enjoy a comparative advantage in these two product areas. Both these types of products require intensive and prolonged selling effort, and one wonders whether Canadian manufacturers who tend to be smaller than those in larger industrial nations may establish better customer relationships. Their smaller size may enable these relation-ships to be more direct, personal and flexible.

But explanations other than comparative advantage are quite possible. The domestic market for capital equipment is quite unstable, for instance, which could encourage managers to diversify into counter cyclical markets abroad. Components are sold in mar-kets where there are only a small number of customers. That could make it easy for component suppliers to enter foreign markets.

In contrast to components and capital equipment, systems type products were below average performers in export markets. Again, any explanation is highly speculative. But as a rather small industrial nation, Canada may not have the variety of skills and product lines to compete with larger nations in supplying integrated systems.

All in all the differential performance of product types suggests a fascinating area for further research. The results of this study again confirm findings of the earlier investigation of McGuinness and Little (1981a). Generally, little is known about this phenomenon which could make a major contribution to a country's industrial strategy. So far industrial strategy schemes in Canada have touched upon product types only to the extent of emphasizing high technology and perhaps de-emphasizing products that depend upon scale economies.

In contrast to product types, market characteristics had a rela-tively minor influence on foreign sales intensities. Only in markets where the degree of competition and price cutting were severe, were exports depressed. These market conditions seem to cause firms to emphasize short-term survival at the expense of future growth through innovation and market development. One cannot help but feel that competition of this intensity is destructive in the longer term.

Other types of markets, however, seemed to have no particular impact on foreign sales performance. This implies that nearly all types of markets be they mature or youthful, growing or stagnant, can provide an adequate home market foundation on which to build international sales.

CONCLUSIONS

The results of this study tend to contradict conventional wisdom and downplay the importance of R & D to trade. R & D intensity had its usual statistically significant correlation to foreign sales but the magnitude of the relationship was pragmatically unimportant. Moreover, lurking in the background as more fundamental causal factors were market conditions that determined much of the variation in R & D levels.

In spite of these findings it would be reckless to downgrade R & D too much as a contributor to trade. But perhaps a more balanced view is needed. Instead of the rather overwhelming emphasis on R & D alone as a quick route to greater international competitiveness, R & D needs to be seen as one factor in a mix of important elements. For instance, it is clear that new products of all types outperform more established ones in foreign markets. Yet R & D is only one input to the new product development process and may not be the most important one. It is the totality of skills used in the innovative process that matter. The intensity of R & D may, in fact, not be a reliable indicator of either the amount or quality of innovative work going on in an organization.

Similarly, this study has found that those firms that are larger and more dominant than their competitors tend to have above average exports. Certainly R & D could be encouraged as a means to helping firms achieve dominance. But R & D would be only one of the many factors involved, and there is no indication in this study that dominance required above average R & D intensities.

Government policy, then, should be to promote innovation and encourage the more dominant firms in all markets to become more export oriented. R & D should be treated as just one of many elements involved in attaining these goals.

One aspect to which government policy should devote fresh attention is the impact of product types on exports. The much above average export performance of components and capital equipment suggests that certain types of products could be emphasized in national strategies. This kind of comparative advantage is virtually unexplored and may deserve more attention from those who wish to understand trade flows.

10

Technology Transfer and Export Marketing Strategies: The LDC Perspective

Gurprit S. Kindra

The process of technology diffusion and its impact on socio-economic growth and international trade is of vital concern to multi-national enterprises (MNEs), the subsidiaries of such MNEs based in less developed countries (LDCs), and the LDCs and developed countries as economic entities.

The term "technology" has come to include a number of things. Some conceive of technology as patents, licenses, blueprints and trademarks. Others view technology in terms of products, equipment and machinery. Yet others regard technology as techniques: advertising, management, manufacturing, and so forth. In fact, technology is a combination of human know-how and equipment. Equipment includes all kinds of tools, machinery, buildings and vehicles as well as process technology. Technological know-how includes functional skills (including marketing, management and export promotion), information and knowledge about equipment, market know-how, and organizational know-how as well as product and process knowledge. Since knowledge itself leads to the creation of machinery as well as further knowledge, it is the decisive factor. Furthermore, since knowledge is held in human beings, technological capacity necessarily calls for an increase in the number of human beings with technological know-how as well as an improvement in the knowledge level already possessed by workers. It should be noted that technological know-how is inappropriate and in many instances useless unless there is a critical mass of knowledge, equipment, and market and financial factors. This point will be developed further in the latter part of this chapter.

Although much of the media and political discussion is focused on technology transfer from developed countries to LDCs, the two proxies for technology transfer—royalties and direct overseas investment—indicate that most technology exchanges occur between developed countries. For example, a survey conducted by the United Nations shows that in 1968 the United States received a total of $1,246 million in royalties and fees of which only $420 million came from LDCs (Basche and Duerr 1975, p. 1). Similarly, U.S. direct investment in developing countries in 1973 amounted to less than 25 percent of its total overseas investment (UNCTAD 1981, p. 15). A study by Mansfield and Romeo (1980) indicates that newer technologies go first to developed country subsidiaries followed by LDC subsidiaries and LDC joint ventures. (See also Caves 1981, p. 14.)

Our aim in this chapter is to (a) establish the critical role of technology imports and diffusion in the economic and developmental transformation of less developed countries; (b) establish the role of LDC government in the decision making process regarding technology acquisition; and (c) explore the process and stages of technology diffusion and provide a blueprint for export marketing strategies.

TECHNOLOGICAL DEPENDENCE OF LDCs

The process of technology diffusion is preceded by technology invention and technical innovation. Because most innovations are labor saving in nature, their payoff is highest in countries with a high value for human time. (The average wage of a skilled worker in five LDCs was U.S. $0.45 per day; see Gunder 1981, p. 181.) Also, an innovation has the highest prospect of success in high income areas where the potential market is large and willing to pay premium price for the new product. Further, in the early stages of production the manufacture is small scale, fluid, somewhat experimental and therefore localized. Therefore, not only are most innovations confined to high income countries,[1] but also the initial production and consumption occurs in the high income market.

The virtually total dependence of LDCs on developed countries for technology is a result of several other asymmetries: In education—LDCs have an overall literacy rate of under 40 percent and a lack of appreciation for technical knowledge; in capital—LDCs have very limited access to it; they account for 75 percent of the world's population but only 20 percent of its income; in incentive—there are few benefits to be derived from innovative activities; in skills—there are few opportunities to acquire skills by learning-by-doing; and in means of production—the infrastructure to manufacture capital goods is inadequate. A survey of 128 business leaders of 45 countries indicated a dire need to raise the technological levels of LDCs and confirmed the dependence of LDCs on developing nations for the needed know-how (Basche and Duerr 1975, p. 1).

The technological dependence of LDCs has imposed heavy costs on these nations. It is estimated that LDCs currently pay close to $10,000 million for patent licenses, trademarks, patent know-how and technical services to developed countries each year (Richardson 1979, p. 153). The indirect costs, for example, the overpricing on imports of intermediate goods, markups, and profits on capitalization of technological know-how are probably even higher. Yet, the returns to LDCs from technology transfers have not been insignificant. National output per capita is a reasonable indicator of the success of technology transfer, since improved productivity and overall output increases are the main consequence of technology acquisition. From 1950 to 1975, the total real output of LDCs grew at a rate of 5 percent per year (UNCTAD 1981, p. 7). This growth rate is higher than the historical growth rate of developed countries and five times the growth rate of LDCs during the early twentieth century. Another major indicator of technological capability is the domestic manufacture of capital goods. From 1960 to 1975 the manufacture of capital goods in LDCs was ahead of imports for such goods. This development is important because it not only reduces the total impact of foreign exchange constraints imposed by heavy costs of technology acquisition but also increases the scope of international trade and economic development. Other indirect and peripheral indicators of technology diffusion, e.g., fertilizer consumption, per capita energy consumption, number of vehicles in use per 10,000 population, and railway freight traffic also indicate a marked growth in LDCs compared to the rest of the world from the period 1960 to 1976 (UNCTAD 1981, p. 16).

Therefore, given the heavy cost of acquiring new technology and the potential for its accrued benefits, it is imperative that economic development of LDCs be closely coordinated with a well thought out system and policy of technology acquisition and international trade. This point is developed further in the following pages.

LDCs: TECHNOLOGY TRANSFER, TRADE
AND ECONOMIC DEVELOPMENT

Economic growth results from some combination of labor increase, capital increase, and productivity increase. In LDCs one-third of the economic growth is attributable to productivity factors as opposed to approximately one-half in the case of developed countries. A recent study indicates that the four semi-industrialized LDCs (Hong Kong, Singapore, Korea and Taiwan) followed a growth pattern that relied heavily on the contribution of productivity improvements rather than labor or capital growth (Chen 1979). This is a particularly significant finding because most LDCs aspire to model their economies after these four nations and Japan.

Two major sources of productivity increases are technology acquisition and application and economies of scale in production. A third source, improved labor performance, may be viewed as a function of successful technological change. It should be noted that technological know-how is the only productivity factor with no natural limits. Thus, in the initial stages of industrial development productivity increases result from rising levels of capital and human investment, education, and the shift of resources to the more productive industrial sectors, regardless of technological change. As the LDC moves closer to limits of such resources, however, technological improvement is the only resourse that remains untapped and fortunately unlimited in potential.

As indicated earlier, the per capita output of LDCs grew at a rate of 5 percent during the period 1950–75. Yet, converted into dollars, per capita GDP in 1975 for all LDCs was $460 compared to $5,130 in developed countries. Expressed in terms of GDP per labor unit, the comparable figures are $1,230 and $12,290, a ratio of 1 to 10 (UNCTAD 1981, p. 19). It has also been estimated that for LDCs to reach the 1975 level of developed market-economy countries by the year 2000 they need an annual percentage per capita growth rate of 10.1 (UNCTAD 1981, p. 21). Can a technological chasm of this size be overcome? The Japanese experience in the 1950s and 1960s indicated that technology gaps can be narrowed effectively by the diffusion process leading to economic development. From 1950 to 1971 Japan spent approximately $3 billion on technology acquisition and currently enjoys the highest sustained rate of productivity increase. However, the crucial factor that allows the productivity increases to be translated into economic development is a sustained growth in exports. This is particularly true for non-OPEC LDCs with large oil imports and rising debt service charges. It has been estimated that in the period 1971–81 LDC debt charges have increased at an annual rate of 26 percent—from $11 billion in 1971 to $112 billion in 1981. On the other hand, the external debt of LDCs increased by only 20 percent over the same period (OECD *Observer* 1981, p. 7). Also over the period 1970–80, for all LDCs the ratio of net fuel imports as a percent of total exports increased from 9.1 to 28.7 (Wallich 1981, p. 21). In countries like India at the present time, approximately 50 percent of export earnings are absorbed by oil imports. When debt service charges are added to oil imports, by the year 2000, 80 percent of export earnings will be absorbed by these two obligations for all non-OPEC LDCs. Such a pessimistic projection may be proven wrong, however, if external markets are opened further to LDCs and trade barriers and quotas substantially diminished leading to vigorous trade, and (given the recent breakthrough in energy efficient products) emphasis is placed on importing up-to-date technologies.

In the 1960s and early 1970s Organization for Economic Cooperation and Development (OECD) countries experienced rapid economic growth, and world trade grew almost twice as fast as industrial production (IP). Currently, the world trade is growing at approximately the same rate as IP and the picture is one of general economic slump in all three trade zones—the United States, Europe, and Japan (Chase Manhattan 1979, p. 96). The dynamic growth of a number of LDCs in the last few years resulted from abundant labor, technology availability, and access to economically vigorous OECD markets. In 1978, as a group, OECD member countries imported approximately 10 billion dollars' worth of electrical appliances and machinery from LDCs (OECD 1981, p. 4). It is clear from Table 10.1 that although there is a trend toward greater imports from LDCs, their share in the total imports of all manufactures is merely 10.1 percent. Further, imports from LDCs are dominated by a few countries only—particularly Taiwan, Hong Kong, and Singapore. In 1970, for example, while imports of manufactures from these three nations were in excess of $10 billion each, Mexico, India, Israel, and Yugoslavia traded below the $4 billion mark (OECD 1981, p. 7).

In view of the tremendous financial drain on LDCs resulting from oil payments, debt service charges, and purchase of capital goods, it is imperative that Organization for Economic Cooperation and Development and other external markets remain open to them. Although the Ottawa Summit of OECD governments' pledge to further open their markets to LDCs is a welcome sign, a concerted effort on the part of these nations is needed to collaborate in the areas of

TABLE 10.1

Share of Imports from LDCs in Total OECD Imports of Manufactures
(percent)

	1970	1976	1977	1978	1979
Chemicals	4.5	3.9	4.1	3.2	4.1
Iron and steel	2.9	4.3	4.2	4.6	5.5
Textiles	13.0	17.1	17.0	19.8	20.5
Clothing	27.4	44.0	42.8	45.5	44.7
Footwear, leather goods and furs	16.4	31.9	31.6	34.5	33.9
Non-electrical machinery	0.8	2.2	2.4	2.7	2.9
Electrical machinery and appliances	5.3	12.6	13.2	15.4	17.2
Road motor vehicles	0.2	0.6	0.6	1.1	1.1
Other transport equipment	2.0	3.9	5.3	8.2	5.5
Other manufactures	6.8	9.5	10.3	11.1	11.1
All manufactures	5.3	8.7	9.0	9.9	10.1

Source: Reprinted from OECD *Observer*, March 1981, No. 109, p. 7.

economic and technological assistance. In the years to come, it is critical for LDCs to make at least substantial progress toward improvement of their system and policy of technology acquisition and diffusion and international trade infrastructure—particularly in the area of export market strategies.

TECHNOLOGY IMPORT OPTIONS

At the present time there is no generally accepted indicator of technology transfer. However, transfer of technology is believed to be strongly related to LDC imports of machinery, their payments for technical services and licenses, and direct foreign investment in LDCs.

During 1970–79 there was a 10 percent (real terms) yearly growth in OECD world exports of machinery and equipment to LDCs. This represented over 40 percent of total OECD exports in the area of machinery and equipment. During the same period payment for licenses, and technical and commercial services increased by 4 percent each year (in real terms). The third indicator of technology transfer, direct foreign investment, increased at approximately 3.9 percent per year (in real terms). Financial flows, another indicator of technology transfer, increased substantially during this period. Borrowing by LDCs increased at an annual rate of 10 percent (in real terms) during the period. It has been estimated that the United States, Japan, France, the United Kingdom and Germany supply approximately 70 percent of the technology imported by LDCs (OECD 1981, p. 5). The following discussion deals with different means of technology transfer.

Licensing Agreements. These are agreements whereby the licensor provides know-how, copyrights, patents or trademarks in return for royalties, a percentage of sales or profits, or a lump sum fee. In most cases the licensor does not cede property rights; it merely provides specific rights of use of a given technological know-how. International franchising is an example of licensing agreement whereby the technology bundle provides know-how, trademark, training programs, and geographical monopoly.

Joint Ventures. Two types of joint ventures are common in developing countries. First are those in which equity is held more or less half-and-half by the LDC based partner(s) and the multinational corporation(s). The exact distribution of shares may be determined by each partner's contribution in the areas of technology, capital, machinery, managerial skills, and so forth. The second are those that involve more than one LDC in the technology transfer agreement.

Joint ventures are preferred by countries with the basic infrastructure of management and production because they normally lead to sharing of profits, assets, risks and, most important of all, technology. Such agreements are particularly appealing when they involve the so-called phaseout clause. Under such a clause it is agreed that over a specified period of time ownership gradually will be transferred to the LDC partner. Thereafter, the multinational corporation (MNC) partner may function as a consultant, minority stockholder, or simply draw a fixed royalty. International marketing is one area in which the MNC partner is likely to be actively involved even after the phaseout is complete. Joint ventures have been the cornerstone of India's commercial developmental program because of the long-run economic and political appeal of such agreements.

Turnkey Operations. Under such product-in-hand agreements the supplier is usually responsible for completely installing and operationalizing a given industrial complex. The first turnkey agreements appeared in the early 1960s and were being used by only a small number of LDCs toward the end of the decade. The late 1970s brought a resurgence of turnkey agreements mainly due to the vast recycling of petrodollars through large contracts by OPEC countries for industrial plants.

Training and Development Contracts. These agreements call for the MNC to provide training for local personnel when need arises because of advances in learning in any of the areas of operation. Such contracts may be modified in the following two ways. First, training of local personnel may be part of a larger package of a management contract. In this case, the MNC initially provides a complete package of management functions including planning, organizing, directing, controlling, motivating and maintaining a viable training and development program. Gradually, the management authority is handed over to the LDC country personnel. In some cases, the LDC party may wish to retain the MNC party as an independent observer to monitor the performance of the new enterprise for a specified period of time. Second, training of local personnel may be a part of a multiparty contract package whereby one or more other groups (from an LDC or IC) are providing plant and machinery, capital, technology, and so forth. Such multiparty contracts may also take the form of subcontracting, particularly for turnkey projects.

International Subcontracting. This usually involves a MNC based in a developed country that contracts one or more firms in one or more LDCs to manufacture parts or assemble them. All inputs are provided by the MNC, and it retains all marketing rights—in the LDCs as well as the MNC home country.

Multiparty Industrial Cooperation Agreements. Under such agreements three or more parties get together to perform a project in a LDC. A major difference between such agreements and multiparty contracts discussed above is that in the former case one or more parties represent Communist-bloc economies in addition to one or more MNCs from a developed country and one or more parties from the host LDC. Such agreements often take place on a turnkey basis. The parties representing the centrally planned economies usually provide equipment, low technology, and skilled labor. The Western MNCs usually contribute high technology and electronic equipment, and the LDC partner provides raw materials and engineering skills for the construction of the plant.

THE ROLE OF GOVERNMENT

Technology diffusion does not take place in a vacuum. Transfer of know-how occurs effectively when specific government policies encourage research and educational programs in related areas of finance, administration, and international economics.

A review of governmental policy framework in regard to technology transfer indicates that no systematic steps have been taken by most LDCs to promote such transfers. It should be noted that although several developing country governments offer help in the form of tax incentives to attract foreign investment, technical and financial assistance, investment insurance, and establishment of central development corporations, there is an underlying lack of coordination among the objectives of various measures. Furthermore, there is no indication that such objectives, indeed, complement the priorities of LDCs.

FIGURE 10.1

Technology Acquisition Decision Process

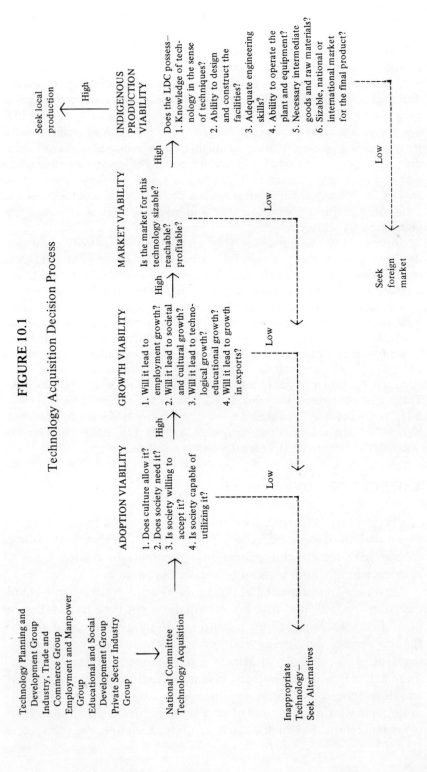

A healthy assimilation of foreign know-how is first and foremost conditional upon a societal climate of receptivity to new ideas. Strong measures are needed in LDCs, particularly India, Pakistan, and most African nations, to foster interest in invention and innovation. Such measures could include village extension programs, TV and radio shows, modifications of primary school curricula and establishment of centers for the promotion of invention and innovation. The many engineering colleges in India should promote a curriculum that highlights the developmental benefits of technology assimilation. Further, such engineering and technical colleges could provide consulting service to the community on a regional basis.

Next, to encourage innovative diffusion of technology, a strong package of financial and nonfinancial incentives must be present Patent protection, provision of risk capital, soft taxes on profits and capital gains, and adequate financial stipends will go a long way in encouraging a potential entrepreneur. Such incentives should be available to both individuals and organizations. Steps must also be taken to create an atmosphere in which it becomes desirable for financial institutions to provide risk capital.

On the government side, there is great need for developing the capacity for meaningfully evaluating various technology options (discussed earlier), assessing various sources (including domestic) of supply, and negotiating for maximum benefits and least costs for the import of a technology. Critical considerations in the cost-benefit analysis include appropriateness[2] of the new technology and potential for local diffusion. Myopic and emotionally motivated actions such as defensive import substitution are not technologically progressive and are likely to be unsuccessful in the long run.

It should be noted that, although by the mid-1970s advanced LDCs (e.g., Mexico, India, Brazil, South Korea, and the Philippines) had significantly improved their position as technology importers (through the formation of technology transfer centers, industrial property institutes, foreign investment legislations, technology transfer pacts, and so on), three major inadequacies remain. One, although most of these countries (particularly India) have a variety of research and development organizations, the vital link between technology importation and its local promotion and diffusion is largely unexplored and ineffective. Two, with regard to the technology acquisition process, there is little or no coordination between various groups and organizations that are directly or indirectly knowledgeable about and affected by a given technology transfer. And three, the actual framework for determining the appropriateness of a technology acquisition is inadequate or lacking.

Figure 10.1 envisions a national decision making committee composed of representatives of various groups involved with technology acquisition. To determine the suitability of acquiring a certain technology, the committee systematically explores the possibility of local acceptance of the new technology—its impact on domestic economic, sociocultural and educational growth, the profitability of the domestic market, and indigenous production potential. If adoption, growth, or market viability is low, the technology in question is inappropriate and alternatives must be sought. On the other hand, if all three viabilities are high, the committee explores the possibility of local production leading to the final outcome of either acquisition from foreign sources or domestic production. As indicated earlier, a number of LDCs have developed policy measures to deal with the transfer of technology; the above scheme provides a framework for coordinating the objectives underlying the various policy initiatives and matching indigenous needs with such measures.

PROCESS OF AGGREGATE OF
TECHNOLOGY DIFFUSION/ADOPTION

Figure 10.2 develops a paradigm to illustrate factors that encourage/retard the domestic aggregate diffusion of a new technology. The environment affecting the rate of diffusion is divided into three groupings: governmental factors, conditional factors and adopter characteristics. Each of these groups, in turn, affects the answer to five critical questions relating to the new technology. The more change a new technology requires in the existing sociocultural norms and patterns of behavior, the greater is the resistance to its adoption. If the new technology is clearly advantageous in terms of expected profits, it will be adopted sooner. Also, the easier it is to understand, relate to and explain the new technology, the higher will be the rate of adoption. The more a new technology lends itself to trialability, sampling, and so on, the less the perceived risk and the extent of commitment will be and therefore the rate of adoption will be higher. And finally the degree to which the benefits of the new technology can be effectively displayed or demonstrated will enhance the rate of adoption. The actual adoption process—awareness, interest, evaluation, trial and action—is therefore highly influenced by the conditions relating to the imported technology. Generally, impersonal mass

FIGURE 10.2

Technology Adoption Process

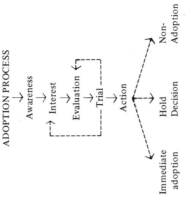

ADOPTION PROCESS

Awareness
↓
Interest
↓
Evaluation ←
↓   ← Trial
Action
↓
Immediate ← Hold → Non-
adoption   Decision   Adoption

CHARACTERISTICS OF ADOPTERS

1. Educational level
2. Attitudes toward innovation in general and the technology under consideration in particular
3. Sociocultural norms
4. Professionalization
5. Bank of conceptual skills

GOVERNMENTAL FACTORS

1. Technology and developmental plans
2. Barrier or Incentive System
3. Communications and other dissemination infrastructure
4. Access to necessary finances

CONDITIONAL FACTORS

1. Existing and forecasted trade and economic conditions
2. Political support
3. Opinion leadership and reference visibility
4. Relative sophistication of existing core and peripheral indigenous technologies: knowledge and equipment

TECHNOLOGY FACTORS
AFFECTING LOCAL ADOPTION

Does/Is the new technology:

1. Compatible with domestic sociocultural norms?
2. Relatively simple to use and understand?
3. Can it lead itself to trialability?
4. Possess clear and obvious relative advantage?
5. Lend itself to effective advertising, publicity and world-of-mouth?

FIGURE 10.3

Adoption Curve

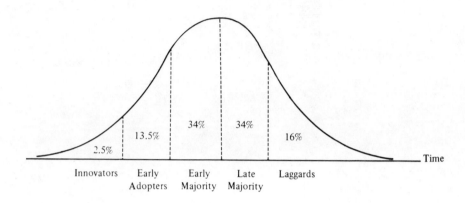

media devices are more effective during the awareness, interest, and often evaluation stages; the later stages benefit more from word-of-mouth, and local face-to-face encounters with information disseminators.

The distribution of enterprises over time that adopt a given technology will follow the bell shaped curve shown in Figure 10.3. Normally a few highly innovative and risk prone enterprises adopt at first, rapidly followed by others. Figure 10.3 indicates that the rate finally diminishes as only a few potential adopters are left in the nonadopter category. Innovators are defined as the first 2.5 percent of businesses or individuals to adopt the innovation; laggards are the final 16 percent to adopt. The next section of this chapter explores the technology diffusion process within an individual firm and makes recommendations for export strategies at various stages of the process.

INTRAFIRM TECHNOLOGY DIFFUSION AND EXPORT MARKETING STRATEGIES

Technology diffusion at the level of an individual firm has received little emphasis from researchers. One reason for this is that while most models of diffusion are based on the concept of productive efficiency, the core of the literature in the area deals with life cycle of new products. In other words, the product life cycle (PLC) theory provides limited guidance in the way of empirical research when technology is understood to include equipment such as tools and machinery as well as know-how in various functional, organizational and information areas. Second, although the PLC theory, as represented by the works of Vernon (1966) and Wells (1972), is an innovative extension of the earlier works of marketing researchers[3] it ignores the significance of marketing variables like promotion and product differentiation for export development. In other words, two products that are similarly in the maturity stage of the PLC are likely to show different export potential because of their differences from a marketing perspective. Although some researchers, notably Findlay (1978), de la Torre (1972) and Krugman (1979) have provided useful insights into the two issues, two specific questions remain unanswered.

What is the typical pattern of technology assimilation[4] within an LDC based firm? At what point in the diffusion process is the local firm ready to take over critical market and product design decisions, promotion and pricing decisions, and export decisions?

In order to answer the first question the following hypothesis was formulated: the learning curve for a firm assimilating a new technology is nonlinear and has the characteristic shape shown in Figure 10.4. The theoretical basis for this hypothesis was consolidated by surveying about 95 experienced technical managers of a consumer electronics industry in a LDC. The survey was accomplished by open-ended personal and telephone interviews administered over a period of four months in 1978. The survey sought the subjective opinions and perceptions of these managers on matters involving productivity change over time, relative success of employee training and development programs, competitive environment, technical information flow, governmental and political influence, and export marketing problems and opportunities. In addition to providing the theoretical basis for the above hypothesis, the interviews provided critical insights into the question of appropriate export marketing strategies at various stages of technology assimilation.

Based on the information obtained, four stages of technology assimilation were identified, namely: (1) Do-how stage; (2) Do-why stage; (3) Know-how stage; and (4) Know-why stage. Each stage has found to be characterized by a gradual internalization of activities and decisions that had been performed earlier by the MNC. In an earlier study (Kindra and Goyal 1981), the hypothesized shape of the diffusion curve was operationalized and tested. The study using data relating to a Canadian MNC and its operations in a LDC over a 10 year period tentatively confirmed the shape of the hypothesized learning curve shown in Figure 10.4. We will describe the four

FIGURE 10.4

Diffusion Curve of a Firm in LDC

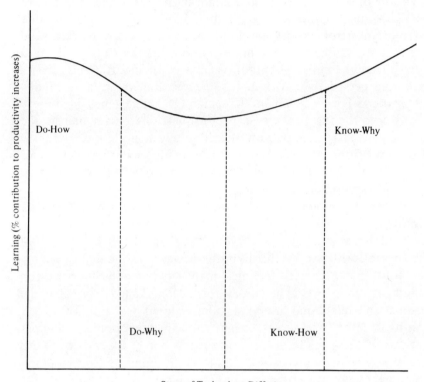

Stage of Technology Diffusion

technology-assimilation stages and then discuss the strategic options open to LDC export firms at each stage.

It should be noted that the firm's learning curve embraces more than individual learning by repetition of a work task; it describes a more complete organism—namely, the collective absorption of knowledge of many people, all striving to perform common tasks with increasing efficiency.

Table 10.2 schematically presents the four stages of technology assimilation and how they relate to the familiar marketing strategy variables of product, price, promotion, distribution, and post-purchase service. The exhibit shows the degree to which various responsibilities within the marketing strategy areas fall on the company in the various stages of technology diffusion. These relationships were identified on the basis of the above-mentioned interviews and studies of various case histories.

TABLE 10.2

Stages of Exports Market Development

	Product			Price		Promotion			Distribution		Post-Purchase Service		
	Core-product decision	Augmented product decision	Quality control	Price to retailer	Price to consumer	To Local importers	To retailers	To consumers	To retailers	To distributors	Warranty & guaranty	Missionary selling	Marketing research
Do-how	1	0	0	0	0	1	0	0	0	0	0	0	1
Do-why	2	1	1	0	0	1	0	0	0	0	1	1	1
Know-how	2	1	1	1	1	2	1	0	1	1	1	1	1
Know-why	2	2	2	2	1	2	2	1	1	2	2	1	2

Note: 0 = No involvement; 1 = partial responsibility; 2 = full responsibility.

Do–how Stage. During this phase, the employees of the firm become familiar with the basic skills: for example, fitting, turning and milling skills in the machine tool industry. In the case of product technologies, manpower will progressively become familiar with assembly operations. In process technologies (such as fertilizer plants), the people become familiar with the operating characteristics of the process. The important requirements of skilled people in this stage will be to handle different jobs and perform multiple functions. This stage provides the groundwork for further assimilation; hence, the need to have a strong foundation cannot be over-emphasized.

During this stage, the firm is in no position to seek exports. Their export business, if any, is initiated by a MNC searching for a low cost production facility. The firm at this stage typically lacks the skill and the market and product know-how to make independent export decisions. In almost all cases, the local producer in this stage is merely a seller of production capacity.

Do–why Stage. The local company usually evolves into the second stage—particularly when the technology is new, complex, and guarded. When the technology in question is simple, time-tested, and easily accessible, however, the company may begin operations in the second stage.

During this stage, skilled people develop their skills further primarily by learning-by-doing. Technical personnel also acquire specialized knowledge of certain key aspects of the manufacturing process especially in the area of critical inputs and distributor relations. In this stage, the company tries to reduce its dependence on the "imported" technology and usually identifies local suppliers and/or simpler endogenous manufacturing processes. Another important feature at this stage is the attempt at diversification of product range by minor modifications such as adaptation of a two-speed lathe to a three-speed lathe in a machine tool firm.

At this stage, the firm is in a position to exhibit samples, organize a basic marketing department and make attempts to move into the export arena. Such attempts typically will include contacting importers by mail, getting listed in the relevant trade directories, calling on importers visiting the LDC and, to some degree, participating in trade shows and exhibitions in the importing countries.

Trained personnel by now have acquired skills to train others and the firm is self-sufficient in operating skills.

Know–how Stage. At this point, the firm focuses on development from within although assimilation of technology is still taking place in the areas of design, packaging, quality control, and promotional subtleties. Product modifications at this stage are the "product to product" type as, for example, making the product of better quality or redesigning and manufacturing similar products capable of satisfying additional consumer needs. These modifications result from learning by research applied to specific problems. By this time the technical base of the local environment is sufficiently geared to provide the services required by the firm. Reliable suppliers of standard parts and ancillaries for intermediate inputs are established or identified. Further, both suppliers and manufacturer have become quality conscious toward the product. Quality consciousness is reinforced by the consumers, thereby setting the pace for technological improvements.

At this stage, we have a marketer of products and not a seller of production capacity. In the clothing industry, a firm at this stage will start to take full responsibility for design, create its own brand names, ship goods directly to their destination and become conscious of its marketing deficiencies. The main tool of competition in the clothing industry at this stage is quality control and efficient distribution, whereas in the consumer electronics and shoe industry, it is still price. The leaders of the industry at this stage start to emphasize "pull" based marketing strategies in order to command premium prices.

LDC based firms at this stage have access to many of the style changes and technological advances taking place at the MNCs. Except for a few leaders in the industry, however, adoption of these innovations is restrictive—mainly because of an incomplete grasp of marketing factors and the absence of sophisticated strategic planning. From this stage onward, the firm needs to take a multidisciplinary approach to development and diversification, that is, it must invest in related areas of science and technology. A machine tool company, for example, draws heavily from the fields of electronics, aeronautics, hydraulics, and space technology and must keep abreast of the developments in these areas.

Know–why Stage. This transformation from the third stage to the fourth is most difficult to achieve. This transformation is brought about through a slow and evolving process to which contributions of academic institutions, government and the firm are equally important. Learning by research is a risky endeavor in this stage, since the outcome is more uncertain than in the know–how stage where research is more specific than fundamental. The main functions of learning by research in this phase are:

To Translate a Concept into Products. An example would be to convert the concept of noncutting metal removal process to an electrochemical machine.

To Use the Same Product for Different Concepts or Applications. An example would be the adoption of electronic controls developed for computers as control systems for machine tools.

Very few firms in LDCs will reach this stage affecting such major transformations. The Japanese experience, however, indicates that firms in this stage will become indistinguishable from the MNCs in the importing countries. At this stage the circle has gone a full turn from a "push" based, production capacity to "pull" oriented consumer franchise. A company at this stage will organize a sophisticated marketing research department and employ advertising agencies and other services much as the importing firms do.

Not all firms strive for this stage; neither may it be desirable. Many firms (particularly the small ones) are content to follow the leader. Others, discouraged by the heavy financial requirements (particularly in the capital intensive industries) may concentrate only on selected areas and "purchase" technology improvements from the more adventurous firms.

Strategic Options for LDC Exporters. The following strategy options will be discussed from the perspective of an individual firm. We will, for example, not concern our analysis with the politically colored goals of the government such as macroeconomic development and fair allocation of scarce resources to different industrial sectors.

From the perspective of LDC firms, the evolution from the do-how to know-how stage is clearly attractive because it places the firm in a position to command large profits based on its unique skills (rather than merely on production capacity). The resources invested in efforts to acquire such skills is quickly mitigated by the intraorganization diffusion of know-how. It is, however, not clear whether a move to the know-why stage is always desirable. The know-why stage requires heavy investment, major structural changes, and strong credit support from governmental as well as nongovernmental sources. In general, an ability to face high risk and absorb major losses is a major prerequisite for entry into the know-why stage.

It is at the know-how stage that the firm faces the option of either foregoing short-run profits and concentrating on the long-run success of standardized products or paying greater attention to expansion and/or improvement of the present product line. The latter strategy works best when large retail outlets in the importing country can and will buy directly from the producer. On the other hand, the former strategy will require the producer to proceed to the know-why stage—particularly when the market is dominated by "middlemen" who threaten to cut off the do-how-stage firm's access to the retailers. The Indian ready-made garment export industry is currently faced with a similar decision. In the face of an increasing number of dominant import houses, the know-how-stage exporters are being forced to open overseas marketing offices and showrooms, establish and maintain contact with retailers, and perform a full range of promotional and post-purchase maintenance activities.

A vast majority of the do-how-, do-why-, and know-how-stage firms in the garment export inductry in India rely extensively on the letter of credit (LC) to bolster their working capital. The know-why-stage firm essentially loses the LC option because it delivers goods directly to its branch office in the importing country where the products will be offered at whatever terms exist at that time. Without the LC "benefit," and in the absence of strong financial support either from within or outside the firm, many know-how-stage firms could not take on the risk of financing work in process and maintaining viable promotional, products handling, and distribution systems. This significantly reduces the chances of their entry into the know-why stage.

It should be noted that in the case of high technology based products like computers and calculators, the problems of the know-how stage firm trying to enter the know-why stage are even more acute because relative to clothing: (1) calculators and computers are high priced items, (2) establishment of a strong national brand name is necessary, and (3) very heavy R and D expenditures are required. It is specifically because of these reasons that the government run Hindustan Machine and Tools (HMT), despite strong efforts, has failed to establish itself as a stage IV exporter of wristwatches. To cite another instance in 1970, the know-how stage firms of Italy and West Germany controlled over 34 percent of the world calculator market. However, with the Japanese firms' successful and forceful entry into the know-why stage in 1968–69 and the consequent reluctance of large retailers as well as consumers to buy "no name" Italian/West German calculators and the inability of Italian/West German firms to enter the know-why stage because of poor marketing/financial backing, their combined share of the world market declined to 1 percent in 1977 (U.S. Department of Commerce, 1966–77). Since the know-why stage consumes large amounts of precious foreign exchange, the governments of LDCs are generally reluctant to provide grants/loans that may be "better" spent on, for example, agricultural machinery.

To summarize, the know-why stage entry may be unnecessary when most of the following conditions exist:

- The nature of the product is such that it is low cost and relatively standardized.
- No competitor exists in or plans to enter the know-why stage in the foreseeable future.
- The technological base is stable and not complex.
- Marketing conditions and nature of the product do not require strong brand positioning.
- Links with major retailers are strong and mature.

Alternatively, when most of the above conditions are absent, a firm may have no choice except to make an eventual move to the know-why stage. Without a strong financial, marketing, and entrepreneurial backup, the move to stage IV is likely to be unsuccessful. One alternative to this fatal push into the know-why stage is to attempt persisting in the know-why stage by specializing in and catering to the low priced market. A manufacturer of stereo equipment, for example, can last in the know-how stage by maintaining the position as the "lowest" cost supplier in the industry. Once this distinction is lost, the firm either must move to stage IV and attempt to establish a national brand name or eventually perish.

At least three topics touched upon this section need to be developed further. One is the nature of the relationship between the goals of a LDC and LDC firm; two, the relationship between market structure and strategic alternatives; and three, an assessment of alternative strategies purely from a LDC governmental perspective.

SUMMARY, CONCLUSIONS AND FUTURE RESEARCH

The first section of this chapter established the fact that LDCs are heavily dependent on industrially advanced nations for their technology needs. Reasons include asymmetries in the areas of education, skills, incentives, and production infrastructure. The second section explored the impact of technology transfer on the trade and economic development patterns of LDCs. It was concluded that given the large payments for oil imports and debt service charges, LDCs must continue to seek international trade vigorously for economic development. The third section sought the various technology import options available to LDCs. The fourth section dealt with the question of technology appropriateness and provided a decision making framework for technology acquisition. It was concluded that an overall planning procedure for technology acquisition is an integral component of national development efforts on the part of LDCs. The fifth section provided a paradigm to illustrate various factors that encourage/retard the domestic diffusion of a new technology. It was suggested that the speed with which an individual firm adopts an innovation is strongly influenced by technology characteristics like compatability with sociocultural norms, degree of sophistication of the new technology, the obviousness of its relative advantage, inherent communicability of the acquired technology, and the degree to which it can be tried before the final decision to acquire. The last section dealt with the diffusion of technology within a LDC based firm and provided a case study that tentatively established and explored various stages in the diffusion process. This section also provided a rudimentary blueprint for export marketing strategies for local firms at each stage in the diffusion process.

Several topics touched upon in this chapter need to be developed further. As indicated at the end of the sixth section the nature of the relationship between LDC goals and LDC based firms' goals, as well as an assessment of alternative export strategies from a purely governmental perspective are areas that need to be further explored. The possibility of cooperation by firms within various LDCs as well as the viability of establishing a "technology bank"[5] operated by and for LDCs should be researched. Several manifestations of the concept of LDCs "technology bank" may be to provide such nations with some control over their technology imports, strengthen their negotiating capacity, ensure a certain degree of technology appropriateness, and reduce duplication of technology imports by member LDCs—thereby making such acquisitions more affordable. There is also a need for a comprehensive study of the role of small and medium firms in technology diffusion and exports promotion. And finally, the question of how economic and technological aid from the industrialized nations can be funneled toward a viable trade and development policy needs to be explored in depth.

Over the next two decades LDCs will experience upheavals similar in magnitude to the ones experienced by the West during the Industrial Revolution. It is in anticipation of such transformations that LDCs must give top priority to developing the capacity to import, diffuse and invent technologies and relate the same to trade and development policies and programs.

NOTES

1. Only 6 percent of the 3.5 million worldwide patents are granted by LDCs; 84 percent of these are owned by foreigners.

2. An appropriate technology may be defined as one which utilizes domestic inputs to the greatest extent, satisfies local consumption needs, is nonthreatening to the domestic sociocultural system, and has the least negative environmental impact.

3. For excellent discussions on PLC research in marketing see Buzzell (1966: 46–64); Cox (1967: 375–84); Levitt (1965: 81–94); Polli and Cook (1969: 385–400); and Wasson (1968: 36–43).

4. Technology assimilation should be viewed here as the embodiment of functional knowledge by the company personnel.

5. The term "technology bank" in this context refers to a regional organization specializing in the accumulation of technological capacity (in the form of know-how, blueprints, patents, equipment, and trained manpower) and its orderly flow to contributing member nations.

11

Canadian Multinational Enterprises and Developing Countries

Alan M. Rugman

INTRODUCTION

As a wealthy and resource rich nation Canada has started to come of age in international business. Many years of dependence on foreign (mainly U.S.) capital have led to much foreign ownership of Canadian secondary manufacturing industry. Yet now, for a variety of economic and political reasons, a remarkable change in investment patterns is taking place.

It is becoming evident that Canadian based multinational enterprises (MNEs) are growing rapidly and that Canadian foreign direct investment in the United States and in developing nations (especially the Caribbean) is increasing rapidly. Indeed, the resource based Canadian MNEs are among the most aggressive and dynamic firms active in the Western economies, and their importance is likely to increase in the future.

Canada has always been the largest trading partner of the United States, traditionally exceeding the value of trade of Japan or any European nation. It is now clear that the tendency of government to restrict and regulate trade is leading to the replacement of trade by organizations such as MNEs. Therefore, in this world of market imperfections, Canadian based MNEs will replace lost trading opportunities and will continue to link the economies of the United States and Canada. Yet the distinctive nature of foreign direct investment is that the ownership is more visible in the host (traditionally the U.S.) nation—so the presence of Canadian MNEs will become more visible; indeed, it is already apparent that "the Canadians are coming."

166 ● Multinationals and Technology Transfer

This chapter reports and analyzes data on the growth and performance of the largest Canadian based MNEs over the 1970–79 period. Tables 11.1 and 11.2 summarize data on the sizes, foreign operations and performance of these MNEs. The return on equity of these MNEs is compared with the profit rates of U.S., European and Japanese MNEs of similar size in Table 11.3. Reasons for significant differences in earnings are examined. The economic impact of Canadian MNEs on the home and host countries is investigated. The resource intensive and service nature of Canadian MNEs is considered as part of the general theory of MNEs developed in Rugman (1980, 1981a). New implications for an understanding of MNEs are drawn out on the basis of the empirical and theoretical work reported in the chapter. The chapter advances substantially upon the rather cursory treatment of some Canadian based MNEs in the recent book by Litvak and Maule (1981).

CANADIAN MNEs AS ECONOMIC ORGANIZATIONS

The theory of the MNE applies equally well to Canadian based as to U.S. based MNEs. I have demonstrated elsewhere (Rugman 1980) that the MNE is explained by internalization theory. Although this statement was made for large U.S. based MNEs, it is just as appropriate for the newly emerging Canadian based MNEs. This is the first and key point in understanding the role of Canadian based MNEs— they are explained by the same theory as other MNEs.

The MNE is a producer of goods and/or services; it employs local workers; may or may not use local capital; and markets its output mainly in the host nation. Yet all of these purely economic activities are the result of normal, cost conscious business decisions; they are not activities directly related to the economic goals or political aspirations of the host nation. Nor should they be. The MNE is an economic organization, not a social agency. It owes no allegiance to the host nation or to the home nation for that matter. Its only interest as a good corporate citizen is in keeping a good business partnership with local consumers, producers and (in today's regulated world) political figures.

Canadian based MNEs have the same responsibilities to their shareholders as do U.S., European or Japanese based MNEs. The Canadian MNE is obliged to operate in an efficient manner, that is, to maximize profits subject to relevant local cost conditions. The MNE can use its internal market to exploit a firm-specific advantage abroad, and it cannot neglect the risks of alternative contractual arrangements when it makes the foreign investment decision. If the host nation chooses to impose regulations on the MNE, this forces the firm to consider alternative locations in order to minimize costs.

At the margin the social and political objectives of a host nation, as reflected in its controls and regulations on the MNE, may force the MNE to an alternative site or cause it to cancel or postpone its foreign investment. To this extent there is a potential conflict of interests between the nation state and the MNE. Yet the MNE is a regulation taker, not a regulation maker; and the dependence of the MNE on the whim of local political leaders will serve to make it risk averse in its choice of location. Thus political risk and perceptions of social, cultural or psychic distance are the major elements in the information cost set of the MNE. There is no reason to believe that Canadian based MNEs have any superior method of forecasting political or other risks when compared to MNEs of other nations. So Canadian MNEs will behave in the same economic manner as all other MNEs.

If we turn from a strictly economic viewpoint and begin to incorporate political economy effects then the situation becomes more complex and, indeed, may yield no model solutions or predictions. To some extent the MNE reflects the political hue of its parent government. Perhaps in some developing nations Canadian based MNEs are thought to be less capitalist (that is, market oriented) than U.S. based ones, but the logic for this is doubtful. With the exception of Cuba, Canadian political actions toward developing nations have been very similar to those of the United States. Indeed, it is difficult for foreigners to distinguish between American and Canadian foreign policy or between Americans and Canadians as individuals.

Canadian foreign policy is frequently observed to follow the broad lines laid out in Washington, D.C. This is natural and not difficult to justify since the economic and political interests of the two North American nations are closely related. The U.S. economy dominates the Canadian one to the extent that an independent economic and especially monetary policy is impossible for Canada. Interest rates and the foreign exchange rate are determined simultaneously for the United States and Canada. The major economic indicators tend to move in tandem, with only small lags in Canadian variables. The integration of the North American economy means that the operations of the U.S. based and Canadian based MNE will be virtually identical.

The implications of internalization theory in a Canadian context are now examined briefly. Rugman (1981a) develops the theory of internalization in more detail. This theory can be used to consider the explicit choice to be made by a Canadian based MNE between the three classic options of exporting, foreign direct investment (FDI) and licensing. Exporting takes place when conditions for free trade exist and country specific factors are permitted to be dominant. FDI occurs when exporting is denied, for example by tariffs, and when a firm or ownership-specific advantage exists. Licensing represents all nonequity forms of participation in foreign markets and occurs only when the risk of dissipation of the firm-specific advantage has fallen to an acceptable level.

In a Canadian context the theory of internalization applies quite well. It predicts that exporting to the United States (the closest market in geographical terms) will be chosen when conditions of free trade operate and when export marketing (M*) costs are low. However, when tariffs or other entry barriers are imposed by the United States, then FDI is required and the additional cost of FDI (A*) needs to be compared with M* and the risk of dissipation (D*). The firm-specific advantage of Canadian MNEs will reflect the resource intensive nature of Canada's country specific advantage. They will seek to minimize D*, which occurs when their firm-specific advantages in resources is at risk. Canadian MNEs are thereby behaving in the same manner as U.S. MNEs with a firm-specific advantage in R and D.

More specifically it can be hypothesized that the firm-specific advantage of Canadian MNEs is in resource management. It builds upon the efficient manipulation of technology required for resource based industries. Thus the largest Canadian MNEs are in the resource sector or in support of this sector.

The core skill of a Canadian MNE lies in its ability to assemble a package of firm-specific advantages in resource management and to use them to overcome obstacles placed in the way of distributing these resources. Such obstacles are usually put in place by government regulations, tariffs and nontariff barriers, effective tax rate differentials, and other market imperfections.

The next section attempts to identify the largest Canadian firms engaged in international business. It is difficult to separate the firms that are exporting from those engaged in foreign direct investment since the primary statistical indicator available is the ratio of foreign (F) to total (T) sales. Clearly the (F/T) ratio does not distinguish between export (X) sales and sales by foreign subsidiaries (S). I attempt to make this distinction in the following tables whenever data are available; yet in many cases I am forced to assume that a high (F/T) is an indicator of multinationality, even when most of the F comes from X rather than S. The reader should be alert to this empirical constraint imposed by the data.

THE PERFORMANCE OF THE CANADIAN MULTINATIONALS

The political, cultural and social environment within which an MNE operates will have an important effect on its performance. The measurements of performance generally available, however, are economic rather than social ones; examples are rates of return on assets, return on sales, or return on stockholders' equity. The reason that such economic indicators are used is that the MNE is an economic rather than a social institution and investors are ultimately interested in the profitability of the organization.

The impact of foreign MNEs on host countries such as Canada is large and affects many aspects of the nation's social fabric; yet, since the MNE is a business rather than a social agency, its very existence depends upon a satisfactory economic performance over time. It is essential to observe, therefore, the rate of return for MNEs and to examine if it is being affected by the increasing amount of government regulation of multinationals.

The economic impact of Canadian based MNEs is also revealed best by assessment of their performance. Profitability is a summary indicator of the success (or failure) of the MNE relative to its competitors in the home and foreign nations. From the viewpoint of the Canadian MNEs, good and stable profits satisfy their shareholders and the general public. This assumes that the latter are well informed about the purely economic role of the MNEs and do not expect the MNEs to contribute to social objectives better achieved by tax-subsidy (that is, redistributional) systems.

In Table 11.1 the largest 28 Canadian based MNEs are identified. They are ranked in decreasing order of size, measured by sales for 1978. The MNE is defined as a firm with either subsidiaries in one or more foreign countries or with a rate of foreign (F) to total (T) sales of greater than 20 percent. Foreign sales include exports (X) of the parent firms plus sales by overseas subsidiaries (S). Data on X, S, and the (F/T) ratio are reported in Table 11.1.

Further attention will be confined to the largest 17 Canadian based MNEs for which data are available and for which the (F/T)

TABLE 11.1

Size and Degree of Multinationality of the Largest Canadian MNEs

Name of company	Sales (millions) T	Exports (millions) X	Subsidiary sales S	Foreign sales (millions) F = X + S	(F/T) percent	Number of countries with a foreign subsidiary
Canadian Pacific Ltd.	6,617	NA	NA	NA	NA	4*
Alcan Aluminum	3,711	222.7	2820.4*	3043.1*	82*	31*
Massey-Ferguson	2,925	204.8	2544.75*	2749.55*	94*	34*
Canada Packers	1,878.4*	NA	NA	281.0	15*	9*
Seagram Co. Ltd.	2,273*	NA	NA	NA	$94^{\dagger x}$	34*
Inco	2,083*	833.2	1041.5*	1874.7*	90*	24*
MacMillan Bleodel	2,005*	621.6	982.5*	1604.1*	80*	5*
Steel Co. of Canada	1,776*	NA	NA	NA	$12^{\dagger x}$	13*
Noranda Mines	1,691*	NA	NA	NA	$75^{\dagger x}$	30*
Northern Telecom ~	1,505*	150.5	617.1	676.6*	51*	18*
Moore Corporation	1,323*	13.23	1190.7*	1836.03*	91*	30*
Abitibi Price	1,293*	60.8	NA	862.46*	67*	4*
Domtar Ltd.	1,241	NA	NA	377.7	30	7
Genstar	1,143	NA	NA	244.6	21	14
Dominion Foundries	1,120	NA	NA	NA	$10^{\dagger x}$	2
Consolidated Bathurst	1,807	NA	NA	NA	58^{y}	NA
Hiram Walker	1,041	NA	NA	NA	$88^{\dagger x}$	NA
Molson	951.1	NA	NA	NA	$4^{\dagger x}$	2
Cominco	901	404.6	296.6	701.2	78	31
Dominion Bridge	886	NA	NA	NA	$33^{\dagger x}$	20
Algoma Steel	864	NA	NA	NA	$22^{\dagger x}$	8
Labatt	839	NA	NA	NA	$7^{\dagger x}$	NA
B.C. Forest Products	704	NA	NA	NA	82^{y}	1
Dominion Textiles	560	NA	NA	NA	$40^{\dagger x}$	25
Canron	400	NA	NA	NA	NA	19
Emco	225	NA	NA	NA	NA	9
Maclean Hunter	221	NA	NA	33.1	15	12
National Sea Products	217	NA	NA	NA	52^{z}	4

Notes: All figures are for 1978, except those shown by x, for 1976; y, for 1979; and z for 1980. NA = Not available.

Sources:

Annual Reports

John M. Stopford, John H. Dunning, and Klaus O. Haberich, *The World Directory of Multinational Enterprises* (London: Macmillan, 1980); otherwise obtained from annual reports. These data are shown by an *.

I. A. Litvak and C. J. Maule, *The Canadian Multinationals* (Toronto: Butterworths, 1981). These data are shown by a †.

United Nations, Economic and Social Council, *Transnational Corporations in World Development: A Re-Examination* (U.N. 1978:05692).

ratio is greater than 20 percent. These constraints lead to the exclusion of the largest holding company, Canadian Pacific (although two of its subsidiaries are included, namely Cominco and Algoma Steel). Also excluded are: Canada Packers, Steel Co., Dominion Foundries, Molson, Labatt and the smallest five firms listed in Table 11.1. These firms were included originally since they have a subsidiary in one or more foreign nations, but they are not able to meet the (F/T) minimum requirement as well. Also excluded from attention are the subsidiaries of foreign owned MNEs, such as General Motors (Canada), and so forth.

The degree of multinationality of Canadian firms is striking. Nine of the 17 have an (F/T) ratio of 70 percent or more. In contrast there are only five European based MNEs with an (F/T) in excess of 70 percent while only one of the largest 17 U.S. based MNEs has an (F/T) ratio greater than this amount. None of the ten largest Japanese MNEs approached this figure. One reason for this may be the small size of the domestic market, which tends to bias upward the ratio of foreign to domestic operations.

As a group the 17 Canadian MNEs are smaller, in terms of sales, than both the largest 17 U.S. and European MNEs. All but one of the Canadian MNEs have sales of less than 3,000 million dollars in 1978, whereas all of the largest 17 U.S. and European MNEs have sales over 5,000 million. Six of the largest ten Japanese MNEs also have sales over this amount, and all ten have sales over 3,000 million.

Another interesting facet of the Canadian MNEs is that 11 of the U.S., European and Japanese MNEs are in secondary manufacturing and use more R and D, technology and capital in general. The staples theory which has explained Canadian economic theory so well (see Rugman 1980) may be applicable in this context. Instead of exports of resource staples such as fur, fish, timber, wheat or minerals, the modern regulated world economy now requires that foreign markets be serviced by resource based Canadian MNEs. Yet the MNEs are merely a substitute for former resource exports, now that the latter are denied by market imperfections.

As background information on the similarity between Canadian and U.S. based MNEs I report data on the profits of Canadian MNEs. To place the findings in perspective it should be noted that, over the decade 1970–79, the mean profit rate for the 50 largest U.S. based MNEs was 12.98, with a standard deviation of 4.38. The mean profit rate for the 50 largest non-U.S. MNEs was 9.54, with a standard deviation of 4.31. The figures are reported in Rugman (1981a) in Tables 7.1 and 7.2, where a more detailed discussion of the methodology also appears. The ratio of foreign to total sales (F/T) is an index of multinationality. Where the cut off point is made depends on the theoretical underpinnings of the work; here it is 20 percent or more.

The performance of the 17 largest Canadian based MNEs is reported in Table 11.2. The firms selected are those listed in Table 11.1, which is confirmed by rankings in *Fortune* in their annual directory of the largest non-U.S. industrial corporations. Data were collected on the profits of the 17 firms for the last ten years; specifically, the rate of return on equity (net income over stockholders' equity) was calculated for each year. The sources used were mainly annual reports but these data were then checked against *Fortune* and the annual *Financial Post Survey*.

TABLE 11.2

Means and Standard Deviations of Return on Equity
for the 17 Largest Canadian Multinationals 1970–1979

	Mean	Standard Deviation	(F/T)
Alcan Aluminum	10.85	6.08	82
Massey–Ferguson	7.68	5.88	94
Seagram	9.00	1.69	94^x
Inco	11.98	5.88	90
Noranda Mines	15.14	6.66	75^x
MacMillan Bloedel	9.75	6.32	80
Northern Telecom	13.72	5.88	51
Moore	15.86	3.24	91
Domtar	11.18	7.93	30
Abitibi Price	9.61	6.88	67
Cominco	13.74	7.94	78
Genstar	13.96	4.61	21
Consolidated Bathurst	11.24	9.35	58^y
Dominion Bridge	13.01	5.05	33^x
Algoma Steel	10.37	3.25	22^x
Hiram Walker	11.52	1.49	88^x
B.C. Forest Products	16.59	9.17	82^y
Av. Mean 11.41		Av. Dev. 5.72	

Note: All (F/T) figures are for 1978 except those shown by x (for 1976) and y (for 1979).

Source: Annual Reports, various.

TABLE 11.3

Comparative Performance of Canadian and Non-Canadian MNEs

	Rate of Return on Equity, Percent 1970–1979	
	Mean	Standard Deviation
A		
17 largest Canadian MNEs	11.41	5.72
17 largest U.S. MNEs	13.06	4.02
17 largest European and Japanese MNEs	10.48	4.49
B		
10 largest Canadian MNEs	11.48	5.64
10 largest U.S. MNEs	13.36	3.07
10 largest European MNEs	10.52	5.58
10 largest Japanese MNEs	9.97	3.84

Sources: A. M. Rugman, "The Internal Markets and Economic Performance of European Multinational Enterprises," mimeo, 1981; Table 11.2.

The interpretation of the mean profit rate of 11.64 for the group of Canadian MNEs in Table 11.2 is clear. There is no indication of excess profits. The mean return of 11.41 is not significantly different from that of the 50 largest U.S. MNEs (which earned 12.98), nor is it much greater than the 50 largest non-U.S. MNEs (at 9.54). Although the standard deviation is greater (at 5.72) than for these other groups, there is no significant difference after allowing for the variation in the size of the groups. Overall, the performance of Canadian based MNEs is fully consistent with the implications of internalization theory. While some of these MNEs are involved in developing nations and others are not, we can conclude at this stage that there is no material effect on the performance of the Canadian based MNEs, whatever market they service.

Table 11.3 permits us to make a more detailed comparison between the profits of Canadian MNEs and MNEs based in other nations. Using data reported elsewhere on U.S. and European MNEs it is possible to compare the profits of the largest 17 MNEs from these nations with those from Canada. The Canadian MNEs' mean profit of 11.40 percent falls between that of U.S. MNEs at 13.06 per-

TABLE 11.4

The Largest Canadian Industrials

Rank in *Fortune*		Percentage Foreign Ownership	Sales (U.S. million)
32	General Motors of Canada	100	6,772
36	Ford Motor of Canada	89	6,024
44	Canadian Pacific	35	5,581
56	Imperial Oil	71	4,830
74	Alcan Aluminum	61	3,771
101	Massey-Ferguson	45	2,925
114	Chrysler Canada	100	2,520
133	Gulf Canada	60	2,237
148	Inco	38	2,083
178	MacMillan Bloedel	4	1,759
184	Canada Packers	–	1,733
202	Steel Co. of Canada	–	1,557
209	Noranda Mines	6	1,483
233	Seagram	–	1,347
238	Moore	–	1,323
240	Northern Telecom	55	1,320
271	Texaco Canada	91	1,172
282	Canada Development Corp.	–	1,145
290	Abitibi Paper	–	1,136
297	International Thompson Organization	–	1,107
301	Domtar	–	1,088
331	Dominion Foundries and Steel	not listed	983
334	Canadian General Electric	92	968
340	Consolidated Bathurst	12	946
394	Labatt	–	769
410	Molson	–	740
430	Hiram Walker-Gooderham & Worts	–	672
435	Imasco	47	664
466	British Columbia Forest Products	41	618
468	Husky Oil	69	617
494	DuPont of Canada	75	581

Notes: Percentage foreign owned = percentage of shares held outside Canada (*Financial Post* 500, June 1981).

Source: Fortune: The largest non-U.S. industrials, 1979.

cent and European MNEs at 10.48 percent, but the standard deviation of the Canadian MNEs is slightly higher than that of the other two groups. A similar picture emerges if the Japanese MNEs are included; here data limitations restricted the comparison to the largest ten MNEs.

It is apparent from the data of Table 11.3 that the Canadian MNEs exhibit no unusual performance behavioral patterns. Their position between the U.S. and European/Japanese MNEs is of interest; indeed, the Canadian MNEs perform better than might have been anticipated, given their smaller size and resource intensity relative to the MNEs of other nations.

To place the Canadian MNEs in perspective I report in Table 11.4 details of the largest Canadian corporations, both foreign owned and Canadian owned. It is apparent that the subsidiaries of U.S. MNEs in Canada, such as General Motors, Ford, Imperial Oil and others are not much larger than the Canadian owned MNEs such as Canadian Pacific, Alcan, Massey-Ferguson, and so on. This indicates that there is no size bias affecting Canadian MNEs per se; they are just small relative to other nations' MNEs because Canada itself is a relatively small economy.

INVOLVEMENT OF CANADIAN MNEs
IN DEVELOPING NATIONS

Having identified the major Canadian MNEs and examined their performance over the last ten years, this section turns to an investigation of the role of Canadian based MNEs in developing nations. The data repeated here are rather exploratory in nature. There has been almost no prior published work in this area and the data sources are limited.

The main sources of information used are the annual reports of the Canadian MNEs. These provide details of the major product lines of the MNEs and their areas of foreign market penetration. An analysis of this basic information is seen to reveal some useful generalized statements about the average degree of involvement of Canadian MNEs in developing nations.

To set the Canadian involvement in perspective a similar analysis is undertaken of the annual reports of the largest U.S. based MNEs. It is found that U.S. MNEs are more heavily involved in developing nations. Then the resource intensive nature of the Canadian MNEs is contrasted with the manufacturing intensity of U.S. MNEs. The

TABLE 11.5

Canadian MNEs in Developing Countries

Company	Main products	Total number of developing countries in which involved	Operations in developing countries
Alcan	Aluminum and bauxite	16	Jamaica, Bermuda, Brazil, Mexico, Venezuela, Malaysia, Trinidad, Argentina, Colombia, Uruguay, Ghana, Guinea, Nigeria, India, Indonesia, Thailand
Massey-Ferguson	Farm and industrial machinery; diesel engines; construction machinery	10	Brazil, Mexico, Iran, Argentina, Turkey, India, Pakistan, Rhodesia, Libya, Peru
Seagram Co. Ltd.	Spirits and wines; oil and gas	5	Brazil, Mexico, Venezuela, Argentina, Costa Rica
Inco	Nickel; batteries (principally dry cell); formed metals	3	Brazil, Indonesia, Guatemala
MacMillan Bloedel	Forest products	1	Hong Kong
Noranda Mines	Mining, smelting and refining of gold, zinc, lead, copper, silver, and aluminum; and forest products	7	Mexico, Venezuela, Brazil, Philippines, Nicaragua, Colombia, Nigeria
Northern Telecom	Telecommunications equipment	6	Singapore, Hong Kong, Brazil, Malaysia, Eire, Turkey

Company	Products		Countries
Moore Corporation	Paper and office products	15	Barbados, Brazil, Hong Kong, Iran, Jamaica, Malaysia, Mexico, Venezuela, Costa Rica, El Salvador, Guatemala, Lebanon, Puerto Rico, Rhodesia, South Korea
Abitibi Price	Forest products	0	—
Domtar Ltd.	Paper and pulp; construction materials; chemicals	0	—
Genstar	Construction materials; chemicals; marine transportation and towing	1	Bermuda
Consolidated Bathurst	Newsprint; kraft pulp, kraft paper; lumber; glass	0	—
Hiram Walker	Spirits	2	Argentina, Rhodesia
Cominco	Mining, milling, smelting and refining of nonferrous metals	1	India
Dominion Bridge	Heavy industrial equipment	4	Bermuda, Greece, Bahrein, Philippines
Algoma Steel	Coke; iron and steel	0	—
Dominion Textiles	Textiles and related products	0	—

Sources: Moody's Industrial Manual, 1979; J. M. Stoppard, J. H. Dunning, and K. O. Haberich, The World Directory of Multinational Enterprises (London: Macmillan, 1980).

TABLE 11.6

U.S. MNEs in Developing Countries

Company	Total number of developing countries in which involved	Developing countries involved
Exxon	25	Bahamas, Brazil, Chile, Panama, Jamaica, Saudi Arabia, Iran, Malaysia, Hong Kong, Argentina, Colombia, Nicaragua, El Salvador, Libya, India, Eire, Greece, Lebanon, Senegal, Pakistan, Indonesia, Malagasy, Kenya, Thailand, Liberia
Mobil	32	Bahamas, Barbados, Bavaria, Bermuda, Brazil, Burundi, Chile, Colombia, Egypt, Ghana, Greece, Guinea, Hong Kong, Iraq, Kenya, Liberia, Malaysia, Iran, Saudi Arabia, Singapore, Qatar, Indonesia, Turkey, Libya, Nigeria, Cyprus, Lebanon, Philippines, Sierra Leone, Senegal, Abu Dhabi
Ford Motor	12	Mexico, Venezuela, Brazil, Singapore, Taiwan, Argentina, Philippines, Thailand, Egypt, Malaysia, Puerto Rico, Uruguay
Texaco	20	Brazil, Iran, Hong Kong, Saudi Arabia, Panama, Guatemala, Puerto Rico, Chile, Ivory Coast, Greece, South Korea, Angola, Trinidad, Paraguay, Ghana, Indonesia, Turkey, Bahamas, Ecuador, Egypt
Standard Oil of California	14	Bermuda, Bahamas, Nigeria, Panama, Liberia, Indonesia, South Korea, Philippines, Lebanon, Pakistan, Kenya, Rhodesia, Bahamas, Iran
Gulf Oil	6	Taiwan, Bahamas, Liberia, Nigeria, Panama, Puerto Rico
IBM	25	Bahamas, Brazil, Mexico, Hong Kong, Singapore, Taiwan, Venezuela, Malagasy, Israel, Nigeria, Zaire, Argentina, Bolivia, Chile, Colombia, Costa Rica, Panama, Peru, Indonesia, South Korea, Philippines, Thailand, Uruguay, Ecuador, Guatemala

Company		
Standard Oil (Indiana)	16	Taiwan, Brazil, Bermuda, Singapore, Iran, South Korea, Liberia, Egypt, India, Trinidad, Colombia, Guatemala, Pakistan, Philippines, Taiwan, India
International Telephone & Telegraph	7	Hong Kong, Bermuda, Brazil, Argentina, Philippines, Indonesia, Puerto Rico
Shell Oil	6	Brazil, Malaysia, Saudi Arabia, Singapore, Egypt, Philippines
Conoco	10	Iran, Malaysia, Taiwan, Egypt, Indonesia, Libya, Thailand, Tunisia, Abu Dhabi, Bahamas
Chrysler	5	Mexico, Brazil, Panama, Peru, Argentina
Occidental Petroleum	6	Brazil, Colombia, Panama, Peru, Argentina, Liberia
Phillips Petroleum	16	Venezuela, Iran, Bolivia, Colombia, Ghana, Ivory Coast, Morocco, India, Indonesia, Philippines, Nigeria, Egypt, Nicaragua, Chile, Mexico, Puerto Rico
Dow Chemical	24	Hong Kong, Malaysia, Saudi Arabia, Iran, Taiwan, Singapore, Brazil, Venezuela, India, Indonesia, South Korea, Thailand, Greece, Panama, Colombia, Costa Rica, Guatemala, Ecuador, El Salvador, Peru, Chile, Argentina, Bermuda, Mexico
Union Carbide	20	Hong Kong, Iran, Malaysia, Singapore, Venezuela, Brazil, Argentina, Colombia, Costa Rica, Ecuador, Ghana, Greece, India, Indonesia, Ivory Coast, Kenya, Philippines, Thailand, Puerto Rico, Sudan
United Technologies	12	Argentina, Brazil, Egypt, Zambia, Venezuela, Peru, Mexico, Lebanon, Kenya, Iran, India, Hong Kong

Sources: Moody's Industrial Manual, 1979; J. M. Stoppard, J. H. Dunning, and K. O. Haberich, The World Directory of Multinational Enterprises (London: Macmillan, 1980).

reasons for the different performance and involvement of Canadian MNEs, as compared to U.S. MNEs, are then explored.

The 17 largest Canadian based MNEs and their operations in developing nations are now examined. Of these, several MNEs have no foreign operations in developing nations, namely, Abitibi Price, Domtar, Consolidated Bathurst, Algoma Steel and Dominion Textiles. These are excluded from further examination, leaving a total of 12 MNEs with some degree of foreign involvement in developing nations, as reported in Table 11.5. Firms are included if they have foreign operations in one or more developing nations. Yet only six of these MNEs have operations in five or more developing nations. These are: Alcan, Massey-Ferguson, Seagram, Noranda Mines, Northern Telecom and Moore. As a group the 17 largest Canadian MNEs have at least 75 separate operations in developing countries for a mean involvement of 4.18 operations per MNE.

In contrast, the largest 17 U.S. based MNEs are all active in developing nations, as reported in Table 11.6. Every single one of them is active in at least five developing nations and the mean involvement for the group of 17 U.S. MNEs is 14.96.

The reasons for the relative lack of Canadian involvement in developing nations compared to U.S. MNEs can only be speculated upon. Such reasons may be found in the relatively smaller size of the Canadian MNEs; their concentration in resource and primary sectors rather than in secondary manufacturing; their relative newness as MNEs in comparison to the more established U.S. MNEs; and related factors which depend upon the special characteristics of Canadian MNEs in comparison to U.S. ones. Perhaps the most likely reason is backward vertical integration to secure supplies of raw materials, a classic market advantage of the MNE, first noticed by Hymer (1976). This seems to apply to Alcan and Noranda. Forward vertical integration to secure market seems to be applicable to the cases of Massey-Ferguson for farm machinery, Seagram for liquor, Moore (which is active in office equipment) and Northern Telecom in telecommunication goods.

Clearly, these firm-specific explanations are closely intertwined with country specific factors. Canada is a smaller, newer and more resource intensive nation than the United States; so its MNEs reflect these country specific factors. It may also be that purely economic explanations of the Canadian MNEs' involvement in developing nations is less relevant than the perceived political, cultural, historical and other noneconomic distinctions between Canada and the United

TABLE 11.7

Performance of Canadian MNEs and Degree of Involvement
in Developing Nations

	Average standard deviation	Average mean	Mean per unit of standard deviation
Six MNEs having no operations in developing nations	6.20	10.42	1.68
Six MNEs having operations in more than one, but less than five developing nations	5.21	12.33	2.37
Six MNEs having operations in five or more developing nations	4.82	11.96	2.48

Sources: Tables 11.2 and 11.5, and *Annual Reports.*

States or Britain. Until fairly recently Canada was possibly still regarded as a colonial nation, either dependent upon Britain or the United States. Thus, Canadian MNEs have lacked a distinctive identity as, to some extent, does Canada itself.

Table 11.7 is based upon data from Tables 11.2 and 11.5. It provides some scanty evidence in support of the international diversification hypothesis. It is apparent that the risk of earnings (as proxied by the standard deviation of profits) decreases as the extent of multinational activity increases. The mean per unit of standard deviation increases from 1.68 with MNEs with no foreign operations in developing nations to 2.37 for MNEs with some foreign operations and up to 2.48 for MNEs with foreign operations in five or more developing nations. In conclusion, the Canadian based MNEs appear to benefit from their involvement in developing nations; indeed, the more involved they are the greater the degree of risk reduction that is observed.

ECONOMIC IMPACT OF CANADIAN MNEs

The economic impact of Canadian based MNEs is of interest to both the home and host nations. As demonstrated in the last section, the economic impact of the new resource based MNEs on the home economy is adequately revealed by an evaluation of their performance. It was found that the profits of Canadian MNEs are in line with those of MNEs from other home nations such as the United States, Japan and Europe. The distinctive feature of the Canadian based MNEs is that they are resource intensive, even though their embodiment of this country specific advantage does not permit these MNEs to earn excessive profits.

In the process of operating as MNEs, the Canadian based firms provide indirect economic benefits to Canada. The economic impact of U.S. multinationals has been studied by many authors. One of the more comprehensive studies is that of the Brookings team of Bergsten, Horst and Moran (1978). A similar study for Canadian based MNEs has not been undertaken, although Langdon (1980) examined the impact of Canadian MNEs on developing nations. One of the indirect economic benefits of MNEs occurs in the form of substituting for free trade, which is otherwise denied by tariffs and related market imperfections. In this manner the Canadian based MNEs help the balance of payments, although a precise evaluation of this indirect economic effect is not attempted here. Similarly, there are indirect effects on employment, tax revenues, industry structure, competition and so on. These effects can only be analyzed by a social benefit cost analysis; yet, as I have argued elsewhere (Rugman 1980), such an analysis itself confuses equity with efficiency considerations.

Benefit cost analysis is a technique derived from welfare economics and is thereby restricted to evaluation of efficiency aspects of a general equilibrium system in which a given income distribution is assumed. It is a technique which cannot be applied readily to analyze the essentially distributional issues of primary interest to governments. In a world of market imperfections, many regular markets do not exist, and the use of "social" benefit cost analysis to evaluate the indirect impact of Canadian MNEs on the home economy is conceptually difficult, if not redundant. As the MNE makes an internal market in response to market imperfections, it is necessary only to evaluate the economic performance of the MNE. It is redundant to attempt to analyze the indirect effects of the MNE since the making of an internal market is itself a sufficient condition for efficiency. The mere existence of Canadian based MNEs indicates that Canada benefits from the process of internalization, a process which bypasses inefficient market imperfections.

Basically the same argument applies when we analyze the second issue, namely the economic impact of Canadian MNEs on host nations. However, the use of internalization theory is complicated by the fact that Canadian MNEs operate in developing nations where distributional considerations are of greater concern than in the host nation. There is a large literature which suggests that MNEs are responsible for some transfer of technology to developing nations. Yet it is apparent that MNEs will find it difficult to unbundle the package of technological, managerial and financial skills which make up their firm-specific advantages. The concern of developing countries at the perceived insufficient secondary spillover and linkage effects of MNEs is misplaced since the transfer of technology takes place at the consumer level, that is, it is embodied in the product. The presence of the MNE in a host nation substitutes for trade or licensing alternatives and reflects the relative cost advantage of this mode over the two alternative modes of servicing the host economy.

Mansfield and Romeo (1980) conducted a study of technology transfer over the 1960–78 period with a sample of 31 U.S. based multinationals: 26 drawn at random from the *Fortune 500*, two from the *Second 500*, and three others. They found the age of the technology transferred for a total of 65 cases, where age is defined as the years elapsed between the time of transfer abroad and the date the technology was first introduced in the United States. They found that the mean age of technologies transferred to subsidiaries in developing countries is nearly ten years whereas it is only six years for the transfer to subsidiaries in developed nations (the precise means are 9.8 and 5.8 years, respectively). The mean age for transfers by licensing or joint ventures is even higher at 13.1 years.

These findings support the implications of internalization theory, as the MNEs are transferring their newest technologies overseas through affiliates (where the risk of dissipation is reduced) and using licensing or joint ventures only at a later stage in the life of the technology when it is becoming more a standard product. It is also predicted by internalization theory that the newer technologies will first go to developed countries, since they may well be inappropriate or costly to adapt in developing countries. Only at a later stage is it profitable for MNEs to transfer technology to developing nations; yet such transfers do indeed take place and the internal market of the MNEs achieves this worldwide transfer of technology without any help from governments.

* this is not tech transfer as intended -- re: acquisition of ownership of productive capital = control

As argued above, there is no theoretical reason to suspect that the results of this study of U.S. based MNEs will differ if a comparable study were done for Canadian based MNEs. The activities of both U.S. and Canadian MNEs are explained adequately by the general theory of internalization. The main theme of this chapter is that Canadian MNEs behave in the same manner as U.S. based MNEs; they are both economic entities. There is no evidence in their similar overall economic performance to indicate that internalization theory is not an adequate explanation of their activities.

Naturally the subject of the relationship of Canadian MNEs with the home and host nations is a larger one than I have chosen to explore in this chapter. My focus upon the economic aspects of MNEs is a deliberate one; this is the area in which I believe the modern theory of the MNE can be applied to derive some useful insights for public policy. My neglect of the political aspects of MNEs is deliberate; I have no special insights to offer in this area. Similarly, I do not discuss the important role of Canadian financial intermediaries in developing nations, especially in the Caribbean. This is a topic to be explored in other papers. Finally, I do not discuss the role of private financial capital flows.

My topic might be thought to overlap with that of part of the works by Frank (1980), or Bergsten, Horst and Moran (1978), on technology transfer to developing nations. I, however, have made the fundamental assumption that the MNE does not exist primarily to transfer technology; instead, this is the job of the nation state. Governments are responsible for the economic development of their countries and attempts to unbundle the package of technology brought in by foreign private MNEs are doomed to failure given the different objectives of the MNE (efficiency) versus the nation state (equity). MNEs should be analyzed on the grounds of economic efficiency only, and the best method to do such an analysis is by the consistent applications of internalization theory.

Canadian public policy toward MNEs confuses efficiency and equity objectives. The governments of other advanced and most developing nations also fall into the same trap, so the North–South debate is in many ways a dialogue of the deaf. All governments have a propensity to favor protective devices such as tariffs, quotas, exchange controls, export subsidies, and so on for some particular pressure group within their society. In this world of government imposed market imperfections the MNE is an organization with enough market power to bypass most of the regulations imposed by governments. Its success in arbitraging the imperfections of national markets is remarkable. The recent emergence of Canadian based MNEs is entirely predictable given the imperfect nature of today's world economy.

Like other MNEs, the Canadian based MNEs are responsible for some alleviation of the loss of world welfare that might otherwise be experienced by the continuation and even extension of protective measures and restrictions by most nations. The MNE is not a complete substitute for free trade, but it is an organization with a remarkable degree of adaptability. The creation of internal markets by MNEs to some extent makes up for the closed markets imposed by restrictive government policies. These efficiency aspects of MNEs were the primary focus of this chapter.

Bibliography

Adams, W., and Dirlam, J. "Big Steel, Invention and Innovation." *The Quarterly Journal of Economics* 80(2) (1966): 167-89.

Aharoni, Yair. *The Foreign Investment Decision Process.* Cambridge, Mass.: Harvard University Press, 1966.

Allen, T. J. *Transferring Technology to the Firm: A Study of the Diffusion of Technology in Irish Manufacturing Industry.* Paper No. 942-77, Sloan School of Management. Cambridge, Mass.: MIT Press, 1977.

Allen, T. J., and Cooney, S. "Institutional Roles in Technology Transfer." *R&D Management* 4 (1975): 41-51.

Alsegg, Robert J. *Control Relationship Between American Corporations and Their European Subsidiaries.* New York: American Management Association, 1971.

Arrow, Kenneth J. "Vertical Integration and Communication." *The Bell Journal of Economics* 6(1) (1975): 173-83.

Baldwin, R. E. "Determinants of the Commodity Structure of U.S. Trade." *American Economic Review* 61 (March 1971): 126-46.

Basche, J. R., and Duerr, M. G. "International Transfer of Technology—A World-wide Survey of Chief Executives." *The Conference Board* Report No. 671, New York, 1975.

Baumann, H. G. *The Diffusion of the Basic Oxygen Process in the U.S. and Canadian Steel Industries, 1955-69,* Research Report No. 7303. London: University of Western Ontario, 1973.

Beigie, Carl. "The Political Economy of Canada-United States Free Trade." In K. C. Dhawan, H. Etemad and R. Wright (eds.). *International Business: A Canadian Perspective.* Don Mills, Ontario: Addison-Wesley, 1981.

Bergsten, C. Fred, Horst, Thomas, and Moran, Theodore H. *American Multi-nationals and American Interests.* Washington, D.C.: The Brookings Institution, 1978, Chapter 10.

Bernhardt, T. I. "Diffusion of Catalytic Techniques Through a Population of Medium Size Petroleum Refining Firms." *Journal of Industrial Economics* 29(1) (November 1980): 50-65.

Berry, B. J. L. "Hierarchical Diffusion: The Basis of Bones, Developmental Filtering and Spread in a System of Growth Centres." In P. W. English and R. C. Mayfield (eds.). *Man, Space and Environment.* New York: Oxford University Press, 1972.

Biersteker, Thomas J. *Distortion or Development?* Cambridge, Mass.: MIT Press, 1978.

Bones, Herman P. "Are Foreign Subsidiaries More Innovative?" *Foreign Investment Review* 3 (1980): 20-23.

Bourgault, Pierre, and Crookell, Harold. "Commercial Innovation in Secondary Industry." *Business Quarterly* (Autumn 1979): 56-64.

Branson, W. H. "U.S. Comparative Advantage: Some Further Results." *Brookings Papers on Economic Activity* 3 (1971).

Buckley, P. J. "The Modern Theory of the Multinational Enterprise." *Management Bibliographies and Reviews* 5 (1979): 171-85.

——. "New Theories of International Business: Some Unresolved Issues." Mimeographed. Presented at a Conference on Strategic Factors in the Growth of International Business, Reading, England (March 1982).

Buckley, P. J., and Casson, Mark. "The Optimal Timing of a Foreign Direct Investment." *The Economic Journal* 91 (1981): 75-87.

Business Latin America. "How U.S. Bank Regulators Assess Country Risk and What They Find." (July 25, 1977): 233-35.

Business Week. "Survey of Corporate Research and Development Spending: 1975." (June 28, 1976): 62-76.

Business Week. "Brazil: Even Components Must Be Brazilianized." (January 24, 1977): 34.

Business Week. "Survey of Corporate Research and Development Spending: 1976." (June 27, 1977): 62-84.

Business Week. "*Business Week*'s R & D Scoreboard: 1977." (July 3, 1978): 58-77.

Business Week. "A U.S. Damper on World Recovery." (November 1981).

Buzzell, Robert D. "Competitive Behavior and Product Life Cycle." In John S. Wright and Jack L. Goldstucker (eds.). *New Ideas for Successful Marketing.* Chicago: American Marketing Association, 1966.

Canada, Defense Research Board. *The Defense Industrial Research Program.* Ottawa: Defense Research Board, 1968.

Canada, Department of Industry, Trade and Commerce. *Defense Industry Productivity Program.* Ottawa: Information Canada, 1973a.

Canada, Department of Industry, Trade and Commerce. *New Principles of International Business Conduct.* Ottawa: Department of Industry, Trade and Commerce, 1975.

Canada. *Directory of Scientific and Research Establishments in Canada.* Ottawa: Department of Industry, Trade and Commerce, 1977.

Canada, Dominion Bureau of Statistics. *Industrial Research and Development Expenditures in Canada 1973-1975.* Ottawa: Queen's Printer, 1976.

Canada, Foreign Investment Review Agency. *Selected Readings in Canadian Legislation Affecting Foreign Investment in Canada, Part 1: Federal Laws and Regulations as of October 1977.* FIRA Papers No. 2. Ottawa: Department of Supply and Services, 1977.

Canada, Ministry of State for Science and Technology. *R & D in Canadian and Foreign-controlled Manufacturing Firms.* MOSST Background Paper No. 9. Ottawa: Department of Supply and Services, 1979.

Canada, Ministry of State for Science and Technology. *R & D Policies, Planning and Programming*. MOSST Background Paper No. 13. Ottawa: Department of Supply and Services, 1981.

Canada, Statistics Canada. *Industrial Research and Development Expenditure in Canada*. Ottawa: Information Canada, 1976. Cat. No. 13-203.

Canada, Statistics Canada. *Inter-Corporate Ownership 1975*. Ottawa: Department of Supply and Services, 1978. Cat. No. 61-517.

Canada, Statistics Canada. *Corporations and Labour Unions Returns Act, 'Report for 1975, Part I—Corporations*. Ottawa: Queen's Printer, 1978.

Canada, Statistics Canada. *Inter-Corporate Ownership 1978-79*. Ottawa: Department of Supply and Services, 1979a. Cat. No. 61-517.

Canada, Statistics Canada. *Annual Review of Science Statistics 1978*. Ottawa: Queen's Printer, 1979b.

Canada, Statistics Canada. *Corporations and Labour Unions Returns Act, Report for 1977, Part I—Corporations*. Ottawa: Queen's Printer, 1980.

Canadian Senate Committee on Foreign Affairs. *Canada-United States Relations*. Ottawa: Queen's Printer, 1978.

Casson, Mark. *Alternatives to the Multinational Enterprise*. London: Macmillan, 1979.

Chandler, Alfred D., Jr. *The Visible Hand*. Cambridge, Mass.: Harvard University Press, 1977.

Caves, Richard E. *Diversification, Foreign Investment and Scale in North American Manufacturing Industries*. Ottawa: Information Canada for the Economic Council of Canada, 1975.

——. "Multinational Enterprises and Technology Transfer." Second Dalhousie Lecture in International Business, unpublished paper, October 1981.

Chase Manhattan Bank Study. *Dun's Review* (March 1979).

Chen, Edward K. Y. *Hyper-Growth in Asian Economies: A Comparative Study of Hong Kong, Japan, Korea, Singapore, and Taiwan*. London: Macmillan, 1979.

Chiang, Alpha C. *Fundamental Methods of Mathematical Economics*. New York: McGraw-Hill, 1967.

Comanor, W. S. "Market Structure, Product Differentiation, and Industrial Research." *Quarterly Journal of Economics* 81 (1967): 639-67.

Cooper, R. G., and Little, B. "Determinants of Market Research Expenditures for New Industrial Products." *Industrial Marketing Management* 6 (1977): 103-12.

Corporations and Labour Unions Returns Act (CALURA). Ottawa, 1977.

Cox, William E., Jr. "Product Life Cycles as Marketing Models." *Journal of Business* (October 1967): 375-84.

Crookell, Harold, and Caliendo, John. "International Competitiveness and the Structure of Secondary Industry." *The Business Quarterly* (Autumn 1980): 58-64.

Crookell, Harold, and Wrigley, Leonard. "Canadian Response to Multinational Enterprise." *Business Quarterly* (Spring 1975): 58-66.

Curhan, J. P., Davidson, W. H., and Suri, R. *Tracing the Multinationals*. Cambridge, Mass.: Ballinger, 1977.

Curhan, J. P., and Vaupel, J. W. *The Making of Multinational Enterprise—A*

Sourcebook of Tables Based on a Study of 187 Major U.S. Manufacturing Corporations. Boston: Graduate School of Business Administration, Harvard University, 1969.

Cyert, R. M., and March, J. G. *A Behavioral Theory of the Firm.* Englewood Cliffs, N.J.: Prentice-Hall, 1963.

Daly, Donald J. *Canada's Comparative Advantage.* Economic Council of Canada, Discussion Paper No. 135 (August 1979).

Daly, Donald J., MacCharles, Donald C., and Altwasser, Wendy. *The Canadian Business Review* (1982).

Daniels, J. E., Ogram, E. W., Jr., and Radebaugh, Lee H. *International Business Environments and Operations.* Reading, Mass.: Addison-Wesley, 1976.

Dauphin, Roma. *The Impact of Free Trade in Canada.* Ottawa: Information Canada for the Economic Council of Canada, 1978.

Davidow, Joel. "Extraterritorial Application of U.S. Antitrust Law in a Changing World." *Law and Policy in International Business* 8(4) (1976): 895-912.

Davidson, W. H., and McFetridge, D. G. "International Technology Transactions and the Theory of the Firm." Mimeographed. Carleton University, Ottawa (1980).

Davies, S. *The Diffusion of Process Innovations.* Cambridge: Cambridge University Press, 1979.

Davis, Howard. "Technology Transfer Through Commercial Transactions." *Journal of Industrial Economics* (December 1977).

de la Torre, J. R. "Marketing Factors in Manufactured Exports from Developing Countries." In L. T. Wells (ed.). *The Product Cycle and International Trade.* Cambridge, Mass.: Harvard University Press, 1972.

Delupis, Ingrid. *Finance and Protection of Investment in Developing Countries.* New York: Halsted Press, 1973.

De Melto, Dennis P., McMullen, K. E., and Wills, R. M. *Preliminary Report: Innovation and Technological Change in Five Canadian Industries.* Discussion Paper No. 176. Ottawa: Economic Council of Canada, 1980.

"Developing Countries and the Oil-Price Shock." *OECD Observer* 109 (March 1981).

Duerr, Michael G. "R & D in the Multinational Company." *Managing International Business.* New York: National Industrial Conference Board, 1970.

Dunning, John H. "Trade, Location of Economic Activity and the MNE: A Search for an Eclectic Approach." In B. Ohlin, P. Hesselborn, and P. M. Wijkman (eds.). *The International Allocation of Economic Activity.* London: Macmillan, 1977.

——. "Explaining Changing Patterns of International Production: In Defence of the Eclectic Theory." *Oxford Bulletin of Economics and Statistics* 41 (1979): 269-95.

Economic Council of Canada. *Looking Outward: A New Trade Strategy for Canada.* Ottawa: Information Canada, 1975.

Etemad, Hamid. "A Game Theoretic Approach to Host Country-Multinational Enterprise Relationships: Policy Implication." McGill Working Paper, 1980.

——. "Environmental Risk: Is it Possible to Plan for It?" Presented at 1981 AIB Annual Meeting, Montreal. McGill Working Paper, 1982a.

——. "World Product Mandating in Perspective." *Proceedings* of the Administrative Sciences Association of Canada—International Business Division, Ottawa, 1982.

Export Promotion Review Committee. *Strengthening Canada Abroad* (The Hatch Report). Ottawa: Department of Industry, Trade and Commerce (November 1979).

Findlay, R. "Relative Backwardness, Direct Foreign Investment, and the Transfer of Technology: A Simple Dynamic Model." *Quarterly Journal of Economics* 92 (February 1978): 1-16.

Fischer, William A., and Behrman, Jack N. "The Co-ordination of Foreign R and D Activity by Transnational Corporations." *Journal of International Business Studies* 10 (Winter 1979): 28-35.

Fisher, C. "Urban to Rural Diffusion of Opinions in Contemporary America." *American Journal of Sociology* 84 (July 1978): 151-59.

Fisher, W. D. *Clustering and Aggregation in Economics.* Baltimore: Johns Hopkins University Press, 1969.

Frank, Isaiah. *Foreign Enterprises in Developing Countries.* Baltimore: Johns Hopkins University Press, 1980.

Frankl, Roslyn. "A Cross Section Analysis of Research and Development Intensity in Canadian Industries with Particular Reference to Foreign Control." Mimeographed. Ottawa: Department of Industry, Trade and Commerce, Economic Policy and Analysis Division, May 1979.

Freeman, C. "Technical Innovation and British Trade Performance." In F. Blackaby (ed.). *De-industrialization.* London: Heineman Education Books, 1979.

Giddy, Ian H., and Rugman, Alan M. "A Model of Trade, Foreign Direct Investment, and Licensing." Columbia Graduate School of Business Working Paper , 274a, 1979.

Giersch, Herbert (ed.). *On the Economics of Intra-Industry Trade.* Tuebingen: J. B. Mohr, 1979.

Globerman, Steven. "Market Structure and R and D in Canadian Manufacturing Industries." *Quarterly Review Economics and Business* 13(2) (1973): 227-45.

——. *Technological Diffusion in Canadian Manufacturing Industries.* Research Report No. 17, Technological Innovation Studies Programme. Ottawa: Department of Industry, Trade and Commerce, 1974.

——. "Technological Diffusion in Canadian Tool and Die Industry." *Review of Economics and Statistics* (1975).

——. "Canadian Science Policy and Technological Sovereignty." *Canadian Public Policy* 4(1) (Winter 1978): 34-45.

Gold, B. "Technological Diffusion in Industry: Research Needs and Shortcomings." *The Journal of Industrial Economics* 29(3) (1981): 247-67.

Gorecki, P. K., and Stanbury, W. T. (eds.). *Perspectives on the Royal Commission on Corporate Concentration.* Scarborough: Butterworth and Company (Canada), 1979.

Grabowski, H. G. "The Determinants of Industrial Research and Development: A Study of the Chemical, Drug and Petroleum Industries." *Journal of Political Economy* 76(2) (March/April 1968): 292-306.

—— and Baxter, N. D. "Rivalry in Industrial Research and Development." *Journal of Industrial Economics* 21(3) (July 1973): 209-35.

Gray, Herb. *Foreign Direct Investment in Canada.* Ottawa: Information Canada, 1972.

Grilliches, Z. "Hybrid Corn: An Exploration in the Economics of Technological Change." *Econometrica* 25(4) (October 1957): 501-22.

Gruber, W. H., Mehta, S., and Vernon, R. "The R & D Factor in International Trade and International Investment of United States Industries." *Journal of Political Economy* 75 (February 1967): 20-37.

—— and Vernon, R. "The Technology Factor in a World Trade Matrix." In R. Vernon (ed.). *The Technology Factor in World Trade.* New York: National Bureau of Economic Research (distributed by Columbia University Press), 1970.

——. *The Export Performance of Six Manufacturing Industries.* New York: Praeger, 1977.

Grunfeld, Y. Z., and Grilliches, Z. "Is Aggregation Necessarily Bad." *Review of Economics and Statistics* (February 1960): 1-13.

Gunder, Frank A. *Crisis in the Third World.* New York: Holmes and Mesier, 1981.

Gunnemann, Jon P. (ed.). *The Nation-State and Transnational Corporations in Conflict.* New York: Praeger, 1975.

Hagerstrand, T. "Aspects of the Spatial Structure of Social Communication and the Diffusion of Information." In P. W. English and R. C. Mayfields (eds.). *Man, Space and Environment.* New York: Oxford University Press, 1972.

Hamberg, Daniel. *R and D: Essays in the Economics of Research and Development.* New York: Random House, 1966.

Hatch Report. *Strengthening Canada Abroad.* Department of Industry, Trade and Commerce: Export Promotion Review Committee (November 1979).

Hay, D. R. "A Canadian University Experience in Technological Innovation and Entrepreneurship." *Technovation* 1 (1981): 43-55.

Helleiner, Gerald K. "Transnational Corporations and Trade Structures: The Role of Intra-Firm Trade." In Herbert Giersch (ed.). *On the Economics of Intra-Industry Trade.* Tuebingen: J. B. Mohr, 1979.

Heller, Robert, and Willet, Norris. *The European Revenge.* New York: Scribner and Sons, 1975.

Hewitt, Gary K. "Research and Development Performed Abroad by U.S. Manufacturing Multinationals." *Kyklos* 33(2) (1980a): 308-27.

——. "Research and Development Performed in Canada by American Manufacturing Multinationals." Mimeographed. Halifax: Centre for International Business Studies, Dalhousie University, 3 (1980b).

Hirsch, Seev. *Location of Industry and International Competitiveness.* Oxford: Clareton Press, 1967.

——. *The Export Performance of Six Manufacturing Industries: A Comparative Study of Denmark, Holland, and Israel.* New York: Praeger, 1971.

——. "An International Trade and Investment Theory of the Firm." *Oxford Economic Papers* 28 (July 1976): 258-70.

Horst, T. "The Industrial Composition of U.S. Exports and Subsidiary Sales to the Canadian Market." *American Economic Review* 62 (March 1972): 39-45.

Hough, G. W. *Technology Diffusion.* Mt. Airy, Md.: Lomond Books, 1975.

Howe, J. D., and McFetridge, D. G. "The Determinants of R and D Expenditures." *Canadian Journal of Economics* 9(1) (1976): 57-71.

Hubbs, George J. "Global Product Mandating: Does it Pay?" Speech prepared for the *Financial Times*/Corpus Conference on World Product Mandating: Survival in the Post-GATT Environment (Toronto, October 5-6, 1981).

Hymer, Stephen H. *The International Operations of National Firms: A Study of Direct Foreign Investment.* Cambridge, Mass.: MIT Press, 1976.

Kamien, Morton I., and Schwartz, Nancy L. "Market Structure and Innovation: A Survey." *Journal of Economic Literature* 13(1) (1975): 1-37.

Katzman, M. T. "Paradoxes in the Diffusion of a Rapidly Advancing Technology: The Case of Solar Photovoltaics." *Technological Forecasting and Social Change* 19 (1981): 227-36.

Keesing, D. B. "The Impact of Research and Development on United States Trade." *Journal of Political Economy* 75 (February 1976): 38-47.

Killing, John Peter. *Manufacturing Under License in Canada.* Ph.D. Dissertation, School of Business Administration, University of Western Ontario, 1975.

——. *International Business—A Canadian Perspective.* Don Mills, Ontario: Addison-Wesley, 1981.

Kindra, G. S., and Goyal, S. K. "An Investigation of a Model of Technology Diffusion in LDCs." Unpublished paper, 1981.

Klein, L. R. "Macroeconomics and the Theory of Rational Behaviour." *Econometrica* 14 (1946): 93-108.

Kobrin, Stephen J. "Political Risk: A Review and Reconsideration." *Journal of International Business Studies* (Spring 1979): 68-80.

——. "Assessing Political Risk Overseas." *Wharton Magazine* (Winter 1981): 25-31.

Koizumi, T., and Kopecky, K. J. "Economic Growth, Capital Movements and the International Transfer of Technical Knowledge." *Journal of International Economics* (1977).

Komus, David W. *Modelling the Multinational Corporation.* Unpublished Ph.D. Thesis, University of Edinburgh, 1981.

Krugman, Paul R. "A Model of Innovation, Technology Transfer and the World Distribution of Income." *Journal of Political Economy* 87 (April 1979): 253-66.

——. "Intra-Industry Specialization and the Gains from Trade." *Journal of Political Economy* 89 (October 1981): 959-73.

Kujawa, Duane. "Foreign Sourcing Decision Under Duty to Bargain Under the NLRB." *Law and Policy in International Business* (1972): 497ff.

Lake, A. W. "Technology Creation and Technology Transfer by Multinational Firms." *Research in International Business and Finance—An Annual Compilation of Research*, 1 (1979).

Langdon, Steven W. *Canadian Private Direct Investment and Technology Marketing in Developing Countries.* Ottawa: Economic Council of Canada, 1980.

Leroy, G. "Multinational Product Planning: An Innovation Diffusion Perspective." In *Multinational Product Management, Proceedings,* American Marketing Association/Marketing Science Institute Research Workshop, Cambridge, Mass., 6 (August 1976): 1–8.

Levitt, Theodore. "Exploit and Product Life Cycle." *Harvard Business Review* (November/December 1965): 81–94.

Lilien, G. L. "The Implications of Diffusion Models for Accelerating the Diffusion of Innovation." *Technological Forecasting and Social Change* 17 (1980): 339–51.

Lithwick, N. H. *Canada's Science Policy and the Economy.* London: Methuen, 1969.

Litvak, I. S., and Maule, C. J. *The Canadian Multinationals.* Toronto: Butterworths, 1981.

Lodge, Lorne J. "Global Product Mandating: A Business Perspective." Speech prepared for the *Financial Times*/Corpus Conference on World Product Mandating: Survival in the Post-GATT Environment (Toronto, October 5–6, 1981).

Lowinger, T. C. "The Technology Factor and the Export Performance of U.S. Manufacturing Industries." *Economic Inquiry* 13 (1975): 221–36.

Mahajan, V., and Peterson, R. A. "Innovation Diffusion in a Dynamic Potential Adopter Population." *Management Science* 24(15) (November 1978): 1589–97.

Malkiel, B. G. "Risk and Return: A New Look." Working Paper No. 700, National Bureau of Economic Research, Cambridge, Mass., 1981.

Mansfield, Edwin. *Industrial Research and Technological Innovation.* New York: W. W. Norton, 1968.

———. "International Technology Transfer: Rates, Benefits, Costs and Public Policy." Mimeographed. Presented at the Allied Social Sciences Meetings, Washington, D.C. (December 1981).

Mansfield, E., Rapoport, J., Schnee, J., Wagner, S., and Hamburger, M. *Research and Innovation in the Modern Corporation.* New York: Macmillan, 1971.

Mansfield, E., Rapoport, J., Romeo, A., Villani, E., Wagner, S., and Husic, F. *The Production and Application of New Industrial Technology.* New York: W. W. Norton, 1977.

Mansfield, Edwin, and Romeo, Anthony. "Technology Transfer to Overseas Subsidiaries by U.S. Based Firms." *Quarterly Journal of Economics* XCV(4) (December 1980): 737–50.

Marshall, H., Southard, Jr., F., and Taylor, K. *Canadian-American Industry, A Study in International Investment.* New York: Russell & Russell, 1936.

Martin, F., Swan, N., Banks, I., Barker, G., and Beaudry, R. *The Interregional Diffusion of Innovations in Canada*. Economic Council of Canada, Ottawa: Supply and Services Canada, 1979.

MacCharles, Donald C., and Wolf, Bernard M. "Statistics Canada's Flirtation with Mercantilism." *Canadian Public Policy* (forthcoming).

McFetridge, D. G. *Government Support of Scientific Research and Development: An Economic Analysis*. Toronto: Ontario Economic Council, 1977.

———. "The Choice of Technology Transfer Mechanism: A Theoretical and Empirical Analysis." Prepared for the Economic Council of Canada, mimeographed. Ottawa: Carleton University, 1981.

———, and Weatherby, L. J. *Notes on the Economics of Large Firm Size*. Study No. 20, Royal Commission on Corporate Concentration. Ottawa, 1977.

McGuinness, Norman W., and Little, Blair. "The Impact of R & D Spending on the Foreign Sales of New Canadian Industrial Products." *Research Policy* 10 (January 1981a): 78-98.

———. "The Influence of Product Characteristics on the Export Performance of New Industrial Products." *Journal of Marketing* 45 (1981b): 110-22.

McMullen, K. "A Model of Lag Lengths for Innovation Adoption by Canadian Firms." Discussion Paper 216. *Economic Council of Canada*, 1982.

Metcalfe, J. S. "Impulse and Diffusion in the Study of Technical Change." *Futures* 13(5) (October 1981): 347-59.

"Ministerial Declaration on Future Policies for Science and Technology." *The OECD Observer* 110 (May 1981).

Mitchell, Paul. "Infrastructure and International Marketing Effectiveness." *Columbia Journal of World Business* (Spring 1979): 91-101.

Moody's Industrial Manual. Volumes I & II. New York: Moody's Investors Service, 1976.

Mowery, D., and Rosenberg, N. "The Influence of Market Demand Upon Innovation: A Critical Review of Some Recent Empirical Studies." *Research Policy* 8(2) (1979): 102-53.

"Multinational Corporations and Developing Countries." *The Conference Board* Report 767, New York, 1979.

Nabseth, L., and Ray, G. F. (eds.). *The Diffusion of New Industrial Processes*. London: Cambridge University Press, 1974.

National Research Council. *Industrial Research Assistance Program, Information for Applicants*. Ottawa: Department of Supply and Services, 1978.

National Science Foundation. *Research and Development in Industry, 1975*. Washington, D.C.: U.S. Government Printing Office, 1977.

Nickell, Stephen P. *The Investment Decisions of Firms*. Cambridge: Cambridge University Press, 1978.

Norris, K., and Vaizey, J. *The Economics of Research and Technology*. London: George Allen and Unwin, 1973.

"North-South Technology Transfer: The Adjustments Ahead." *The OECD Observer* 109 (March 1981).

OECD Observer, The. "The Case of the Least Developed Countries—A Challenge to Global Solidarity." No. 112 (September 1981).

OECD Observer, The. "The Third World—Aid and Trade." No. 113 (November 1981).

O'Keefe, J., and Dingeldein, D. "Research in Western Canada." *Canadian Research* (January 1982): 31-52.

Ontario, Ministry of Industry and Tourism. *The Report of the Advisory Committee on Global Product Mandates.* Toronto, December 1980.

Palda, K. S., and Pazderka, B. *Approaches to an International Comparison of Canada's R&D Expenditures.* Ottawa: Supply and Services, 1982.

Penrose, Edith R. *The Growth of the Firm.* Oxford: Blackwell, 1959.

——. "International Patenting and the Less Developed Countries." *The Economic Journal* (September 1973).

Polli, Rolando, and Cook, Victor. "Validity of the Product Life Cycle." *Journal of Business* (October 1969): 385-400.

Porter, Michael E., and Zannetos, Zenon S. "Administrative Regulation Versus Market Regulation in the Diversified Company." MIT, Sloan School of Management Working Paper 987-78 (April 1978).

Prahalad, C. K., and Doz, Yves L. "An Approach to Strategic Control in MNEs." *Sloan Management Review* 22(4) (Summer 1981): 5-14.

Prasad, A. J. "Technology Transfer to Developing Countries Through MNCs." *Research in International Business and Finance* 2 (1981).

"Protectionism vs. Economic Policy." *The OECD Observer* 115 (March 1982).

Proulx, Pierre-Paul. "Integration and Mandates." *Policy Options* 3(2) (March/April 1982): 28-32.

Richardson, Jacques. *Integrated Technology Transfer.* Mt. Airy, Md.: Lomand Books, 1979.

Ringbakk, K. A. "Strategic Planning in Turbulent International Environment." *Long Range Planning* (June 1976): 2-10.

Robinson, J. N. "Is it Possible to Assess Political Risk?" *The Banker* (January 1981): 71-81.

Robinson, Richard. *International Business Management.* Hinsdale, Ill.: Dryden Press, 1978.

Romeo, A. A. "Interindustry and Interfirm Differences in the Rate of Diffusion of an Innovation." *Review of Economics and Statistics* 57(3) (August 1975): 311-19.

Ronstadt, Robert C. *Research and Development Abroad by U.S. Multinationals.* New York: Praeger, 1977.

——. "International R & D: The Establishment and Evolution of Research and Development Abroad by Seven U.S. Multinationals." *Journal of International Business Studies* 8(1) (1978): 7-24.

Rosenberg, N. "Factors Affecting the Diffusion of Technology." *Explorations in Economic History* 10(1) (Fall 1972): 3-33.

Rugman, Alan M. *International Diversification and the Multinational Enterprise.* Lexington and Toronto: D. C. Heath, 1979.

——. "Internalization as a General Theory of Foreign Direct Investment." *Weltwirtschaftliches Archiv* 116(2) (1980a): 365-79.

———. *Multinationals in Canada: Theory, Performance and Economic Impact.* Boston: Martinus Nijhoff, 1980b.

———. *Inside the Multinationals: The Economics of Internal Markets.* New York: Columbia University Press, 1981a.

———. "The Internal Markets and Economic Performance of European Multinational Enterprises." Dalhousie Discussion Paper in International Business, 9 (May 1981b).

———. "Canadian Multinational Enterprises and Developing Countries." Dalhousie Discussion Paper in International Business (June 1981c).

———. "Research and Development by Multinational and Domestic Firms in Canada." *Canadian Public Policy* 7 (Autumn 1981d): 606.

———. "Multinational Enterprises and World Product Mandates." Mimeographed. Presented at a seminar of the Economic Council of Canada, Ottawa (May 1982).

Rumelt, P. R. *Strategy Structure and Economic Performance.* Cambridge, Mass.: Harvard University Press, 1974.

Rutenberg, David P. "Global Product Mandating." In K. C. Dhawan, Hamid Etemad and Richard Wright (eds.). *International Business: A Canadian Perspective.* Don Mills, Ontario: Addison-Wesley, 1981.

Safarian, A. E. *Foreign Ownership of Canadian Industry, 1966.* 2nd ed. Toronto: University of Toronto Press, 1973.

Safarian, A. E., and Daly, J. "Foreign Ownership and Industrial Behaviour: A Comment on 'The Weakest Link.'" *Canadian Public Policy* 5 (Summer 1979): 318-35.

Scherer, F. M. "Firm Size, Market Structure, Opportunity and Output of Patented Inventions." *American Economic Review* 55 (1965): 1097-1125.

———. *Industrial Market Structure and Economic Performance.* 2nd ed. Chicago: Rand McNally, 1980.

Schumpeter, J. A. *Capitalism, Socialism and Democracy, 1947.* 3rd ed. New York: Harper and Row, 1950.

Science Council of Canada. *Multinationals and Industrial Strategy: The Role of World Product Mandates.* Ottawa: Science Council of Canada (September 1980).

Science Council of Canada. *The Adoption of Foreign Technology by Canadian Industry.* Proceedings of a Workshop. Ottawa: Science Council, 1981.

Searby, Daniel M. "Doing Business in the Mideast: The Game is Rigged." *Harvard Business Review* (January-February 1976): 53-63.

Shapiro, Daniel M. *Foreign and Domestic Firms in Canada.* Toronto: Butterworths, 1980.

Shaw, R. W. "Investment and Competition from Boom to Recession: A Case Study in the Processes of Competition—The Dry Cleaning Industry." *Journal of Industrial Economics* 21(3) (July 1973): 308-25.

Simon, H. A. *Administrative Behavior.* New York: Macmillan, 1975.

Spence, A. Michael. "The Economics of Internal Organization: An Introduction." *Bell Journal of Economics* 6(1) (Spring 1975): 163-72.

Stewart, F. "Production and Consumption Patterns." *Third World* (March/April 1975).

Stirling Hobe Corporation. *International Transfer of Semiconductor Technology.* Prepared for U.S. Department of Labor, Bureau of International Labor Affairs, October 1978.

Stopford, J. M., and Wells, L. T., Jr. *Managing the Multinational Enterprise/ Organization of the Firm and Ownership of the Subsidiaries.* New York: Basic Books, 1972.

———, Dunning, John H., and Haberich, Klaus O. *The World Directory of Multinational Enterprises.* London: Macmillan, 1980.

Sutton, C. J. "The Effect of Uncertainty on the Diffusion of Generation Computers." *Journal of Industrial Economics* 23(4) (June 1975): 273-80.

Swan, P. "The International Diffusion of an Innovation." *Journal of Industrial Economics* 22(1) (September 1973): 61-69.

"Technology Transfer: Appropriate?" *The Economist* (March 1979).

Teece, David J. "Internal Organization and Economic Performance: An Empirical Analysis of the Profitability of Principal Firms." *Journal of Industrial Economics* (1981).

Terpstra, V. "Research on Product Policy of U.S. Multinationals." In *Multinational Product Management, Proceedings.* American Marketing Association/Marketing Science Institute Research Workshop, Cambridge, Mass., 8 (August 1976): 1-25.

Thomas, M. D., and LeHeron, R. B. "Perspectives on Technological Change and the Process of Diffusion in the Manufacturing Sector." *Economic Geography* 51(3) (July 1975): 231-51.

Tilton, John E. *International Diffusion of Technology: The Case of Semiconductors.* Washington, D.C.: Brookings Institution, 1971.

UNCTAD, Committee on Transfer of Technology. *U.N. Publication* TD/B/C.6/30 Geneva, 1978a.

UNCTAD, Committee on Transfer of Technology, *U.N. Publication* TD/B/C.6/33 Geneva, 1978b.

UNCTAD, Committee on Transfer of Technology, *U.N. Publication* TD/B/C.6/63 (Summary), Geneva, 1980a.

UNCTAD, Committee on Transfer of Technology, *U.N. Publication* TD/B/C.6/64 (Summary), Geneva, 1980b.

UNCTAD, Committee on Transfer of Technology, *U.N. Publication* TD/B/C.6/70 Geneva, 1980c.

UNCTAD, "Planning the Technological Transformation of Developing Countries." *U.N. Publication* TD/B/C.6/50, 1981.

United Nations, Economic and Social Council. *Transnational Corporations in World Development: A Re-examination.* U.S., 1978:05692.

U.S. Department of Commerce. "Industrial Outlook Report of the Business Machines." Various issues.

Utterback, J. M. "The Dynamics of Product and Process Innovation in Industry." In C. T. Hill and J. M. Utterback (eds.). *Technological Innovation for a Dynamic Economy.* New York: Pergamon Press, 1979a.

——. "Product and Process Innovation in a Changing Competitive Environment." In M. J. Baker (ed.). *Industrial Innovation: Technology, Policy, Diffusion.* London: Macmillan, 1979b.

—— and Abernathy, William J. "Dynamic Model of Process and Product Innovation." *OMEGA 4, The International Journal of Management Science* 3(6) (1975): 639-56.

Vernon, Raymond. "International Investment and International Trade in the Product Cycle." *Quarterly Journal of Economics* 80(2) (1966): 190-207.

——. "Multinational Enterprises and National Governments: Exploration of an Uneasy Relationship." *Columbia Journal of World Business* (Summer 1976): 9-16.

——. "The Product Cycle Hypothesis in a New International Environment." *Oxford Bulletin of Economics and Statistics* 41 (1979): 255-67.

——. "The R and D Factor in International Trade and International Investment of United States Industries." *Journal of Political Economy* 75 (1967).

Villard, H. H. "Competition, Oligopoly and Research." *Journal of Political Economy* 66 (1958): 483-97.

Von Hippel, E. *Role of the Initial User in the Industrial Goods Innovation Process.* Report prepared for the National Science Foundation, MIT Sloan School of Management, July 1978.

Wallender III, Harvy W. "Developing Country Orientations Toward Foreign Technology in the Eighties: Implications for New Negotiation Approaches." *Columbia Journal of World Business* (Summer 1980).

Wallich, Christine. "An Analysis of Developing Country Adjustment Experience in the 1970's: Low-Income Asia." *World Bank Staff Working Paper* 487, Washington, D.C., 1981.

Wasson, C. R. "How Predictable are Fashion and Other Product Life Cycles?" *Journal of Marketing* (July 1968): 36-43.

Weichman, Erlik. "Integrating Multinational Marketing Activities." *Columbia Journal of World Business* (Winter 1974): 7-16.

Wells, Louis T. "International Trade: The Product Life Cycle Approach." In L. T. Wells (ed.), *The Product Life Cycle and International Trade.* Cambridge, Mass.: Harvard University, 1972.

——. "Negotiating with Third World Governments." *Harvard Business Review* (January-February 1977): 72-80.

Wetzel, W. E. "Technovation and the Informal Investor." *Technovation* 1 (1981): 15-30.

Whitman, Marina von Neumann. "International Trade and Investment: Two Perspectives." *Essays in International Finance* 143 (July 1981): 23.

Wilkinson, Bruce W. *Canada's International Trade: An Analysis of Recent Trends and Patterns.* Montreal: The Canadian Trade Committee, Private Planning Association of Canada, 1968.

——. *Canada in the Changing World Economy*. Montreal: C. D. Howe Research Institute, Canada-U.S. Prospects Series, 1980. Appendix D.

Williamson, Oliver E. *Markets and Hierarchies: Analysis and Anti-Trust Implications.* New York: The Free Press, 1975.

Wilson, R. W., Ashton, P. K., and Egan, T. P. *Innovation, Competition and Government Policy in the Semiconductor Industry*. Lexington, Mass.: Lexington Books, 1980.

Witten, Mark. "Branch Plants Bear New Fruit." *Canadian Business* (November 1980).

Wolf, Bernard M. "World Product Mandates and Canada-United States Free Trade." Mimeographed. Paper to NAESA, Washington, D.C. (December 1981).

——. "Statistics Canada's Flirtation with Mercantilism." *Canadian Public Policy* (forthcoming).

Wonnacott, Ronald J. *Canadian Trade Options*. Ottawa: Information Canada for the Economic Council of Canada, 1975.

Wood, A. R., and Elgie, R. J. *Early Adoption of Manufacturing Innovations*. London: University of Western Ontario, School of Business Administration, Research and Publication Division, 1976.

"World Bank Report Notes that Inflation, Recession, Oil Prices Dim World Growth Prospects." *Business America: The Journal of International Trade* (September 1980).

Wortzel, L., and Wortzel, H. "Export Marketing Strategies for NIC and LDC-Based Firms." *Columbia Journal of World Business* (Spring 1981): 51–60.

Wrigley, Leonard. *Divisional Autonomy and Diversification*. Doctoral Dissertation, Harvard Business School, 1970.

Index

Abernathy, W. J., 131
Adams, W., 55
Alexander, J. A., 2-6
Allen, T. J., 56
Alsegg, R. J., 108
Arrow, K. J., 77

Baldwin, R. E., 126
Basche, J. R., 143-44
Baumann, H. G., 55
Behrman, J. N., 77, 96
Beigie, C. E., 110
Bergsten, C. F., 182, 184
Bernhardt, T. I., 54
Berry, B. J. L., 52
Bourgault, P., 76
Branson, W. H., 126
Buckley, P. J., 98

Caliendo, J., 76
Canada: branch plants (or trun-
    cated operations), 1, 75, 92-93,
    95-96, 102, 109-11, 113, 119,
    121, 136, 138; federal govern-
    ment, 80; foreign policy, 167;
    host nation, 73, 109; public pol-
    icy, 184-85; regulatory control,
    109-11, 166-67, 169. See also
    industry; research and develop-
    ment, R & D grants; world
    product mandate
Canadian Ministry of State for Sci-
    ence and Technology (MOSST),
    37
Canadian multinational enterprises,
    10, 167; comparison with U.S.
    MNEs, 171-73, 175, 180; eco-
    nomic impact, 182-83; foreign
    ownership, 165; performance of,
    169, 171-73, 175, 180; resource
    based, 165-66, 180-82; role in

[Canadian MNEs]
    developing nations, 175-81.
    See also comparative advantage;
    multinational enterprises
Casson, M. C., 21, 74
Caves, R. E., 143
Chandler, A. D., 77
Chen, E. K. Y., 145
comparative advantage (or country
    specific advantage), 102-3, 115-
    16, 140, 168, 180-82
Cooper, R. G., 60
Corporations and Labour Unions
    Returns Act (CALURA), 27, 30-
    31
Crookell, H., 76, 81

Daly, D. J., 28
Daniels, J. E., 111
Davidson, W. H., 63
Davies, H., 54-55
de la Torre, J. R., 154
Delupis, I., 109
De Melto, D. P., 65
Dirlam, J., 55
Duerr, M. G., 36, 143-44
Dunning, J. H., 74, 83

Economic Council of Canada, 51, 57,
    65, 110
economies of scale. See scale econ-
    omies
Etemad, H., 6-7, 76, 109
European Economic Community,
    101
exporting, 21, 168. See also research
    and development; foreign sales;
    technology, transfer

Findlay, R., 155
Fischer, W. A., 77, 96

Searby, D. M., 109
Southard, F., 39
Spence, A. M., 77
Statistics Canada, 27, 30, 37, 40
Stopford, J. M., 38
Sutton, C. J., 54

tariffs, 92-93, 110, 113, 168;
   nontariff barriers, 92, 110, 113,
   168; protection, 92-93
Taylor, K., 39
technology, 51, 142-43; diffusion,
   142-46; diffusion curve, 155-56;
   source of, 69; technological advance, 28-29; transfer, 1, 9, 77-
   78, 144, 146-47, 149, 151-52,
   155, 163, 182-84. *See also* innovation; less developed countries;
   research and development
Terpstra, V., 64
tests of determinants of R & D:
   multivariate regression analysis,
   37, 39-46; net revenue model, 13-
   20; simultaneous equation model,
   33
Tilton, J. E., 54
trade, 146, 168; barriers, 92, 100,
   110; free trade, 92-93, 102, 116,
   168; international trade, 103-4,
   144, 162-63; intra-industry trade,
   103. *See also* scale economies;
   tariffs

UNCTAD, 143-45
Utterback, J. M., 51, 62, 131

Vernon, R., 12, 51, 109, 126, 131,
   155

Von Hippel, E., 56

Wallich, C., 146
Weatherby, L. J., 28
Weichman, E., 117
Wells, L. T., 38, 57, 109, 155
Wetzel, W. E., 58
Whitman, M. von Neumann, 103
Wilkinson, B. W., 126
Willat, N., 117
Williamson, O. E., 77
Wills, R. M., 65
Wilson, R. W., 60
Witten, M., 76
Wolf, B. M., 6-7, 76
world product mandate (WPM), 1-2,
   6, 73, 91, 136, 138; advantages
   of, 74-75, 86, 115-16; changes in
   subsidiary operations, 119-20,
   122; costs and benefits, 101-2;
   country specific factors, 83;
   decentralized R & D, 7, 84-86,
   96-98, 103; firm specific advantage, 6, 76, 82-83; goals, 79-81,
   91, 104; host country relations,
   111, 113; and internalization, 74-
   75, 77; policy implications of, 74-
   76, 81-82, 84-85; product rationalization, 93, 103; R & D grants,
   81-82, 98; scope, definition of, 7,
   79-81, 91, 93-94, 113; strategy,
   6-7, 74, 78-84, 94-101, 116-19.
   See also Canada, branch plants
Wonnacott, R. J., 92

Zannetos, Z. S., 77

204

About the Editor and Contributors

ALAN M. RUGMAN is Professor of Business Administration and Director of the Centre for International Business Studies at Dalhousie University. On several occasions he has been a Visiting Professor in the Graduate School of Business of Columbia University. Dr. Rugman has written three books on the multinational enterprise and edited another book. He is the author of numerous articles on aspects of international business and finance, some of which have appeared in the *Journal of International Business Studies* and the *Journal of Economics and Business*.

Dr. Rugman holds a B.A. Hons. from the University of Leeds, an M.Sc. from the University of London, and a Ph.D. from Simon Fraser University.

JUDITH A. ALEXANDER is Associate Professor and Chairperson of the Department of Economics, University of Regina. Dr. Alexander has published in the *Journal of Economic Theory, Atlantis, The Collected Papers of Cliff Lloyd* and the *Canadian Journal of Economics*.

Dr. Alexander holds a B.A. from the University of Calgary and an M.A. and Ph.D. from Simon Fraser University.

JOCELYN M. BENNETT is a Research Assistant at the Centre of International Business Studies, Dalhousie University. She has published in *Policy Options*.

Ms. Bennett holds a B.Sc. from McGill University and is a candidate for the LLB/MBA degree in 1985 at Dalhousie University.

HAMID G. ETEMAD is Assistant Professor of the Faculty of Management, McGill University. Dr. Etemad has published a book on *International Business: A Canadian Perspective* and articles that are forthcoming in the *Journal of International Business Studies*.

Dr. Etemad holds a M.Eng., M.Sc., M.B.A., and a Ph.D., all from the University of California at Berkeley.

GARY K. HEWITT is Assistant Professor of Commerce at the University of Saskatchewan. Previously he taught in the Department of Economics, Concordia University, and before that in the Faculty of Commerce and Business Administration, University of British Columbia. He has published in *Kyklos.*

Dr. Hewitt holds a B. Comm. from the University of British Columbia and an M.Phil. and Ph.D. from Yale University.

GURPRIT S. KINDRA is an Assistant Professor of Marketing at the University of Ottawa. Dr. Kindra has published in numerous proceedings and is the author of forthcoming articles in the *International Journal of Production Research* and the *Journal of Academy of Marketing Science.* He is also a contributor to and editor of a forthcoming book on *Marketing in Developing Countries.*

Dr. Kindra holds a B.Sc. from Dalhousie University, an M.B.A. from NWMSU, and a Ph.D. from the University of Iowa.

DAVID W. KOMUS is a Program Analyst with the Department of Community Services and Corrections of the Province of Manitoba. He has published in *Public Finance.*

Dr. Komus holds a B.A. from the University of Manitoba, an M.A. from Queen's University, and a Ph.D. from the University of Edinburgh.

NORMAN W. McGUINNESS is an Associate Professor of Business Administration at Acadia University, Nova Scotia. Dr. McGuinness has done extensive research into the impact of innovation and R & D on exports. His articles on the subject have appeared in *The Journal of Marketing* and in *Research Policy.*

Dr. McGuinness holds a B.Eng. from McGill University and an M.B.A. and Ph.D. from the University of Western Ontario.

KATHRYN E. McMULLEN is a Research Economist with the Economic Council of Canada, Ottawa, Ontario. She is also a sessional lecturer with the Department of Geography, Carleton University, Ottawa, teaching a course on technological change, the multinational enterprise, and economic growth.

Ms. McMullen holds a B.A. and an M.A. from Carleton University, Ottawa, Ontario.

BERNARD M. WOLF is Associate Professor of Economics in the Faculties of Administrative Studies and Glendon College of York

University, Toronto. He has also been associated with the Management Centre of the University of Bradford, England. Dr. Wolf is a specialist in international economics and international business. His articles have appeared in the *Journal of Industrial Economics* and *Canadian Public Policy*.

Dr. Wolf holds a B.A. from Queens College of the City University of New York and an M.A. and Ph.D. from Yale University.